NINETEENTH-CENTURY
HOMOSEXUALITY: A SO

Nineteenth-century Writings on Homosexuality collects together texts concerned with same-sex desire in the nineteenth and early twentieth centuries. This comprehensive sourcebook ranges widely, both generically and chronologically, and includes prose, poetry, fiction, history and polemic from 1810 to 1914. Containing a general introduction, section headnotes, extensive information on the genesis and publication of the texts, a bibliography of primary and secondary source material, and sections on the Law, Science, Love, and Sex, this book provides a unique picture of the diversity and daring of writing about same-sex desire at a time when all such acts were illegal. *Nineteenth-century Writings on Homosexuality* includes writing on

- trials and scandals
- censorship and homophobia
- personal and cultural histories
- love and friendship
- lesbianism
- aestheticism and decadence
- sexual tourism and colonialism
- cross-class desire
- sodomy and sadomasochism

Bringing together for the first time in one volume a wide range of primary source material, this fascinating book includes many texts out of print since the last century, and unavailable outside specialised academic libraries.

Chris White is lecturer in Literature at Bolton Institute. She is the co-editor with Elaine Hobby of *What Lesbians Do in Books*, and has published a number of essays on nineteenth-century homosexuality and lesbianism.

NINETEENTH-CENTURY WRITINGS ON HOMOSEXUALITY: A SOURCEBOOK

EDITED BY
CHRIS WHITE

London and New York

First published 1999
by Routledge
11 New Fetter Lane, London EC4P 4EE

Simultaneously published in the USA and Canada
by Routledge
29 West 35th Street, New York, NY 10001

Typeset in Sabon by Routledge
Printed and bound in Great Britain by
TJ International Ltd, Padstow, Cornwall

British Library Cataloguing in Publication Data
A catalogue record for this book is available from the British Library

Library of Congress Cataloging in Publication Data
Nineteenth-century writings on homosexuality: a sourcebook
[compiled by] Chris White.
p.   cm.
1. Homosexuality–Great Britain–Literary collections.
2. Homosexuality–Great Britain–History–19th century–Sources.
3. Lesbians–Great Britain–History–19th century–Sources.
4. Gay men–Great Britain–History–19th century–Sources.
5. Lesbians–Great Britain–Literary collections.
6. Gay men–Great Britain–Literary collections.
7. English Literature–19th century.
8. Gay men's writings, English.
9. Lesbians' writings, English.
10. Gays' writings, English.
I. White, Chris, 1963–.
PR1111.H57L68   1 999   98–45703
820.8'0353–dc21   CIP

ISBN 0–415–15305–0 (hbk)
ISBN 0–415–15306–9 (pbk)

CONTENTS

CONTENTS

CONTENTS

ACKNOWLEDGEMENTS

I have incurred a large number of debts in the course of this research. The work could not have been completed without the assistance and expertise of the staff of Bolton Local Studies and Archives Department; the British Library, in particular the staff of the Rare Books Room; Cambridge University Library; John Rylands Library in Manchester; New York Public Library; the Hallward and Law Libraries of Nottingham University; and Sheffield City Archives.

I am very grateful to the Bolton Institute of Higher Education for providing the sabbatical which allowed this work to be completed nearly on time, and to my students at Bolton for asking difficult questions about some of the material included here.

This work has benefited from the scrutiny and criticism of many individuals, including Joseph Bristow, Angela Leighton, Suzanne Raitt, Tim Youngs and especially Simon Shepherd, to whom I owe and give particular thanks.

To three people I would like to acknowledge very large debts indeed: Bill Overton, for the time and trouble he has taken in tracking down and translating obscure Latin references and other recherché matters; Norman Vaughton, for being there; and Elaine Hobby for her loving patience, tireless support, practical assistance and stubbornness. Thank you. The errors are, of course, all mine own.

GENERAL INTRODUCTION
Strategies for liberation

The laws of God, the laws of man,
He may keep that will and can;
Not I: let God and man decree
Laws for themselves and not for me;
And if my ways are not as theirs
Let them mind their own affairs.
Their deeds I judge and much condemn,
Yet when did I make laws for them?
Please yourselves, say I, and they
Need only look the other way.
But no, they will not; they must still
Wrest their neighbour to their will,
And make me dance as they desire
With jail and gallows and hell-fire.
And how am I to face the odds
Of man's bedevilment and God's?
I, a stranger and afraid
In a world I never made.
They will be master, right or wrong;
Though both are foolish, both are strong.
And since, my soul, we cannot fly
To Saturn or to Mercury,
Keep we must, if keep we can,
These foreign laws of God and man.[1]

The keynote of nineteenth-century homosexuality is struck by Oscar Wilde in the witness box in 1895 speaking at length of 'the love that dare not speak its name'.[2] Such a paradox can be seen to represent the fissures that are opened up in a culture which conceives of homosexual sex as 'the mute sin', that which cannot be named by true Christians, and a culture which is increasingly, through the course of the century, under sustained and varied assault by those who are only too keen to speak and name their love. This speaking and

1

naming occurs in code, in private, under guise of scientific truth written for experts and specialists, but also breaks out into the public domains of high art, historical certainty, social hygiene and responsibility to the empire.

Much effort and energy is put by those in power into controlling and punishing any outbreak of what is seen simultaneously as disease and evil. The homosexual is classified and determined by every available model of under-standing: legal, religious, medical, moral. He poses the greatest threat to the stability and progress of society. His sexual non-productiveness is collapsed into social and industrial non-productiveness. He is extraneous and a source of a deadly contagion to the majority. The body of the homosexual is seen as a reflection of his soul, or vice versa. Both mind and body are lax, puffy, decayed and morbid through self-indulgence and affinity to things of the street and the animal kingdom, made effeminate and languid by too long an association with all things French. Such men were not wanted in England.

> An empire such as ours requires as its first condition an Imperial Race – a race vigorous and industrious and intrepid. Health of mind and body exalt a nation in the completion of the universe. The survival of the fittest is an absolute truth in the conditions of the modern world.[3]

This book documents the responses of homosexuals themselves to the understandings and treatments to which they were subject.

By tracking the terminology employed to label same-sex sexual acts between 1822 and 1885, the shifting conceptualizations of the acts and the identities associated with those acts become apparent. Prior to 1869 the terms available to name sexual acts or sexual relationships between persons of the same sex were circumlocutory avoidances of naming the beast, mere insults or those names which borrowed from the certainties of Old Testament wrath. Thus, a criminal charge was often framed as an unnatural offence, and reported as 'disgusting depravity' (see Candler and Doughty, p. 32 below), or 'monstrous feats' (see R v. Nicoll, p. 40 below). These men were invariably wretches, intent on committing filthy acts through filthy lusts, to the detriment of social order, family happiness and racial health. In the ringing phrase of Robert Holloway, writing about the Vere Street brothel (see p. 9 below), these men were 'the sweepings of Sodom [and] the spawn of Gomorrah', so detestable a race that a *Times* editorial called for any offence to be punishable with instant death. There is a strong savour of it being the civilized thing to do to put these animals out of their misery, and certainly of it being necessary to preserve the purity and uprightness of British culture. Sodomy, in the legal framework prior to 1885, is conceptualized as being the same kind of thing as bestiality, since the laws defined and redefined in 1831 and 1861 address sodomy, attempted sodomy and bestiality as unnatural offences of equal weight and grossness. With the Criminal Law Amendment Act of 1885, sexual acts between men are, instead, bracketed with prostitution and offences against the age of consent, a concept which persisted up to and including the 1967 Sexual Offences Act. Apocryphally, there has never been any law relating to sexual acts between women, because Queen Victoria declined to believe such things were possible, although a clause in the 1861 Offences Against the Person Act provided scope for a woman to be convicted of an indecent assault on another woman in the twentieth century.[4]

Every publication, every utterance on same-sex desire, is made in the context of a culture which saw such acts and desires as 'abominable', even after the death penalty fell into disuse after 1836. In the context of the hate and vitriol, both discursive and practical, other words and other frameworks were needed for a liberationist discourse. Science became the mainstay of the nascent liberation movement, and from the middle of the nineteenth century a new vocabulary began to be invented, by those who had a vested interest in being treated as healthy, law-abiding human beings, usually borrowing from the scientific discourses of classification, biological determinism and moral neutrality. The fundamental tenet of this framework is that same-sex desire is inborn, and thus neither acquired (the result of a perverse and immoral challenge to the norm), nor a corrupting threat to the normal majority, who are as secure and natural in their sexual identities as homosexuals are in theirs. It is impossible to know to what extent these theorists genuinely believed in the theory of innate homosexuality, or to what extent it was a vital strategic device in arguing for toleration and acceptance. Whatever the case, the logical consequence of the innate theory is that it is absurd to regard as a punishable offence what has been created by nature and her laws.

This model was most vigorously developed in Germany, and the most notable of the Germans writing in this field were Krafft-Ebing and Ulrichs, who proposed that homosexuals were made that way by nature, that they were as natural and normal as heterosexuals, and should be treated so by the law. Such works argue for a biological predisposition, down to the level of body-shape and the appearance of the genitals. Male homosexuals tend to have bodies and genitals that are more like women's, and female homosexuals are intrinsically more male in their physical make-up and mental inclinations than their heterosexual counterparts. Ulrichs and Krafft-Ebing do, however, demonstrate fundamental disagreements about the cause of homosexuality. While Krafft-Ebing incorporated many of Ulrichs' ideas (from his twelve pamphlets, 'Researches on the riddle of love between men', published between 1864 and 1879) into his book, *Psychopathia Sexualis* (1889), particularly that of innate, inborn characteristics, he argued that all sexual deviations were a product of hereditary degeneration of the central nervous system. Ulrichs, however, represented homosexuals as a separate species of human being, a third sex, whom he named Uranians or urnings, where the men had a feminine soul in a man's body, and the women a masculine soul in a woman's body. (For a more detailed discussion of Ulrichs's elaborate classificatory system, with its four sub-categories of urning, see John Addington Symonds, *A Problem in Modern Ethics*, p. 71 below.) This formulation was further developed by Magnus Hirschfeld in his concept of the 'intermediate sex', which sits between the two standard ones of men and women. Hirschfeld pursued the work of classification by producing photographs which exemplified the three physical types. The photograph of the Uranian in the 1903 issue of the Yearbook of Hirschfeld's Scientific Humanitarian Committee has broad female hips, although no breasts, nor any discernible genitals, but it does wear a mask.

Many of the words and definitions developed by these theorists are laborious in construction, derived from classical mythology, or from a carefully 'scientific' differentiation of normal and abnormal instincts. The term which has persisted into modern language, 'homosexuality' (which will be used throughout this book as both historically valid and comprehensible to the modern reader), was coined in 1869 by a man named Benkert, who has gone down in history as a Hungarian doctor, but who was neither Hungarian, nor a doctor, but rather a Swedish campaigner for the rights of those he called 'homosexuals'. The extent to which the names mattered is marked by Edward Carpenter's etymological dispute with Benkert's 'bastard' word, half-Latin, half-Greek, and his preferred, all-Greek, 'homogenic'.[5] (Benkert added the word 'heterosexuality' to the language in 1870, a word Carpenter showed no interest in challenging.) While science offers the promise of neutrality and objectivity, where it is being used strategically it also produces a great deal of confusion as to what precisely causes what. In 1862, Ulrichs wrote:

> Sexual dualism, which is universally present in embryonic form in every individual, simply reaches a higher degree of expression in hermaphrodites and uranians than in the ordinary man and woman. With uranians, this level of expression merely takes a different form than with hermaphrodites.[6]

Ulrichs's apparently rigid boundaries between one type and another here collapse to reveal that homosexuality potentially exists in everyone, undermining any hope of maintaining the façade that toleration of Uranians posed no threat to the established norms of society. But those remarks were made in a private letter, and as such reveal the difference between what can be said in public and what may be admitted in private.

Much of the effort of the German theorists was directed towards changing the legal position of homosexuals, instigated by a steady and then abrupt erosion of the legal equality between heterosexual and homosexual acts from the 1860s onwards. In the wake of the French Revolution and the adoption in France of the Napoleonic Code, which placed homosexuality on the same legal basis as heterosexuality, some German states also made homosexual acts legal. But, by 1869, other German states were independently beginning to strengthen the law against homosexuality, and in 1871 Paragraph 175 was passed by the Reichstag, making homosexual acts between men a criminal offence. Paragraph 175 was the object of attack for all those with an interest in the treatment of homosexuals, and scientific analysis was explicitly directed towards producing a more 'rational' law. The relationship between the output of German liberationists and those working in Britain reveals the extent to which British pronouncements and campaigning are far more tentative. Analysis of the legal position of male homosexuals appears as though it were an afterthought to the main objective and truthful depiction of homosexuality, and emphasis falls far more on distinguishing between good homosexuals and bad perverts, making an implicit appeal to the state to be tolerant to those who can be no different from what they are. The opening paragraph of the principal British publication on homosexuality, *Sexual Inversion*, is a cautious definition of the distinction between identity and acts.

> Congenital sexual inversion – that is to say, sexual instinct turned by inborn constitutional abnormality towards persons of the same sex – is a comparatively rare phenomenon….Sexual attraction between persons of the same sex, due merely to the accidental absence of the natural objects of sexual attraction, is, on the other hand, of universal occurrence among all human races and among most of the higher animals.[7]

There is an apparent mis-match between the strict classificatory systems and pathological emphasis of this sexological science, and the often explicit arguments for equality and tolerance. To what extent the sexologists genuinely believed in their degrees of difference between someone who was 'truly' homosexual and

5

someone who might indulge from time to time, is impossible to know. But either as a statement of truth, or as a strategic position, it speaks to systems of absolute knowledge and certainty by utilizing the language and thought-structures of empirical science, thus demanding to be believed as fact, a useful position in cultures where homosexuals were blamed, condemned and executed for performing acts against nature, since here nature is recruited to support such 'deviant' acts.

The development of more positive terms does not preclude the continued use of the pejorative terms, which persist throughout the nineteenth century and beyond. But in many ways, the language of science seems as redolent of condemnation as that of the law courts and the editorial. Talk of perversion and inversion appears to be a long way from an unapologetic defence of the desire and the act. But such campaigns began from where they were, living in a culture which could refer to them as 'the spawn of Gomorrah and the sweepings of Sodom', and which, in the 1820s, was putting their kind into the public pillory for them to be all but beaten to death.

What the writings in this book demonstrate is the variety and inventiveness of strategies, genres and other textual devices developed to talk about same-sex desire. The material in Chapters 3 to 6 is organized by type, by the method or approach used to articulate personal and public concerns. Dominant ideology has its say in the first two chapters, through the venting of its spleen in Chapter 1 and through its legal devices and practices in Chapter 2. After that, all the voices are of those who have a vested interest in having the condition of homosexuals and lesbians improved. The method of organization is not chronological, but rather moves further and further away from the discourses of the normative and dominant. Chapter 3 gives a range of examples of texts which deploy scientific language and structures of understanding, with the aim of having the law altered and the minds of doctors, with their approaches of cold showers or behavioural therapy, challenged and changed. Chapter 4, the largest by far, maps the mechanisms and methodologies of appropriating mainstream culture to demonstrate the historical and cultural contributions homosexuals have made. Thus, Shakespeare, Michelangelo, Plato and many others are co-opted to the cause, as homosexual writers set out both to challenge their invisibility and to create a framework of social value for their desires and feelings. Chapter 5 is a collection of love poetry by men and women, where the tone is less apologistic than the treatments of Shakespeare's sonnets, and more inclined to celebrate the possibilities of homosexual relationships. Yet in these texts it is possible to see working the stresses and pressures of the legal and social status quo on the day-to-day experiences of individuals, who articulate desire without a hope of it being requited, and who expect to be condemned by those they desire. Chapter 6 takes virtually no recognizance of the norms of society whatever, as a series of sexually explicit texts demonstrate the gap between what was permitted and what actually could happen or be articulated.

Unsurprisingly, it is these texts which have the most marginalized position in terms of their production and publication. Where some of the love poems appeared in mainstream books and magazines, much of Chapter 5 and all of Chapter 6 emerges from the practices of private or anonymous publication, these texts being destined for a self-selecting audience. Some of the material in this book was never published at all, while some appeared in editions as small as twenty-five from private presses. Some, particularly the poetry of the 1890s, was produced from publishing houses which specialized in manufacturing very beautiful, very expensive little books. One such example is the Bodley Head, founded in the 1880s by John Lane, who published Oscar Wilde, John Gray, Theodore Wratislaw, Arthur Symons and others who put in appearances in this book. The status of such a publishing firm and its public image are perfectly captured by Aubrey Beardsley, who habitually referred to the firm as the 'Sodley Bed' in his letters. Because these things were written does not mean that it was all right for them to be written and published. 'Going public' is an activity fraught with danger, as the circumlocutions, defensiveness, censorship and limited printings of many of these texts reveal. But cleverly, subtly, blatantly, cautiously or secretly, these men and women went public.

A more detailed discussion of each method and genre of strategic opposition will be found at the beginning of each chapter. While there are far more texts which treat of male homosexuality, texts concerned with lesbians have not been consigned to their own distinct chapter, but will be found in the chapters where they most logically belong.

Editorial principles

Wherever possible, texts have been included in their entirety. With some very long prose and poetic works, extracts have been made, with the aim of giving an accurate and undistorted sense of what the whole text would contain. Where material has been omitted, this is clearly marked in the text with an ellipsis. To avoid confusion, in a small number of instances where the original texts contain an ellipsis, this is indicated in the endnotes. The endnotes, which are gathered together at the end of the book, are explanatory, providing translations, bibliographical information, notes on the history of the publication of the text and matters of that kind. Unless otherwise indicated, translations are those of the editor or made for the editor. The 'textual footnotes', indicated by the # sign, are those notes which belong to the texts themselves, as they were originally published; these are gathered together at the end of the relevant chapters. Where the textual footnotes themselves have required editorial notes, I have included this information in square brackets. Certain texts have required extensive explanatory notes: to reduce the level of notation, I have silently completed short titles in both texts and footnotes. For example, *Symp.* in the original appears here as *Symposium*. Emendations to texts are restricted to these changes. Otherwise, texts appear precisely as they do in the original, including the spelling, punctuation and style. In order to avoid an unwieldy bibliographical apparatus, duplication and unnecessary referencing, texts appear with sufficient bibliographical information to enable the reader to pursue them further, if they wish. The bibliography at the end of the book is restricted, therefore, to useful, important or interesting secondary works, and editions of primary texts that are accessible, rather than the original publications, which often exist only in a handful (or fewer) of specialist libraries.

1 THE MUTE SIN

This chapter gathers together a variety of texts which express hatred, contempt, mockery, outrage or a desire to string up on sight those who are variously termed the sweepings of Sodom, margeries, pooffs, detestable wretches and epicene. The genre of vitriol spans the 'mere reporting' of a mob's attempt to lynch a group of men arrested for same-sex activities, through Gilbert and Sullivan's parodic treatment of the perceived effeminacy of those surrounding Wilde and Water Pater, to the apoplectic spleen of O'Brien's attack on Edward Carpenter and threat to denounce him to the police.

The phrase 'the mute sin' becomes a legalistic term (as can be seen in Deacon's *Digest,* included in Chapter 2), but begins life as a religious term in *Peccatum Mutum* (the mute sin), a work on sodomy by a seventeenth-century theologian, Father Sinistrari. He, amongst prolonged discussion of what constitutes sodomy and how women might commit it with one another, asserts that 'torture by fire against a Sodomite must be by all means practised among us', and 'one tempted with Sodomy, if he has no other way of avoiding it, can with impunity kill his tempter'.[1] Such sentiments are not so different from those of nineteenth-century pundits.

The Vere Street brothel case, 1810

The Times, 13 July 1810

The existence of a Club, or Society, for the purpose so detestable and repugnant to the common feelings of our nature, that by no word can it be described without committing an outrage upon decency, has for some time been suspected by the Magistrates of Bow-street; who cautiously concealing the odious secret, abstained from taking any steps on the information they had received, until an opportunity should offer of surprising the whole gang. About 11 o'clock last Sunday evening, three separate parties of the patrole,[2] attended by constables, were detached from Bow-street on this service....The enterprize was completely successful. – We regret most deeply, that the information given at the office was found to be so accurate, that the Officers felt themselves justified in seizing no fewer than 23 individuals, at a public-house, called the White Swan, in Vere-street, Clare-market.

'The detestable wretches', *The Times*, 30 September 1810

At the Middlesex Sessions, Clerkenwell, on Saturday the 22d, seven of the infamous and detestable wretches lately taken at the Swan, in Vere-street, viz. *William Amos*, alias *Fox*, *James Cooke, Philip Ilett, William Thomson, Richard Francis, James Done*, and *Robert Aspinal*, were tried, and all found guilty. Amos, having been twice before convicted of similar offences and punished, was sentenced to three years imprisonment, and to stand once in the pillory, in the Haymarket, opposite Panton-street. Cooke, the keeper of the house, Ilett, Thomson, Francis, and Done, were each sentenced to two years imprisonment, and the pillory in the same place; and Aspinal, as not having appeared so active as the others, to one year's imprisonment only.

James McNamara, a low vulgar Irishman, seemingly a bricklayer's labourer, and *Thomas Walker*, a squalid looking lad, about 17, a soldier in the first regiment of the Guards, were tried for a similar crime, at a public-house, in White Hart-yard, Drury-lane, on the 11th instant; and *George Horiby*, a cobler, and *John Cutmore*, a soldier, were indicted for a similar crime, at the Star and Crown public-house, in Broadway, Westminster, on the 21st July. – All four were caught in the fact. – Macnamara, Horiby and Cutmore were sentenced each to twelve months solitary confinement; and Walker to six months solitary confinement.

On sentence being pronounced on these wretches, they were all hand-cuffed, and tied to one chain in Court, and ordered to Cold Bath-fields Prison. On leaving the Court, a numerous crowd of people, who had collected at the door, assailed them with sticks and stones, which the constables could not completely prevent, although they were about forty in number, and told them to make the best of their way to prison, and they all immediately ran off to it, which they reached in a few minutes, and the constables, by blockading the streets, prevented the most fleet of their assailants from molesting them during their inglorious retreat.

'The pillorying of the Vere-street Club', *The Times*, 28 September 1810

The disgust felt by all ranks of society at the detestable conduct of these wretches occasioned many thousands to become spectators of their punishment. At an early hour the Old Bailey was completely blockaded, and the increase of the mob about 12 o'clock put a stop to the business of the Sessions. The shops from Ludgate-hill to the Haymarket were shut up, and the streets lined with people, waiting to see the offenders pass....Shortly after twelve, the *ammunition wagons* from the neighbouring markets appeared in motion. These consisted of a number of carts which were driven by butchers' boys, who had previously taken care to fill them with the offal, dung, &c, appertaining to their several slaughter-houses. A number of hucksters were also put in requisition,[3] who carried on their heads baskets of apples, potatoes, turnips, cabbage-stalks, and other vegetables, together with the remains of divers dogs and cats. The whole of these were sold to the populace at a high price, who spared no expence to provide themselves with the necessary articles of assault....Cook received several hits in the face, and he had a lump raised on upon his eye-brow as large as an egg. Amos's two eyes were completely closed up; and when they were untied, Cook appeared almost insensible....It is impossible for language to convey an adequate idea of the universal expressions of execration, which accompanied these monsters on their journey; it was fortunate for them that the weather was dry, had it been otherwise, they would have been smothered. From the moment the cart was in motion, the fury of the mob began to display itself in showers of mud and filth of every kind. Before the cart reached Temple-bar, the wretches were so thickly covered with filth, that a vestige of the human figure was scarcely discernible....In the name of decency and morality, for the sake of offended Heaven itself, we exhort our Legislators to take this subject into their most serious consideration in the ensuing Session. The monsters must be crushed, or the vengeance of Heaven will fall upon the land. Annihilation to so detestable a race can no otherwise be effected than by making every attempt of this abominable offence punishable with instant death, without benefit of clergy. The present punishment cannot surely be considered commensurate to an offence so abhorrent, and so shocking to human nature; besides, is it not dreadful to have female delicacy and manly feeling shocked, and the infant mind perhaps polluted by such disgusting spectacles, and the conversations to which they unavoidably give rise?

The White Swan, Vere Street, as described in *The Phoenix of Sodom, or the Vere Street Coterie. Being an Exhibition of the Gambols Practised by the Ancient Lechers of Sodom and Gomorrah, embellished and improved with the Modern Refinements in Sodomitical Practices, by the Members of the Vere Street Coterie, of detestable Memory*, printed by Robert Holloway, 1813

The fatal house in question was furnished in a style most appropriate for the purposes it was intended. Four beds were provided in one room, another was fitted up for a ladies dressing-room with a toilette and every appendage of rouge &c &c. A third room was called the 'Chaple', where marriages took place, sometimes between a *female grenadier*, six feet high, and a *petit maitre*[4] not more than half the height of his beloved wife! These weddings were solemnized with all the mockery of bridemaids and bride-men; and the nuptials were frequently consummated by two, three or four couples, in the same room, and in the sight of each other! Incredible as this circumstance may appear the reader may depend it is all provable: – the upper part of the house was appropriated to wretches who were constantly waiting for casual customers; who practised all the allurements that are found in a brothel by the more natural description of prostitutes, and the only difference consisting in that want of decency that subsists between the most profligate men and depraved women. Men of rank and respectable situations in life might be seen wallowing either in or on the beds with wretches of the lowest description: but the perpetration of the abominable act, however offensive, was infinitely more tolerable than the shocking conversation that accompanied the perpetration; some of which, Cook has solemnly declared to me, was so odious, that he could not either write, or verbally relate. It seems many of these wretches were married; and frequently when they are together, make their wives, who they call *Tommies*, topics of ridicule; and boast of having compelled them to act parts too shocking to think of....It seems the greater part of these reptiles assume feigned names, though not very appropriate to their calling in life: for instance, Kitty Cambric is a Coal Merchant; Miss Selina a Runner at a Police office;[5] Black-eyed Leonora, a Drummer;[6] Pretty Harriet, a Butcher; Lady Godina, a Waiter; the Duchess of Gloucester, a gentleman's servant; Duchess of Devonshire, a Blacksmith; and Miss Sweet Lips, a Country Grocer. It is a generally received opinion, and a very natural one, that the prevalency of this passion has for its object effeminate delicate beings only: but this seems to be, by Cook's account, a mistaken notion; and the reverse is so palpable in many instances, that the Fanny Murry, Lucy Cooper, and Kitty Fisher, are now personified by an athletic Bargeman, an Herculean Coal-heaver, and a deaf tyre Smith.[7] Some of the parties came a great distance, even so much as 30 miles, to join the festivity, and elegant amusements of grenadiers, servants, waiters, drummers, and all the Catamite[8] brood, kneaded into human shape, from the sweepings of Sodom, with the spawn of Gomorrah.

It may naturally be supposed that this vice is more expensive than any other, and is the vortex that engulphs the property of men, whose acquaintance are astonished at the mode of their getting rid of their fortunes. I remember a man, who had a place of great emolument, a considerable sum of ready money, and thirty thousand pounds, the fortune of an ill-fated woman whom he married; all of which vanished without a trace of its destination....There is scarcely any description of men, but some individual is comprehended in the associates of this vice; even men in the sacerdotal garb[9] have descended from the pulpit to the gully-hole[10] of breathing-infamy in Vere-street, and other places for similar vice: but I must spare myself and my readers the ungracious task of pursuing, in detail, circumstances that almost chill the blood to think of, and afflict me with the same sensation that a crimping knife[11] on my side would create. – I will therefore briefly consider the origin and progress of this crime, which is so detestable, that the law of England blushes to name it....From the best authority that can be gathered, this crime was first introduced into England about the year 1315, by a sect of heretics called Lollards;[12] whose intent it was, among other most damnable doctrines, was to subvert the Christian faith; for from a note on the Parliamentary Rolls it is said, 'A Lollard has committed the sin not to be named among Christians', which seems to be the first authentic account of it in England. Many years previous to the reign of Geo. I the sin was permitted without any exemplary punishment: – but about the 12th year of that reign a number of those wretches were apprehended, and convicted of the most abominable practices, some of whom were put to death; which gave a check to the evil for some time.

We will now come to the prevalency of the crime in the present age. About five and twenty years ago, there existed a society of the same order with the Vere-street gang, in the City of Exeter, most of whom were men of rank and local situation; they were apprehended, and about fifteen of them tried; and, though they were acquitted by the letter of the law, the enraged multitude was so convinced of their guilt, that, without any respect for their rank, they burnt them in effigy.

'H. Smith' [William Dugdale],[13] 'A few words about margeries – the way to know the beasts – their haunts etc.', from *Yokel's Preceptor: or, More sprees in London!*, c. 1850

The increase of these monsters in the shape of men, commonly designated *Margeries, Pooffs,* etc., of late years, in the great metropolis, renders it necessary for the sake of the public, that they should be made known. The punishment generally awarded to such miscreants is not half severe enough, and till the law is more frequently carried to the fullest extent against them, there can be no hopes of crushing the bestiality. The wretches are too well paid – they being principally, it is well known, supported by their rich companions – to care a jot about a few months' imprisonment. Why has the pillory been abolished? Would it not be found very salutary for such beasts as these? for can they be too much held up to public degradation and public punishment? Will the reader credit it, but such is nevertheless the fact, that these monsters actually walk the streets the same as the whores, looking out for a chance!

Yes, the Quadrant,[14] Fleet-street, Holborn, the Strand, etc., are actually thronged with them! Nay, it is not long since, in the neighbourhood of Charing Cross, they posted bills in the window of several respectable public houses cautioning the public to 'Beware of Sods!'

They generally congregate around the picture shops,[15] and are to be known by their effeminate air, their fashionable dress, etc. When they see what they imagine to be a chance, they place their fingers in a peculiar manner underneath the tails of their coats, and wag them about – their method of giving the office.[16]

A great many of them flock the saloons and boxes of the theatres, coffee-houses, etc.

We could relate many instances of the gross bestiality of the practices of these wretches, but think it would be occupying too much of the reader's time on so disgusting a subject. One or two anecdotes of them, we cannot, however, resist the temptation of relating.

The Quadrant is thronged by a number of the most notorious Margeries, who turn out daily and nightly to look for their living the same as the blowens.[17] One of these is nicknamed 'Fair Eliza'. This fellow lives in Westminster, and keeps his fancy woman, who does not scruple to live upon the fruits of his monstrous avocation. Another fellow, called 'Betsy H — ,' who walks the Strand, Fleet-street, and St Martin's-court, is a most notorious and shameless poof. He is not unfrequently to be found at free-and-easys,[18] where he spouts smutty recitations. His father was a notorious cock-bawd,[19] and when he died he bequeathed his two sons a bawdyken[20] each. One of the sons got a *situation*, we believe, for *borrowing* something[21] – the other soon floored[22] his knocking shop,[23] and then took to the streets. He has been imprisoned several times, and yet he persists in following his beastly pursuits.

There have been also many fellows of this description in the theatrical profession, who have yet been considered respectable members of society. We could mention the names of several, but will, out of compassion only, withhold them. A certain wealthy showman, it was suspected, did not so well respect a certain 'purty'[24] actor of his, without good reasons for so doing: and it is well known, that a wretch, who was in the habit of perpetrating the French characters at a theatre notorious for its horses[25] and *asses*,[26] over the water, was one of the same disgusting and most abominable fraternity.

But we will leave this disgusting subject, again cautioning the respectable portion of the human race to beware of these wholesale abominable traders in this bestiality.

Anon, 'A celebrated slang consarn,[27] as chaunted[28] at various lush cribs',[29] from *The Rummy Cove's*[30] *Delight, c.* 1833

Ye wives when you marry, of course you expect
That your husbands with something in front will be deck'd;
And should he be gifted with what's rather small,
It's better than if he had nothing at all.
But the story I tell you is true, 'pon my life,
It's found out a woman has married a wife,
Who was strong, who was hearty, was stout and was tall,
But to please her poor spouse she had – Nothing at all.

She liv'd as a groom, and the housemaid she wed,
And the very first night that they went into bed,
The wife she did turn round her face to the wall,
For she knew that the husband had – No – thing at all.

15

Then they laid all the night, and no doubt they both sigh'd,
For a good strapping drayman their charms to divide;
'Twas very provoking it so did befall,
That one for the other had – Nothing at all.

In a dockyard this husband did work for some years,
Undiscover'd to be a female, it appears;
And but for an accident, there is no doubt,
This secret of secrets had ne'er been found out
But it happen'd one day, that this female did die,
And the searchers were sent for, who quickly did spy,
That instead of a three-square gimblet[31] or awl,[32]
She'd a-a what-do-ye-call-it, – a nothing at all.

Gilbert and Sullivan, Bunthorne's recitative and song, from *Patience; or, Bunthorne's Bride, an entirely new and original aesthetic opera*, Act 1, first performed April 1881

[*As soon as he is alone,* BUNTHORNE[33] *changes his manner and becomes intensely melodramatic*]

Am I alone,
And unobserved? I am!
Then let me own
I'm an aesthetic sham!
This air severe
Is but a mere
Veneer
This cynic smile
Is but a wile
Of guile!
This costume chaste
Is but good taste
Misplaced!

Let me confess!

A languid love for lilies does *not* blight me!
Lank limbs and haggard cheeks do *not* delight me!
I do *not* care for dirty greens
By any means.
I do *not* long for all one sees
That's Japanese.
I am *not* fond of uttering platitudes
In stained-glass attitudes.
In short, my mediaevalism's affectation,
Born of a morbid love of admiration!

If you're anxious for to shine in the high aesthetic line as a man of
    culture rare,
You must get up all the germs of the transcendental terms, and plant them
    everywhere.
You must lie upon the daisies, and discourse in novel phrases of your
    complicated state of mind,
The meaning doesn't matter if it's only idle chatter of a transcendental kind.
And everyone will say,
As you walk your mystic way,
'If this young man expresses himself in terms too deep for *me*,
Why what a very singularly deep young man this deep young man must be!'

Be eloquent in praise of the very dull old days which have long since passed
    away,
And convince 'em, if you can, that the reign of good Queen Anne[34] was
    Culture's palmiest day.
Of course you will pooh-pooh whatever's fresh and new, and declare it's crude
    and mean,
For Art stopped short in the cultivated court of the Empress Josephine.[35]
And everyone will say,
As you walk your mystic way,
'If that's not good enough for him which is good enough for *me*,
Why what a very cultivated kind of youth this kind of youth must be!'

Then a sentimental passion of a vegetable fashion must excite your languid
    spleen,
An attachment *à la Plato*[36] for a bashful young potato, or a not-too-French
    French bean!
Though the Philistine may jostle, you will rank as an apostle in the high
    aesthetic band,

If you walk down Piccadilly with a poppy or a lily in your mediaeval hand.
And every one will say
As you walk your flowery way,
'If he's content with a vegetable love, which would certainly not suit *me*,
Why what a most particularly pure young man this pure young man must be!'

Eliza Lynn Linton, from 'The Epicene Sex', *The Girl of the Period and Other Social Essays*, London, 1883

There has always been in the world a kind of woman who one scarcely knows how to classify as to sex; men by their instincts, women by their form, but neither men nor women as we regard either in the ideal. In early times they were divided into two classes; the Amazons who, donning helmet and cuirass,[37] went to the wars that they might be with their lovers, or perhaps only for an innate liking for rough work; and the tribe of ancient women, so withered and so wild, who should be women yet whose beards forbade men so to account them, and for whom public opinion usually closed the controversy by declaring that they were witches – that is, creatures so unlike the rightful woman of nature that only the devil himself was supposed to be answerable for them. These particular manifestations have long since passed away, and we have nowadays neither Amazons learning the goose-step in our barrack-yards, nor witches brewing hell-broth on Scottish moors; but we have the Epicene sex all the same – women who would defy the acutest social Cuvier[38] among us to classify, but who are growing daily into more importance and making continually fresh strides in their unwholesome way.

Possessed by a restless discontent with their appointed work, and fired with a mad desire to dabble in all things unseemly, which they call ambition; blasphemous to the sweetest virtues of their sex, which until now have been accounted both their own pride and the safeguard of society; holding it no honour to be reticent, unselfish, patient, obedient, but swaggering to the front, ready to try conclusions in aggression, in selfishness, in insolent disregard of duty, in cynical debasement of modesty, with the hardest and least estimable of men they emulate – these women of the doubtful gender have managed to drop all their own special graces while unable to gather up any of the more valuable virtues of men....They have taken greatly of late to public speaking all round; and some among them seem only easy when they are standing before a crowd, to be admired if they are pretty, applauded if they are pert, and, in any case, the centre of attraction for the moment....Think of the woman's-right woman, with her hybrid costume and her hard face, showing society how it can be saved from destruction only by throwing the balance of power into the hands of women – by the nobler and brighter instincts of the oppressed sex swamping that rude, rough, masculine element which has so long mismanaged matters....The leering approbation of men never over-nice in thought and now heated with wine, such as are always to be found at public dinners, is an infliction from which we should have imagined any woman with purity and self-respect would have shrunk with shame and dismay. But women who take to after-dinner speeches cannot be either nervous or fastidious.

Perhaps it is expecting too much of women of this kind if we ask them to consider themselves in relation to men's liking. They profess to despise the masculine animal they are so fond of imitating, and to be careless of his liking; holding it a matter of supreme indifference whether they are to his taste or not. But it may as well be said plainly that the disgust which we may presume the normal healthy woman feels for men who paint and pad and wear stays and work Berlin work[39] – men who give their minds to chignons and costumes; who spy after their maids' love-letters, and watch their boys as cats watch mice – men who occupy themselves with domestic details they should know nothing about; who look after the baby's pap-boat[40] and cinders in the dust-heap, and can call the various articles of household linen by their proper names – the disgust which the womanly woman feels for them is exactly that which the manly man feels for the epicene sex....If there were any special work which they could do better than manly men or feminine women, we could understand their economic uses, and accept them as eminently unlovely outgrowths of a natural law, but at least necessary and natural. But they are not wanted. They simply disgust men and mislead women, and those women who they do not mislead in their own they often influence too strongly in the other direction by way of reaction, rendering them sickly in their sweetness, and weak rather than womanly....Let men be men, and women women, sharply, unmistakably defined; but to have an ambiguous sex which is neither the one nor the other, possessing the coarser passions and instincts of men without their strength and better judgement, and the position and privileges of women without their tenderness, their sense of duty, or their modesty, is a state of things that we should like to see abolished by public opinion, which alone can touch it.

M. D. O'Brien, from *Socialism and Infamy: the Homogenic or Comrade Love Exposed: An Open Letter in Plain Words for a Socialist Prophet*, private publication, Sheffield, 1909

M. D. O'Brien, an inhabitant of Dronfield, near Sheffield, wrote to the *Yorkshire Post* on a number of occasions, attacking Edward Carpenter for all manner of crimes and social offences, this personal crusade culminating in the publication of *Socialism and Infamy*, privately, in two versions, in 1909. The extracts below are indicative of the bulk of the second, longer pamphlet, which is concerned with homosexuality and its social and religious evils. He repeatedly accuses Carpenter of breaking Section 11 of the 1885 Criminal Law Amendment Act, the same piece of legislation under which Wilde was successfully prose-cuted. Socialism and homosexuality are, in O'Brien's terms, inherently related, since in his eyes, Carpenter is making socialism inevitable by inciting the masses to homosexuality. In addition to these targets, O'Brien attacks Carpenter for repudiating marriage; for wanting to make women into 'unpro-fessional prostitutes'; for approving of the Factory Acts; and for declining to debate with him any of the issues raised by *Homogenic Love*, *Towards Democracy* [41] or *Iolaus*. [42]

To Edward Carpenter.
When a brilliant, distinguished, and influential Prophet and Leader in the Socialist Party, acting in conjunction with a Socialist Printing and Publishing Firm, [43] *privately circulates, not only among a few scientific friends only, but among his followers and admirers in all classes, a Pamphlet in which he advo-cates Criminal Practices that sink human beings below the level of the beasts, and make for social destruction, is it to the interest of Society that the fact should be made public? In what other way can this deadly poison be success-fully fought against?*

If the filthy thing were correctly named it would be called *Homogenic Lust*, or desire for carnal intercourse with one's own sex – a morbid appetite, the product probably of cultivation, which sinks those who possess it to the lowest depths of depravity, as well as of slavery to the perishable flesh of other people, that it is possible for a human creature to fall to. It is to such agents... of an infernal power that St. Paul refers when he says, 'Wherefore God gave them up in the lusts of their hearts to uncleanness, that their bodies should be dishonoured among them. For they exchanged the truth of God for a lie, and worshipped and served the creature rather than the Creator, who is blessed for ever. Amen. For this reason God gave them over to degrading passions; for their women exchanged the natural function for that which is unnatural, and in the same way also the men abandoned the natural function of women and burned in their desire toward one another, men with men committing indecent acts and receiving in their own persons the due penalty of their error. And just as they did not see fit to acknowledge God any longer, God gave them over to a depraved mind, to do those things which are not proper, being filled with all unrighteousness, wickedness, greed, evil; full of envy, murder, strife, deceit, malice; *they are* gossips, slanderers, haters of God, insolent, arrogant, boastful, inventors of evil, disobedient to parents, without understanding, untrustworthy, unloving, unmerciful; and, although they know the ordinance of God, that those that practice such things are worthy of death, they not only do the same, but also give hearty approval to those who practice them.' – *The Epistle of Paul the Apostle to the Romans*, Chapter I, 24–32[44]....You and your Homogenic 'Comrades' will bear with civilization, and will make some outward show of conforming to the decencies and moralities which it requires, until all of you are numerous and powerful enough to arise and sweep it away; just as a cancer may be said to bear with the body in which it has rooted itself until, in course of time, it has grown and grown and spread and spread to such an extent as to seize, so to speak, upon a vital part of the body, when its work of effective destruction will begin, and will go on until it has killed its unfortunate victim, it necessarily at the same time destroys the essential condition of its own life by cutting short the life of the host on whose blood it depends for its food. But no sensible man allows a cancer to go on growing until it has increased to this dangerous extent; he cuts it clean out of his body as quickly as he is able to do so, and thus sacrifices its life to preserve his own.

Do you think that the practice of *Homogenic Love* is likely to promote either the moral, the mental, or the physical welfare of Sheffield? Do you think it is calculated to make Sheffield's citizens better husbands, better fathers, or better sons? Is this vice good for Sheffield, or is it bad for Sheffield? Even looking at it from the extremely low and unworthy standpoint of pounds, shillings, and pence, is it a sound investment for the steel city's sons to invest in? Is it fitted to make mechanics more skilful, intelligent, and inventive? Will it increase the industry and efficiency of merchants, organisers, managers, and directors of labour, or of commercial travellers who have to compete for orders in all parts of the civilized world? Is the infamy which is said to have brought destruction upon Sodom and Gomorrah likely to bring in one form or another anything less than destruction upon the trade of Sheffield? Answer these questions, vile poisoner, if you can. If the city which for more than twenty years you have done your utmost to injure did its duty it would rise as one man and crush both you and the whole of your infernal crew....Are you going to tell me that the infamy which is said to have spelt ruin for the Cities of the Plain[45] can be either practised, preached, or even tolerated for a single moment by any man who honestly endeavours to seek that Kingdom of God, a Kingdom that is within the mind itself, and one, moreover, which can only be known and enjoyed in so far as the mind is free from pollution by such vile lusts as those which prompt the slaves of this so-called *Homogenic Love* to indulge themselves in their homosexual but indescribable practices?

Will anybody dare to stand up in any public place, before any public audience in this country, and tell me that homosexuality in any shape or form, to any extent or degree, is good for any person, at any time, under any circumstances whatever? The practice is entirely without excuse. It is condemned by reason, by Scripture, and by the law of the land. No argument that will hold water can be put forward in favour of it. It stands in the same category as the mysterious sin against the Holy Ghost, for which there is said to be no forgiveness either in this life or in any other.[46] And yet there is reason for believing that it is gaining ground in this country, but more especially in Sheffield and the surrounding district. For you cannot have lived near here for more than twenty years, cannot have exerted your pernicious influence as you have exerted it, cannot have been visited during that period as you have been visited by thousands of persons of both sexes, and cannot have craftily circulated your abominable pamphlet, as you probably have circulated it, without producing some effect among the most depraved portions of all classes of people in these parts....*Homogenic Love* is a social pestilence, and to save Society from its destructive ravages is a duty lying upon all who seek their own good along with that of each individual citizen is, if he did but know it, inseparably bound up....Already in Sheffield, if reports speak correctly men are in some cases being followed and molested by vile wretches who carry out practically the unnatural homosexuality which you preach. Charges of the same kind have also been made from a number of quite independent quarters against a teacher of your infamy who lives but a few miles distant from that city, although it is only fair to say that the charges against this man are not so numerous as those which have been made against the man who lives with him, and who he has no doubt corrupted both by his practice and by his precept. These charges are not pressed home simply because those who make them do not like their names to be mixed up with anything that is so vile and loathesome. Such is the awful fruit already appearing in just that part of the country in which you have planted and watered your homosexual tree – a tree which was planted at least fifteen years ago, if not earlier and which has no doubt been watered ever since by you and your comrades. The most serious charge against the man to whom I have just referred is made by a man who had to climb through one of his windows, when his door was fastened, in order to escape from his homosexual attentions. Ultra-sociability of this demonstrative kind may be agreeable to Socialists, but Individualists do not want it, and do not mean to have it. Let the comrades keep all of it for themselves....The practice of your vile homosexuality quite unfits its slaves for the duties of the married state, and causes them to turn from their wives to the male 'comrades,' who are more capable of satisfying their unnatural appetites. Angels and ministers of grace defend us! This is the comrade love's effect upon the comrades! Are these diseased people fit to be at large? Ought not their homosexual lusts to be treated in a lunatic asylum, or in a lethal chamber?...What vicious, effeminate, and unnatural creatures all men would become if they tried to reduce to practice your vile teaching! The treatment of a man as if he were a woman, the kissing, fondling, and embracing of him by another person of his own sex is as unnatural and as great a sin against reason as it is possible for any human act to be. I am aware that according to your ideas, and according to those of Walt Whitman, the shameless and corrupt American whom you follow in the matter (as well as, so far as I can see, in everything else) no possible human action, how vile and unbecoming soever it may be, is or ever can be unnatural. Men may sink themselves far below the wild beasts of the forest; there is no depravity to which they may not descend, and by which they may not defile themselves; yet still according to your notions, and according to the notions of the erotic and diseased school to which you belong. When they do this they will only be doing what is perfectly natural, and quite as natural as other human conduct. In the sensual Paradise which you offer to your followers, not only is every possible human action to be considered perfectly natural, but there is to be no distinction between virtue and vice, right and wrong, good and evil....Therefore go you, O charming and fascinating hypocrite – charming and fascinating as the infernal serpent who is said to have seduced the Mother of mankind – to you who can see so clearly the mote of jealous exclusiveness in your brother's eye, but cannot or will not see in your own eye the beam of monstrous lust which you lie in calling love – to you I say – Go! false Prophet; corrupter and misleader of youth and inexperience; destroyer of purity, and chastity, and honour; disseminator of filth and dirt vomited up

23

from the foul pit of sin and death; agent of Hell, and enemy of the human race – Go! breaker of sacred pledges, traitor to the Master whom you once acknowledged to be Divine, and whose cause as a Minister of the Gospel you once promised to serve; Go! vile underminer of the work and example of good parents, good guardians, good teachers, good friends, good neighbours, and good fellow-citizens; go with your abandoned disciples, both males and females, your bands of 'comrades, friends, and lovers' – as you call them – to some country where it is legal for you and them to practice the indescribable infamies which, in your legal productions, you have sought to justify, and even to glorify! This country will soon be too hot to hold both you and them. Begone! the whole pack of you, and let us never see your faces again.[47]

2 LAW

In this chapter are a selection of legal cases from 1822 to 1895, incorporated with specific legal clauses and commentaries on the meaning and execution of justice in relation to unnatural offences, gross indecency, attempted sodomy, sodomy and episodes which may be seen to emanate from the so-called 'blackmailer's charter' that the law on sodomy was seen to be. Two of these narratives can be seen as consequences of the opprobrium in which same-sex relationships between men were held. In the case of R v. Attrell, and the suicide of the Marquess of Londonderry (better known by his courtesy title of Lord Castlereagh), threats of exposure and extortion are derived from the fears of any man of being accused of an unnatural offence, since he could not hope to escape such an accusation without some of the mud sticking. The self-destruction of the Marquess of Londonderry clearly depicts the power of such a taint, whether or not it has any substance. The somewhat comic episode of Mr Baring Wall, MP's nocturnal encounter with a policeman reveals the extent to which an ostensibly respectable member of society must prove his respectability, rather than the offence he may have committed being proved. Whatever the legal technicalities, in practice these men are guilty until proven innocent, and while Wall may have walked from the court a free and stainless man, the case of a fellow MP, William John Bankes, shows another side to the response to public scandal. Bankes was arrested and charged in 1833 for an act of indecency performed with a soldier in a public lavatory outside Westminster Abbey. At Bankes's trial he had, amongst others, the Duke of Wellington as a character witness, and was acquitted. However, in 1841 he was arrested for indecent exposure, bailed to appear in court and fled abroad, to die in Venice in 1856. Perhaps one arrest might be perceived as bad luck, but a second would smack of guilt, whatever the truth.

Indecent exposure and public indecency were offences that brought public shame. Sodomy was met with much sterner punishment. The legal position of sodomy undergoes a number of changes across the century, both in terms of legislation, but also in terms in actual practice. In 1828, the statute that made death the penalty for all acts of sodomy, whether with human beings or animals, that had been on the books since the time of Henry VIII, was re-enacted, and in 1831 the same clauses were re-enshrined in a new piece of legislation. But, while the death penalty was not removed from the statute books until 1861, no executions were carried out after 1836 for sodomy, buggery, bestiality or any capital offence other than treason and murder. Thus, there is a gap between legal conditions and legal practices, and, while a number of the men whose cases are included below are apparently condemned to death, they are not executed. Finding out what did happen to them has proved singularly difficult. Once found guilty, they disappear from the public gaze, unless there is some element of celebrity or notoriety in their case.

Sexual acts between men after 1861 are placed within the same conceptual framework as rape, in discussions of proof. But consent is of no relevance whatever. The only difficulties for the law are in proving the act or the attempt at the act, and in deciding what constitutes a completed act – hence the anxiety about whether intromission or ejaculation needs to have occurred for the act to be named sodomy, or is merely attempted sodomy, with its differential penalty. The overall impression from the legal debates up to 1861 is that, on the whole, the law would prefer to inflict the death penalty for sodomy, but, because of the difficulty of proof, there is a regrettable reluctance on the part of juries and judges to give the judgement against the sodomite, and thus it is better to have a sentence of life imprisonment for the offence, in the hope that it would be more willingly deployed. The Labouchere amendment to the 1885 Criminal Law Amendment Act seems to have been an effort to reinscribe the insistence of society on the unacceptability of these acts with renewed vigour, by connecting homosexual acts with concerns of far more significance to society than bestiality. So an act originally intended to deal with issues of prostitution and the age of consent became, under Labouchere's insistent debating in the Commons, a new tool with which to repress the burgeoning visibility of homosexuality, of which the most famous victim was Oscar Wilde. His prosecution was a watershed for writers and activists concerned with the social and legal treatment of same-sex desire, and in the aftermath of the 1895 trials, those who did not flee abroad generally fell silent. The chapter concludes with an activist, John Addington Symonds's, analysis of and recommendations for the legal position of homosexuals, one of the few to say anything even remotely publicly on the subject after Wilde's prosecution. His comments come from a privately published pamphlet destined for a selected audience of scientists and those who might have been able to influence the law, and he responds to moral, religious and social scruples, point by careful point, in, for him, a penultimate bid to make things better.

Offences Against the Person Act 1828, Section 16[1]

That every person convicted of the abominable crime of Buggery either with Mankind or with any Animal, shall suffer death as a Felon.

Edward E. Deacon, from *Digest of the Criminal Law of England*, 1831

1. Sodomy is that horrible sin against nature, and the ordinance of the Almighty,[#1] which the English law (in the language of the indictment for the offence) most fitly describes as one not even to be named amongst Christians. The least notice, that could be taken of this detestable crime, would certainly be the best; but those who profess to expound the criminal law, as well as those whose duty is to administer it, must not shrink from the task, disgusting though it be, of explaining with clearness and precision that dreadful crime, of which the inevitable consequence is death to those convicted of it, besides indelible and lasting infamy to their names, – which the slightest suspicion of the least propensity to, drives them as pestilential outcasts from society, – and which, even to mention by its odious appellation, is pollution to the lips that utter it, or the pen transcribing it. But the offence, revolting as it is, must be defined: – it is a carnal knowledge committed against the order of nature by man with man, or in the same unnatural means with woman, or by man or woman in any manner with beast.

2. To the credit of the law of England, this abominable crime, ever since it was introduced into this country by the Lombards,[2] has been visited with the *penalty of death* – a punishment, which is sanctioned by the voice of nature and of reason, as well as the express law of God....

6. The nature of the evidence, to prove the actual commission of this offence, [is] the same as in cases of rape....But in proportion as this crime is the more detestable, so the proof ought to be, if any thing, the more clear and undeniable. It is an offence, as Sir W. Blackstone well observes, of so dark a nature, so easily charged, and the negative so difficult to be proved, that the accusation should be most clearly and satisfactorily made out. For if strictly and impartially proved, it ought to be as strictly and impartially punished; but if the accusation is false, the miscreant, who prefers the charge, deserves a punishment only inferior to that of the crime itself.

7. To constitute the offence, the act must be in that part of the body where sodomy is usually committed; therefore, the act committed in a child's mouth by a wretch, who was tried at Warwick assizes in 1817, was held not to amount to the offence in law. R v Jacobs, R & R, 331.

8. An admission by a prisoner indicted for this offence, that he had committed the same crime at another time, and with another person, and that his natural inclination was towards such practices, was held inadmissible in evidence; as being foreign to the point in issue, and to the immediate charge on which the person was indicted. R v Cole, 1 Phil, 195....

12. The mere solicitation also to the commission of the crime, is, in itself, an indictable offence, without any overt act indicative of the attempt to commit it.

Humphry W. Woolrych,[3] 'Sodomy and bestiality', from *The History and Results of the Present Capital Punishments in England*, 1832

From the consideration of rapes upon infants, cruelties at which every man of moral energy must shudder, we descend by an easy transition to the lowest and deepest shades. Justly, indeed, have writers shewn their hatred of the most abominable propensities of nature, but whilst they have declared their resolution to make the least possible mention of those deeds, it has been found impossible to avoid such explanations as the subject itself demands. We shall follow their example of brevity, but must record fearlessly our opinion upon the expediency of punishing with death the crime '*inter Christianos non nominandum*'. [#2] The truth is, that notwithstanding the most inexorable strokes of justice, the horrid propensity has multiplied among us lately. And yet, while we cannot but allow this, we are enabled to admit, on the other hand, that if a man be not indicted capitally, juries will do their duty, and will consign an offender to the oblivion which he deserves. Thus the expediency of punishing the crime capitally, is nullified by the results of severity, on the one hand, and of the mitigated proceedings on the latter. Still there remains the consideration of the divine command. And there is no doubt but that, in the sight of God, it is a most grievous and awful sin, and that His holy eyes must turn away from such a violation of His own image with disgust. There is not any question, also, but that He ordered the immediate execution of the Sodomite, or unnatural person; but in the very same chapter, there is an equal denunciation against adultery, cursing of mother and father, soothsaying, incantations, and diviners. Will it be urged, that adultery and abuse of parents should be forthwith punished with death? The reason fails at once, and it is not necessary to dwell upon the subject....Education, *moral* and *political*, will lessen this offspring of indecency. It will lead to the multiplication of capital, with comfort and *economy*; it will endear the ties of legitimate and *prudent* marriages; and, above all, will ensure that command of temper, which while it controls natural, will also restrain unlawful lusts. The baser herd, if any there shall be, will then take refuge in a corner. Beset by the more stinging pains of *moral outlawry*, they will tremble at the very sight of heaven; and, as their ranks thin through disease and death, few, – none, perhaps, will succeed them; for the glory of universal intelligence will shine, and men at large will have LEARNT THE RESPECT DUE to their natures.

I. Table of Convictions and Executions, in
   London, for Sodomy, from 1699–1755
   (*Parl. Papers* 1819, viii, p. 146)

Year	Con.	Ex.
1725–6	2*	2
1727–8	1	1
1729–30	1	1
Totals	4	4

*It appears, however, that there were two other convictions, and another execution in this year. In fact there was a gang of these bad persons, and the witness against them, an accomplice, deposed to the singular fact, that he had been abominally connected with three of them, and they were all executed. There were several acquittals, and many cases of misdemeanour; but for the honour of human nature, the crimes of this kind from 1699 to 1755, have no mentionable proportion to those of rape, although we do not propose, of course, to justify the latter offence.

II. Table of Convictions and Executions for
Sodomy and Bestiality, from 1756–1830, for
London and Middlesex (*Parl. Papers*, 1819,
viii, p. 156)

Years	Con.	Ex.
1757	1	0
1761	1	0
1770	1	1
1772	1	0
1776	2	2
1796	1	1
1797	1	0
1803	1	1
1804	1	0
1806	1	1
1808	1	0
1809	1	1
1810	2	2
1814	1	1
1815	1	1
1816	2	2
1819	1	1
1820	1	1
1822	3	3
1828	2	0
Totals	28	18

III. Convictions and Executions for Similar Offences, on the Circuits

Years	Con.	Ex.
Home 1689–1718 *nil*		
Home 1755–1817	15	13
Western 1770–1818	7	4
Oxford 1799–1819 *Lent Assizes*	3	no return of ex.
Midland 1805–1817	3	0
Norfolk 1768–1818	4	3
Durham 1755–1819 *Lent Assizes nil*		
Lancaster 1805	5	5
Lancaster 1810	1	1
Northern 1804–1817	1	0

The fall of the Marquess of Londonderry, 1822 (Revd John Richardson, from *Recollections, Political, Literary, Dramatic, and Miscellaneous, of the Last Half-Century*, 1855)

Everybody knows the manner of the death of the Marquess of Londonderry; and a variety of motives have been assigned for the commission of the rash act by which it was caused. I will relate what my informant stated he had received from the mouth of a noble lord still living, with whom the Marquess was on terms of social intimacy, and with whom he was connected by political ties. He asserted that this account was authentic, and might be relied upon....The Marquess, in returning from the House of Commons to his abode in St. James's-square, occasionally, when the night was fine, preferred walking to riding home in a carriage. He was on these occasions, as most other persons were at that time, and to some degree at the present time, assailed by the importunities of that unfortunate class of females who live by what is called 'picking up' gentlemen in the street. To the importunities of some of these women he was, in an evil hour, induced more than once to listen....The Marquess, like many others who do things it were better they should leave undone, no doubt flattered himself that he could do them with impunity, and that they into whose society he was tempted to enter were ignorant of his name, rank, and position. No doubt such was the case at the commencement of the intercourse. It was not long before it was discovered who the gentleman was who, in his walk from the House of Commons to St. James's-square, was in the habit of listening to the syrens of the streets, and advantage was taken of the discovery, which terminated in the fatal catastrophe of self-immolation. One night the Marquess accompanied to a receptacle of debauchery one of these wanderers, and was shown into an apartment of the den. It is difficult to describe the scene that ensued. In a very short time he found to his horror that his companion was not a female, as he had supposed, but a youth dressed in female attire, and disguised to pass as a female. He had no time for reflection or delay as to what course to take; the door of the room was forced open, a couple of villains rushed in, and accused him of being about to commit an act from which nature shrinks with horror; adding at the same time, that they knew perfectly well who he was. The purport of the accusation was palpable, and, unfortunately, in the intensity of the crisis, the Marquess lost his presence of mind and his courage. He adopted the course which they suggested, and gave them all the money he had about him to secure his immediate escape. This course was precisely what they had plotted to bring about; they had secured their victim; he was in their power, and they were resolved to let him know that their silence could only be obtained by full compliance with their extortionate demands.

Day after day did these miscreants station themselves by the iron railings with which the inclosure of St. James's-square is surrounded, opposite the windows of the residence of the Marquess, and take the opportunity, by signs and motions whenever he appeared, to let him know that they had not yet forgotten the scene which they had contrived. Driven almost to distraction by this persecution, he made known his case, with all the circumstances, to the late Duke of Wellington, and to another nobleman. By them he was advised to give the wretches into custody at once, avow the full facts, and extricate himself from further disgusting thraldom. He had not the resolution to follow this advice. He shrunk from the consequences which the painful disclosure of what was really to be deplored in his conduct might produce on the feelings of his wife; and in a moment of distraction adopted the desperate remedy which was to extricate him from his prosecutors and himself.[4]

Candler and Doughty, *The Times*, 14 September 1822

Disgusting Depravity – On Monday last *Benjamin Candler*, late valet to the Duke of Newcastle, was committed to Lincoln Castle, by Sir R. Heron, Bart., charged with an unnatural offence. On the same day was committed to the same place by the Alderman of Grantham, *William Arden, Esq.*, of Great Pultney-street, Golden-square, London, charged with the same offence; and on Tuesday was committed to the Castle, by the Alderman of Grantham, *John Doughty*, of Grantham, joiner, charged with the same. A discovery of the abominable intercourse which had been carried on it, it is stated, was made through the circumstance of a letter from Grantham, intended for the valet at Clumber, but accidentally not addressed on the outside, falling into the hands of the Duke of Newcastle. His Grace, on discovering the nature of the contents, proceeded with due caution for furthering the purposes of justice, and the consequence has been the commitment of the above persons to Lincoln Castle for trial at the next assizes. The person committed as an *Esquire*, was apprehended in London after the first examination of the others at Grantham, and was brought down in safe custody in one of the mail coaches on Sunday morning. We understand that he had apartments at Grantham during the last hunting season.

The Bishop of Clogher and the soldier (extract of report of the Metropolitan Court of Armagh, 21 October 1822)

This cause of office was this day called on for hearing in the presence of his grace, the lord primate, and of four of his suffragan bishops...and of other distinguished and respectable personages. The bishop of Clogher having been thrice called in open court, did not appear; and in pain of his contumacy and contempt, the cause was proceeded in to a hearing and to its final determination....The canons are referred to in the pleading, and particularly the 42nd of those canons, by which he was and is bound as the law of his conduct and adoption. That canon particularly prohibits the commission of those offences, of which he stands charged, under the heaviest penalties of the law; and it is for the violation of that canon, and under its authority, that the cause of deprivation is now proceeded in against him. The particular facts, which constitute that offence, are fully detailed in the pleading and written evidence. That evidence is now permanent and recorded; and it fully evinced the existence of those evil habits and propensities of that unhappy man, with which he then stood charged, and which formed the foundation of that sentence which was to be pronounced against him. It also proved the fatal and depraved purposes for which he associated himself with a private soldier, wholly beneath him in rank and station, as the unworthy and vicious partner of his depravity and guilt. The place chosen by him for that base purpose was also unfitted to him as a prelate of the church, and man of high rank and station; it was a common alehouse, situate in St Alban's-place, in the city of Westminster. In his career of vice, he was very fortunately stopped, before he had perpetrated the last foul act, or crime, which he himself designed; and by which, if committed, his life would have been forfeited to the offended law of the country. Being found by the watchman and others, in a situation disgraceful and degrading to him, he was made a prisoner, in order to be removed to the watch-house of the district. He endeavoured, but in vain, to dissuade them from their purpose. On his removal, and close to that public-house in which he had been detected and arrested, he was seen and recognized by a respectable gentleman of Ireland, who, from his previous knowledge of his dress, person, and appearance, proved his identity. He had upon him at the time his usual and proper dress, as a bishop or dignitary of the church. There was no disguise or concealment upon his person or appearance. That circumstance had created an early suspicion and observance of him and his actions on that night, and contributed, with many other circumstances proved in this cause, which under other circumstances might have been difficult of attainment and of proof. In his way to the watch-house, he was surrounded and insulted by many persons, who pressed upon him, and, in a situation degrading to himself and his high office, he approached to and passed the gates of Carlton Palace. What his sensation and sentiments were, or must have been on that occasion, may be conceived; he must have then felt that he was 'fallen'. That feeling he himself displayed in a strong convulsive, but ineffectual struggle for his release and enlargement – a circumstance, too, which is of value in the ascertainment of his guilt and identity.

Extract from the memoirs of Lord Greville, commenting on the Bishop's case

The affair of the Bishop has made a great noise....Lord Sefton went to see the Soldier in prison. He says he is a fine soldierlike man and has not the air which these wretches usually have. The Bishop took no precautions, and it was next to impossible he should not have been caught. He made a desperate resistance when taken, and if his breeches had not been down they think he would have got away. It seems that the soldier will be proceeded against with the greatest vigour, and the Magistrate is much blamed for having taken such small bail as that which he required. The Duke will not spare the Soldier. Lord Lauderdale said the other day that the greatest dissatisfaction would pervade the public mind at the escape of the Bishop and the punishment of the Soldier, and the people, who cannot discriminate, or enter into nice points of law, will only see in such apparent injustice a disposition to shield an offender in the higher classes of society from the consequences of his crime, while the law is allowed to take its course with the more humble culprit. He said that he would have exacted the greatest bail of the Bishop that has ever been taken; this was £20,000 which was taken of Sir Thomas Picton.

R v. Robert Reekspear, 1832[5]

The prisoner was convicted before Mr. Justice Gasalee of sodomy.

The prosecutor, who was fourteen years old, swore that he was on South Sea Common on the 28th of July, at half-past three o'clock in the afternoon, that the prisoner took him by the collar, and threw him down amongst some furze. He then detailed the circumstances of the offence, which were strong to show penetration, and distinctly proved emission, but not during penetration, the prisoner having been interrupted.

The learned Judge left it to the jury to say, whether there had been penetration, stating that, if so, the crime was complete under the new act. The jury were of the opinion there had been, and found the prisoner guilty. The learned Judge passed sentence, but afterwards, as it appeared that there was no emission *in corpore*, *Jacob's case*, Russ. & Ry. 331, and in consequence of the opinion of Mr. Justice Taunton in *Rex v. Russell*, 1 M. & M. 122, the learned judge respited the execution till the 12th May, to give time to take the opinion of the Judges, whether the conviction was proper.

In Easter Term, 1832, all the Judges…met, and, on consideration of this case unanimously held the conviction right.[6]

The convict Attrell, *The Times*, 11 February 1833

William Thomas Attrell, who is to suffer death in the Old Bailey on Tuesday, was convicted at the October sessions of extorting money from Mr. Pearsall, of the India-house, under the threat of preferring an infamous charge against him. It appeared on the trial that he accosted Mr. Pearsall as he was walking along Cornhill, and claimed an acquaintance. Mr. Pearsall denied all knowledge of him, but persisted in walking with him, and finally demanded money, under the threat above alluded to; and Mr. Pearsall, under the influence of fear and agitation, went into a shop and borrowed 5s., which he gave to him. In the next moment another man, supposed to be a companion of Attrell's, came from the other side of the street, and made a similar demand; upon which Attrell said, 'It's all right; the gentleman has no money now, but I know where he lives, and I'll call upon him on Monday morning.' He did so, and Mr. Pearsall had a police-officer in attendance, who took him into custody. At the trial he attempted to justify his conduct, but the Court considered his defence an aggravation of his crime, and the jury having pronounced him guilty, he was sentenced to death. The delay in his execution was occasioned by some legal point, which had been reserved, with the respect to the framing of the indictment, and not because any doubt existed as to his guilt. From the frequency of offences of this description, it is said the Government has signified that, whenever a clear case is made out, the execution of the offender must inevitably follow.

Attrell was convicted of highway robbery accompanied by extortion and executed at Newgate on 12 February 1833. He wrote the following letter from the condemned cell on 11 February to the Reverend Cotton.

In my present unfortunate situation I am bound, as a duty to my fellow sinners, to guard them against the horrors of there wicked ways, perticulary to all young men, as sinful habits has brought me to this dreadful and untimely end. May they take warning by my unhappy fate, and attend to going to church or chapel, and they will not only hear it, but concider it as the salvation of there soals, as the neglecting of agoin to church or chapel has brought me to my late sinful life. Thos. Attrell.

R v. Wall, Court of the King's Bench, Westminster, 11 May 1833 (*The Times*, 13 May 1833)

A full special jury was sworn in this case.

Mr. Clarkson appeared on the part of the prosecution; Sir J. Scarlett, Mr. Adolphus, and Mr. C. Phillips were for the defendant.

Mr. Clarkson addressed the jury. This was an indictment preferred against Charles Baring Wall, Esq. [MP for Guildford], for an indecent assault. The defendant had pleaded that he was not guilty. The charge was one of so very serious a nature, and so deeply affecting the character and reputation of the defendant, that he (Mr. Clarkson) was quite sure he should receive the full and patient attention of the jury while he stated to them the circumstances out of which the prosecution arose; and he hoped that in giving a short detail of the facts, he should not only save time, but assist them in forming a correct judgement upon the case. The indictment imputed to the defendant that he had been guilty of one of the basest acts which it was possible to imagine – that of endeavouring to induce a person previously innocent to commit an abominable offence. There were three counts in the indictment, two of which charged the defendant with doing certain acts for the purpose of inducing the prosecutor to commit an abominable offence, and the third count charged him with a common assault. At the time the offence was alleged to have been committed the prosecutor, John Palmer, was a policeman of the D division, No. 122. He was a person of fair frame, a fact which in this case was of the utmost importance. He need hardly tell the jury that his (prosecutor's) circumstances were such that it had not been without considerable inconvenience he was able to procure even so humble an individual as himself (Mr. Clarkson) to lay the case before them. The defendant was a gentleman of rank, fortune, and fashion, moving in the highest and best circles of society – a gentleman whose character up to the time when this charge was made was free from reproach or suspicion. From the station he held he was, of course, able to throw around himself the protection of the ablest lawyers....The prosecutor was without professional assistance except what he (Mr. Clarkson) had been able to afford him; and he felt himself called upon to perform a most painful duty, – but painful as the duty was, he should not flinch from presenting the case to the jury. If they should find reason to doubt the prosecutor's statement, he called upon them in God's name to acquit the defendant, and it would afford him great pleasure to find that they believed him to be not guilty. If they believed the whole story to be a fabrication, let the consequences rest upon the prosecutor's head; but if, as reasonable men, judging from what they knew of the practices of the world, they had reason to be convinced that this was not a fabrication of the man's mind, then he knew full well that a special jury of England, whatever were the rank or station of the accused, would perform a painful duty firmly.

John Palmer, the prosecutor, examined. – On the 28th of February last, I was on duty in Harley-street. I was in police force, letter D, 122. About a quarter before one in the morning Mr B. Wall came up to me. I had never seen him before. He asked me what it was o'clock. I told him about a ¼ to 1. He said, 'It's a b–y fine morning, is it not?' I said, 'Yes, Sir, it's a fine morning.' He then asked me of what religion I was. I told him I was of no religion in particular, any more than the rest of us. He then said, 'D–n and – all the – religions, it is all a humbug; a parcel of boys, 14 or 15 years of age, are sent to college, and brought up to govern the country.' He asked what regiment I had belonged to, and whether I had belonged to the guards. I said, 'No.' He said, 'You're not allowed to take money, are you?' I said, 'No.' He said 'If I was to chuck a shilling on the pavement, would you pick it up?' I said 'No.' He said, 'D–n and

– the b–y system. I hate it, don't you?' I said, I did not. With that I was going away; he caught hold of my hand and squeezed it, and put a shilling into it, and (Here the witness described what took place). I did not know what he meant, and I had scarcely time to speak before he put half-a-crown into my hand; I said something which I can't recollect; when he put the shilling into my hand, he pulled his coat to one side, and (Here the witness described a most disgusting action) he had hold of my hand, and again acted in an indecent manner. I took hold of him by the collar, and said, 'B– you, do you think I am a – or what.' I took hold of him by the collar, and said he should go to the watch-house. He said something which I can't recollect. I took him to the corner of Cavendish-square. He put another shilling into my hand and said something about his character and wanted me to let him go. I said 'No; I would sooner let a gang of burglars go than I would you.' He then said, 'If you'll leave go of me, I'll walk quietly.' I let go of him, and he walked till he got to the middle of Cavendish-square, when he tried to run away. I then took hold of the collar and cuff of his coat, and said, that he should go the watch-house. He then said, 'If you'll let me go, I'll give you anything.' I said, it's no use; I tell you, as I told you before, I would rather let a gang of burglars go than I would you.' I then took him till I got into Henrietta-street, Cavendish-square; and nearly opposite Old Cavendish-street he caught hold of the railings, repeating several times, if I would let him go he would give me anything. I took him to the watch-house in Marylebone-lane.

Cross-examined by Sir James Scarlett. – I had been two years in the police; nothing of the same sort ever happened to me before; I have heard of similar things having happened to other policemen, but I never knew of any charge being made….It was my right hand he took hold of; I did not understand what he at first meant; the shilling and half-crown were in my hand at the same time; I had looked at the shilling while he put his hand in his pocket for the half-crown; I did not ask him what he meant; perhaps a minute or a minute and a half passed; it was all done almost in an instant; I did not pull my hand away, because I did not know what he was going to do; I did not know what to make of him; he had on a dirty drab great-coat and a handkerchief round his neck; I believe he pulled my hand up; I was confused at his goings on; I knew it was not a manly trick; when he gave me the second shilling I did not look at it until I got across Cavendish-square; I then put it in my pocket; I might have been more or less than ten minutes in conversation with him before I laid hold of his collar; I did not knock him down, because he did not strike me.

James Fell. – I was chief clerk to the magistrates, and took the examination of the prosecutor. Mr. Wall was then called upon to know if he had anything to say in answer. What he said I took down. He said, 'I confess to having stopped the witness, and I acknowledge that I gave him a shilling, and afterwards half-a-crown. All the rest of the man's statement is a fabrication. I never touched him, nor did he touch me, except when I put the shilling into his hand. This occurred at the lower end of Harley-street. It is also true that I gave him money to let me go; for I said, it would not be a question whether it was a weak charge or a strong one, but that it was sufficient to make the charge to blast me forever. When I gave him the half-crown I walked away, and I was much surprised when he followed and seized me. I then gave him, I thought, a sovereign, and was greatly surprised when I found, at the station-house, that I had only given him a shilling. I walked away, and was much surprised when he came and took me.'

This was the case for the prosecution.

Sir James Scarlett then addressed the jury for the defendant. He need not tell them who Mr. B. Wall was; but he might state that he had been educated at Eton, and Oxford, and that shortly after he came of age he was elected member of Parliament. He was a man well-known, – his friends were firmly attached to him, – his manners were dignified, – his language, of all men, the furthest from anything improper, blasphemous, or seditious. It was impossible for them to believe the story they had heard unless they supposed that Mr. Wall had been habituated to such language and to such conduct. Did they believe it possible that a man like Mr. Wall, for the first time in his life, should be betrayed into the gratification of an unnatural propensity at that hour of the morning, with a total stranger, in a public street, accompanied by language and acts which would be a proof of the most abandoned habits and long systematic vice? Here was a member of Parliament going out of the House of Commons at a late hour at night to take the fresh air, having, all at once, a passion for a policeman – a stranger who he had never seen before, and bestowing upon him a shilling. Such was the story of the policeman, who would have the jury believe that he did not know what Mr. Baring Wall meant when he squeezed his hand and gave him the shilling. Was the story probable? The man admitted that he looked at the shilling, that afterwards a half-crown was put into his hand, and that then the indecencies in question were committed....He would call their attention to Mr. Wall's character, even from his boyhood. It would be proved that he never had been heard to utter a blasphemous or immoral word of any kind; and yet the policeman would have them believe, that Mr. Wall burst out, all at once, with the most disgraceful language and that, too, at a time when he was not even labouring under any influence, being perfectly sober. The jury would find, by the evidence, that there was not a more fastidious man than Mr. Wall with regard to his person, never allowing even his servant to be in the room when he was washing, and being always remarkable for chasteness of feeling. Mr. Wall had always been noted for decency, propriety of behaviour, and reserved habits; and his education was such to imbue him with the feelings of religion and morality. If Mr. Wall should be convicted after the jury had heard the evidence he could adduce, no man would be safe from such a charge – no man who walked the streets at twelve o'clock at night could secure himself from the designs of a policeman.[7] The Lord Chief Justice was about to sum up the evidence, when the jury intimated that they thought it unnecessary to trouble his Lordship. They then turned round for a minute or two, and returned a verdict of *Not Guilty*. The verdict having been recorded, one of the jurymen said the jury were of the opinion that the defendant's character was entirely spotless.

R v. Nicoll, *The Times*, 5 August 1833

Home Circuit, Croydon, August 3rd.
Crown Side (Before Mr. Justice Parke)
Captain Henry Nicoll, who, our readers may remember, was one of the unnatural gang to which the late Captain Beauclerk belonged, and which latter put an end to his existence, was convicted on the clearest evidence of the capital offence. The statement by the boy Lawrence, with whom the offence was alleged to have been committed, was clear and credible, and it was confirmed by the evidence of a person connected with Captain Beauclerk, who had heard the prisoner boast to Beauclerk of the monstrous feats he had performed. The prisoner was perfectly calm and unmoved throughout the trial, and even when sentence of death was passed upon him. In performing the duty of passing sentence on the prisoner, Mr. Justice Parke told him that it would be inconsistent with his duty if he held out the slightest hope that the law would not be allowed to take its severest course.

Execution, *The Times*, 15 August 1833

Yesterday morning Henry Nicoll, late captain on the retired list of the 14th Regiment of Infantry, was executed at Horsemonger-lane Gaol. He was tried and found guilty of an unnatural offence at the late Surrey assizes, and in the course of the trial it was proved in evidence that he belonged to a gang of which Beauclerk, who, it may be recollected, committed suicide some time since in the county gaol, formed one of the parties. Nicoll meditated self-destruction himself, as will appear from what occurred after his condemnation. As soon as the trial was over, which took place on Friday, the 2d. inst., and lasted from 9 o'clock in the morning until 8 at night, he was conveyed from the Court-house at Croydon to Horsemonger-lane, and on his arrival at the gaol he was questioned by Elmes, the head turnkey, as to whether he had any instrument in his possession; in reply to this question Nicoll energetically declared that he had not. The turnkey, however, suspected this declaration, and insisted upon a strict search before he was placed in the condemned cell, and immediately commenced it. Nicoll, on finding the turnkey was determined, then began himself to turn his pockets inside out, in order to convince him of the truth of his asseveration; but the turnkey, on a minute inspection, discovered, concealed in the lining of the collar of his coat, a long nail, which was sharpened at the point like a lancet, and with which there was very little doubt he intended to destroy himself. How he became possessed of this instrument there was no means of ascertaining; at all events, it was impossible that he could have sharpened it in the manner it was found, and the supposition is, that it was conveyed to him in some way or other by the other prisoners. Nicoll had entered the army at an early period of life, and formerly belonged to the 72nd, from which he exchanged into the 14th Foot, and with this regiment had seen a good deal of service abroad. He was very respectably connected, one of his brothers having served the office of High Sheriff of Bedfordshire some years ago, and, had the former lived, he would have become entitled to some property arising from the manor of Studham, in the above county. From the period of his conviction up to the morning of the execution he conducted himself with great propriety of conduct in the gaol, and paid the utmost attention to the devotional exercises performed by the chaplain, to whom he had acknowledged the justness of his sentence on several occasions. The night previous to execution he slept soundly for some hours, and on awaking and enquiring the hour appeared anxious for the arrival of the sheriff and the executioner. At 9 o'clock precisely the unhappy man was led from his cell to the place of execution, which is immediately over the entrance into the gaol, and, after a short time spent in prayer, the drop fell and he soon ceased to exist. A large concourse of persons assembled to witness the execution, and amongst the spectators a number of females also presented themselves, and by their shouts manifested their abhorrence of the criminal. The body having been suspended the usual time was taken down and delivered over to the surgeons of one of the Borough hospitals for dissection.

R v. Gatehouse and Dowley, October 1848[8]

Central Criminal Court, October 31 1848 (Before the Common Serjeant)
Indecency – Intent to commit sodomy – indictment

Quære, *whether an indictment which charges two persons with meeting in a room for the purpose of committing sodomy, and with laying their hands upon each other for the purpose of committing sodomy, alleges an offence.*

An indictment which charges two persons with meeting in a room for the purpose of committing with each other filthy acts, and with exposing to each other their private parts in pursuance of such purpose, with intent to excite in each other filthy lusts, is bad, as showing no criminal offence.

The indictment against the prisoners was as follows:–

'Central Criminal Court, to wit the jurors for our Lady the Queen upon their oath present that Edwin Gatehouse, late of the parish of Lambeth, in the county of Surrey, and within the jurisdiction of this court, labourer, and William Dowley, late of the same place, labourer, being persons of depraved and unnatural dispositions, in the 12th year of the reign of our Sovereign Lady Victoria, by the grace of God of the united kingdom of England and Ireland, Queen, defender of the faith, with force and arms, at the parish aforesaid, in the county aforesaid, and within the jurisdiction of the said court, in a certain room there unlawfully and wickedly did meet, and were then together for the purpose of committing with each other that most detestable horrid, and abominable crime called buggery; and did then and there unlawfully and wickedly lay their hands upon each other with intent then and there feloniously, wickedly, diabolically, and against the order of nature to commit and perpetrate with each other the detestable, horrid, and abominable crime aforesaid. To the great displeasure of Almighty God, to the evil example of all others in the like case offending, and against the peace of our Lady the Queen, her crown and dignity. And the jurors aforesaid, upon their oath aforesaid, do further present that the said Edwin Gatehouse and William Dowley, being such evil disposed persons as aforesaid, afterwards (to wit) on the day and year aforesaid, with force and arms at the parish aforesaid, in the county aforesaid, and within the jurisdiction of the said court, unlawfully and wickedly did meet, and then and there were together in a certain room for the purpose and with the intent of committing and perpetrating with each other there divers nasty, wicked, filthy, beastly, and unnatural acts and practices; and that the said Edwin Gatehouse and William Dowley, in pursuance of such purpose and intent, unlawfully, wickedly, and indecently did then and there expose their naked private parts to each other, and did also then and there place their hands upon and take hold of and feel the naked private parts of each other, with intent then and there to excite and stir up in the minds of each other divers filthy, beastly, and unnatural lusts and desires, to the great scandal and subversion of religion, morality, decency and good order, and against the peace of our Lady the Queen, her crown and dignity.'

At the close of the case for the prosecution, *Ballantine*, for the prisoner, Gatehouse, objected that neither of these counts disclosed any offence. The second count was clearly bad within the principle of the cases recently decided. It did not allege that the place where the exposure took place was public; and even if it was public, the exposure was only to one person, which was not sufficient. Indecency, to be criminal, must be in a public place, and in the sight of divers of her majesty's subjects. The first count also was bad. It did not aver an attempt to commit buggery, but a mere intention accompanied by an act indicative of that intention. Such intention was not criminal. To constitute an offence, some act in pursuance of such intention, and as a commencement to the actual crime of buggery, must be shown.

The Common Serjeant.– The judges have not yet expressly decided that the second count is bad, but in accordance with the cases which have been decided, I think they would hold it be bad. I shall therefore tell the jury that, as to that count, they must against acquit the prisoners. An intent to commit sodomy, must, I think, be charged and proved. But this is, in my opinion, done in the first count; and at present, I see no reason for holding that that count is bad. But before judgement is given, I will consult some of the judges; and, if necessary, reserve the point for the consideration of all the judges.

The jury found the prisoners *Guilty on the first count.*

Judgement was respited.[9]

R v. Allen, December 1848[10]

At the December Sessions of the Central Criminal Court Henry Allen was tried, before Mr. Baron Rolfe, for an unnatural crime.

The first count charged that the said Henry Allen in and upon one John Wood feloniously did lay his hands, and then and there feloniously, wickedly, and diabolically, and against the order of nature, did carnally know, and then and there feloniously, wickedly, and diabolically, and against the order of nature, with the said John Wood did commit and perpetrate the detestable, abominable and horrid crime of, &c &c.

The second count charged that the prisoner feloniously, wickedly, and diabolically, and against the order of nature, was consenting to, and did permit and suffer the said John Wood feloniously, wickedly, and diabolically, and against the order of nature, to have a venereal affair with him, the said Henry Allen, and then and there feloniously, wickedly, and diabolically, and against the order of nature, to carnally know him, the said Henry Allen, and with him the said Henry Allen, then and there feloniously, wickedly, and diabolically, and against the order of nature, to commit the diabolical, abominable and horrid crime aforesaid against the form of, &c.

The facts proved were, that the prisoner induced John Wood, a boy of twelve years of age, to have carnal knowledge of his person – the prisoner having been the pathic in the crime.

The jury found the prisoner guilty, but the learned Baron felt some doubt whether the facts supported either count, and requested the opinion of the Judges on the case.

On the 20th of January, 1849, Lord Denman C. J., Parke B., Alderson B., Cottman J., and Coleridge J., being present, Lord Denman said, that the Court were unanimously of the opinion that the conviction was right.[11]

Offences Against the Person Act 1861

Unnatural offences

61. Whosoever shall be convicted of the abominable crime of buggery, committed either with mankind or with any animal, shall be liable, at the discretion of the court, to be kept in penal servitude for life or for any term not less than ten years.[#3]

62. Whosoever shall attempt to commit the said abominable crime, or shall be guilty of any assault with intent to commit the same, or of any indecent assault upon any male person, shall be guilty of a misdemeanour, and being convicted thereof shall be liable, at the discretion of the court, to be kept in penal servitude for any term not exceeding ten years and not less than three years, or to be imprisoned for any term not exceeding two years, with or without hard labour.

R v. Boulton, Park, Hurt and Fiske, 1870

The outline of the case for the prosecution was this: for some two or three years certain persons, alleged to have been some of the defendants – principally, it was said, Boulton and Park – had exhibited themselves at public places, dressed sometimes as women and sometimes as men, and supposed by the police to be women. They were seen at the Alhambra, at the Surrey and Strand Theatres, at the Casino in Holborn, in the Burlington Arcade, in Regent-street, in the Haymarket, and at the Oxford and Cambridge boat-race. As early as 1867 Boulton was seen walking in the Haymarket with one of the defendants who had absconded [William Somerville, Martin Luther Cumming, C. H. Thompson], dressed in women's clothes, and with painted face. Disturbances ensued, and some of the parties were taken before a magistrate, and bound over to keep the peace. But again they were seen at various places – at the Alhambra, for instance – where their conduct gave great offence, and whence they were three or four times turned out; nevertheless they returned again and again; and so they were seen in the Burlington Arcade, and were there also turned out. They promenaded Regent-street and the Haymarket at night until late hours in the morning, and made acquaintances. Their headquarters appear to have been at 13, Wakefield-street, Regent-square, where they had an extensive wardrobe of female attire and female ornaments. In April, 1870, a young gentleman named Mundell made their acquaintance at the Surrey Theatre, and took them to be women. He was taken into custody with them, and was one of the witnesses for the prosecution, and the first witness to be called. The lodgings at Wakefield-street were searched, the female dresses were found, letters were discovered, and inquiries were made which led to the present prosecution....The Attorney-General remarked on the extreme sorrow he felt at being compelled to take part in such a prosecution. But he was without any choice in the matter, the revelations in the Police Courts having rendered it imperatively necessary that the public apprehensions in respect of the charges involved should be satisfied....Having explained the general nature of the charge against the defendants, the learned Attorney-General said it would be admitted that Boulton and Park had frequently worn women's clothes for the purpose of taking part in private theatricals, still it would be for the jury to say whether persistent conduct such as that with which they were charged could be explained away by the theory that they had been guilty of a mere foolish freak....The case ended with a verdict of 'Not Guilty' against the defendants.

When the Lord Chief Justice summed up, he expressed his disapprobation of the form in which the case had been brought before the Court. 'We are trying the defendants,' he said, 'for conspiring to commit felonious crime, and the proof of it, if it amounts to any thing, amounts to proof of the actual commission of the crime, it is not the proper course to charge the parties with conspiring to commit it'....Coming to the actual facts of the case, the learned judge remarked that what had been proved against the defendants Boulton and Park was sufficient to stamp them with the deepest disgrace, although they might not have had any felonious intention. Their going, for example, to the ladies' rooms at theatres and other public places was an offence which the legislature might justly visit with corporal punishment....The jury took about an hour to consider their verdict, and when it was delivered there was a burst of applause in Court.

The defendant Boulton fainted on hearing the verdict.

R v. Ransford, Court of Criminal Appeal, 14 November 1874[12]

A count in an indictment charged that the prisoner unlawfully, wickedly, and indecently did write and send to H. a letter, with intent thereby to move and incite H. to attempt and endeavour, feloniously and wickedly to commit an unnatural offence, and by the means aforesaid did unlawfully attempt and endeavour to incite H. to attempt to commit the crime aforesaid:

Held, that the count charged was an indictable misdemeanour.

The evidence was, that H. was a boy at school, and that he had received two other letters from the prisoner, which he read, but that when he received the one mentioned in the above count he did not read it, nor was he in any way aware of its contents, but handed it over to the school authorities:

Held, that the sending the letter proved the attempt to incite, although it might be doubtful whether it could be said to amount to inciting or soliciting, inasmuch as H. was not aware of its contents.

The prisoner was tried at the September Sessions of the Central Criminal Court, 1874, upon the following indictment:

First count. – That at the time of committing the offence hereinafter in this count mentioned, one William D'Arcy Gardiner O'Halloran was a youth of the age of fourteen years, and was a scholar in the school of Christ's Hospital, and was under the care, custody, and control of the Governors of Christ's Hospital, in the city of London, and was then being educated in the said school in the principles of religion, morality, and virtue, with the object that he might thereafter, when beyond the care and control of the said Governors, enter into the society of his fellow men, and be received by them as a man of honourable, manly, and virtuous habits, and that Edward Ransford, being a person of wicked, immoral, and depraved mind and disposition, with intent to debauch the said William D'Arcy Gardiner O'Halloran, and to vitiate and corrupt his mind, on the 5th of September, 1874, unlawfully and wickedly did write and send, and cause and procure to be written and sent to the said William D'Arcy Gardiner O'Halloran, a certain lewd and indecent letter, in the words and figures following, that is to say:

Henderson's, Oakley-square, 5th Sept. 1874.

Dear O'Halloran, – The fates have hitherto prevented us from meeting, owing to my engagements. On Wednesday next, all being well, I shall meet you positively in the South Transept of St. Paul's. I shall be there between 2½ o'clock and 2¾: we can then settle where to go. How long can you stay out in the evening? Answer by return.– Yours truly, P de la R. Harrison.

I shall only be here tomorrow, and therefore a post-office is my safest address.

(The conclusion of the letter is unfit for publication.)

That the said Edward Ransford, in manner and by the means aforesaid, did unlawfully and wickedly endeavour to corrupt the morals of the said William D'Arcy Gardiner O'Halloran, with lewd, immoral, and wicked inclinations and desires, and to induce and persuade him to commit fornication and divers other immoral and wicked acts and practices, he the said William D'Arcy Gardiner O'Halloran then being such scholar as aforesaid, and so being under the care, custody and control of the said Governors, in manifest violation and corruption of the morals of the said William D'Arcy Gardiner O'Halloran and other liege subjects of our said lady the Queen. To the evil example, &c.

Second count. –...That the said Edward Ransford, being a person of wicked, immoral, and depraved mind and disposition, and seeking to debauch, vitiate, and corrupt the minds and morals of the children and other young persons being scholars in the said school, and so to hinder and prevent the said body corporate in their endeavours to instruct the said children and young persons in the principles [of virtue, religion and morality], on the day and in the year aforesaid, unlawfully and wickedly did write and send, and cause and procure to be written and sent to the said school, a certain lewd and indecent letter, addressed to one William D'Arcy Gardiner O'Halloran, then being one of the scholars in the said school, and which letter was and is the letter set forth in the first count of this indictment.

Third count. – That the said Edward Ransford…did attend at the premises of the said Christ's Hospital in London aforesaid, with the avowed object and design of procuring a personal interview with the said William D'Arcy Gardiner O'Halloran, and by false representations and fraudulent means to take and remove the said William D'Arcy Gardiner O'Halloran from and out of the care, custody, and control of the said governors, and to get him, the said William D'Arcy Gardiner O'Halloran into the custody and control of the said Edward Ransford, with the intent that he the said William D'Arcy Gardiner O'Halloran was so in his custody and control, should commit a certain felony with him the said William D'Arcy Gardiner O'Halloran, to wit, feloniously, wickedly, diabolically, and against the order of nature, to commit and perpetrate with each other the detestable and abominable crime of buggery, against, &c.

Ninth count. – That the said Edward Ransford, being a person of wicked and abandoned mind and disposition, and wholly lost to all sense of decency, chastity, and morality, and unlawfully and wickedly desiring, contriving, and intending, as much as in him lay, to vitiate, debauch, and corrupt the minds and morals of the liege subjects of our said lady the Queen, and to poison and infect the minds of the youth of this kingdom, on the 23rd of March….

The following facts were proved:

The prisoner sent, knowing their contents, three letters to a boy of the age of fourteen years, and the boy received the same….The last two letters were each on two pieces of paper – one such that it might be shown by the boy to anyone, the other intended to be read by the boy only. He read the first and second letters. He did not read the third, nor either part of it, nor in any way knew its contents, handing both parts unread to the authorities of the school where he was.

It was objected that the counts were bad, and that there was no evidence in support of them.

The jury found the prisoner guilty.

I respited judgement, and reserve for the opinion of the Court of Criminal Appeal whether any one or more, or all of the counts, is or are good, and whether there is evidence in support of any good count.

If there is no good count, or no good count in support of which there is evidence, the conviction is to be quashed; otherwise it is to stand as to such count or counts as is or are good, and in support of which there is evidence. (Signed) G. Bramwell.

No counsel appeared for the prisoner.

Straight (*Gill* with him) for the prosecution. – The conviction ought to be affirmed. It is submitted that the letter of the 5th of September, with its inclosure, justified the verdict of guilty. The first three counts allege that O'Halloran was a boy of tender years at Christ's Hospital School, and was under the care and custody of the governors thereof, and was there being educated in the said school in the principles of religion, morality and virtue.... KELLY, C.B. Without discussing the validity of those counts, have you not some count which will raise the point distinctly, whether what the prisoner did was an attempt to commit a misdemeanour? The 4th count charges that the prisoner did solicit and incite O'Halloran to commit an unnatural offence. In *Rex* v. *Higgins* (2 East, 5) it was held, that to solicit a servant to steal his master's goods is a misdemeanour, though it is not charged in the indictment that the servant stole the goods, nor that any other act was done except the soliciting and inciting. That case was recognised as law in *Reg.* v. *Gregory* (10 Cox, C. C. 459), where it was held that to solicit and incite a person to commit a felony, though no felony be in fact committed, is a misdemeanour. Here the solicitation was complete as soon as the letter was posted....POLLOCK, B. Was, then, the third letter with its inclosure, an act done with a criminal intent? I think that the sending of it to a boy with a criminal intent was a criminal act done, though the letter was not seen by the boy. *Conviction affirmed.*[13]

The Wilde trials, 1895

On 18 February 1895 the Marquess of Queensbury left a card for Oscar Wilde with the porter of the Albermarle Club. It read: 'To Oscar Wilde posing as a somdomite', the misspelling apparently a product of his rage at the relationship between Wilde and his son, Lord Alfred Douglas, which he had repeatedly threatened to make public. Wilde, against the advice of friends, started an action for libel against Queensbury, which came to court in April. Queensbury maintained that he could prove his assertion to be true, and in the course of this first trial Wilde gave sufficient hostages to fortune for his libel action to collapse, not least in the exchange (included below) concerning why he had not kissed Walter Grainger. Queensbury, in his plea of justification, accused Wilde of committing sodomy and gross indecency with ten named young men, and an unspecified number of unnamed young men. In addition, the statement on the card was supported with accusations concerning Wilde's writing, and these parts of the justification are included below. On 5 April Wilde was arrested at the Cadogan Hotel and charged with

gross indecency, the names of his alleged partners and victims being virtually identical to those in Queensbury's plea. Two sample indictments of the
twenty-five accusing him of committing gross indecency with named individuals
are included below. He was tried twice with Alfred Taylor, the owner of a male
brothel, the first criminal trial being abandoned after the jury were unable to
reach a verdict after a month of deliberations. The second criminal trial
resulted in a guilty verdict on both men, and Wilde was sentenced to the
maximum penalty under the 1885 Act.

The texts in this section include portions of trial transcripts, letters and
poems which were used to prove the case against Wilde, newspaper edito-
rials on the trials and the verdict, and material from the aftermath, written by
Wilde from Reading Gaol, and by Lord Alfred Douglas a quarter of a century
later. In these last documents, and in the extended letter *De Profundis*, Wilde
writes as a ruined man, divorced by his wife and cut off from his children,
who will die, in exile and poverty, in Paris. Douglas, on the other hand, shows
a remarkable facility for rewriting history.

Letters from Wilde to Lord Alfred Douglas

These, and the two poems by Douglas cited below, were introduced as
evidence by prosecution counsel in Queensbury's trial for libel, and subsequently in the criminal prosecution of Wilde.

My Own Boy,

Your sonnet is quite lovely, and it is a marvel that those rose-leaf lips of
yours should have been made no less for music of song than for madness of
kisses. Your slim gilt soul walks between passion and poetry. I know
Hyacinthus, whom Apollo loved so madly, was you in Greek Days.

Why are you alone in London, and when do you go to Salisbury? Do go
there to cool your hands in the grey twilight of Gothic things, and come whenever you like. It is a lovely place – it only lacks you; but go to Salisbury first.

Always, with undying love,

Yours, Oscar.

Dearest of all Boys,

Your letter was delightful, red and yellow wine to me; but I am sad and out
of sorts. Bosie, you must not make scenes with me. They kill me, they wreck
the loveliness of life. I cannot see you, so Greek and gracious, distorted with
passion. I cannot listen to your curved lips saying hideous things to me....

I must see you soon. You are the divine thing I want, the thing of grace and beauty; but I don't know how to do it. Shall I come to Salisbury? My bill here is £49 for a week. I have also got a new sitting-room....Why are you not here, my dear, my wonderful boy? I fear I must leave – no money, no credit, and a heart of lead.

Your Own Oscar.

Queensbury's plea of justification filed by the defendant in Regina (Wilde) v. Queensbury

Second Plea

The said Oscar Fingal O'Flahertie Wills Wilde in the month of July in the year of our Lord One thousand eight hundred and ninety did write and publish and cause and procure to be printed and published with his name upon the title page thereof a certain immoral and obscene work in the form of a narrative entitled 'The Picture of Dorian Gray' which said work was designed and intended by the said Oscar Fingal O'Flahertie Wills Wilde and was understood by the readers thereof to describe the relations intimacies and passions of certain persons of sodomitical and unnatural habits tastes and practices.

And that in the month of December in the year of our Lord One thousand eight hundred and ninety-four was published a certain other immoral and obscene work in the form of a magazine entitled 'The Chameleon' which said work contained divers obscene matters and things relating to the practices and passions of persons of sodomitical and unnatural habits and tastes and that the said Oscar Fingal O'Flahertie Wills Wilde published his name to the contents sheet of the said magazine as its first and principal contributor and published in the said magazine certain immoral maxims as an introduction to the same under the title of 'Phrases and Philosophies for the Use of the Young'....The said Oscar Fingal O'Flahertie Wills Wilde was a man of letters and a dramatist of prominence and notoriety and a person who exercised a considerable influence over young men, that the said Oscar Fingal O'Flahertie Wills Wilde claimed to be a fit and proper person to give advice and instruction to the young and had published the said maxims hereinbefore mentioned...and that the said Oscar Fingal O'Flahertie Wills Wilde had committed the offences aforementioned and the said sodomitical practices for a long time with impunity and without detection wherefore it was for the public benefit and interest that the matter contained in the said alleged libel should be published and that the true character and habits of the said Oscar

Fingal O'Flahertie Wills Wilde should be known that the said Oscar Fingal O'Flahertie Wills Wilde might be prevented from further committing such offences and further debauching the liege subjects of our said Lady the Queen.

First trial, second day, 4 April 1895, Carson cross-examining Wilde

Carson: Do you know Walter Grainger?

Wilde: Yes.

Carson: How old is he?

Wilde: He was about sixteen when I knew him. He was a servant at a certain house in High Street, Oxford, where Lord Alfred Douglas had rooms. I have stayed there several times. Grainger waited at table. I never dined with him. If it is one's duty to serve, it is one's duty to serve; and if it is one's pleasure to dine, it is one's pleasure to dine.

Carson: Did you ever kiss him?

Wilde: Oh, dear no. He was a peculiarly plain boy. He was, unfortunately, extremely ugly. I pitied him for it.

Carson: Was that the reason why you did not kiss him?

Wilde: Oh, Mr Carson, you are pertinently insolent.

Carson: Did you say that in support of your statement that you never kissed him?

Wilde: No. It is a childish question.

Carson: Did you ever put that forward as a reason why you never kissed the boy?

Wilde: Not at all.

Carson: Why, sir, did you mention that this boy was extremely ugly?

Wilde: For this reason. If I were asked why I did not kiss a door-mat, I should say because I do not like to kiss door-mats. I do not know why I mentioned that he was ugly, except that I was stung by the insolent question you put to me and the way you have insulted me throughout this hearing. Am I to be cross-examined because I do not like it?

Carson: Why did you mention his ugliness?

Wilde: It is ridiculous to imagine that any such thing could have occurred under any circumstances.

Carson: Then why did you mention his ugliness, I ask you?

Wilde: It was a flippant answer.

Extract from 'The case ends with a verdict against Oscar. Sir Edward Clarke asks to withdraw from the prosecution', *Evening News*, 5 April 1895

The Wilde case is sinking deeper and deeper into a foul morass where it becomes increasingly difficult to follow it. The fine verbal fencing of the first day has done little to relieve the horrible darkness of the succeeding passages of the trial, and even the Old Bailey recoiled with loathing from the long ordeal of terrible suggestion that occupied the whole of yesterday when the cross-examination left the artistic literary plane and entered the dim-lit, perfumed rooms where the poet of the beautiful joined with valets and grooms in the bond of the silver cigarette case. And when Oscar Wilde left the box the little light that had relieved the awful sombreness of the picture died out, as Mr. Carson went on to paint a horrid nocturne of terrible suggestions, a thing of blackness, only half defined, but wholly horrible.

Indictment against Wilde, 26 April 1895

Central Criminal Court. The Jurors for our Lady the Queen upon their oath present that –

First Count.
Oscar Fingal O'Flahertie Wills Wilde on the fourteenth day of March in the year of our Lord one thousand eight hundred and ninety-three at the Parish of Saint John the Baptist Savoy in the County of London and within the jurisdiction of the said Court being a male person unlawfully did commit acts of gross indecency with another male person to wit one Charles Parker against the form of the statute in such case made and provided and against the peace of our said Lady the Queen her Crown and dignity.

Twenty-fourth Count.
And the jurors aforesaid do further present that the said Oscar Fingal O'Flahertie Wills Wilde and Alfred Taylor on the first day of September in the year of our Lord one thousand eight hundred and ninety-three at the Parish of St. Margaret's Westminster in the County of London and within the

jurisdiction of the said Court unlawfully did conspire combine confederate and agree together that the said Alfred Taylor should unlawfully procure the commission of acts of gross indecency by the said Oscar Fingal O'Flahertie Wills Wilde being a male person with divers other male persons whom he the said Alfred Taylor should procure for the said unlawful purpose against the form of the statute in such case made and provided and against the peace of our said Lady the Queen her Crown and dignity.

Lord Alfred Douglas, 'Two Loves', *The Chameleon*, December 1894

I dreamed I stood upon a little hill,
And at my feet there lay a ground, that seemed
Like a waste garden, flowering at its will
With buds and blossoms. There were pools that dreamed
Black and unruffled; there were white lilies
A few, and crocuses, and violets
Purple or pale, snake-like fritillaries
Scarce seen for the rank grass, and through green nets
Blue eyes of shy pervenche winked in the sun.
And there were curious flowers, before unknown,
Flowers that were stained with moonlight, or with shades
Of Nature's wilful moods; and here a one
That had drunk in the transitory tone
Of one brief moment in a sunset; blades
Of grass that in an hundred springs had been
Slowly but exquisitely nurtured by the stars,
And watered with the scented dew long cupped
In lilies, that for rays of sun had seen
Only God's glory, for never a sunrise mars
The luminous air of Heaven. Beyond, abrupt,
A grey stone wall, o'ergrown with velvet moss
Uprose; and gazing I stood long, all mazed
To see a place so strange, so sweet, so fair.
And as I stood and marvelled, lo! across
The garden came a youth; one hand he raised
To shield him from the sun, his wind-tossed hair
Was twined with flowers, and in his hand he bore

A purple bunch of bursting grapes, his eyes
Were clear as crystal, naked all was he,
White as the snow on pathless mountains frore,
Red were his lips as red wine-spilth that dyes
A marble floor, his brow chalcedony.
And he came near me, with his lips uncurled
And kind, and caught my hand and kissed my mouth,
And gave me grapes to eat, and said, 'Sweet friend,
Come I will show you thee shadows of the world
And images of life. See from the South
Comes the pale pageant that hath never an end.'
And lo! within the garden of my dream
I saw two walking on a shining plain
Of golden light. The one did joyous seem
And fair and blooming, and a sweet refrain
Came from his lips; he sang of pretty maids
And joyous love of comely girl and boy,
His eyes were bright, and 'mid the dancing blades
Of golden grass his feet did trip for joy;
And in his hand he held an ivory lute
With strings of gold that were as maidens' hair,
And sang with voice as tuneful as a flute,
And round his neck three chains of roses were.
But he that was his comrade walked aside;
He was full sad and sweet, and his large eyes
Were strange with wondrous brightness, staring wide
With gazing; and he sighed with many sighs
That moved me, and his cheeks were wan and white
Like pallid lilies, and his lips were red
Like poppies, and his hands he clenched tight,
And yet again unclenched, and his head
Was wreathed with moon-flowers pale as lips of death.
A purple robe he wore, o'erwrought in gold
With the device of a great snake, whose breath
Was fiery flame: which when I did behold
I fell a-weeping, and I cried, 'Sweet youth,
Tell me why, sad and sighing, thou dost rove
These pleasant realms? I pray thee speak me sooth
What is thy name?' He said, 'My name is Love.'

Then straight the first did turn himself to me
And cried, 'He lieth, for his name is Shame,
But I am Love, and I was wont to be
Alone in this fair garden, till he came
Unasked by night; I am true Love, I fill
The hearts of boy and girl with mutual flame.'
Then sighing, said the other, 'Have thy will,
I am the love that dare not speak its name.'

Lord Alfred Douglas, 'In Praise of Shame', *Chameleon*, 1894

Last night unto my bed methought there came
Our lady of strange dreams, and from an urn
She poured live fire, so that mine eyes did burn
At sight of it. Anon the floating flame
Took many shapes, and one cried: I am Shame
That walks with Love, I am most wise to turn
Cold lips and limbs to fire; therefore discern
And see my loveliness, and praise my name.

And afterwards, in radiant garments dressed
With sound of flutes and laughing of glad lips,
A pomp of all the passions passed along
All the night through; till the white phantom ships
Of dawn sailed in. Whereat I said this song,
'Of all sweet passions Shame is loveliest.'

Section 2, Criminal Law Amendment Act, 1885

Any male person who, in public or private, commits, or is a party to the commission of, or procures, or attempts to procure the commission by any male person of, any act of gross indecency shall be guilty of misdemeanour, and being convicted shall be liable at the discretion of the Court to be imprisoned for any term not exceeding two years, with or without hard labour.

Second trial, fourth day, Gill cross-examines Wilde

Gill: The next poem is one described as 'Two Loves'. It contains these lines:–

'Sweet youth,
Tell me why, sad and sighing, dost thou rove
These pleasant realms? I pray thee tell me sooth,
What is thy name?' He said, 'My name is Love,'
Then straight the first did turn himself to me,
And cried, 'He lieth, for his name is Shame.
But I am Love, and I was wont to be
Alone in this fair garden, till he came
Unasked by night; I am true Love, I fill
The hearts of boy and girl with mutual flame.'
Then sighing said the other, 'Have thy will,
I am the Love that dare not speak its name.'

Was that poem explained to you?

Wilde: I think that is clear.
Gill: There is no question as to what it means?
Wilde: Most certainly not.
Gill: Is it not clear that the love described relates to natural love and unnatural love?
Wilde: No.
Gill: What is the 'Love that dare not speak its name'?
Wilde: 'The Love that dare not speak its name' in this century is such a great affection of an elder for a younger man as there was between David and Jonathan, such as Plato made the very basis of his philosophy, and such as you find in the sonnets of Michelangelo and Shakespeare. It is that deep, spiritual affection that is as pure as it is perfect. It dictates and pervades great works of art like those of Shakespeare and Michelangelo, and those two letters of mine, such as they are. It is in this century misunderstood, so much misunderstood that it may be described as the 'Love that dare not speak its name', and on account of it I am placed where I am now. It is beautiful, it is fine, it is the noblest form of affection. There is nothing unnatural about it. It is intellectual, and it repeatedly exists between an elder and a younger man, when the elder man has intellect, and

57

the younger man has all the joy, hope and glamour of life before him. That it should be so the world does not understand. The world mocks at it and sometimes puts one in the pillory for it.

Oscar Wilde to Lord Alfred Douglas, 20 May 1895

My child, today it was asked to have the verdicts rendered separately. Taylor is probably being judged at this moment, so that I have been able to come back here. My sweet rose, my delicate flower, my lily of lilies, it is perhaps in prison that I am going to test the power of love. I am going to see if I cannot make the bitter waters sweet by the intensity of the love I bear you. I have had moments when I thought it would be wiser to separate. Ah! moments of weakness and madness! Now I see that that would have mutilated my life, ruined my art, broken the musical chords which make a perfect soul. Even covered with mud I shall praise you, from the deepest abysses I shall cry to you. In my solitude you will be with me. I am determined not to revolt but to accept every outrage through devotion to love, to let my body be dishonoured so long as my soul may always keep the image of you. From your silken hair to your delicate feet you are perfection to me. Pleasure hides love from us but pain reveals it in its essence. O dearest of created things, if someone wounded by silence and solitude comes to you, dishonoured, a laughing-stock to men, oh! you can close his wounds by touching them and restore his soul which unhappiness had for a moment smothered. Nothing will be difficult for you then, and remember, it is that hope which makes me live, and that hope alone. What wisdom is to the philosopher, what God is to his saint, you are to me. To keep you in my soul, such is goal of this pain which men call life. O my love, you whom I cherish above all things, white narcissus in an unmown field, think of the burden which falls to you, a burden which love alone can make light. But be not saddened by that, rather be happy to have filled with an immortal love the soul of a man who now weeps in hell, and yet carries heaven in his heart. I love you, I love you, my heart is a rose which your love has brought to bloom, my life is a desert fanned by the delicious breeze of your breath, and whose cool springs are your eyes; the imprint of your little feet makes valleys of shade for me, the odour of your hair is like myrrh, and wherever you go you exhale the perfumes of the cassia tree.

Love me always, love me always. You have been the supreme, the perfect love of my life; there can be no other.

I decided that it was nobler and more beautiful to stay. We could not have been together. I did not want to be called a coward or a deserter. A false name, a disguise, a hunted life, all that is not for me, to whom you have been revealed on that high hill where beautiful things are transfigured.

O sweetest of all boys, most loved of all loves, my soul clings to your soul, my life is your life, and in all the worlds of pain and pleasure you are my ideal of admiration and joy.

Oscar.

Mr Justice Wills's sentencing speech

Wills: Oscar Wilde and Alfred Taylor, the crime of which you have been convicted is so bad that one has to put stern restraint upon one's self to prevent one's self from describing, in language which I would rather not use, the sentiments which must rise to the breast of every man of honour who has heard the details of these two terrible trials. That the jury have arrived at a correct verdict in this case I cannot persuade myself to entertain the shadow of a doubt; and I hope, at all events, that those who sometimes imagine that a judge is half-hearted in the cause of decency and morality because he takes care no prejudice shall enter into the case, may see that that is consistent at least with the utmost sense of indignation at the horrible charges brought home to both of you.

It is no use for me to address you. People who can do these things must be dead to all sense of shame, and one cannot hope to produce any effect upon them. It is the worst case I have ever tried. That you, Taylor, kept a kind of male brothel it is impossible to doubt. And that you, Wilde, have been the centre of a circle of extensive corruption of the most hideous kind among young men, it is equally impossible to doubt.

I shall, under such circumstances, be expected to pass the severest sentence that the law allows. In my judgement it is totally inadequate for such a case as this. The sentence of the Court is that each of you be imprisoned and kept to hard labour for two years.

Wilde: And I? May I say nothing, my lord?[14]

Editorial, *News of the World*, 26 May 1895

The Wilde case is over, and at last the curtain has fallen on the most horrible scandal which has disturbed social life in London for many years. The cries of

'Shame!' with which the sentence pronounced by Mr. Justice Wills was received, indicate that a certain section of the public in court regarded the verdict with disfavour, and that feeling will very possibly be shared by a section of the public outside. But it is well to remember, that the jury are in a position to form the best and honest opinion. They have heard all the evidence and seen the witnesses in the box, while outsiders have only had newspaper reports – necessarily containing the barest suggestion of the facts – to guide them. Yet even those who have read the reports and have taken the trouble to understand what lies behind the lines, cannot but feel that Wilde and his associate – no whit more outcast and disreputable than the erstwhile apostle of aestheticism himself – have got off lightly. Society is well rid of these ghouls and their hideous practices. Wilde practically confessed his guilt at the outset, and the unclean creatures with whom he chose to herd specifically owned that the charges were true. It is at a terrible cost that society has purged itself of these loathsome importers of exotic vice, but the gain is worth the price, and it is refreshing to feel that for once, at least, justice has been done.

Front page editorial, *The Star*, 27 May 1895

Beyond an expression of deep regret that a brilliant career should have come to so terrible an end, we have two, and only two, comments to make upon the Wilde case. The first is that if this trial had not resulted in a conviction the law relating to such offences might as well have been erased from the Statute-book. Judge and jury alike are to be congratulated upon the unflinching discharge of a grave responsibility. Our second comment is that the lesson of the trial ought not to be lost upon the headmasters, and all others who are responsible for the morals, of public schools. It rests with them, more probably than with anybody else, to exorcise this pestilence.

Oscar Wilde to Robert Ross, 23 or 30 May 1896, from Reading Gaol

Dear Robbie, I could not collect my thoughts yesterday, as I did not expect to see you till today. When you are good enough to come and see me will you always fix the day? Anything sudden upsets me.

You said that Douglas was going to dedicate a volume of poems to me. Will you write to him at once and say he must not do anything of the kind. I could not allow or accept such a dedication. The proposal is revolting and grotesque.

Also, he has unfortunately in his possession a number of letters of mine. I wish him at once to hand all these without exception over to you; I will ask you to seal them up. In case I die here you will destroy them. In case I survive I will destroy them myself. They must not be in existence. The thought that they are in his hands is horrible to me, and though my unfortunate children will never of course bear my name, still they know whose sons they are and I must try and shield them from the possibility of any further revolting disclosure or scandal.

Also, Douglas has some things I gave him: books and jewellery. I wish these to be also handed over to you – for me. Some of the jewellery I know has passed out of his possession under circumstances unnecessary to detail, but he has still some, such as the gold cigarette-case, pearl chain and enamelled locket I gave him last Christmas. I wish to be certain that he has in his possession nothing that I ever gave him. All these are to be sealed up and left with you. The idea that he is wearing or in possession of anything I gave him is peculiarly repugnant to me. I cannot of course get rid of the revolting memories of the two years I was unlucky enough to have him with me, or of the mode by which he thrust me into the abyss of ruin and disgrace to gratify his hatred of his father and other ignoble passions. But I will not have him in possession of my letters or gifts. Even if I get out of this loathsome place I know that there is nothing before me but the life of a pariah – of disgrace and penury and contempt – but at least I will have nothing to do with him nor allow him to come near me.

So you will write at once to him and get these things: until I know they are in your possession I will be more miserable than usual. It is I know an ungracious thing to ask you to do, and he will perhaps write to you in terms of coarse abuse, as he did to Sherard[15] when he was prevented from publishing more of my letters, but I earnestly beg of you not to mind. *As soon* as you have received them please write to me, and make part of your letter just like your other, with all its interesting news of literature and the stage. Let me know why Irving[16] leaves the Lyceum etc, what he is playing: what at each theatre: who did Stevenson[17] criticize severely in his letters: anything that will for an hour take my thoughts away from the one revolting subject of my imprisonment.

In writing to Douglas you had better quote my letter fully and frankly, so that he should have no loophole of escape. Indeed he cannot possibly refuse. He has ruined my life – that should content him. O.W.

Inscription on Wilde's tombstone

Oscar Wilde
Oct. 16th 1854 – Nov. 30th 1900.
Verbis meis addere nihil andebant et super
illas stillabat eloquium meum.[18]
Job. xxix 22
R.I.P.

Lord Alfred Douglas, from *Without Apology*, 1938

To sum up all I have said about him, I will say that I think he was a man of enormous genius, and that his work is quite certain to survive indefinitely, and will be read and loved by countless thousands in the future, long after the names of his present-day detractors are forgotten. I will also say that in spite of his sad moral lapses he was essentially a man of 'good will', because he was kind and charitable, in the Catholic sense, and generous and loyal to his friends, and never really an enemy of the light....I have long since got past the stage in which I consider that I have anything to defend or apologize for in my conduct to and about Wilde after his release from prison. The plain truth is that if I had been the Archangel Gabriel I could not possibly have acted better towards him than I did. I gave everything and received nothing, except abuse from *soi-disant* friends. People who do not approve of what I did are welcome to do the other thing. I care no more for their opinion now than I did at the time....The cruelty of the world was then what it always is and always will be. I was the only person in the world who wanted him, out of pure friendship and compassion, and the world, having driven him out of every other refuge, proceeded to smoke him out of this last asylum also.[19]

The prime mover in all the intrigue to separate us was Robert Ross. He was, in this, as in everything else connected with Wilde, the villain of the piece.

John Addington Symonds, 'Suggestions on the subject of sexual inversion in relation to law and education', from *A Problem in Modern Ethics*, 1896

i. The laws in force against what are called unnatural offences derive from an edict of Justinian, A.D. 538. The Emperor treated these offences as criminal, on the grounds that they brought plagues, famines, earthquakes, and the destruction of whole cities, together with their inhabitants, upon the nations who tolerated them.

ii. A belief that sexual inversion is a crime against God, nature, and the state pervades all subsequent legislation on the subject. This belief rests on (1) theological conceptions derived from the Scriptures; (2) a dread of decreasing the population; (3) the antipathy of the majority for the tastes of the minority; (4) the vulgar error that antiphysical desires are invariably voluntary, and the result either of inordinate lust or of satiated appetites.

iii. Scientific investigation has proved in recent years that a very large proportion of persons in whom abnormal sexual inclinations are manifested possess them from their earliest childhood, that they cannot divert them into normal channels, and that they are powerless to get rid of them. In these cases, then, legislation is interfering with the liberty of individuals, under a certain misconception regarding the nature of their offence.

iv. Those who support the present laws are therefore bound to prove that the coercion, punishment, and defamation of such persons are justified either (1) by any injury which these persons suffer in health of body or mind, or (2) by any serious danger arising from them to the social organism.

v. Experience, confirmed by scientific observation, proves that the temperate indulgence of abnormal sexuality is no more injurious to the individual than a similar indulgence of normal sexuality.

vi. In the present state of over-population, it is not to be apprehended that a small minority of men exercising sterile and abnormal sexual inclinations should seriously injure society by limiting the increase of the human race.

vii. Legislation does not interfere with various forms of sterile intercourse between men and women: (1) prostitution, (2) cohabitation in marriage during the period of pregnancy, (3) artificial precautions against impregnation, (4) and some abnormal modes of congress with the consent of the female. It is therefore an illogical position, when it interferes with the action of those who are naturally sterile, on the ground of maintaining the numerical standard of the population.

viii. The danger that unnatural vices, if tolerated by the law, would increase until whole nations acquired them, does not seem to be formidable. The position of women in our civilization renders sexual relations among us occidentals different from those of any country – ancient Greece and Rome, modern Turkey and Persia – where antiphysical habits have hitherto become endemic.

ix. In modern France, since the promulgation of the Code Napoleon, sexual inversion has been tolerated under the same restrictions as normal sexuality. That is to say, violence and outrages to public decency are punished, and minors are protected. But adults are allowed to dispose as they like of their own persons. The experience of nearly a century shows that in France, where sexual inversion is not criminal *per se*, there has been no extension of it through society. Competent observers, like agents of police, declare that London, in spite of our penal legislation, is no less notorious for abnormal vice than Paris.

x. Italy, by the Penal Code of 1889, adopted the principles of the Code Napoleon on the point. It would be interesting to know what led to this alteration of the Italian law. But it cannot be supposed that the results of the Code Napoleon were not fully considered.

xi. The severity of the English statutes render them almost incapable of being put into force. In consequence of this the law is not unfrequently evaded, and crimes are winked at.

xii. At the same time our laws encourage blackmailing upon false accusation; and the presumed evasion of their execution places from time to time a vile weapon in the hands of unscrupulous politicians, to attack the Government in office. Examples: the Dublin Castle Scandals of 1884,[20] the Cleveland Street Scandals of 1889.[21]

xiii. Those who hold that our penal laws are required by the interests of society must turn their attention to the higher education. This still rests on the study of the Greek and Latin classics, a literature impregnated with paederastia. It is carried on at public schools, where young men are kept apart from females, and where homosexual vices are frequent. The best minds of our youth are therefore exposed to the influences of a paederastic literature, at the same time that they acquire the knowledge and experience of unnatural practices. Nor is any trouble taken to correct these adverse influences by physiological instruction in the laws of sex.

xiv. The points suggested for consideration are whether England is still justified in restricting the freedom of adult persons, and rendering certain abnormal forms of sexuality criminal, by any real dangers to society: after it has been shown (1) that abnormal inclinations are congenital, natural, and ineradicable in a large percentage of individuals; (2) that we tolerate sterile intercourse of various types between the two sexes; (3) that our legislation has not suppressed the immorality in question; (4) that the operation of the Code Napoleon for nearly a century has not increased this immorality in France; (5) that Italy, with the experience of the Code Napoleon to guide her, adopted its principles in 1889; (6) that the English penalties are rarely inflicted to their full extent; (7) that their existence encourages blackmailing, and their non-enforcement gives occasion for base political agitation; (8) that our higher education is an open contradiction to the spirit of our laws.[4]

Textual footnotes

1 Leviticus, xx, 13, 15, 16.
2 So called, because at the coming of Christ the Pagans were unusually given up to such practices, and the apostles strongly commended their converts not *even to mention* those as well as other indecencies.
3 For this offence penal servitude is now substituted for that of death (recorded) under the old law. The alteration has this advantage, the culprit and the public now at once know the punishment to be undergone, whereas before they were in ignorance of it, they only knew that death would *not* be inflicted; hence one of the great purposes of punishment – example to others was unfulfilled.
4 It may not be superfluous to recapitulate the main points of English legislation on this topic. (1) Sodomy is a felony, defined as the carnal knowledge (per anum) of any man or of any woman by a male person; punishable with penal servitude for life as a maximum, for ten years as a minimum. (2) The attempt to commit sodomy is punishable with ten years' penal servitude as a maximum. (3) The commission, in public or in private, by any male person with another male person, of 'any act of gross indecency', is punishable with two years' imprisonment and hard labour.

3 SCIENCE

The major British work of the 1890s which deals in scientific terms with the causes and practices of homosexuality is Havelock Ellis and John Addington Symonds's *Sexual Inversion*. Ellis was at work on a multi-volume work of sexological analysis of all possible sexual practices, entitled *Studies in the Psychology of Sex*, and the first volume in the original series dealt with homosexuality. Subsequent volumes considered such things as onanism, fetishism, urolagnia and the cultural variability of sexual taboos, and were all solely authored by Ellis. For volume one, however, he sought a knowledge-able collaborator and wrote to Symonds proposing a joint publication. *Sexual Inversion* is, consequently, a curious hybrid, because, as can be seen from Symonds's letter to Ellis (see p. 90 below), they did not actually agree on fundamental points of scientific interpretation. But the book as a whole relies on the apparatus of empiricism, a substantial part of it being made up of detailed case histories, to prove that inverts were born so and could not help it.

The fate of the original work and subsequent British editions of it was rather unfortunate. The book first appeared in German in 1896 out of Leipzig as *Das Konträre Geschlechtsgefühl von Havelock Ellis und John Addington Symonds*, and in English in 1897, published by Wilson & Macmillan, 16 John St, Bedford Row, London, a wholly fictitious firm. The contents and presentation of these two editions is virtually identical, with 'A problem in Greek ethics' and 'Ulrichs' views' both signed by Symonds. The German edition also contained Symonds's 'Soldatenliebe und Verwandtes', which was omitted from every subsequent publication. Symonds died in 1896 and at the publication in April 1897 of *Sexual Inversion* his family protested and threatened legal action for defamation. Ellis reissued the book in October 1897, having recalled as many of the edition as he could, but by no means all. This second version was substantially the same, containing the same chapters and appendices, but had no reference at all to Symonds, either as joint author or contributor. But Ellis's problems did not end there. In 1898 the work was caught up by accident in the so-called Bedborough Trial, the prosecution of Thomas Bedborough, owner of the bookshop of the Adult League (an organization campaigning for the legal recognition of relationships outside of marriage and for the children of those relationships to have legal equality with the offspring of married people) for selling obscene material. Police officers working under cover purchased a copy of *Sexual Inversion* amongst other books. The book itself was not prosecuted for obscenity, and as a result neither Ellis nor any of his expert witnesses were permitted to give evidence at the trial. Following the success of the prosecution, Ellis, in the privately published *A Note on the Bedborough Trial*, announced that he would never publish on sexology again in Britain, and also defended his motives in publishing *Sexual Inversion*:

> The incriminated passages, when read out in court, proved to be simple statements of fact, mostly from the early life of the cases of inversion recorded in the volume, and my responsibility for them merely lay in the fact that I judged them to contain, in bald uncoloured language, the minimum of definite physical fact required in such a book, if it is to possess any scientific value at all....In its final English shape it expresses my most mature convictions on the subject it treats; the opinion of judicious friends had been obtained at doubtful points, and every sentence carefully weighed. Errors of fact or opinion may possibly be found, but there is not a word which on moral grounds I feel any reason to regret or withdraw....The numerous letters of gratitude for the work, and strong support of its objects, which have reached me from the thinkers and social reformers, men and women, I refrain from more than mentioning....In submitting to these conditions an author puts his publisher and printer into an unmerited position of danger, he risks the distortion of his own work while it is in progress; and when he has written a book which is approved by the severest and most competent judges he is tempted to adapt it to the vulgar tastes of the policeman.[1]

All subsequent editions of *Sexual Inversion* and other works by Ellis on any aspect of sexuality were published in Philadelphia, and Symonds's name was never publicly linked with the work again.

Symonds's pamphlet, *A Problem in Modern Ethics*, published in 1891, is the precursor to his collaboration with Ellis on *Sexual Inversion*. It was published privately in a limited edition of ten copies, and claimed by Symonds to be intended only for close friends and sympathetically interested experts in medicine and science. It is an educational and propagandist text intended to shift the terms of the debate about sexual inversion, and as such is both a survey of European and American writings on homosexuality, and a presentation of his own ideas about the inadequacies of the theories propounded in such writings. The core argument running through the entire text is that, while homosexuality or inversion is an eternal given, understandings of homosexuality are culturally produced and thus subject to change over history and between cultures. In this way, he rejects the dominant culture's judgements on homosexuality as a symptom of social malaise or cultural or racial corruption. At the same time, he constructs himself as a sexologist, the person who knows the truth by virtue of the objective methodologies of scientific inquiry. From this position he produces science as the means of truly understanding what is a fixed and universal part of human sexuality, and which has an essence which is not provisional or culturally produced, as the explanations of it are. Amongst the theories he rejects are those of disease and degeneracy, external androgyny and physical defect, heredity and effeminacy. Instead, he presents homosexuality as natural and straightforward, because it is innate. It may be innocent and uncorrupt, or it may be exclusively sexually and morally corrupt, just like heterosexuality, and it is this which represents the key move in his argument. Heterosexuality is given primacy, as the original and normative manifestation of the balance of femininity and masculinity in the individual, and inversion is a distorted version of that same relationship, which represents a move to put heterosexuality and homosexuality on the same footing: they occupy the same discursive, conceptual space, and this marks his argumentation as fundamentally different to the more apologetic, defensive models of his European predecessors. The last third of the extract here is a remarkable *tour de force* of rhetoric, using Ulrichs to speak all the criticisms of hypocrisy and to refute objections to equality. This was a note of confidence he was rarely able to strike again, and never in any of his mainstream publications, where, as can be seen from others of his works included in this volume, his writing is distorted by fears and distinctions between one kind of homosexual and another. This text is also distinguished by being the most detailed engagement in English with the theories of sexual inversion.

Classification of types is the prime interest of the pseudonymous 'Xavier Mayne'[2] in his private publication of 1909, *The Intersexes*, which, in the Preface, he asserts 'is addressed particularly to the individual layman, intelligently inclined to social sciences; whether he has any immediate reason to study simisexuality, or none'. In addition to adumbrating his own theories on inversion (and developing his own jargon), he provides the reader with an extensive and detailed questionnaire for them to determine their own position along his spectrum of perversion. For him it is a matter of degree of inversion, rather than a simple either/or. What might sound negative or damning in his vocabulary and theorization, actually emerges as a somewhat bizarre recommendation of the Uranian as the most highly developed, civilized, intelligent, creative brand of human being, although with a marked oversensitivity to pain, both physical and emotional. Such virtues do not, however, extend to the female of the species, the Uraniad, who combines the worst of masculinity with a lack of all the finer traits of femininity, and who is in addition sexually unsatisfied and likely to be found in a lunatic asylum. This is not so very different from the account of female inversion to be found in *Sexual Inversion*, where lesbians are seen as both failed men and failed women.

Females are entirely absent from what is arguably the oddest of the scientific texts, not included here because it was published in French in Paris, Marc-André Raffalovich's *Uranism and Uni-sexuality: A Study of Different Manifestations of Sexual Instinct* (1896). Raffalovich's model of inversion is all but impossible to disentangle from the turgid prose which seems a product of reasonable English being translated into very bad French. A representative passage may be translated as follows:

> Inversion, whether congenital or acquired, is very common amongst the poor, amongst coarse people. This exhaustion moreover is as frequent amongst them as it is in the educated classes; alcoholism, syphilis are found everywhere, bad diet, an excess of privation and suffering, or of brutality, bestiality, have comparable effects to those that dyspepsia and neurasthenia[3] have amongst the rich. If these causes act in one class they act in another. Reading the Classics is replaced by low conversation, the liberty of children and grown ups by promiscuity. It is probably more difficult for a man of the people to realize his inversion in good time, he probably makes more attempts at heterosexuality before his recognition, but that's all the difference there is. Boys of the common people are exposed much more to seduction than boys in the superior classes: nights spent in the bed of an older boy or of a man often end up in mutual masturbation. If they are heterosexual it stops there, but if they are inclined to unisexuality they persist in it. Prisons, penal colonies, cells, shared work, workshops, are just as much places of unisexuality as the promiscuity of big towns.

Raffalovich seems to have taken a much more cultural or environmental line on the causes of inversion. He also incorporates a strong element of blame, even accusation, of those who choose to indulge their tendencies.

This chapter concludes with what might seem thoroughly bad science, with extracts from two papers given by Edith Ellis (wife of Havelock Ellis) to the Eugenics Education Society in 1911. Whatever the political implications of such a belief may be, Ellis here uses eugenics, supposedly concerned with breeding the fittest and best race by removing all deviant and deficient elements from the breeding pool, to argue that 'nature' has a purpose and a reason for these abnormals, of which she was one. That purpose appears to be that these people are favoured by Nature, since, if they are not preoccupied with producing biological children, they can serve the greater good by creating 'spiritual children', works of art and tasks of social benefit.

Edmund Gosse, 'Neurasthenia', *Collected Poems*, 1911

Curs'd from the cradle and awry they come,
    Masking their torment from a world at ease;
On eyes of dark entreaty, vague and dumb,
    They bear the stigma of their souls' disease.

Bewildered by the shadowy ban of birth,
    They learn that they are not as others are,
Till some go mad and some sink prone to earth,
    And some push stumbling on without a star;

And some, of sterner mould, set hard their hearts,
    To act the dreadful comedy of life,
And wearily grow perfect in their parts; –
    But all are wretched and their years are strife.

The common cheer that animates mankind,
    The tender general comfort of the race,
To them is colour chattered to the blind,
    A book held up against a sightless face.

Like sailors drifting under cliffs of steel,
    Whose fluttering magnets leap with lying poles,
They doubt the truth of every law they feel,
    And death yawns for them if they trust their souls.

The loneliest creatures in the wash of air,
    They search the world for solace, but in vain;
No priest rewards their confidence with prayer,
    And no physician remedies their pain.

Ah! let us spare our wrath for these, forlorn,
    Nor chase a bubble on the intolerant wave;
Let pity quell the gathering storm of scorn,
    And God, who made them so, may soothe and save.

John Addington Symonds, from
A Problem in Modern Ethics, 1896

From Chapter 2, 'Vulgar errors'

Gibbon's remarks[4] upon the legislation of Constantine, Theodosius, and Justinian supply a fair example of the way in which men of learning and open mind have hitherto regarded what, after all, is a phenomenon worthy of cold and calm consideration. 'I touch,' he says, 'with reluctance, and despatch with impatience, a more odious vice, of which modesty rejects the name, and nature abominates the idea.' After briefly alluding to the morals of Etruria, Greece, and Rome, he proceeds to the enactment of Constantine: 'Adultery was first declared to be a capital offence...the same penalties were inflicted on the passive and active guilt of paederasty; and all criminals, of free or servile condition, were either drowned, or beheaded, or cast alive into the avenging flames.' Then, without further comment, he observes: 'The adulterers were spared by the common sympathy of mankind; but the lovers of their own sex were pursued by general and pious indignation.' 'Justinian relaxed the punishment at least of female infidelity: the guilty spouse was only condemned to solitude and penance, and at the end of two years she might be recalled to the arms of a forgiving husband. But the same Emperor declared himself the implacable enemy of unmanly lust, and the cruelty of his persecution can scarcely be excused by the purity of his motives. In defiance of every principle of justice he stretched to past as well as future offences the operations of his edicts, with the previous allowance of a short respite for confession and pardon. A painful death was inflicted by the amputation of the sinful instrument, or the insertion of sharp reeds into the pores and tubes of most exquisite sensibility.' One consequence of such legislation may be easily foreseen. 'A sentence of death and infamy was often founded on the slight and suspicious evidence of a child or a servant: the guilt of the green faction, of the rich, and of the enemies of Theodora, was presumed by the judges, and paederasty became the crime of those to whom no crime could be imputed.'[5]

This state of things has prevailed wherever the edicts of Justinian have been adopted into the laws of nations. The Cathari, the Paterini, the heretics of Provence, the Templars, the Fraticelli, were all accused of unnatural crimes, tortured into confession, and put to death. Where nothing else could be adduced against an unpopular sect, a political antagonist, a wealthy corporation, a rival in literature, a powerful party-leader, unnatural crime was insinuated, and a cry of 'Down with the pests of society' prepared the populace for a crusade.

It is the common belief that all subjects of sexual inversion have originally loved women, but that, through monstrous debauchery and superfluity of naughtiness, tiring of normal pleasure, they have wilfully turned their appetites into other channels. This is true about a certain number. But the sequel of this Essay will prove that it does not meet by far the larger proportion of cases, in which such instincts are inborn, and a considerable percentage in whom they are also inconvertible. Medical jurists and physicians have recently agreed to accept this as a fact.

It is a common belief that a male who loves his own sex must be despicable, degraded, depraved, vicious, and incapable of humane or generous sentiments. If Greek history did not contradict this supposition, a little patient enquiry into contemporary manners would suffice to remove it. But people will not take this trouble about a matter, which like Gibbon, they 'touch with reluctance and despatch with impatience'. Those who are obliged to do so find to their surprise that 'among the men who are subject to this deplorable vice there are even quite intelligent, talented, and highly-placed persons, of excellent and even noble character'. The vulgar expect to discover the objects of their outraged animosity in the scum of humanity. But these may be met with every day in the drawing-rooms, law-courts, banks, universities, mess-rooms; on the bench, the throne, the chair of the professor; under the blouse of the workman, the cassock of the priest, the epaulettes of the officers, the smock-frock of the ploughman, the wig of the barrister, the mantle of the peer, the costume of the actor, the tights of the athlete, the gown of the academician.

It is the common belief that one, and only one, unmentionable act is what the lovers seek as the source of their unnatural gratification, and that this produces spinal disease, epilepsy, consumption, dropsy, and the like. Nothing can be more mistaken, as the scientifically reported cases of avowed and adult sinners amply demonstrate. Neither do they invariably or even usually prefer the *aversa Venus*;[6] nor, when this happens, do they exhibit peculiar signs of suffering in health. Excess in any venereal pleasure will produce diseases of nervous exhaustion and imperfect nutrition. But the indulgence of inverted sexual instincts within due limits, cannot be proved to be especially pernicious. Were it so, the Dorians and Athenians, including Sophocles, Pindar, Æschines, Epaminondas, all the Spartan kings and generals, the Theban legion, Pheidias, Plato, would have been one nation of rickety, phthisical,[7] dropsical[8] paralytics. The grain of truth contained in this vulgar error is that, under the prevalent laws and hostilities of modern society, the inverted passion has to be indulged furtively, spasmodically, hysterically; that the repression of it through fear and shame frequently leads to habits of self-abuse; and that its unconquerable solicitations sometimes convert it from a healthy outlet of the sexual nature into a morbid monomania. It is also true that professional male prostitutes, like their female counterparts, suffer from local and constitutional disorders, as is only natural.

It is the common belief that boys under age are especially liable to corruption. This error need not be confuted here. Anyone who chooses to read the cases recorded by Caspar–Liman,[9] Caspar in his Novellen,[10] Krafft-Ebing, and Ulrichs, or to follow the developments of the present treatise, or to watch the manners of London after dark, will be convinced of its absurdity. Young boys are less exposed to dangers from abnormal than young girls from normal voluptuaries.

It is the common belief that all subjects from inverted instincts carry their lusts written in their faces; that they are pale, languid, scented, effeminate, painted, timid, oblique in expression. This vulgar error rests upon imperfect observation. A certain class of such people are undoubtedly feminine. From their earliest youth they have shown marked inclination for the habits and the dress of women; and when they are adult, they do everything in their power to obliterate their manhood. It is equally true that such unsexed males possess a strong attraction for some abnormal individuals. But it is a gross mistake to suppose that all the tribe betray these attributes. The majority differ in no detail of their outward appearance, their physique, or their dress from normal men. They are athletic, masculine in habits, frank in manner, passing through society year after year without arousing a suspicion of their inner temperament. Were it not so, society would have long ago have had its eyes opened to the amount of perverted sexuality it harbours.

The upshot of this discourse on vulgar errors is that popular opinion is made up of a number of contradictory misconceptions and confusions. Moreover, it has been taken for granted that 'to investigate the depraved instincts of humanity is unprofitable and disgusting'. Consequently the subject has been imperfectly studied; and individuals belonging to radically different species are confounded in one vague sentiment of reprobation. Assuming that they are all abominable, society is content to punish them indiscriminately. The depraved debauchee who abuses boys receives the same treatment as the young man who loves a comrade. The male prostitute who earns his money by extortion is scarcely more condemned than a man of birth and breeding who has been seen walking with soldiers.

From Chapter 7, 'Literature – polemical'

It can hardly be said that inverted sexuality received a serious and sympathetic treatment until a German jurist, named Karl Heinrich Ulrichs, began his long warfare against what he considered to be prejudice and ignorance upon a topic of the greatest moment to himself. A native of Hanover, and writing at first under the assumed name of Numa Numantius, he kept pouring out a series of polemical, analytical, theoretical, and apologetical pamphlets between the years 1864 and 1870. The most important of these works is a lengthy and comprehensive Essay entitled 'Memnon. Die Geschlechtsnatur des mannliebenden Urnings. Eine naturwissenschaftliche Darstellung. Schleiz, 1868'. Memnon may be used as the text-book of its author's theories; but it is also necessary to study earlier and later treatises – Inclusa, Formatrix, Vindex, Ara Spei, Gladius Furens, Incubus, Argonauticus, Prometheus, Araxes, Kritische Pfeile – in order to obtain a complete knowledge of his opinions, and to master the whole mass of information he has brought together.

The object of Ulrichs in these miscellaneous writings is two-fold. He seeks to establish a theory of sexual inversion upon the basis of natural science, proving the abnormal instincts are inborn and healthy in a considerable percentage of human beings; that they do not owe their origins to bad habits of any kind, to hereditary disease, or to wilful depravity; that they are incapable in the majority of cases of being extirpated or converted into normal channels; and that the men subject to them are neither physically, intellectually, nor morally inferior to normally constituted individuals. Having demonstrated these points to his own satisfaction, and supported his views with a large induction of instances and a respectable show of erudition, he proceeds to argue that the present state of the law in many states of Europe is flagrantly unjust to a class of innocent persons, who may indeed be regarded as unfortunate and inconvenient, but who are guilty of nothing which deserves reprobation and punishment. In this second and polemical branch of his exposition, Ulrichs assumes, for his juristic starting-point, that each human being is born with natural rights which legislation ought not to infringe but protect. He does not attempt to confute the utilitarian theory of jurisprudence, which regards laws as regulations made by the majority in the supposed interests of society. Yet a large amount of his reasoning is designed to invalidate utilitarian arguments in favour of repression, by showing that no social evil ensues in those countries which have placed abnormal sexuality upon the same footing as the normal, and that the toleration of inverted passion threatens no danger to the well-being of nations.

After this prelude, an abstract of Ulrichs' theory and his pleading may be given, deduced from the comparative study of his numerous essays.

The right key to the solution of the problem is to be found in physiology, in that obscure department of natural science which deals with the evolution of sex. The embryo, as we are now aware, contains an undetermined element of sex during the first months of pregnancy. This is gradually worked up into male and female organs of procreation; and these, when the age of puberty arrives, are generally accompanied by corresponding male and female appetites. That is to say, the man in an immense majority of cases desires the woman, and the woman desires the man. Nature, so to speak, aims at differentiating the undecided foetus into a human being of one or the other sex, the propagation of the species being the main object of life. Still, as Aristotle puts it, and as we observe in many of her operations, 'Nature wishes, but has not always the power.' Consequently, in respect of physical structure, there comes to light imperfect individuals, so-called hermaphrodites, whose sexual apparatus is so far undetermined that many a real male has passed a portion of his life under a mistake, has worn female clothes, and has cohabited by preference with men. Likewise, in respect of spiritual nature, there appear males who, not withstanding their marked masculine organisation, feel from the earliest childhood a sexual proclivity toward men, with a corresponding indifference for women. In some of these abnormal, but natural, beings, the appetite for men resembles the normal appetite of men for women; in others it resembles the normal appetite of women for men. That is to say, some prefer effeminate males, dressed in feminine clothes and addicted to female occupations. Others prefer powerful adults of an ultra-masculine stamp. A third class manifest their predilection for healthy young men in the bloom of adolescence, between nineteen and twenty. The attitude of such persons toward women also varies. In genuine cases of inborn sexual inversion a positive horror is felt when the woman has to be carnally known; and this horror is of the same sort as that which normal men experience when they think of cohabitation with a male. In others the disinclination does not amount to repugnance; but the abnormal man finds considerable difficulty in stimulating himself to the sexual act with females, and derives a very imperfect satisfaction of the same. A certain type of man, in the last place, seems to be indifferent, desiring males at one time and females at another.

In order to gain clearness in his exposition, Ulrichs has invented names for these several species. The so-called hermaphrodite he dismisses with the German designation of *Zwitter*. Imperfect individuals of this type are not to be considered, because it is well known that the male or female organs are never developed in one and the same body. It is also, as we shall presently discover, an essential part of his theory to regard the problem of inversion psychologically.

The normal man he calls *Dioning*, the abnormal man *Urning*. Among Urnings, those who prefer effeminate males are christened by the name of *Mannling*; those who prefer powerful and masculine adults receive the name of *Weibling*; the Urning who cares for adolescents is styled a *Zwischen-Urning*. Men who seem to be indifferently attracted by both sexes, he calls *Uranodioninge*. A genuine Dioning, who, from lack of women, or under the influence of special circumstances, consorts with persons of his own sex, is denominated *Uraniaster*. A genuine Urning, who has put restraint upon his inborn impulse, who has forced himself to cohabit with women, or has perhaps contacted marriage, is said to be *Virilisirt* – a virilised Urning.

These outlandish names, though seemingly pedantic and superfluous, have their technical value, and are necessary to an understanding of Ulrichs' system. He is dealing exclusively with individuals classified by common parlance as males without distinction. Ulrichs believes that he can establish a real natural division between men proper, whom he calls *Dioninge*, and males of an anomalous sexual development, whom he calls *Urninge*. Having proceeded so far, he finds the necessity of distinguishing three broad types of the Urning, and of making out the crosses between Urning and Dioning, of which he also finds three species. It will appear in the sequel that whatever may be thought about his psychological hypothesis, the nomenclature he has adopted is useful in discussion, and corresponds to well-defined phenomena, of which we have abundant information. The following table will make his analysis sufficiently plain:–

Broadly speaking, the male includes two main species: Dioning and Urning, men with normal and men with abnormal instincts. What, then, constitutes the

The Human Male

(1) Man or Dioning	Uraniaster, when he has acquired the tastes of the Urning
(2) Urning	Mannling Weibling
	Zwischen-Urning Virilized Urning
(3) Uranodioning	
(4) Hermaphrodite	

distinction between them? How are we justified in regarding them as radically divergent?

Ulrichs replies that the phenomenon of sexual inversion is to be explained by physiology, and particularly by the evolution of the embryo. Nature fails to complete her work regularly and in every instance. Having succeeded in differentiating a male with full-formed sex organs from the undecided foetus, she does not always effect the proper differentiation of that portion of the physical being in which resides the sexual appetite. There remains a female soul in a male body. *Anima muliebris virili corpore inclusa*, is the formula adopted by Ulrichs; and he quotes a passage from the 'Vestiges of Creation', which suggests that a male is a more advanced product of sexual evolution than the female. The male instinct of sex is a more advanced product than the female instinct. Consequently men appear whose body has been differentiated as masculine, but whose sexual instinct has not progressed beyond the feminine stage.

Ulrichs' own words ought to be cited upon his fundamental part of his hypothesis, since he does not adopt the opinion that the Urning is a Dioning arrested at a certain point of development; but rather that there is an element of uncertainty attending the simultaneous evolution of physical and psychical factors from the indeterminate ground-stuff. 'Sex,' says he, 'is only an affair of development. Up to a certain stage of embryonic existence all living mammals are hermaphroditic. A certain number of them advance to the condition of what I call man (Dioning), others to what I call woman (Dioningin), a third class become what I call *Urning* (including *Urningin*). It ensues therefrom that between these three sexes there are no primary, but only secondary differences. And yet true differences, constituting sexual species, exist as facts.' Man, Woman, and Urning – the third being either a male or a female in whom we observe a real and inborn, not an acquired or a spurious, inversion of appetite – are consequently regarded by him as the three main divisions of humanity viewed from the point of view of sex. The embryonic ground-stuff in the case of each was homologous; but while the two former, Man and Woman, have been normally differentiated, the Urning's sexual instinct, owing to some imperfection in the process of development, does not correspond to his or her sexual organs.

The line of division between the sexes, even in adult life, is a subtle one; and the physical structure of men and women yields indubitable signs of their emergence from a common ground-stuff. Perfect men have rudimentary breasts. Perfect women carry a rudimentary penis in their clitoris. The raphé[11] of the scrotum shows where the aperture, common at first to masculine and feminine beings, but afterwards only retained in the female vulva, was closed up to form a male. Other anatomical details of the same sort might be adduced. But these will suffice to make thinking persons reflect upon the mysterious dubiety of what we call sex. That gradual development, which ends in normal differentiation, goes on very slowly. It is only at the age of puberty that a boy distinguishes himself abruptly from a girl, by changing his voice and growing hair on parts of the body where it is not usually found in women. This being so, it is surely not surprising that the sexual appetite should sometimes fail to be normally determined, or in other words, should be inverted.

Ulrichs maintains that the body of an Urning is masculine, his soul feminine, so far as sex is concerned. Accordingly, though physically unfitted for coition with men, he is imperatively drawn towards them by a natural impulse. Opponents meet him with this objection: 'Your position is untenable. Body and soul constitute one inseparable entity.' So they do, replies Ulrichs; but the way in which these factors of the person are combined in human beings differ extremely, as I can prove by indisputable facts. The body of a male is visible to the eyes, is measurable and ponderable, is clearly marked in its specific organs. But what we call his soul – his passions, inclinations, sensibilities, emotional characteristics, sexual desires – eludes the observation of the senses. This second factor, like the first, existed in the undetermined stages of the foetus. And when I find that the soul, this element of instinct and emotion and desire existing in a male, has been directed in its sexual appetite from earliest boyhood towards persons of the male sex, I have the right to qualify it with the attribute of femininity. You assume that soul-sex is indissolubly connected and inevitably derived from body-sex. The facts contradict you, as I can prove by referring to the veracious autobiographies of Urnings and to known phenomena regarding them.

Such is the theory of Ulrichs; and though we not incline to his peculiar mode of explaining the want of harmony between sexual organs and sexual appetite in Urnings, there can be no doubt that in some way or other their eccentric diathesis must be referred to the obscure process of sexual differentiation. Perhaps he antedates the moment at which the aberration sometimes takes in origin, not accounting sufficiently for imperative impressions made on the imagination or the senses of boys during the years which precede puberty.

However this may be, the tendency to such inversion is certainly inborn in an extremely large percentage of cases. That can be demonstrated from the reports of persons whose instincts were directed to the male before they knew what sex meant. It is worth extracting passages from these confessions. (1) 'As a schoolboy of eight years, I sat near a comrade rather older than myself; and how happy was I when he touched me. That was the first indefinite perception of an inclination which remained a secret for me till my nineteenth year.' (2) 'Going back to my seventh year, I had a lively feeling for a schoolfellow, two years older than myself; I was happy when I could be as close as possible to him, and in our games could place my head near his private parts.' (3) 'At ten years of age he had a romantic attachment for a comrade; and the passion for people of his own sex became always more and more marked.' (4) Another confessed that 'already at the age of four he used to dream of handsome grooms.' (5) A fifth said: 'My passion for people of my own sex awoke at the age of eight. I used to enjoy my brother's nakedness; while bathing with other children, I took no interest at all in the girls, but felt the liveliest attraction towards boys.' (6) A sixth dates his experience from his sixth or seventh year. (7) A seventh remembers that 'while yet a boy, before the age of puberty, sleeping in the company of a male agitated him to such an extent that he lay for hours awake'. (8) An eighth relates that 'while three years old, I got possession of a fashion book, cut out the pictures of men, and kissed them to tatters. The pictures of women I did not care to look at'. (9) A ninth goes back to his thirteenth year, and a school friendship. (10) A tenth records the same about his seventh year. (11) An eleventh says that his inverted instincts awoke in early childhood, and that from his ninth year onward he fell over and over again in love with adult men. (12) A twelfth spoke as follows: 'So far back as I can remember, I was always subject to this passion. Quite as a child, young men made deeper impression on me than women or girls. The earliest sensual perturbation of which I have any recollection was excited by a tutor, when I was nine or ten, and my greatest pleasure was to be allowed to ride astride upon his leg.' (13) A thirteenth: 'From the earliest childhood I have been haunted by visions of men, and only of men; never has a woman exercised the least influence over me. At school I kept these instincts to myself, and lived quite retired.' (14) A fourteenth can recollect 'receiving a distinctly sensual impression at the age of four, when the manservants caressed him.' (15) A fifteenth says that at the age of thirteen, together with puberty, the inversion of appetite awoke in him. (16) A sixteenth confesses that he felt an unconquerable desire for soldiers in his thirteenth year. (17) A seventeenth remembers having always dreamed only of men; and at school, he says, 'when my comrades looked at pretty girls and criticised them during our daily promenades, I could not comprehend how they found anything to admire in such creatures'. On the other hand, the sight and touch of soldiers and strong fellows excited him enormously. (18) An eighteenth dates the awakening of passion in him at the age of eleven, when he saw a handsome man in church;

and from that time forward his instinct never altered. (19) A nineteenth fell in love with an officer at the age of thirteen, and since then always desired vigorous adult males. (20) A twentieth confessed to have begun to love boys of his own age, sensually, when only eight years of age. (21) A twenty-first records that, when he was eight, he began to crave after the sight of naked men.

In addition to these cases a great many might be culled from the writings of Ulrichs, who has published a full account from his own early experience. 'I was fifteen years and ten and a half months old,' he says, 'when the first erotic dream announced the arrival of puberty. Never before that period had I known sexual gratification of any kind whatever. The occurrence was there-fore wholly normal. From a much earlier time, however, I had been subject to emotions, partly romantic, partly sensual, without any definite desire, and never for one and the same young man. These aimless yearnings of the senses plagued me in my solitary hours, and I could not overcome them. During my fifteenth year, while at school in Detmold, the vague longing took a twofold shape. First, I came across Norman's 'Säulenordnungen,'[12] and there I was vehemently attracted by the figure of a Greek god or hero, standing in naked beauty. Secondly, while studying in my little room, or before going to sleep, the thought used suddenly and irresistibly to rise up in my mind – If only a soldier would clamber through the window and come into my room! I then painted in my fancy the picture of a splendid soldier of twenty to twenty-two years old. And yet I had no definite idea of why I wanted him; nor had I ever come in contact with soldiers. After two years of this, I happened to sit next to a soldier in a post-carriage. The contact with his thigh excited me to the highest degree.' Ulrichs also relates that in his tenth year he conceived an enthusiastic and romantic friendship for a boy two years his senior.

That experiences of the kind are very common, every one who has at all conversed with Urnings knows well. From private sources of unquestionable veracity, these may be added. A relates that, before eight years old, reverie occurred to him during the day, and dreams at night, of naked sailors. When he began to study Latin and Greek, he dreamed of young gods, and at the age of fourteen, became deeply enamoured of the photograph of the Praxitelian Eros[13] in the Vatican. He had a great dislike for physical contact with girls; and with boys was shy and reserved, indulging in no acts of sense.[14] B says that during his tenderest boyhood, long before the age of puberty, he fell in love with a young shepherd on one of his father's farms, for whom he was so enthusiastic that the man had to be sent to a distant moor. C at the same early age, conceived a violent affection for a footman; D for an officer, who came to stay at his home; E for the bridegroom of his eldest sister.

In nearly all the cases here cited, the inverted sexual instinct sprang up spontaneously. Only a few of the autobiographies record seduction by an elder man as the origin of the affection. In none of them was it ever wholly overcome. Only five out of the twenty-seven men married. Twenty declare that, tortured by the sense of their dissimilarity to other males, haunted by shame and fear, they forced themselves to frequent public women soon after the age of puberty. Some found themselves impotent. Others succeeded in accomplishing their object with difficulty, or by means of evoking the images of men on whom their affections were set. All, except one, concur in emphatically asserting the superior attraction which men have always exercised for them over women. Women leave them, if not altogether disgusted, yet cold and indifferent. Men rouse their strongest sympathies and instincts. The one exception just alluded to is what Ulrichs would call an Uranodioning. The others are capable of friendship with women, some even of aesthetic admiration, and the tenderest regard for them, but not of genuine sexual desire. Their case is literally an inversion of the ordinary.

Some observations may be made on Ulrichs' theory. It is now recognized by the leading authorities, medical and medico-juristic, in Germany, by writers like Casper–Liman and Krafft-Ebing, that sexual inversion is more often than not innate. So far, without discussing the physiological and metaphysical explanations of this phenomenon, without considering whether Ulrichs is right in his theory of *anima muliebris inclusa in corpore virili*, or whether heredity, insanity, and similar general conditions are to be held responsible for the fact, it may be taken as admitted on all sides that the sexual diathesis in question is in a very large number of instances congenital. But Ulrichs seems to claim too much for the position he has won. He ignores the frequency of acquired habits. He shuts his eyes to the force of fashion and depravity. He reckons men like Horace and Ovid and Catullus, among the ancients who were clearly indifferent in their tastes (as indifferent as the modern Turks) to the account of Uranodionings. In one word, he is so enthusiastic for his physiological theory that he overlooks all other aspects of the question. Nevertheless, he has acquired the right to an impartial hearing, while pleading in defence of those who are acknowledged by all investigators of the problem to be the subjects of an inborn misplacement of the sexual appetite.

Let us turn, then, to the consideration of his arguments in favour of freeing Urnings from the terrible legal penalties to which they are at present subject, and, if this were possible, from the no less terrible social condemnation to which they are exposed by the repugnance they engender in the normally constituted majority. Dealing with these exceptions to the kindly race of men and women, these unfortunates who have no family ties knotted by bonds of mutual love, no children to expect, no reciprocity of passion to enjoy, mankind, says Ulrichs, has hitherto acted just in the same way as a herd of deer acts when it drives the sickly and the weakly out to die in solitude, burdened with contumely, and cut-off from common sympathy.

From the point of view of morality and law, he argues, it does not signify whether we regard the sexual inversion of an Urning as morbid or a natural. He has become what he is in the dawn and first emergence of emotional existence. You may contend that he derives perverted instincts from his ancestry, that he is the subject of psychical disorder, that from the cradle he is predestined by atavism or disease to misery. I maintain that he is one of nature's sports, a creature healthy and well organised, evolved in her superb indifference to aberrations from the normal type. We need not quarrel over our solutions of the problem. The fact that he is there, among us, and he constitutes an ever-present factor in our social system, has to be faced. How are we to deal with him? Has society the right to punish individuals sent into the world with homosexual instincts? Putting the question at its lowest point, admitting that these persons are the victims of congenital morbidity, ought they to be treated as criminals? It is established that their appetites, being innate, are *to them* at least natural and undepraved; the common appetites, being excluded from their sexual scheme, are *to them* unnatural and abhorrent. Ought not such beings, instead of being hunted down and persecuted by legal bloodhounds, to be regarded with pitying solicitude as among the most unfortunate of human beings, doomed as they are to inextinguishable longings and life-long deprivation of that which is the chief prize of man's existence on this planet, a reciprocated love? As your laws at present stand, you include all cases of sexual inversion under the one domination of crime. You make exceptions in some special circumstances and treat the men involved as lunatics. But the Urning is neither criminal nor insane. He is only less fortunate than you are, through an accident of birth, which is at present obscure to our imperfect science of sexual determination.

So far Ulrichs is justified in his pleading. When it has been admitted that sexual inversion is usually a fact of congenital diathesis, the criminal law stands in no logical relation to the phenomenon. It is monstrous to punish people as wilfully wicked because, having been born with the same organs and the same appetites as their neighbours, they are doomed to suffer under the frightful disability of not being able to use their organs or gratify their appetites in the ordinary way.

But here arises a difficulty, which cannot be ignored, since upon it is based the only valid excuse for the position taken up by society in dealing with this matter. Not all men and women possessed by abnormal sexual desires can claim that these are innate. It is certain that the habits of sodomy are frequently acquired under conditions of exclusion from the company of persons of the other sex – as in public schools, barracks, prisons, convents, ships. In some cases they are deliberately adopted by natures tired of normal sexual pleasure. They may even become fashionable and epidemic. Lastly, it is probable that curiosity and imitation communicate them to otherwise normal individuals at a susceptible moment of development. Therefore society has the right to say: Those who are the unfortunate subjects of inborn sexual inversion shall not be allowed to indulge their passions, lest the mischief should spread and a vicious habit should contaminate our youth. From the utilitarian point of view, society is justified in protecting itself against a minority of exceptional beings whom it regards as pernicious to the general welfare. From any point of view, the majority is strong enough to coerce to inborn instincts and to trample on the anguish of a few unfortunates. But, asks Ulrichs, is this consistent with humanity, is it consistent with the august ideal of impartial equity? Are people, sound in body, vigorous in mind, wholesome in habit, capable of generous affections, good servants of the state, trustworthy in all the ordinary relations of life, to be condemned at law as criminals because they cannot feel sexually as the majority feel, because they find some satisfaction for their inborn wants in ways which the majority dislike?

Seeking a solution of the difficulty stated in the foregoing paragraphs, Ulrichs finds it in fact and history. His answer is that if society leaves nature to take her course, with the abnormal as well as with the normal subjects of sexual inclination, society will not suffer. In countries where legal penalties have been removed from inverted sexuality, where this is placed upon the same footing as the normal – in France, Bavaria (?), the Netherlands (?) – no inconvenience has hitherto arisen. There has ensued no sudden and flagrant outburst of a depraved habit, no dissemination of a spreading moral poison. On the other hand, in countries where these penalties exist and are enforced – in England, for example, and in the metropolis of England, London – inverted sexuality runs riot, despite of legal prohibitions, despite threats of prison, dread of exposure, and the intolerable pest of organised *chantage*.[15] In the eyes of Ulrichs, society is engaged in sitting on a safety-valve, which if nature allowed to operate unhindered would do society no harm, but rather good. The majority, he thinks, are not going to become Urnings, for the simple reason that they have not the unhappy constitution of the Urning. Cease to persecute Urnings, accept them as inconsiderable, yet real factors, in the social commonwealth, leave them to themselves, and you will not be the worse for it, and will also not carry on your conscience the burden of intolerable vindictiveness.

Substantiating this position, Ulrichs demonstrates that acquired habits of sexual inversion are almost invariably thrown off by normal natures. Your boys at public schools, he says, behave as though they were Urnings. In the lack of women, at the time when their passions are predominant, they yield themselves up together to mutual indulgences which would bring your laws down with terrible effect upon adults. You are aware of this. You send your sons to Eton and Harrow, and you know very well what goes on there. Yet you remain untroubled in your minds. And why? Because you feel convinced that they will return to their congenital instincts.

When the school, the barrack, the prison, the ship has been abandoned, the male reverts to the female. That is the truth about Dionings. The large majority of men and women remain normal, simply because they were made normal. They cannot find the satisfaction of their nature in those inverted practices to which they yielded for a time through want of normal outlet. Society risks little by the occasional caprice of the school, the barrack, the prison, and the ship. Some genuine Urnings may, indeed, discover their inborn inclination by means of the process to which you subject them. But you are quite right in supposing that a Dioning, though you have forced him to become for a time an Uraniaster, will never in the long run appear as an Urning. The extensive experience which English people possess regarding such matters, owing to the notorious condition of their public schools, goes to confirm Ulrichs' position. Headmasters know how many Uraniasters they have dealt with, what excellent Dionings they become, and how comparatively rare, and yet how incorribly steadfast, are the genuine Urnings in their flock.

The upshot of this matter is that we are continually forcing our young men into conditions under which, if sexual inversion were an acquired attribute, it would become stereotyped in their natures. Yet it does not do so. Provisionally, because they are shut off from girls, because they find no other outlet for their sex at the moment of its most imperious claims, they turn toward males, and treat their younger school-fellows in ways which would consign an adult to penal servitude. They are Uraniasters by necessity and *faute de mieux*.[16] But no sooner are they let loose upon the world than the majority revert to normal channels. They pick up women in the streets, and form connections, as the phrase goes. Some have undoubtedly, in this fiery furnace through which they have been passed, discover their inborn sexual inversion. Then, when they cannot resist the ply of their proclivity, you condemn them as criminals in their later years. Is this just? Would it not be better to revert from our civilisation to

84

the manners of the savage man – to initiate youths into the mysteries of sex, and to give each in his turn the chance of developing a normal instinct by putting him during his time of puberty freely and frankly to the female? If you abhor Urnings, as you surely do, you are at least responsible for their mishap by the extraordinary way in which you bring them up. At all events, when they develop into the eccentric beings which they are, you are the last people in the world who have any right to punish them with legal penalties and social obloquy.

Considering the present state of the law in most countries to be inequitable toward a respectable minority of citizens, Ulrichs proposes that Urnings should be placed upon the same footing as other men. That is to say, sexual relations between males and males should not be treated as criminal, unless they are attended with violence (as in the case of rape), or be carried on in such a way as to offend the public sense of decency (in places of general resort or on the open street), or thirdly be entertained between an adult and a boy under age (the protected age to be decided as in the case of girls). What he demands is that when an adult male, freely and of his own consent, complies with the proposals of an adult person of his own sex, and their intercourse takes place with due regard for public decency, neither party shall be liable to prosecution and punishment at law. In fact he would be satisfied with the same conditions as those prevalent in France, and since June, 1889, in Italy.

If so much were conceded by the majority of normal people to the abnormal minority, continues Ulrichs, an immense amount of misery and furtive vice would be at once abolished. And it is difficult to conceive what evil results would follow. A defender of the present laws of England, Prussia, &c., might indeed reply: 'This is opening a free way to the seduction and corruption of young men.' But young men are surely at least as capable of defending themselves against seduction and corruption as young women are. Nay, they are far more able, not merely because they are stronger, but because they are not usually weakened by an overpowering sexual instinct on which the seducer plays. Yet the seduction and corruption of young women is tolerated, in spite of the attendant consequences of illegitimate childbirth, and all which that involves. This toleration of the seduction of women by men springs from the assumption that only the normal sexual appetite is natural. The seduction of a man by a male passes for criminal, because the inverted sexual instinct is regarded as unnatural, depraved, and wilfully perverse. On the hypothesis that individuals subject to perverted instincts can suppress them at pleasure or convert them into normal appetite, it is argued that they must be punished. But when the real facts come to be studied, it will be found: first, that these instincts are inborn in Urnings, and are therefore in their case natural;

secondly, that the suppression of them is tantamount to life-long abstinence under the constant torture of sexual solicitation; thirdly, that the conversion of them into normal channels is in a large percentage of cases totally impossible, in nearly all where it has been attempted is only partially successful, and where marriage ensues has generally ended in misery for both parties. Ulrichs, it will be noticed, does not distinguish between Urnings, in whom the inversion is admitted to be congenital, and Uraniasters, in whom it has been acquired or deliberately adopted. And it would be very difficult to frame laws which should take cognisance of these two classes. The Code Napoleon legalises the position of both, theoretically at any rate. The English code treats both as criminal, doing thereby, it must be admitted, marked injustice to recognised Urnings, who at the worst are morbid or insane, or sexually deformed, through no fault of their own.

In the present state of things, adds Ulrichs, the men who yield their bodies to abnormal lovers, do not merely do so out of compliance, sympathy, or the desire for reasonable reward. Too often they speculate upon the illegality of the connection, and have their main object in the extortion of money by threats of exposure. Thus the very basest of all trades, that of *chantage*, is encouraged by the law. Alter the law, and instead of increasing vice, you will diminish it; for a man who should then meet the advances of an Urning, would do so out of compliance, or, as in the case of female prostitutes, upon the expectation of a reasonable gain. The temptation to ply a disgraceful profession with the object of extorting money would be removed. Moreover, as regards individuals alike abnormally constituted, voluntary and mutually satisfying relations, free from degrading risks, and possibly permanent, might be formed between responsible agents. Finally, if it be feared that the removal of legal disabilities would turn the whole male population into Urnings, consider whether London is now so much purer in this respect than Paris?

One serious objection to recognising and tolerating sexual inversion has always been that it tends to check the population. This was a sound political and social argument in the time of Moses, when a small and militant tribe needed to multiply to the full extent of its procreative capacity. It is by no means so valid in our age, when the habitable portions of the globe are rapidly becoming overcrowded. Moreover, we must bear in mind that society, under the existing order, sanctions female prostitution, whereby men and women, the normally procreative, are sterilised to an indefinite extent. Logic, in these circumstances, renders it equitable and ridiculous to deny a sterile exercise of sex to abnormal men and women, who are by instinct and congenital diathesis non-procreative.

As a result of these considerations, Ulrichs concludes that there is no real ground for the persecution of Urnings except as may be found in the repugnance by the vast numerical majority for an insignificant minority. The majority encourages matrimony, condones seduction, sanctions prostitution, legalises divorce in the interests of its own sexual proclivities. It makes temporary or permanent unions illegal for the minority whose inversion of instinct it abhors. And this persecution, in the popular mind at any rate, is justified, like many other inequitable acts of prejudice or ignorance, by theological assumptions and the so-called mandates of revelation.

In the next place it is objected that inversed sexuality is demoralising to the manhood of a nation, that it degrades the dignity of a man, and that it is incapable of moral elevation. Each of these points may be taken separately. They are all of them at once and together contradicted by the history of ancient Greece. There the most warlike sections of the race, the Dorians of Crete and Sparta, and the Thebans, organised the love of male for male because of the social and military advantages they found in it. Their annals abound in eminent instances of heroic enthusiasm, patriotic devotion, and high living, inspired by homosexual passion. The fighting peoples of the world, Kelts in ancient story, Normans, Turks, Afghans, Albanians, Tartars, have been distinguished by the frequency among them of what popular prejudice regards as an effeminate vice.

With regard to the dignity of man, is there, asks Ulrichs, anything more degrading to humanity in sexual acts performed between male and male than in similar acts performed between male and female. In a certain sense all sex has an element of grossness which inspires repugnance. The gods, says Swinburne,

Have strewed one marriage-bed with tears and fire,
For extreme loathing and supreme desire.[17]

It would not be easy to maintain that a curate begetting his fourteenth baby on the body of a worn-out wife is a more elevating object of mental contemplation than Harmodius in the embrace of Aristogeiton,[18] or that a young man sleeping with a prostitute picked up in the Haymarket is cleaner than his brother sleeping with a soldier picked up in the Park. Much of this talk about the dignity of man, says Ulrichs, proceeds from a vulgar misconception as to the nature of inverted sexual desire. People assume that Urnings seek their pleasure only or mainly in an act of unmentionable indecency. The exact opposite, he assures them, is the truth. The act in question is no commoner between men and men than it is between men and women. Ulrichs, upon this point, may be suspected, perhaps, as an untrustworthy witness. His testimony, however, is confirmed by Krafft-Ebing, who, as we have seen, has studied sexual inversion long and minutely from the point of view of psychical pathology. 'As regards the nature of sexual gratification,' he writes, 'it must be established at the outset that the majority are contented with reciprocal embraces; the act commonly ascribed to them they generally abhor as much as normal men do; and, inasmuch as they always prefer adults, they are in no sense specially dangerous to boys.' This author proceeds to draw a distinction between Urnings in whom sexual instinct is congenital, and old debauchees or half-idiotic individuals, who are in the habit of misusing boys. The vulgar have confounded two different classes; and everybody who studies the psychology of Urnings is aware that this involves a grave injustice to the latter.

'But, after all,' continues the objector, 'you cannot show that inverted sexuality is capable of any moral elevation.' Without appealing to antiquity, the records of which confute this objection overwhelmingly, one might refer to the numerous passages in Ulrichs' writings where he relates the fidelity, loyalty, self-sacrifice, and romantic enthusiasm which frequently accompany such loves, and raises them above baseness. But, since here again he may be considered a suspicious witness, it will suffice, as before, to translate a brief passage from Krafft-Ebing. 'The Urning loves, idolizes his friend, quite as much as the normal man loves and idolizes his girl. He is capable of making for him the greatest sacrifices. He suffers the pangs of unhappy, often unreturned, affection; feels jealousy, mourns under the fear of his friend's infidelity.' When the time comes for speaking about Walt Whitman's treatment of this topic, it will appear that the passion of a man for his comrade has been idealized in fact and deed, as well as in poetry. For the present it is enough to remark that a kind of love, however, spontaneous and powerful, which is scouted, despised, tabooed, banned, punished, relegated to holes and corners, cannot be expected to show its best side to the world. The sense of sin and crime and danger, the humiliation and repression and distress to which the unfortunate pariahs of inverted sexuality are daily and hourly exposed must inevitable deteriorate the nobler elements in their emotion. Give abnormal love the same chance as normal love, subject it to the wholesome control of public opinion, allow it to be self-respected, draw it from dark slums into the light of day, strike off its chains and set if free – and I am confident, says Ulrichs, that it will exhibit analogous virtues, checkered, of course, by analogous vices, to those with which you are familiar in the mutual love of male and female. The slave has of necessity a slavish soul. The way to elevate is to emancipate him.

'All that may be true,' replies the objector: 'it is even possible that society will take the hard case of your Urnings into consideration, and listen to their bitter cry. But, in the meanwhile, supposing these inverted instincts to be inborn, supposing them to be irrepressible and inconvertible, supposing them to be less dirty and nasty than they are commonly considered, is it not the plain duty of the individual to suppress them, as long as the law of his country condemns them?' No, rejoins Ulrichs, a thousand times no! It is only the ignorant antipathy of the majority which renders such a law as you speak of possible. Go to the best books of medical jurisprudence, go to the best authorities on psychical deviations from the normal type. You will find that these support me in my main contention. These, though hostile in their sentiments and chilled by natural repugnance, have a respect for science, and they agree with me in saying that the Urning came into this world an Urning, and must remain till the end of his life an Urning still. To deal with him according to your code is no less monstrous than if you were to punish the colour-blind, or the deaf and dumb, or albinoes, or crooked-back cripples. 'Very well,' answers the objector: 'But I will quote the words of an eloquent living writer, and appeal to your generous instincts and your patriotism. Professor Dowden observes that "self-surrender is at times sternly enjoined, and if the egoistic desires are brought into conflict with social duties, the individual life and joy within us, at whatever cost of personal suffering, must be sacrificed to the just claims of our fellows."[19] What have you to say to that?' In the first place, replies Ulrichs, I demur in this case to the phrases *egoistic desires, social duties, just claims of our fellows*. I maintain that in trying to rehabilitate men of my own stamp and to justify their natural right to toleration I am not egoistic. It is begging the question to stigmatise their inborn desire as selfish. The social duties of which you speak are not duties, but compliances to law framed in blindness and prejudice. The claims of our fellows, to which you appeal, are not just, but cruelly inequitous. My insurgence against all these things makes me act indeed as an innovator; and I may be condemned, as a consquence of my rashness, to persecution, exile, defamation, proscription. But let me remind you that Christ was crucified, and that he is now regarded as a benefactor. 'Stop,' breaks in the objector: 'We need not bring sacred names into this discussion. I admit that innovators have done the greatest service to society. But you have not proved that you are working for the salvation of humanity at large. Would it not be better to remain quiet, and to sacrifice your life and joy, the life and joy of an avowed minority, for the sake of the immense majority who cannot tolerate you, and who dread your innovation? The Catholic priesthood is avowed to celibacy; and unquestionably there are some adult men in that order who have trampled out the imperious appetite of the male for the female. What they do for the sake of their vow will not you accomplish, when you have so much of good to gain, or evil to escape?' What good, what evil? rejoins Ulrichs. You are again begging the question; and now you are making appeals to my selflessness, my personal desire for tranquility, my wish to avoid persecution and shame. I have taken no vow of celibacy. If I have taken any vow at all, it is to fight for the rights of an innocent, harmless, downtrodden group of outraged personalities. The cross of a Crusade is sewn upon the sleeve of my right arm. To expect from me and from my fellows the renouncement voluntarily undertaken by a Catholic priest is an absurdity, when we join no order, have no faith to uphold, no ecclesiastical system to support. We maintain that we have the right to exist after the fashion in which nature made us. And if we cannot alter your laws, we shall go on breaking them. You may condemn us to infamy, exile, prison – as you formerly burned witches. You may degrade our emotional instincts and drive us into vice and misery. But you will not eradicate inverted sexuality. Expel nature with a fork, and you know what happens. 'That is enough,' says the objector: 'We had better close this conversation. I am sorry for you, sorry that you will not yield to sense and force. The Urning must be punished.'

John Addington Symonds to Henry Havelock Ellis, 1 December 1892

Dear Mr Ellis,

Various pressing occupations have prevented me from replying earlier to your letter of the 14th Nov: which I found here [Davos Platz, Switzerland] upon my return from Venice.

With regard to your proposed plan, I will first consider it in general, and then in detail.

A). I like the principle you have sketched out for our collaboration and for our responsibility in the several parts. All this seems just as it should be. And I think your statement of our object as 'primarily a study of a psychological anomaly' exactly right.

I only doubt whether we are completely agreed as to the part played in the phenomenon by morbidity. This is the most important question. And I apprehend that, while I have been growing to regard these anomalies as sports, that is to say, as an occasional mal-arrangement between the reproductive function and the imaginative basis of desire, you still adhere to the neuro- or psychopathical explanation.

I should be inclined to abolish the neuropathical hypothesis, and also suggestion, on the ground that impaired health in ancestors and suggestion are common conditions of all sexual development, normal and abnormal.

What I mean is this. Considering the wide and impartial distribution of 'Erbliche Belastung',[20] and the comparative infrequency of Sexual Anomaly, I regard neurosis in a Sexual Pervert as a *concomitant* not as a *cause*.

Considering that all boys are exposed to the same order of suggestions (sight of a man's naked organs, sleeping with a man, being handled by a man) and that only a few of them become sexually perverted, I think it reasonable to conclude that these few were previously constituted to receive the suggestion. In fact, suggestion seems to play exactly the same part in the normal and abnormal awakening of sex.

The only cases in which I should be inclined to accept the theory of psychopathy are those extreme ones in which there is a marked *Horror Feminae*. I do not believe that in perfectly natural and unprejudiced persons there is absolute Horror Feminae or Horror niasis. (Apropos of this, did you ever pay attention to the position of the 'Concubinus' in a young Roman noble's household? I could send you some notes I have made on it, if you think fit.) At the end of this letter I will return to this point, and will collect some information I have recently obtained upon the subject.

B). *Introduction*. As you suggest. N.B. In dealing with my 'Problem' when you have to use it, you would always be at liberty to tace [suppress] expressions where it seemed too argumentative or heated.

Chapter i. History. Yes.

Chapter ii. History in Greece. This might well be my own Essay, as you say, with the last pages omitted. (I never meant to publish those, they were intended to impress schoolmasters and Jowett.) I do not think anything important could be added about 'Complete frigidity' or *horror feminae*, because the Greeks recognised the preference of male for male as a matter of course, and were not impressed by cases in which a male confined himself to males. Something may be gleaned from *Straton* and from Glaucus in Plato's *Republic*. (Also from Lucian's *Grôtes*.) But the fact to dwell on about Greeks is that were mostly sensitive to both sexes. They married and went on taking boys. Yes....As to female Sexual Inversion we do not know very much. I think it would have to be alluded to: of course Sappho, then Lucian's Brothel Dialogues. I should notice the fact that while there are numerous paiderastic myths I do not know of one which sanctions female perversion.

Chapter iii. I feel serious difficulty about the history of the Transition to modern times. But it might be done by showing the effect of Justinian's Edicts in making Perversion a *Crime*. Of course I know lots about it in Italy, and could largely increase the list of ancient people you mention. The problem would assume this shape: that in modern history there have been individuals with a specific perversion, frigid to women, or indifferent to them: but that there have also been (especially in the South) very numerous persons who for various reasons preferred the male, though they are potent for the female.

Part ii. 1, 2, 3, 4. These you assign to H. E. quite rightly. Any material you here take from my 'Problem',[21] you would use as you thought best. By the way, I can supply you with duplicate copies of that essay, for scissor use, if you wanted.

Only I feel that it is just in these Chapters that our difficulty of collaboration will be felt. (We must come to some fundamental agreement about neurosis.)

Conclusion. This I would undertake, as you suggest, but should hope to have your assistance in correcting the outlines etc.

One great difficulty I foresee. It is that I do not think it will be possible to conceal the fact that sexual anomaly (as in Greece) is often a matter of preference rather than of fixed physiological or morbid diathesis. This may render the argument *ad legislatores* complicated.

If we succeed in producing this book together, I hope you will allow your name to stand first and mine second, because I feel my own want of scientific equipment. And I think it ought to be published by one of the medical publishers. But about this I am not sure, since one wants the subject to come under the notice of laymen.

John Addington Symonds to Edward Carpenter, 29 December 1892

<u>Private</u>

My dear Carpenter

Thank you much for your letter & the promise of your book.

I will send you my last little book in return. It is called *In the Key of Blue*. I fear you will not find much in it. Look at 'Platonic Love,' 'Clifton,' & the first Essay.

I am so glad that H. Ellis has told you about our project. I never saw him. But I like his way of corresponding on this subject. And I need somebody of medical importance to collaborate with. Alone, I could make but little effect – the effect of an eccentric.

We are agreed enough upon fundamental points. The only difference is that he is too much inclined to stick to the neuropathical theory of explanation.

But I am whittling that away to a minimum. And I don't think it politic to break off from the traditional line of analysis, which has been going rapidly forward in Europe for the last 20 years upon the psychiatric theory. Each new book reduces the conception of neurotic disease.

I mean to introduce a new feature into the discussion, by giving a complete account of homosexual love in ancient Greece. I wrote this some time ago, & had 10 copies of it privately printed. If you like to see it, I will lend you one of my remaining two copies. I should indeed value a word from you about it.

All the foreign investigators from Moreau & Caspar to Moll, are totally ignorant of Greek Customs. Yet it is here that the phenomenon has to be studied from a different point of view from that of psychopathology. Here we are forced to recognize that one of the foremost races in civilization not only tolerated passionate comradeship, but also utilized it for high social and military purpose.

(By the way, in the book I send you, you will find an essay on the subject.)

You raise a very interesting question with regard to physiological grounds for this passion. I have no doubt myself that the absorption of semen implies a real modification of the physique of the person who absorbs it, & that, in these homosexual relations, this constitutes an important basis for subsequent conditions – both spiritual & corporeal.

It is a pity that we cannot write freely on the topic. But when we meet, I will communicate to you facts which prove beyond all doubt to my mind that the most beneficial results, as regards health and nervous energy, accrue from the sexual relation between men: also, that when they are carried on with true affection, through a period of years, both comrades become united in a way which would be otherwise quite inexplicable.

The fact appears to me proved. The explanation of it I cannot give, & I do not expect it to be given yet. Sex has been unaccountably neglected. Its physiological & psychological relations even in the connection between man & woman are not understood. We have no theory which is worth anything upon the differentiation of the sexes, to begin with. In fact, a science of what is the central function of human beings remains to be sought.

This, I take it, is very much due to physiologists, assuming that sexual instincts follow the build of the sexual organs; & that when they do not, the phenomenon is criminal or morbid. In fact, it is due to science at this point being still clogged with religious & legal presuppositions.

Any good book upon homosexual passions advances the sound method of induction, out of which may possibly be wrought in the future a sound theory of sex in general. The first thing is to force people to see that the passions in question have their justification in nature.

My hope has always been that eventually a new chivalry, i.e. a second elevated form of human love, will emerge & take its place for the service of mankind by the side of that other which was wrought out in the Middle Ages.

It will be complementary, by no means prejudicial to the elder & more commonly acceptable. It will engage a different type of individual in different spheres of energy – aims answering to those of monastic labour in common or of military self-devotion to duty taking here the place of domestic cares & procreative utility.

How far away the dream seems! And yet I see in human nature stuff neglected, ever-present – pariah and outcast now – from which I am as certain as I live, such a chivalry could arise.

Whitman, in *Calamus*, seemed to strike the key-note. And though he repudiated (in a very notable letter to myself) the deductions which have logically to be drawn from *Calamus*, his work will remain infinitely helpful.

South-Sea Idylls. C. W. Stoddard. Boston. James R. Osgood. 1873. I got mine from Sampson Low, I think, through Nutt 270 Strand. If you cannot get a copy, let me hear, & I will send you mine. It was suppressed at once in America.

Yours in affection

JAS

Havelock Ellis and John Addington Symonds, from *Sexual Inversion*, first British edition, 1897

Preface

It was not my intention to publish a study of an abnormal manifestation of the sexual instinct before discussing its normal manifestations. It has happened, however, that this part of my work is ready first, and, since I thus gain a longer period to develop the central parts of my subject, I do not regret the change of plan.

It is owing to the late John Addington Symonds that this part of my work has developed to its present extent. I had not at first proposed to devote a whole volume to sexual inversion. It may even be that I was inclined to slur over it as an unpleasant subject, and one that it was not wise to enlarge on. But I found in time that several persons for whom I felt respect and admiration were the congenital subjects of this abnormality. At the same time I realised that in

England, more than in any other country, the law and public opinion combine to place a heavy penal burden and a severe social stigma on the manifestations of an instinct which to these persons who possess it frequently appears natural and normal. It was clear that the matter was in special need of elucidation and discussion. So that when Mr. Symonds, who had long studied this subject, proposed – while still unaware that I was working at the psychology of sex – that we should collaborate in a book on sexual inversion, I willingly entered into correspondence with him regarding the scope and general tendency of the suggested book, and ultimately agreed to the proposal....There can be no doubt that a peculiar amount of ignorance exists regarding the subject of sexual inversion. I know medical men of many years' general experience who have never, to their knowledge, come across a single case. We may remember, indeed, that some fifteen years ago the total number of cases recorded in scientific literature scarcely equalled those of British race which I have obtained, and that before my first cases were published not a single British case, unconnected with the asylum or the prison, had ever been recorded. Probably not a very large number of people are even aware that the turning in of the sexual instinct towards persons of the same sex can ever be regarded as in-born, so far as any sexual instinct is in-born. And very few indeed would not be surprised if it were possible to publish a list of the names of sexually inverted persons. Shortly before Mr. Symonds' death he drew up a list of men of British race whom of his own knowledge or from trustworthy information he knew to be inverted. The list contained fifty-two names, many of them honourably known in Church, State, Society, Art, and Letters. I could supplement this list with another of sexually inverted women, of whom a considerable proportion are widely and honourably known in literature or otherwise, while many of the others are individuals of more than average ability or character.

It cannot be positively affirmed of all these persons that they were born inverted, but in most the inverted tendency seems to be instinctive, and appears at a somewhat early age. In any case, however, it must be realised that in this volume we are not dealing with subjects belonging to the lunatic asylum or the prison. We are dealing with individuals who live in freedom, some of them suffering intensely from their abnormal organisation, but otherwise ordinary members of society.

From Chapter IV, 'Sexual Inversion in Women'

We know comparatively little of sexual inversion in women; of the total number of recorded cases of this abnormality, now very considerable, but a small proportion are in women, and the chief monographs on the subject devote but little space to women.

I think there are several reasons for this. Notwithstanding the severity with which homosexuality in women has been visited in a few cases, for the most part men seem to have been indifferent towards it; when it has been made a crime or a cause for divorce in men, it has usually been considered as no offence at all in women. Another reason is that it is less easy to detect in women; we are accustomed to a much greater familiarity and intimacy between women than between men, and we are less apt to suspect the existence of any abnormal passion. And allied with this cause we have also to bear in mind the extreme ignorance and extreme reticence of women regarding any abnormal or even normal manifestation of their sexual life. A woman may feel a high degree of sexual attraction for another woman without realising that her affection is sexual, and when she does realise it she is nearly always very unwilling to reveal the nature of her intimate experience, even with the adoption of precautions, and although the fact may be present to her that by helping to reveal the nature of her abnormality she may be helping to lighten the burden of it on other women. Among the numerous confessions voluntarily sent to Krafft-Ebing there is not one by a woman. There is, I think, one other reason why sexual inversion is less obvious in a woman. We have some reason to believe that, while a slight degree of homosexuality is commoner in women than in men, and is favoured by the conditions under which women live, well marked and fully developed cases of inversion are rarer in women than in men. This result would be in harmony with what we know as to the greater affectability of the feminine organism to slight stimuli, and its less liability to serious variation....These passionate friendships, of a more or less unconsciously sexual character, are certainly common. It frequently happens that a period during which a young woman falls in love at a distance with some young man of her acquaintance alternates with periods of intimate attachment to a friend of her own sex. No congenital inversion is usually involved....In some cases, on the other hand, such relationships, especially when formed after school life, are fairly permanent. An energetic emotional woman, not usually beautiful, will perhaps be devoted to another who may have found some rather specialised life-work but who may be very unpractical, and who has probably a very feeble sexual instinct; she is grateful for her friend's devotion but may not actively reciprocate it. The actual specific sexual phenomena generated in such cases vary very greatly. The emotion may be latent or unconscious; it may be all on one side; it is often more or less recognised and shared. Such cases are on the borderland of true sexual inversion, but they cannot be included in its region. Sex in these relationships is scarcely the essential and fundamental element; it is more or less subordinate and parasitic. There is often a semblance of a sexual relationship from the marked divergence of the friends in physical and psychic abilities, and the nervous development of one or both the friends is often slightly abnormal. We have to regard such relationships as hyper-trophied friendships, the hypertrophy being due to unemployed sexual instinct.

For many of the remarks which I have made here regarding true inversion in women I am not able to bring forward the justificatory individual instances. I possess a considerable amount of information, but, owing to the tendencies already mentioned, this information is for the most part more or less fragmen-tary, and I am not always free to use it.

A class of women to be first mentioned, a class in which homosexuality, while fairly distinct, is only slightly marked, is formed by the women to whom the actively inverted woman is most attracted. These women differ in the first place from the normal or average woman in that they are not repelled or disgusted by lover-like advances from persons of their own sex. They are not usually attractive to the average man, though to this rule there are many exceptions. Their faces may be plain or ill-made, but not seldom they possess good figures, a point which is apt to carry more weight with the inverted woman than beauty of face....The actively inverted woman differs from the woman of the class just mentioned in one fairly essential character: a more or less distinct trace of masculinity. She may not be, and frequently is not, what would be called a 'mannish' woman, for the latter may imitate men on grounds of taste and habit unconnected with sexual perversion, while in the inverted woman the masculine traits are part of an organic instinct which she by no means always wishes to accentuate. The inverted woman's masculine element may in the least degree consist only in the fact that she makes advances to the woman to whom she is attracted and treats all men in a cool, direct manner, which may not exclude comradeship, but which excludes every sexual relationship, whether of passion or merely of coquetry. As a rule the inverted woman feels absolute indifference towards men, and not seldom repulsion. And this feeling, as a rule, is instinctively reciprocated by men....The brusque, energetic movements, the attitude of the arms, the direct speech, the inflexions of the voice, the masculine straightforwardness and sense of humour, and especially the attitude towards men, free from any suggestion either of shyness or audacity, will often suggest the underlying psychic abnormality to a keen observer. Although there is sometimes a certain general coarseness of physical texture, we do not find any trace of a beard or moustache.

It is probable, however, that there are more genuine approximations to the masculine type. The muscles are everywhere firm with a comparative absence of soft connective tissue, so that an inverted woman may give an unfeminine impression to the sense of touch. Not only is the tone of the voice often different, but there is reason to suppose that this rests on a basis of anatomical modification. At Moll's suggestion, Flatau examined the larynx in twenty-three inverted women, and found in several a very decidedly masculine type of larynx, especially in cases of distinctly congenital origin. In the habits not only is there frequently a pronounced taste for smoking (sometimes found in quite feminine women), but there is also a dislike and sometimes incapacity for needlework and other domestic occupations, while there is often some capacity for athletics. No masculine character is usually to be found in the sexual organs, which are sometimes undeveloped. Notwithstanding these characters, however, sexual inversion in a woman is as a rule not more obvious than in a man. At the same time, the inverted woman is not usually attractive to men. She herself generally feels the greatest indifference to men, and often cannot understand why a man should love a woman. She shows, therefore, nothing of that sexual shyness and engaging air of weakness and dependence which are an invitation to men. The man who is passionately attracted to an inverted woman is usually of rather a feminine type. For instance, in one case present to my mind, he was of some-what neurotic heredity, of slight physique, not sexually attractive to women, and very domesticated in his manner of living – in short, a man who might easily have been passionately attracted to his own sex.

While the inverted woman is cold, or at most comradely, in her bearing towards men, she may become shy and confused in the presence of attractive persons of her own sex, even unable to undress in their presence, and full of tender ardour for the woman who she loves.

The passion finds expression in sleeping together, kissing and close embraces, with more or less sexual excitement, the orgasm sometimes occur-ring when one lies on the other's body; the extreme gratification is *cunnilingus (in lambendo lingua genitalia alterius)*,[22] sometimes called sapphism. There is no connection, as was once supposed, between sexual inversion in women and an enlarged clitoris, which has been very seldom found in such cases, and never, so far as I am aware, to an extent that would permit of its use in coitus with another woman.

The inverted woman is an enthusiastic admirer of feminine beauty, espe-cially of the statuesque beauty of the body, unlike in this the normal woman whose sexual emotion is but faintly tinged by aesthetic feeling. In her sexual habits we rarely find the degree of promiscuity which is not uncommon among inverted men. I am inclined to agree with Moll that homosexual women love more faithfully and lastingly than homosexual men.

From Chapter VI, 'The Theory of Sexual Inversion'

What is sexual inversion? Is it, as many would have us believe, an abominable acquired vice, to be stamped out by the prison? Or is it, as a few assert, a beneficial variety of human emotion which should be tolerated or even fostered? Is it a diseased condition which qualifies its subject for the lunatic asylum? or is it a natural monstrosity, a human 'sport,' the manifestations of which must be regulated when they become anti-social? There is probably an element of truth in more than one of these views. I am prepared to admit that very widely divergent views of sexual inversion are largely justified by the position and the attitude of the investigator. It is natural that the police official should find that his cases are largely mere examples of disgusting vice and crime. It is natural that the asylum superintendant should find that we are chiefly dealing with a form of insanity. It is equally natural that the sexual invert himself should find that he and his inverted friends are not so very unlike ordinary persons. We have to recognise the influence of professional and personal bias and the influence of environment, one investigator basing his conclusions on one class of cases, another on a quite different class of cases. Naturally, I have largely founded my own conclusions on my own cases. I believe, however, that my cases and my attitude towards them justify me in doing this with some confidence. I am not in the position of one who is pleading *pro domo*, nor of the police official, nor even of the physician, for these persons have not yet come to me for treatment. I approach the matter as a psychologist who has ascertained certain definite facts, and who is founding his conclusions on those facts.

The first point which impresses me is that we must regard sexual inversion as largely a congenital phenomenon, or, to speak more accurately, as a phenomenon which is based on congenital conditions. This, I think, lies at the root of the right comprehension of the matter....It must also be pointed out that the argument for acquired or suggested inversion logically involves the assertion that normal sexuality is also acquired or suggested. If a man becomes attracted to his own sex simply because the fact or the image of such attraction is brought before him, then we are bound to believe that a man becomes attracted to the opposite sex only because the fact or the image of such attraction is brought before him. This theory is totally unworkable. In nearly every country of the world men associate with men, and women with women; if association and suggestion were the only influential causes, then inversion, instead of being the exception, ought to be the rule throughout the human species, if not, indeed, throughout the whole zoological series. We would, moreover, have to admit that the most fundamental human instinct is so constituted as to be equally well adapted for sterility as for that of propagation throughout the whole of life. We must, therefore, put aside entirely the notion that the direction of sexual impulse is merely a suggested phenomenon; such a notion is entirely opposed to observation and experience, and will with difficulty fit into a rational biological scheme....If, then, we must postulate a congenital abnormality in order to account satisfactorily for at least a large proportion of sexual inverts, wherein does that abnormality consist? Ulrichs explained the matter by saying that in sexual inverts a male body coexists with a female soul: *anima muliebris in corpore virili inclusa*.[23] Even writers with some pretension to scientific precision, like Magnan[24] and Gley,[25] have adopted this phrase in a modified form, considering that in inversion a female brain is combined with a male body or male glands. This is, however, not an explanation. It merely crystallises into an epigram the superficial impression of the matter. As an explanation it is to a scientific psychologist unthinkable. We only know soul as manifested through body; and, although if we say that a person seems to have the body of a man and the feelings of a woman we are saying what is often true enough, it is quite another matter to assert dogmatically that a female soul, or even a female brain, is expressing itself through a male body. That is simply unintelligible....We can probably grasp the nature of the abnormality better if we reflect on the development of the sexes and on the latent organic bi-sexuality in each sex. At an early stage of development the sexes are indistinguishable, and throughout life the traces of this early community of sex remain. The hen fowl retains in rudimentary form the spurs which are so large and formidable in her lord, and sometimes she develops a capacity to crow, or puts on male plumage. Among mammals the male possesses useless nipples, which occasionally even develop into breasts, and the female possesses a clitoris, which is merely a rudimentary penis, and may also develop. The sexually inverted person does not usually possess any gross exaggeration of these signs of community with the opposite sex. But, as we have seen, there are a considerable number of more subtle approximations to the opposite sex in inverted persons, both on the physical and the psychic side. Putting the matter in a purely speculative shape, it may be said that at conception the organism is provided with about 50 per cent. of male germs and about 50 per cent. of female germs, and that as development proceeds either the male or the female germs assume the upper hand, killing out those of the other sex, until in the maturely developed individual only a few aborted germs of the opposite sex are left. In the homosexual person, however, and in the psychosexual hermaphrodite, we may imagine that the process has not proceeded normally, on account of some peculiarity in the number or character of either the original male germs or female germs, or both; the result being that we have a person who is organically twisted into a shape that is more fitted for the exercise of the inverted than of the normal sexual impulse, or else equally fitted for both.

Thus in sexual inversion we have what may fairly be called a 'sport,' or variation, one of these organic aberrations which we see throughout living nature, in plants and in animals....The sexual invert may thus be roughly compared to the congenital idiot, to the instinctive criminal, to the man of genius, who are all not strictly concordant with the usual biological variation (because this is of a less subtle character), but who become somewhat more intelligible to us if we bear in mind their affinity to variations. Symonds compared inversion to colour-blindness; and such a comparison is reasonable. Just as the ordinary colour-blind person is congenitally insensitive to those red-green rays which are precisely the most impressive to the normal eye...the invert fails to see emotional values patent to normal persons, transferring their values to emotional associations which for the rest of the world are utterly distinct.

Case III

A married woman, 40 years of age. Has been deserted by her husband because of her perverted sexuality. Neurotic history on both sides of the family, and several cases of insanity on mother's side. In this case affinity for the same sex and perverted desire for the opposite sex existed, a combination by no means infrequent. Hypnotic suggestion tried, but without success. Cause was evidently suggestion and example on the part of another female pervert with whom she associated before marriage. Marriage was late – at age of 35.

Case XXVIII

Miss S. age 38, living in a city of the United States of America, a business woman of fine intelligence, prominent in professional and literary circles. Her general health is good, but she belongs to a family in which there is a marked degree of neuropathic element. She is of rather phlegmatic temperament, well poised, always perfectly calm and self-possessed, rather retiring in disposition, with gentle, dignified bearing.

She says she cannot care for men, but that all her life has been 'glorified and made beautiful by friendship with women', who she loves as a man loves women. Her character is, however, well disciplined, and her friends are not aware of the nature of her affections. She tries not to give all her love to one person, and endeavours (as she herself expresses it) to use this 'gift of loving' as a stepping-stone to high mental and spiritual attainments. She is described by one who has known her for several years as 'having a high nature, and instincts unerringly towards high things'.

Case XXVII [26]

Englishman, independent means, aged 52, married. His ancestry is of a complicated character. Some of his mother's forefathers in the last and earlier centuries are supposed to have been inverted.[27]

He remembers liking the caresses of his father's footmen when he was quite a little boy. He dreams indifferently about men and women, and has strong sexual feeling for women. Can copulate, but does not insist on this act; there is a tendency to refined, voluptuous pleasure. He has been married for many years, and there are several children by the marriage.

He is not particular about the class or the age of the men he loves. He feels with regard to older men as a woman does, and likes to be caressed by them. He is immensely vain of his physical beauty; he shuns *paedicatio*[28] and does not much care for the sexual act, but likes long hours of voluptuous communion during which his lover admires him. He feels the beauty of boyhood. At the same time he is much attracted by young girls. He is decidedly feminine in his dress, manner of walking, love of scents, ornaments and fine things. His body is excessively smooth and white, the hips and buttocks rounded. Genital organs normal. His temperament is feminine, especially in vanity, irritability and petty preoccupations. He is much preoccupied with his personal appearance and fond of admiration; on one occasion he was photographed naked as Bacchus. He is physically and morally courageous. He has a genius for poetry and speculation, with a tendency to mysticism.

He feels a discord between his love for men and society, also between it and his love for his wife. He regards it as in part, at least, hereditary and inborn in him.

From Chapter VII, 'Conclusions'

The question of the prevention of homosexuality is a large one, but it is in too vague a position at present to be very profitably discussed. So far as the really congenital invert is concerned, prevention can have but small influence; but, as in a large proportion of cases there is little obvious congenital element, sound social hygiene should render difficult the acquisition of homosexual perversity. What we need first of all is a much greater degree of sincerity concerning the actual facts. The school is undoubtedly the great breeding-place of artificial homosexuality among the general population – at all events in England. Its influence in this respect may have been over estimated, but it is undoubtedly large. It is very unfortunate that school authorities do their best to ignore and conceal the facts. The time is coming, however, when much greater attention to this matter will be insisted on in physicians and others who have the care of boys in large public and other schools....While much may be done by physical hygiene and other means to prevent the extension of homosexuality in schools, it is impossible, even if it were desirable, absolutely to repress the emotional manifestations of sex in either boys or girls who have reached the age of puberty. The only way to render such manifestations wholesome, as well as to prepare for the relationships of later life, is to ensure the adoption, so far as possible, of the methods of co-education of the sexes. This, however, is not the place to insist on the desirability of co-education.

Turning from the prevention of sexual inversion to its medical treatment, so far as I am entitled to any opinion I strongly advocate discrimination, caution and scepticism. I have little sympathy with those who are prepared to 'cure' the invert at any price. Dr. von Schrenck-Notzing, the best known and most successful of these operators, seems to me to serve rather as a warning than as an example. He undertakes even the most pronounced cases of inversion by courses of treatment lasting more than a year, and involving, in at least one case, nearly 150 hypnotic sittings; he prescribes frequent visits to the brothel, previous to which the patient takes large doses of alcohol; by prolonged manipulations a prostitute endeavours to excite erection, a process attended with varying results. It appears that in some cases this course of treatment has been attended by a certain sort of success, to which an unlimited good will on the part of the patient, it is needless to say, has largely contributed. The treatment is, however, usually interrupted by continual back-sliding to homosexual practices, and sometimes, naturally, the cure involves a venereal disease. The patient is enabled to marry and to beget children; how the children turn out it is yet too early to say....While there is, no doubt, a temptation to aid those who are anxious for aid to get rid of their homosexuality, it is not possible to look upon the results of such aid, even if successful, with much satisfaction. Not only is the acquisition of the normal instinct by an invert very much on a level with the acquisition of a vice, but probably it seldom succeeds in eradicating the original inverted instinct. What usually happens is that the person becomes capable of experiencing both impulses, not a specially satisfactory state of affairs.

Moreover, it is often not difficult to prematurely persuade the invert that his condition is changed; his health is perhaps improving, and if he experiences some slight attraction to a person of the opposite sex he hastily assumes that a deep and permanent change has occurred. This may be disastrous, especially if it leads to marriage, as it may do in an inverted man or still more easily in an inverted women. The apparent change does not turn out to be deep, and the invert's position is more unfortunate than his original position, both for himself and for his wife....We can seldom, therefore, safely congratulate ourselves on the success of any 'cure' of inversion. The success is unlikely to be either permanent or complete, in the case of a decided invert; and in the most successful cases we have simply put into the invert's hands a power of reproduction which it is undesirable he should possess. The most satisfactory result is probably obtained when it is possible by direct and indirect methods to reduce the sexual hyperae(diph)sthesia[29] which usually exists when the medical treatment of inversion comes into question, and by psychic methods to refine and spiritualise the inverted impulse, so that the invert's natural perversion may not become a cause of acquired perversity in others. The invert is not only the victim of his own abnormal obsession; he is the victim of social hostility. We must seek to distinguish the part in his sufferings due to these two causes. When I review the cases I have brought forward and the mental history of the inverts I have known, I am inclined to say that if we can enable an invert to be healthy, self-restrained, and self-respecting, we have often done better than to convert him into the mere feeble simalcrum of a normal man.

Xavier Mayne, from *The Intersexes: A History of Simisexualism as a Problem in Social Life*, 1909

Extracts from the main text

Undercurrents of personal interest in understanding sexual impulses

I can offer myself on this occasion only as a finger-post to guide the reader along a road where shapes that will be startling, mystic, beautiful, repulsive, tragic, commonplace, are continually to be seen. It is a highway of human nature hourly traversed by millions, of all ranks; a road foot-worn day by day, since humanity began. But the procession upon it is one extraordinarily, sternly reticent. Perhaps the very reader of these lines may long have been marching, or staggering, with the cortège, half-conscious of his companions far behind him, or at hand on the right or the left, or beyond him. Those who could unriddle the march to him are not likely to speak a word to him. Those who are willing to speak of one or another social or moral phase of the matter, particularly of the more obvious or vulgar aspects, are as a general rule, either insincere or wholly ignorant of the real psychology in what they discuss. And the reader may be the last person in his whole circle of friends to confess that he has a profound personal interest in the topic. Like the Spartan lad, with the gnawing fox hidden under his garment, he may have done nothing more instinctively and carefully, all his life long, than to try to hide from all inter-locuters the anguish that is destroying his peace of mind and life.

Definition of the Uranian

An Uranian, or Urning, a member of the Intersex previously set apart from the major sexes, may be defined as a human being that is more or less perfectly, even distinctively, masculine in physique; often a virile type of fine intellectual, moral and aesthetic sensibilities; but who through an inborn or later-developed prefer-ence feels sexual passion for the male human species. His vita sexualis reverts now vaguely, now with vigorous definiteness to the sex to which he seems naturally to belong, by strict psychological classification. His sexual preference may quite exclude any desire for the female sex; or may exist concurrently with that instinct.

Characteristic traits, types, tastes, tempers, etc. of the Uranian

The Uranian shows a marked tendency to support illnesses more readily than most other individuals, with a feminine ability to bear physical pain. Mental anguish works with severity on him. Outward surroundings are of importance to him; they affect his nervous state keenly. He is usually orderly, often has feminine tastes more or less developed, such as cookery, needlework, and the like. This fact is curiously combined in military individualities, an odd 'incon-sistency'. The Uranian is likely to be passionately fond of children and animals; they are frequently surprisingly attracted to him as if by some mystic understanding. But the Uranian is to be counted a creation not far aloof from the eternal World-Child. (As indicated, the best type of Uranian is not typically pederastic.) He is spontaneously benevolent, tender-hearted, and pacific; with a large and philosophic or other tolerance....He is fond of jewellery and ornaments, beautiful and valuable or not such, according to his aesthetic education. It is significant in him, that while as a type, he tends to avoid giving pain to anyone, or seeing it, he is (another indication of the feminine texture of the uranistic psychos) often passionately interested in the deliberately brutal sports....The uranistic temperament is especially mercurial; now wildly gay, now sombre, easily changed.

The bewildered question: and answer

'Why am I? What am I? Outwardly as a man, inwardly in so much a woman! Able to keep my character and sex as a man before the world and yet with this sexual nature of a woman in me. Why am I cursed thus? What ails me? Am I sick, mad?' So cries some 'inborn' Uranian, bewildered and wretched, when he is alone and can throw down the Mask. So demands he of the confidential physician, if he has decided to visit one, hoping to be 'cured' of his psychologic disorder. Too frequently the doctor, ignorant but confident, talks to him as were he indeed 'diseased,' 'to be cured'; often advises marriage. But any doctor, really anxious to lead the querist not to feel himself solitary, or morally depraved because of his mysterious sexual nature, can give no better reply in most instances, than – 'Friend, you are what you are – an Uranian, one of the Intersex-race. You cannot be cured. You are not alone. There are thousands, tens of thousands, of you. Fear man, if you must: but fear not to face God who has made your kind as it is. Strive to be the best mortal being that you can possibly be.'

How is the Uranian physically satisfied

As to what brings the Uranian his physical gratification and appeasement absurd popular notions are plentiful enough, including those grounded on the ideas of bodily hermaphroditism. There is a general ignorance of this matter among otherwise educated people. The law confuses physical expression of simisexualism, both active and passive. There cannot, of course, be precisely the same bodily conjunction, even when coitus analis or buccal coition[30] are the processes, as when the opposite sexes unite. But the Uranian is satisfied without such perfect physical union. Nude embraces and close contacts

106

genitally as a rule suffice for all the pleasurable sensations of normal sexual intercourse. Mere close embraces, or a coitus inter femora[31] is usually adequate toward complete orgasm by him. Often less than that is needed. For one must remember that the Uranian passion is informed much by a sort of idealism, far more vivid and nervous than the sensation of normalists. The Uranian's instinct demands less of the actual physique. Usual as are buccal onanism, mutual masturbation and so on, they are not invariably instinctive to the Uranian. In his more refined class he is intensely sensitive to a spiritual possession of his friend, his psychic conquest of the beauty of the male. Imagination has a powerful share in even the physical pleasure of all superior simisexualism.

When only is the Uranian capable of 'unnatural' sexualism?

In fact only in one way can the real Uranian be guilty of 'unnatural' acts of sexualism; for we are of course putting aside such obvious offences against nature and humanity as bestiality or the debauchment or physical injury to minors, a forcible sexual intercourse, and so on. Unnatural condition for an Uranian comes when involuntarily he attempts 'normal' intercourse with a woman; with the sex that by nature's decree repels him, that often he loathes in any corporeal relationship. Prostitute, mistress, or wife – then is he indeed guilty of a sin against Nature, violates his sexual Ego, as does the normalist, the completely masculine man, sin against his nature in sexual relations with other than a woman.

General psychology of Uraniad

The Uraniad is met in almost all social situations that show superior moral, intellectual and social traits. She can be highly receptive to aesthetics. Under the latter type, let us remark her intense susceptibility to music, which susceptibility can be blent into merely high nervosity, without any intellectual sense of the art. The Uraniad frequently enters with absorbing earnestness into severe professions of the masculine order. She exhibits more success in meeting their abstract sides than the Uranian does. The Uraniad also is likely to be rather undomestic, and to care relatively little for the personal concerns, for the minutiae of feminine dress, ornament, and so on. She does not seek to attract the man as a lover, but as a comrade and friend. She shrinks from maternity, often with intense repulsion. Many Uraniads are incapable of maternity when the sexual organs otherwise seem wholly normal. Altruism, courage, perseverance, judgement, belong to her moral or intellectual furniture; just as are met rugged male attributes, relish for man's work, man's dress, male amusements, in peasant Uraniads, and other crude types. The Uraniad is unlikely to be a good diplomat; not even of the degree of the normal woman. Her mannish bluntness of speech and of plan disaccord. She lacks intuitions. The Uraniad shows her vaguer inherent femininity by interesting minor traits, such as the fact that she is not distinguished in inventive processes more than is her normal sister. In literature, she is constantly successful. She is a good executive, especially when she has at her side, as in royal and official instances, the physical aid of man. If we pass to the Uraniad who is of the lowest grade of social humanity, whether we meet her in a brothel or prison, she is depravity in the abstract; an *épavée*[32] complete, if fallen into the uttermost social pits.

General aspects of the Uraniad's sexualism

In the Uraniad-love we meet again sudden passions, excited by the mere beauty of another woman; or the more gradual growth of desire. We find the blending of intellectual and moral admirations. We observe the amour's wish for physical possession, with the instinct for the surrender of self, as the only possible completion of the Ego. We find the indifference to male beauty as a sexual feeling, and a coldness or horror as to the man's sexual embraces. There are the jealousies, the struggles, the despairs, the vengeances, the emotional nuances, social dramas of every kind. The physical rapports of Urandism, as contrasted with male simisexual relations, do not allow the bodily satisfactions of the Uraniad to be organically so vivid as the man's. Man's seminal system and its ejaculative process make his pleasure more acutely physical. Again, the Uranian embraces are not necessarily at all dangerous to his nervous system. But the nervous demands of the Uraniad frequently make the gratification of her desires pernicious; disturbing gravely her intellectual and nervous poise.

Parental desires and pre-natal Uranianism

The Uranian and the Uraniad, especially of the higher grades, constantly seem reflexes of pre-natal influences. Their instinct is inborn. The mother's imagination and wish, quite likely sub-conscious during her pregnancy, here can come into plain coincidence with the vita sexualis of her offspring. The similisexualism of the father is repeated in the child. Or sometimes, overpassing a generation, referring the boy or girl back to a remoter ancestor, the mystery of atavism is before us. The organic sex of unborn infants we know as not determined for a considerable period of gestation. Nature herself seems to hesitate, to postpone. The boy comes into the world not obviously affected in his sex as to any virile trait, born with a boy's body and a boy's mind; but unluckily for him endowed with the sexual impulses of a girl. Or the girl, blamelessly feminine in her physique, must go through life yearning for sexual union with a woman. Victims of pre-natal obsession, they may too easily mature, burdened with the intersexual Ego, bewildered as to themselves, at cross-purposes with their environments, occupations, society, moral sentiments, religious notions, with the laws, and all chances of relief.

Professional medicine and Uranianism

A remarkable proportion of physicians and surgeons are homosexual; fully Uranians, or Dionysian-Uranians. The contingent 'census' of any city points this out. Life in the medical schools is not hostile to the instinct. The doctor often loses all sense of sexual charm in the feminine psychos, and a woman's physique ceases to rouse his sexual excitement. This is especially true of doctors devoted to women's diseases. The physician appreciates peculiarly the weakness, the limitations, of feminine psychology. He turns reactively to the richer nature, the masculine. Usually a physician must wear his 'mask' like the rest of the uranistic fraternity. Sometimes when he finds that he cannot do this, he quits his profession, or even quits the world.

The Uraniad as degenerate, criminal and victim

To the Uraniad Intersex, the law to-day has almost nothing to say. Statutes are tacit, as in ages past. Respectable, discreet Uraniads are not in any really unhappy case before the world. Feminosexual relationships may be known or suspected, right and left, in all societies, in all countries. But they seldom excite open comment now-a-days, any more than of old. If a whispered and smiling contempt is shown, it does not usually much injure the social prestige of the objects. While certain crimes quite naturally are in uraniadistic ambients, the blackmailer, robber or assassin, are only exceptionally met. Uraniad amours thrive and prosper, with no spectre of police-courts to trouble them. Boudoirs, baths and brothels are a rendezvous, day by day; immune of penalties. Such matters as bestiality, proxenetism[33] and other special offences are punishable;

109

but within the pale of assenting privacy, the adult Uraniad is a free agent to do what she pleases – when, where and how her sexual passion suggests, be it nobly or indeed degenerately.

Dangerous workings of Uraniadism on woman's nervous status

But if the Uraniad is not nearly so much a social or legal victim as the Uranian, she can suffer a natural penalty for her intersexual existence. Uraniad appetites, and the feminosexual 'type,' are likely to be linked with morbidity of psychos, with undesirable physical conditions – negative or positive – and even with organic disease. The gratification of Uraniad love reacts in many instances, by obviously mischievious influences, on the Uraniad's nervous system. The Uranian passion in adults, or in robust, fairly healthful youth, is not nervously harmful, *per se*. On the contrary, it is largely salutary; particularly if decent, tranquil, regular in expression and idealized by circumstances. The opposite effects can result by feminosexualism. Too often, by it the feminine psychos goes to pieces. The Uraniad significantly helps to fill insane asylums and sanitariums.

Instance: perverted Uranianism [sic], moral deficiencies

In Berlin, not long ago, came a criminal trial against an Uraniad typically of the degenerate moral type, but of no common mind. This was the notable Frau K—; arrested as being a professional bawd in feminosexualism – sapphic 'Kupplerei' with minors – with personal sadism, masochism, fetichism, and a long category of perversities, including the use of her premises as a resort for all sexual clientages. Shocking scenes were described. She had been the associate in letters and science of many eminent scientific writers on sociology, criminology and psychiatric medicine, etc., not only in Germany but also in America and in Italy, including Cesare Lombroso. She was remarkably efficient in certain fields of literature and science. She was punished as was merited, and her career ended.

Extracts from Appendix A

A Categoric Personal Analysis for the Reader –
  'Am I at all an Uranian?'
  'Am I at all an Uraniad?'

As to hereditary circumstances, early youth, etc.

Are you aware of any simisexual traits in your parents? Of your ancestry in general, or of collatoral blood-relatives, either remote, deceased, etc., or living? If so, in what relationship?

Have there been cases of distinct moral deficiency – kleptomania, untruthfulness as a trait, business-dishonesty, tendency to intrigue unscrupulously, eccentricity, etc.?

Have you any idea whether before your birth, or after it, your sex was not quite acceptable to your father or mother; especially to your mother?

Was the process of teething in your case, as far as you can learn, easy – normal and timely?

In early life at school, etc., had you a taste for music, drawing, and other arts?

Was your memory, as a young student, a good one? Did you easily apply it?

As to general physical traits, capacities, etc.

As far as you can now conclude, were you a distinctly beautiful child or youth (or young girl) in your bodily development, apart from your face?

Are your bones and joints large or small?

Are the lines of your bosom flat or curved, compared with the average model of your sex? Is your chest broad or narrow?

Is your wrist flat or round?

Are your fingers pointed or blunt?

Do you write a large or a small handwriting?

Are your feet large or small, broad or narrow; and is the instep high?

Can you readily separate the great toe from its fellows by its *own* force?

Physiognomy, and kindred details

Is your skin soft and fine, rough or thick, sensitive or not, clear or muddy?

Are your skin and body, in general, strongly *odorific*? especially when you are warm? – or of little or no odour at *any* time?

Do you feel bodily pain, especially of merely passing sort, with *special* plainness and nervousness? – as for instance, a slight, sharp blow, a pinch, a cut, etc? Do scars soon disappear?

When coughing, expectorating, swallowing, and so on, is that process always easy, and swift; or often otherwise?

111

Do you whistle well, and naturally like to do so? Do you sing? And how instinctively?

Do you feel at ease in the dress of the opposite sex? When so clad, do you easily and *naturally* pass for a person of that other sex?

Certain distinctively sexual characteristics

Have you in mind a clear or vague ideal of a sexual-companion who would 'perfectly suit' you, but who has not yet been met? Or have you met such an ideal?

Would you say that sexually you were 'haunted' and 'drawn-to' one special type of person? – either outwardly, or in his or her psychic personality?

Is the sort of sexual relation in question, particularly if with an adult, only 'at its best' in proportion to the intellectual, refined, etc., traits of your partner, along with due physical force? Or is it so exclusively physical that, when it is enjoyed and over, you feel no further attraction to the partner?

In sexual relations do you think yourself emphatically potent?

How often should you say that it was necessary for you to have sexual intercourse, in order to be calmed and at ease?

How is the simisexual act performed? Coitus inter femora, coitus ani, amplexus sine coitu, onanismus mutu, onanismus buccalis,[34] etc. etc.? (*Uraniad*, *Sapphism* etc.)

Does imagination, and the idea of enjoying the act with *another* person have any part in the intercourse?

Is ejaculation copious? How often usually repeated?

Are you given to loving where you do *not* respect? Does such feeling last? Has such a person recurrent power over you?

Have you ever been conscious of betraying or guessing by a mere *look*, a brief exchange of glances (quite instantaneous often) that you or another person are homosexuals? This absolutely apart from any gesture or incident that any third person would understand as hinting at simisexualism.

Various moral, temperamental, habitual traits, etc., etc.

Have you ever for the sake of external matters (such as dress, ornaments or other aids to bodily attractiveness) wished you were of another sex than your own?

Have you ever wished that you could change your sex because of more serious reasons? If so, for what ones?

Do you think of yourself as a morally justified, responsibly-acting sort of human creature, apart from any sexual influences on you?

Do you feel so more or less because of your sexual impulses and *vita sexualis*?

Do you believe that the Simisexual when the *best* (but quite indisputedly homosexual) examples are considered, presents a higher or a lower type of human nature?

Mrs Havelock Ellis, from 'Eugenics and the mystical outlook', 1911[35]

If we introduce large and sound ideas in the carrying out of eugenic practices, the loveliness of love and the inner meaning of parenthood may slowly evolve, and Dame Nature get her chance to interpret herself through all her children. Nature has not told us many of her secrets yet, and probably Eugenics may be one of the means she will employ to open our eyes a little wider.

Our object surely is not only to limit the production of the unfit, but to get the best results out of those in the Community who are a bewilderment to the State and who seem unfitted from a eugenic standpoint to propagate. Consider the neurotic and the abnormal, for instance, and also the sane members of insane families. How can we secure that there shall be no waste or ruin for their special powers of work for the race? It is surely an accepted fact that many of the most capable people are neurotic or abnormal. Not only modern life proves it, but history accentuates it, and in the field of art, as in music and the drama, we find the problem in several forms.

According to the severe code of some eugenists, not only an Oscar Wilde, but a Michael Angelo, a Nietzsche, a Chopin, a Tchaikovsky, a Blavatsky, a Rosa Bonheur, a William Blake, and a Mrs Eddy stand in the same class of the neurotic or the abnormal, to say nothing of a vast mass of less distinguished people. Is it not a part of Eugenics and a part of religion to indicate to these people how they can directly aid the improvement of the race – in other words to turn them into allies instead of ostracising them into rebels? The best citizen is surely one who produces, from personal emotion, the finest results for the whole community. It is our duty as advanced citizens to see to it that equality of opportunity for this end is given alike to the normal and abnormal men and women in our midst. Often by a stupid, vindictive, or conventional attitude towards what we do not understand we waste or ruin powers which could otherwise have helped the world, and at the same time produce, through our materialistic and bigoted attitude, much personal suffering….In the near future the average sexual relationship of men to women today will be looked upon with as great an aversion as that for which Oscar Wilde was crucified. For Oscar Wilde was a martyr to unscientific legislation. He was not responsible before Heaven's tribunal as many normal men and women are to-day for their consciously gross sins against both Nature and Love. Wilde's mother, had for nine long months, before he was born, prayed continually for a girl. Her imagination dwelt on this during nearly all her pregnancy. That her prayer was partially granted in that perplexing mixture of artist, man, woman and egotist the world knows as Oscar Wilde was perhaps one of Nature's satires in order to show what we do when we force, through our limited laws and barbaric persecutions, these peculiar people into becoming menaces to the State, through lack of capacity either to understand them or to educate them. After all, the universal scheme may have ulterior ends to serve in producing, through the primitive function of sex, giants or pygmies who have possibly a sacred function in the human scheme. Even in abnormality, in its congenital manifestations, Nature may have a meaning as definite in her universal purpose as the discord is in music to the musician.

Mrs Havelock Ellis, from 'Eugenics and spiritual parenthood', 1911

Invalids, criminals, and abnormals as well as the robust must be given the chance to satisfy their hunger to create. There are surely as many spiritual children in the world as physical ones, and there are as many miscarriages and still-births as in normal parenthood. Our prudish cruelties, our lack of humour and imagination, our fetish worship of crudities and mock moralities, our terror of bogies, and our ignorance of our individual natures make many of us blundering midwives who actually destroy what we are trying to bring into the world. The abnormal has such horror for us, and our dread of being associated with it brings such odium and fear in our minds, that we ignore again and again a problem which is becoming more and more important to face, as it affects the health and well-being of the whole community. It is time we gave not only a word of warning but also a word of help to the class of people we designate as abnormal….Science and Love have proved that there are, and always have been, men who have the souls of women, and women who have the souls of men. This is the true abnormality….The true invert, though often not a criminal in any real sense, is an alien among normal people. He realises that he is the gypsy, the outcast, the sufferer, and it lies with him whether he can also be one of the redeemers of the race. Society does its best, through its distaste for him, to thwart this greater purpose for which he may possibly exist.

This is not a plea to glorify the invert, but to understand him and to put him in his place in relation to Religion, Eugenics and Ideals. The normal, so far as we know anything, is the true harmony in nature, and the invert is the seeming discordant note. But in music the discord has its place. Without it, should we get the perfect harmony? It is possible that inversion and genius have some sort of affinity. They certainly both tend to belong to the neurotic group. Are we then to condemn both genius and inversion at sight and make laws for their crucifixion, or are we to find out the special laws and meaning of these forces in the evolution of the world? Both genius and inversion are capable of being forged into powers instead of remaining menaces, if they are rightly approached and understood....The true invert, under Eugenics combined with ideals, has to face either total renunciation of the physical expression of love, or, if Fate send him a true mate in the form of another alien, then the bond shall be as binding, as holy, and as set for splendid social ends as the bond of normal marriage. There is surely no other solution of this vexed question. Any concession, any compromise with seduction or prostitution, or cheap physical expression, though no worse in many ways in abnormals than normals, but destructive in either, hinders the development of true love, and so the betterment of the human race, which betterment should always be an outcome of personal love. True love is the best thing in the whole world, and if the invert is true to what ought to be his ideals in this matter and refuses to cheapen love on any side, he can thus join hands with eugenist, because their aims will be to diminish unfitness and increase racial possibilities. There is, in the meeting of the eugenist and the invert, an apparently hard word for the latter. It is this: Thou shalt *not* increase and multiply, nor shalt thou concede in matters of desire to what is common, average, or unclean. Spiritual parenthood must be freed from deadly microbes and vicious tendencies, even more than physical parenthood, for it is as glorious a thing to give to the world as a child of love, a work of art, as one with hands and feet.

As we do not understand abnormality as yet, the true invert must stand for the greatest ideal of all. He must lay down his life for the world....The wise thing to do with the invert is to let him follow his *own* best ideals, rather than force him to follow normal ideals for which he not only is not fitted but which would cripple his special powers of work in the eugenic fields of spiritual parenthood.

4 MODES OF DEFENCE

In a society where homosexuals were seen as degenerate, evil, demonic; as gender-traitors, class-traitors, and vicious, dangerous conspirators against health, work and light, those wishing to write about homosexuality as a positive, healthy and productive identity were obliged both to find discreet ways and discrete discourses of speaking about themselves, to each other and the world, and also to invent a literature of their own. Such writing relies on an encoded framework there to be read by those in the know, taking the very best of mainstream culture and turning it to ends that can only be called political. To this is added scientific rationalism, the assertion of observable and verifiable truths about the materially existing world, as a means of providing a defence against moral or spiritual condemnation. Texts which seek to demonstrate how unjustly homosexuals are treated merge classical scholarship with scientific truth, by documenting past examples of political and military heroism and artistic importance, alongside contemporary examples of the pernicious effects of the law on the positive potential of homosexuals who, when they are subjected to the legitimate judgements of science, are seen to be victims, not villains. In three of the texts in this section, Greek myth and scientific classification are allied in the project of promoting the homosexual as a wasted social resource, and of condemning the law as irrational and inhuman. Edward Carpenter's extended essay, *Homogenic Love and its Place in a Free Society* (1894), contains virtually every feature of the cultural/historical argument for the social usefulness and moral decency of the homosexual, which other authors included in this section approach in comparable manner, citing the same examples, reading the same stories in the same way. But Carpenter's lack of defensiveness is unusual. Where Richard Burton, in the 'Terminal essay' to his translation of the *Arabian Nights*, enters anthropological and classical overload, piling example upon instance of how central homosexuality has been to the history of the world, and John Addington Symonds, in *A Problem in Modern Ethics*, pleads, constructs fact by careful fact an argument for the defence, Carpenter's strategies of the collusive we, of sweet reason, of rhetorical questions anticipating a particular answer seem intended to leave the reader no alternative position other than agreement with him, that not only are homosexuals acceptable, they are actually superior. His tentativeness is of a most disingenous kind, in contrast to the more sombre and

116

ponderous arguments produced by John Addington Symonds. Carpenter's use of the words ordinary, normal and natural is both critical and parodic, not least in their repetition, but primarily in the way in which he makes heterosexuality sound so dull. His inclusion of women as a central part of the problem, rather than an extra, or a complete omission, is unusual, though at times he seems to forget they exist. Lesbians are represented in this literature of cultural appropriation solely by Sappho, the poet of Lesbos, and are only to be seen scientifically as morally and physically deficient, even in those texts campaigning for male homosexual equality.

The aim of these texts seems to be to campaign to change the law and attitudes, but the ways in which some of these works appeared undercuts a propagandist agenda, resulting instead in preaching to the converted. Burton's 'Terminal essay' appeared in an appendix to his translation of *The Thousand Nights and a Night*, published by the 'Kamashastra Society' of Benares (in reality Stoke Newington, north London) and available by private subscription only, coming out of the same stable as a cosmopolitan blend of pornography and disreputable French literature manufactured by Leonard Smithers. Symonds's *A Problem in Modern Ethics* appeared in a privately published edition of a hundred copies only, and was 'addressed specially to medical psychologists and jurists'. Precisely the same conditions pertained to his *A Problem in Greek Ethics*. Whether the jurists and psychologists ever read either text is not known. The publication of *Homogenic Love* was attended by considerably more controversy, because it occurred in a public, rather than private domain. When it was printed by the Manchester Labour Party Press, Carpenter's publisher, T. Fisher Unwin, withdrew from sale all his other works and cancelled a contract with him for another work already in press. The mostly whimsical 'The new chivalry' had the most mainstream publication in the rather recherché *The Artist and Journal of Home Culture*, but also the least ambitious intentions. Yet it marks another form of the cultural reappropriation performed by those writing positively about homosexuality. This text shares its satirical edge with Wilde's 'A portrait of Mr. W. H.', which both mocks the bigotry of those who would condemn homosexuality, and also pokes fun at the likes of Symonds and Carpenter, and their soapbox prose. But in the main, the texts which co-opt Greek heroes, biblical precedent, Shakespeare and Marlowe, Walt Whitman and his modern Platonism, and scientific certainty do so either for strategic evidence, or for a language and a frame of reference which allows them to speak about desires and experiences that have no dictionary anywhere else.

The ideal image of the homosexual that emerges from these texts is premised upon the oft-reiterated assertion that there is no intrinsic connection between same-sex desire and same-sex acts. Over and over these writers say, yes, we need physical proximity, but no, we don't need or even want those gross sexual acts which the world thinks is all we are interested in. They may love, esteem and desire those of their own sex, and request or demand that this be legalized, but they express nothing but repulsion and condemnation when sodomy and all its kin are mentioned. A hierarchy of perversion is established which shadows in its structure the distinctions of the law; to what extent the horror concerning sodomy is authentic, a product of the age, or a strategic mollifying of the dominant ideology, is unclear, particularly when examined in relation to the content of the texts in the final section, where sodomy and sadomasochism are celebrated. It was *possible* to write in favour of sodomy, but it may not have been wise. Instead, the reader in search of role models, of writing which offers the promise of empathy, is given a portrait of themselves as brave, honourable, intelligent, physically perfect (or naturally distorted), and capable of being devoted to the needs of society as a whole, to the higher good rather than selfishly concerned with their own mundane family unit.

The common ground between the appropriations of Greek and Renaissance culture, and the adulation visited upon the American poet Walt Whitman, is youth. 'The Greeks had no past,' says John Addington Symonds, 'and the world has now grown old.'[1] The Greeks are therefore young, but more crucially innocent: there is no vice or sin to be found in these socially valued and legitimized forms of homosexual love. Instead of sober maturity and respectability, the reader is offered a catalogue of pairs of classical lovers, brave, handsome, dedicated to social justice and each other. These men are held up as objects of admiration, as exemplars to be emulated. In the multiple accounts included here Greek homosexuality manifests itself at the highest levels of the culture, in philosophy, sculpture, military enterprise, amongst military and political leaders and artists of all kinds. Both structurally and morally, male homosexuality is represented as part of the very best of the best of civilizations, and thus given social and cultural sanction.

Depiction of and pleasure in the male body, naked, or in intimate contact with other male bodies, is legitimized by the myths of gods and heroes, and the art of ancient Greece. In 'Winckelmann', Walter Pater quotes from a letter written by Winckelmann to Friedrich von Berg, with whom he had 'such a friendship'[2] as those which characterized Greek life:

I have noticed that those who are observant of beauty only in women, and are moved little or not at all by the beauty of men, seldom have an impartial, vital, inborn instinct for beauty in art. To such persons the beauty of Greek art will ever seem wanting, because its supreme beauty is rather male than female. But the beauty of art demands a higher sensibility than the beauty of nature.

Greek art is marked out as a domain in which appreciation of male physical beauty is essential to its understanding, and in which those who admire male beauty are of a higher order than, by implication, heterosexuals who can only appreciate the female or 'nature'. In his essay, 'The age of athletic prizemen', a history and analysis of classical Greek sculpture of athletes and wrestlers, Pater connects the statue of the Discobolus (the discus thrower) by Myron with living and breathing English youth. The statue embodies 'all one has ever fancied or seen, in old Greece or on Thames' side, of the unspoiled body of youth, thus delighting itself and others, at that perfect, because unconscious, point of good fortune, as it moves or rests just there for a moment'.[3] This equation between then and now, there and here, can be seen in a number of the texts included below, an equation which is made permissible by the unimpeachable virtue and value of Greek culture and civilization. Underpinning the reworkings of Greek myths and civilization is a belief – strategic or otherwise – in the inferiority of the modern over the ancient. The possibility is held out that if homosexuality in nineteenth-century Britain could take this form, then no one would be justified in condemning such desires.

The earliest text included here, 'Desiderato' by William Cory, best known for the often-anthologized 'Heraklitus', depicts, merely through the association of terms, primarily with the Greekish title of the volume, *Ionica*, in which it appears, a legitimized eroticism for the male. The meaning was clear enough for Symonds to write to Cory after reading *Ionica* and finding it 'went straight to my heart and inflamed my imagination'. The reply to that letter seems to have surprised Symonds:

> It was a long epistle on paiderastia in modern times, defending it and laying down the principle that affection between people of the same sex is no less natural and rational than the ordinary passionate relations. Underneath [Cory]'s frank exposition of this unconventional morality there lay a wistful yearning sadness – the note of disappointment and forced absention.[4]

The link is made between the ancient and the modern, with the modern being articulated through the history and stories of the ancient. Ancient Greek culture offers a model in which relationships between men are not only a given, but are an intrinsic part of the organization of society, its laws, education, military prowess and literature, where women are not citizens, where no reference need be made to the female. The valid binary is not between heterosexual and homosexual, but between good and bad homosexual relationships. Relationships between men are normal. Exemplary relationships between men can save a society from barbarous enemies. The same pairings of famous lovers are cited again and again as evidence of how beneficial and healthy homosexual relationships can be: Pythias and Damon, Achilles and Patroclus, Orestes and Pylades, Heracles and Hylas. They are all proof of purity and innocence in a culture which is young, which has not yet become corrupted by age. The modern is old, decayed, declining, while the ancient is young, vigorous and physically robust, a contrast played upon in Saale's 'Sonnet', where modern youths who strip and dive into a canal 'rise as though/The youth of Greece burst on this latter day'. The youthful ancients are capable of selfless devotion and sacrifice for the greater good, in contrast to the mercantile, grimy modern world whose people think only of their own good, their own pleasures. Such a framework requires the male body to be central to the good these relationships bring. It is always a young, muscular, athletic body containing a mind on higher things, representing a masculinity which is militaristic but never macho. While the *mens sana in corpore sano* can be seen in Edward Cracroft Lefroy's 'A Palaestral Study', which sanctions its celebration of the male body and its concomitant moral strengths by setting the scene in a wrestling-school or gymnasium, the importance of masculine sensibility, or even emotional sensitivity, is fundamental to John Addington Symonds's *A Problem in Greek Ethics*, with its dwelling on the day-to-day delicacies of the normal homosexual relationship. This text offers the fullest and most explicit campaigning version of the reappropriation of ancient Greek culture, but it only champions male relationships, relegating lesbianism to a 'parenthetical investigation', and equating the absence of social value in lesbian relationships with modern degeneracy.

Where men are sensitive and responsive, macho attributes are ascribed instead to lesbians. Their sexuality is active, even predatory, and focused not on the greater good, but on sexual pleasure and the use of a 'monstrous instrument of lust'. Sappho the Lesbian poet offers the only female equivalent to all those famous pairings of male lovers, and she is subject to an appropriation which emphasizes a corrupt, poisonous and luxurious pleasure, as in Swinburne's 'Sapphics'. This poem takes the form of a vision of Aphrodite travelling away from Lesbos, the home of Sappho, and leaving the muses 'sick with anguish' and Sappho singing a song which repels muses, gods and men, in a barren land 'full of fruitless women and music only'. If for Swinburne, like Balzac's *Girl with the Golden Eyes*, Diderot's *The Nun* and

Daudet's *Sappho*, lesbianism is a feeble and unsatisfactory passion, since it excludes men, and its proponents are given to sadistic predation on innocent women, for Michael Field, two women writing under a male pseudonym, relations between women are a given in the Lesbian idyll, and as capable of producing as good or bad relationships as heterosexuality. Such a commonplace is almost unique in contrast to the idealized romanticism of the male equivalents, who are universally muscular, robust, virtuous and, of course, young.

In the editions and analyses of Renaissance texts, the centrality of youthful masculinity is marked by such statements as 'national life was fresh, full, and young, ripe with the masterful spirit of domination, enterprise, reckless daring and adventure'.[5] John Addington Symonds describes Shakespeare, Marlowe, Raleigh and Spenser as 'adolescent giants', referring not to their ages, but to the youthfulness and manly vigour of the English civilization from which their works emerge. The maturity of the Victorian age is exemplified in the 'sense of serious responsibilities'[6] weighing on the head of an aged queen. With an old woman as national figurehead, the insistence on young masculinity as the best of culture, past and present, is an insistence on the non-heterosexual and non-domestic.

Walter Pater epitomizes the method and function of reading the sixteenth and seventeenth centuries in order to claim morality and cultural respectability for homosexuals, in his 'Conclusion' to *The Renaissance*, the effects of which on young men so concerned him that he withdrew it from the second edition (see p. 183 below). Pater criticizes the tendency to 'regard all things and principles of things as inconstant modes of fashion', and looks instead to establish a 'means of affiliation' across history and culture, for those who understand who and what he is talking about in such abstruse and 'jewel-like' prose.

In addition to the broad sweep of the historical picture, biographical details of authors, and elements in their works which imply sensual and emotional relationships between men, are cited and explored and re-made in these texts. Thus Roden Noel presents Thomas Otway as a man who demonstrated 'ardour and constancy [in his] personal attachments', and in whose play, *Venice Preserved*, devoted comradeship is 'forcibly delineated'.[7] Symonds gives a more personal slant to appropriation, in his autobiographical description of his fantasies about Shakespeare's *Venus and Adonis*, where he takes the place of Venus in love with an adolescent Adonis, and 'dreamed of falling back like her upon the grass, and folding the quick-panting lad in my embrace'.[8]

Such efforts of appropriation did not, however, go uncriticized:

Carson: I believe you have written an article to show that Shakespeare's sonnets were suggestive of unnatural vice?

Wilde: On the contrary, I have written an article to show that they are not. I objected to such a perversion being put upon Shakespeare.[9]

In the witness box, defending his public reputation, Oscar Wilde definitively rejects such a reading of his essay, 'A portrait of Mr. W. H.',[10] as attempting to prove the presence of homosexual desire in the sonnets. The essay itself plays self-consciously with ideas of identity, inauthenticity and forgery through a parodic treatment of others' attempts to co-opt the greatest writer to the homosexual cause. The object of his attack are those who looked for antecedents and precedents for their desires in Renaissance texts, like Ernest Dowden's analysis in *Shakspere: His Mind and Art*, like Roden Noel's handling of Thomas Otway's *Venice Preserved*, like John Addington Symonds's adolescent sexual fantasies about Adonis. Rather than presenting the facts of the appropriation, Wilde's text performs the appropriation, making explicit the cultural and personal histories at work in those reading these texts, and then invalidating all that has been said and done by his characters by revealing it as a forgery. In this way he critiques an entire methodology and also the assumed authenticity of evidence and identity that his contemporaries find in Renaissance texts. Where Pater, Dowden, Symonds find continuity and transcendental subjectivity, Wilde shows that there is no tradition, no universal, ahistorical formation of homosexuality which can be recovered, and in doing so succeeds in revealing the strategic nature of all those other readings.

If Greek literature and Shakespeare's sonnets had to be reclaimed to make them amenable to a homosexual reading, the works of Walt Whitman provided a ready-made language and politics of love between men. The poetry and person of the American poet Walt Whitman became the focus of adulation and discipleship amongst a significant number of those writing in Britain about homosexuality as a positive social and sexual identity. Whitman's work, particularly the poems contained in the 'Calamus' section of *Leaves of Grass*, offered a language and a framework in which same-sex relationships were both healthy and socially valuable. What the myths and history of ancient Greece offered in pre-modern role-models and social structures as an institutionalized justification for homosexuality, Whitman's doctrine of 'comradeship' between men of all conditions and classes offered in modern and progressive terms a means of reflecting and guaranteeing that civilization was indeed going forward towards a meritocratic democracy of manhood, thus holding out a future promise of acceptance and equality for homosexuals. Pre-eminent amongst British advocates of Whitman's democratic art were John Addington Symonds and a Bolton-based group who termed themselves the Eagle Street College. Whilst the output of the latter may strike the modern reader as cringingly sentimental, for in writing to and of Whitman they gush romantic hopes and fears for his loving them, individually and collectively, such an emotional masculinity is striking for the last quarter of the nineteenth century. Symonds, however, has another agenda, teasingly played out in an 1890 letter to Whitman included below, where he asks and asks again for Whitman's definitive answer to the question: does 'Calamus' condone homosexuality? The answer came back as an uncompromising 'no', which Symonds transcribes for Edward Carpenter in a search for validation of his own opinion. Carpenter comments, in *Some Friends of Walt Whitman* (see p. 226 below), that the question was a stupid one and Symonds really ought to have known better. Carpenter himself is far less in thrall to the pronouncements of the master, and in *Some Friends of Walt Whitman* he blithely sets out an account of comradeship which makes it straightforwardly sexual, while retaining the unremitting repetition of the healthy mind in a healthy body legitimation of homosexual relationships which Whitman's works seem to vindicate. But many writers, including Carpenter with his assertion that 'thousands of people date from their first reading of them *a new era in their lives*',[11] acknowledged a personal debt to Whitman and his work. Edmund Gosse wrote to Whitman to tell him:

The Leaves of Grass have become a part of my every-day thought and experience....Often when I have been alone in the company of one or other of my dearest friends, in the very deliciousness of nearness and sympathy, it has seemed to me that you were somewhere invisibly near us.[12]

Roden Noel thanked Whitman for the 'proclamation of comradeship',[13] while Symonds eulogizes on the personal impact of the doctrine of comradeship in *Walt Whitman: A Study* (see p. 214 below). Whitman's texts are represented as being the catalyst which enables these men to name themselves, since they see themselves represented in his writing. Whitman and his ideals are posited as the antithesis of all that is morally and sexually reprehensible, and a vivid alternative to popular notions of the homosexual as effeminate, languid, decadent, corrupt. While there are differences in the assessments and uses of Whitman the man and his work, two images of homosexuality emerge from these British critics. First, attempts are made to invent the concept and actuality of the 'good gay citizen', a person who would be socially responsible and respectable, not necessarily in this life, but in an as yet unrealized utopia. Second, discussions of Whitman provide scope to develop an already existing practice of eroticizing relationships between middle-class and working-class men. The writer becomes spokesman for and lover of the workers, who are more valuable and more sexy than they are themselves. (Texts which celebrate the body of the working man will be found in Chapter 6.)

HISTORIES OF THE HOMOSEXUAL

Edward Carpenter, from *Homogenic Love, and its Place in a Free Society*, Manchester Labour Society, 1894

Of all the the many forms that Love delights to take, perhaps none is more interesting (for the very reason that it has been so inadequately considered) than that special attachment which is sometimes denoted by the word Comradeship. In general we may say that the passion of love provides us at once with the deepest problems and the highest manifestations of life, and that to its different workings can be traced the farthest-reaching threads of human endeavour. In one guise, as the mere semi-conscious Sex-love, which runs through creation and is common to man and the lowest animals and plants, it affords a kind of organic basis for the unity of all creatures; in another, as for instance the love of the Mother for her offspring (also to be termed a passion) it seems to pledge itself to the care and guardianship of the growing race; then again in the Marriage of man and woman it becomes a thing of mystic and eternal import, and one of the corner-stones of human society; while in the form of Comrade-love with which this paper is concerned, it has uses and functions which we trust will clearly appear as we proceed.

To some perhaps it may appear a little strained to place this last-mentioned form of attachment on a level of importance with the others, and such persons may be inclined to deny the homogenic or homosexual love[#1] (as it has been called) that intense, that penetrating, and at times overmastering character which would entitle it to rank as a great human passion. But in truth this view, when entertained, arises from a want of acquaintance with the actual facts; and it may not be amiss here, in the briefest possible way, to indicate what the world's History, Literature and Art has to say to us on the whole subject, before we go on to any further considerations of our own. Certainly, if the confronting of danger and the endurance of pain and distress for the sake of the loved one, if sacrifice, unswerving devotion and life-long union, constitute proofs of the reality and intensity (and let us say *healthiness*) of an affection, then these proofs have been given in numberless cases of such attachment, not only as existing between men, but as between women, since the world began. The records of chivalric love, the feats of enamoured knights for their ladies' sake, the stories of Hero and Leander,[14] etc., are easily paralleled, if not surpassed, by the stories of the Greek comrades-in-arms and tyrannicides – of Cratinus and Aristodemus, who offered themselves together as a voluntary sacrifice for the purification of Athens;[15] of Chariton and Melanippus,[#2] who attempted to assassinate Phalaris, the tyrant of Agrigentum;[16] of Diocles who fell fighting in defence of his loved one;[17] or of Cleomachus who in like manner, in a battle between the Chalkidians and Eretrians, being entreated to charge the latter, 'asked the youth he loved, who was standing by, whether he would be a spectator of the fight; and when he said he would, and affectionately kissed Cleomachus and put his helmet on his head, Cleomachus with a proud joy placed himself in the front of the bravest of the Thessalians and charged the enemy's cavalry with such impetuosity that he threw them into disorder and routed them; and the Eretrian cavalry fleeing in consequence, the Chalkidians won a splendid victory.'[#3]

The annals of all nations contain similar records – though probably among none has the ideal of this love been quite so enthusiastic and heroic as among the post-Homeric Greeks. It is well known that among the Polynesian Islanders – for the most part a very gentle and affectionate people, probably inheriting the traditions of a higher culture than they now possess – the most romantic male friendships are (or were) in vogue. Says Herman Melville in *Omoo* (ch. 39), 'The really curious way in which all Polynesians are in the habit of making bosom friends is deserving of remark....In the annals of the island (Tahiti) are examples of extravagant friendships, unsurpassed by the story of Damon and Pythias[18] – in truth much more wonderful; for notwithstanding the devotion – even of life in some cases – to which they led, they were frequently entertained at first sight for some stranger from another island.' So thoroughly recognized indeed were these unions that Melville explains (in *Typee*, ch. 18) that if two men of hostile tribes or islands became thus pledged to each other, then each could pass through the enemy's territory without fear of molestation or injury; and the passionate nature of these attachments is indicated by the following passage from *Omoo*: – 'Though little inclined to jealousy in [ordinary] love-matters, the Tahitian will hear of no rivals in his *friendship*.'

Even among savage races lower down than these in the scale of evolution, and who are generally accused of being governed in their love-relations only by the most animal desires, we find a genuine sentiment of comradeship beginning to assert itself – as among the Balonda[#4] and other African tribes, where regular ceremonies of the betrothal of comrades take place, by the transfusion of a few drops of blood into each other's drinking bowls, by the exchange of names,[#5] and the mutual gift of their most precious possessions; but unfortunately, owing to the obtuseness of current European opinion on this subject, these and other such customs have been but little investigated and have by no means received the attention that they ought.

When we turn to the poetic and literary utterances of the more civilized nations on this subject we cannot but be struck by the range and intensity of the emotions expressed – from the beautiful threnody of David over his friend whose love was passing the love of women,[19] through the vast panorama of the Homeric Iliad, of which the heroic friendship of Achilles and his dear Patroclus forms really the basic theme,[20] down to the works of the great Greek age – the splendid odes of Pindar burning with clear fire of passion, the lofty elegies of Theognis, full of wise precepts to his beloved Kurnus, the sweet pastorals of Theocritus, the passionate lyrics of Sappho, or the more sensual raptures of Anacreon. Some of the dramas of Aeschylus and Sophocles – as the *Myrmidones* of the former and the *Lovers of Achilles* of the latter – appear to have had this subject for their motive;[#6] and many of the prose-poem dialogues of Plato were certainly inspired by it.

Then coming to the literature of the Roman age, whose materialistic spirit could only with difficulty seize the finer inspiration of the homogenic love, and which in such writers as Catullus and Martial could only for the most part give expression to its grosser side, we still find in Virgil a noble and notable instance. His second Eclogue bears the marks of a genuine passion; and, according to some,[#7] he there under the name of Alexis immortalizes his own love for the youthful Alexander. Nor is it possible to pass over in this connection the great mass of Persian literature, and the poets Sadi, Hafiz, Jami, and many others, whose names and works are for all time, and whose marvellous love-songs ('Bitter and sweet is the parting kiss on the lips of a friend') are to a large extent if not mostly addressed to those of their own sex.[#8]

Of the medieval period in Europe we have of course but few literary monuments. Towards its close we come upon the interesting stories of Amis and Amile (thirteenth century), unearthed by Mr. W. Pater[21] from the *Bibliotheca Elzeviriana*.[#9] Though there is historic evidence of the prevalence of the passion we may say of this period that its *ideal* was undoubtedly rather the chivalric love than the love of comrades. But with the Renaissance in Italy and the Elizabethan period in England the latter once more comes to evidence in a burst of poetic utterance,[#10] which culminates perhaps in the magnificent sonnets of Michel Angelo and of Shakespeare; of Michel Angelo whose pure beauty of expression lifts the enthusiasm into the highest region as the direct perception of the divine in mortal form;[#11] and of Shakespeare – whose passionate words and amorous spirituality of friendship have for long enough been a perplexity to hide-bound commentators. Thence through minor writers (not overlooking Winckelmann[#12] in Germany) we pass to quite modern times – in which, notwithstanding the fact that the passion has been much misunderstood and misinterpreted, two names stand conspicuously forth – those of Tennyson, whose 'In Memoriam' is perhaps his finest work, and of Walt Whitman, the enthusiasm of whose poems on Comradeship is only paralleled by the devotedness of his labours for his wounded brothers in the American Civil War.

It will be noticed that here we have some of the very greatest names in all literature concerned; and that their utterances on this subject equal if they do not surpass, in beauty, intensity, and humanity of sentiment, whatever has been written in praise of the other more ordinarily recognized love....This brief sketch may suffice to give the reader some idea of the place and position in the world of the particular sentiment which we are discussing; nor can it fail to impress him – if any reference is made to the authorities quoted – with a sense of the dignity and solidity of the sentiment, at any rate as handled by some of the world's greatest men. And at the same time it will be sure to arouse further questions. It will be evident from the instances given – and there would be no object to ignoring this fact – that this kind of love, too, like others, has its physical side; and queries will naturally arise as to the exact place and purport of the physical in it.

This is a subject which we shall have occasion to consider more in detail in the second part of this paper; but here a few general remarks may be made. In the first place we may say that to all love and indeed to all human feeling there must necessarily be a physical side. The most delicate emotion which plays through the mind has, we cannot but perceive, its corresponding subtle change in the body, and the great passions are accompanied by wide-reaching disturbances and transformations of corporeal tissue and fluid. Who knows (it may be asked) how deeply the mother-love is intertwined with the growth of the lacteal vessels and the need of the suckled infant? or how intimately even the most abstract of desires – namely the religious – is rooted in the slow hidden metamorphosis by which a new creature is really and physically born within the old? Richard Wagner, in a pregnant little passage in his *Communication to my Friends*, says that the essence of human love 'is the longing for utmost physical reality, for fruition in an object which can be grasped by all the senses, held fast with all the force of actual being.'[22] And if this is a somewhat partial sentiment it yet puts into clear language one undoubted relation between the sensuous and the emotional in all love, and the sweet *excuse* which this relation may be said to provide for the existence of the actual world – namely that the latter is the means whereby we become conscious of our most intimate selves.[#13] But if this is true of love in general it must be true of the Homogenic Love; and we must not be surprised to find that in all times this attachment has had some degree of physical expression. The question however as to what degree of physical intimacy may be termed in such a case fitting and natural – though a question which is sure to arise – is one not easy to answer: more especially as in the common mind any intimacy of a bodily nature between two persons of the same sex is so often (in the case of males) set down as a sexual act of the crudest and grossest kind. Indeed the difficulty here is that the majority of people, being incapable perhaps of understanding the *inner* feeling of the homogenic attachment,[#14] find it hard to imagine that the intimacy has any other object than the particular form of sensuality mentioned (i.e. the *Venus aversa*,[23] which appears, be it said, to be rare in all the northern countries), or that people can be held together by any tie except the most sheerly material one – a view which of course turns the whole subject upside down, and gives rise to violent and no doubt very natural disapprobation; and to endless recriminations and confusion.

Into this mistake we need not fall. Without denying that sexual intimacies do exist; and while freely admitting that, in great cities, there are to be found associated with this form of attachment prostitution and other evils comparable with the evils associated with the ordinary sex-attachment; we may yet say that it would be a great error to suppose that the homogenic love takes as a rule that extreme form vulgarly supposed; and that it would also be a great error to overlook the fact that in a large number of instances the relation is not distinctively sexual at all, though it may be said to be physical in the sense of embrace and endearment. While it is not my object in this paper to condemn special acts or familiarities between lovers (since these things must no doubt be largely left to individual judgement, aided by whatever light Science or

Physiology may in the future be able to throw upon the subject) – still I am anxious that it should be clearly understood that the glow of a really human and natural love between two persons of the same sex may be, and often is, felt without implying (as is so often assumed) mere depravity of character or conduct. No one can read the superb sonnets, already mentioned, of Shakespeare and Michel Angelo without feeling, beneath the general mass of emotional utterance, the pulsation of a distinct bodily desire; and even Tennyson, somewhat tenuous and Broad-churchy as he is, is too great a master and too true a man not to acknowledge in his great comrade-poem 'In Memoriam' (see Cantos xiii., xviii., etc.) the passionateness of his attachment – for doing which indeed he was soundly rated by the *Times* at the time of its publication; yet it would be monstrous to suppose that these men, and others, because they were capable of this kind of feeling and willing to confess its sensuous side, were therefore particularly licentious....With these few general remarks, and the conclusion, so far, that while the homogenic feeling undoubtedly demands *some* kind of physical expression, the question what degree of intimacy is in all cases fitting and natural may not be a very easy one to decide – we may pass on to consider what light is thrown on the whole subject by some recent scientific investigations.

That passionate attachment between two persons of the same sex is, as we have seen, a phenomenon widespread through the human race, and enduring in history, has been always more or less recognized; and once at least in history – in the Greek age – the passion rose into distinct consciousness, and justified, or even it might be said glorified, itself; but in later times – especially perhaps during the last century or two of European life – it has generally been treated by the accredited thinkers and writers as a thing to be passed over in silence, as associated with mere grossness and mental aberration, or as unworthy of serious attention.

In latest times however – that is, during the last thirty years or so – a group of scientific and capable men in Germany, France, and Italy – among whom are Dr. Albert Moll of Berlin; Krafft-Ebing, one of the leading medical authorities of Vienna, whose book on *Sexual Psychopathy* has passed into its eighth edition; Dr. Paul Moreau (*des Aberrations du sens Génésique*); Cesare Lombroso, the author of various works on Anthropology; Tarnowski; Mantegazza; K. H. Ulrichs, and others – have made a special and more or less impartial study of this subject: with the result that a quite altered complexion has been given to it; it being indeed especially noticeable that the change of view among the scientists has gone on step by step with the accumulation of reliable information, and that it is most marked in the latest authors, such as Krafft-Ebing and Moll.

It is not possible here to go into anything like a detailed account of the works of these various authors, their theories, and the immense number of interesting cases and observations which they have contributed; but some of the general conclusions which flow from their researches may be pointed out. In the first place their labours have established the fact, known hitherto only to individuals, that *sexual inversion* – that is the leaning of sexual desire to one of the same sex – is in a vast number of cases quite instinctive and congenital, mentally and physically, and therefore twined in the very roots of individual life and practically ineradicable. To Men or Women thus affected with an innate homosexual bias, Ulrichs gave the name of Urning,[#15] since pretty widely accepted by scientists. Too much emphasis cannot be laid on the distinction between these born lovers of their own sex, and that class of persons, with whom they are so often confused, who out of mere carnal curiosity or extravagance of desire, or from the dearth of opportunities for a more normal satisfaction (as in schools, barracks, etc.) adopt some homosexual practices. In the case of these latter the attraction towards their own sex is merely superficial and temptational, so to speak, and is generally felt by those concerned to be in some degree morbid. In the case of the former it is, as said, so deeply rooted and twined with the mental and emotional life that the person concerned has difficulty in imagining himself affected otherwise than he is; and to him at least the homogenic love appears healthy and natural, and indeed necessary to the concretion of his individuality.

In the second place it has become clear that the number of individuals affected with 'sexual inversion' in some degree or other is very great – much greater than is generally supposed to be the case. It is however very difficult or perhaps impossible to arrive at satisfactory figures on the subject, for the simple reasons that the proportions vary so greatly among different peoples and even in different sections of society and in different localities, and because of course there are all possible grades of sexual inversion to deal with, from that in which the instinct is *quite exclusively* directed towards the same sex,[#16] to the other extreme in which it is normally towards the opposite sex but capable occasionally and under exceptional attractions, of inversions towards its own – this last condition being probably among some peoples very widespread, if not universal.

In the third place, by the tabulation and comparison of a great number of cases and 'confessions,' it has become pretty well established that the individuals affected with inversion in marked degree do not after all differ from the rest of mankind, or womankind, in any other physical or mental particular which can be distinctly indicated.[#17] No congenital association with any particular physical conformation or malformation has yet been discovered; nor with any distinct disease of body or mind. Nor does it appear that persons of this class are usually of a gross or specially low type, but if anything rather the opposite – being often of refined sensitive nature and including, as Krafft-Ebing points out (*Psychopathia Sexualis*, seventh ed., p. 227) a great number 'highly gifted in the fine arts, especially music and poetry,' and, as Mantegazza says,[18] many persons of high literary and social distinction. It is true that Krafft-Ebing insists on the generally strong sexual equipment of this class of persons (among men), but he hastens to say that their emotional love is also 'enthusiastic and exalted,'[19] and that, while bodily congress is desired, the special act with which they are vulgarly credited is in most cases repugnant to them.[20]

The only distinct characteristic which the scientific writers claim to have established is a marked tendency to nervous development in the subject, not infrequently associated with nervous maladies; but – as I shall presently have occasion to show – there is reason to think that the validity even of this characteristic has been exaggerated.

Taking the general case of men with a marked exclusive preference for their own sex, Krafft-Ebing says (*Psychopathia Sexualis*, p. 256) 'The sexual life of these Homosexuals is *mutatis mutandis*[24] just the same as in the case of normal sex-love....The Urning loves, deifies his male beloved one, exactly as the woman-wooing man does *his* beloved. For him, he is capable of the greatest sacrifice, experiences the torments of unhappy, often unrequited, love, of faithlessness on his beloved's part, of jealousy, and so forth. His attention is enchained only by the male form....The sight of feminine charms is indifferent to him, if not repugnant.' Then he goes on to say that many such men, notwithstanding their actual aversion to intercourse with the female, do ultimately marry – whether from ethical, as sometimes happens, or from social considerations. But very remarkable – as illustrating the depth and tenacity of the homogenic instinct[21] – and pathetic too, are the records that he gives of these cases; for in many of them a real friendship and regard between the married pair was still of no avail to overcome the distaste on the part of one to sexual intercourse with the other, or to prevent the experience of actual physical distress after such intercourse, or to check the continual flow of affection to some third person of the same sex; and thus unwillingly, so to speak, this bias remained a cause of suffering to the end.

This very brief summary of scientific conclusions, taken in conjunction with the fact (which we have already referred to) that the whole literature and life of the greatest people of antiquity – the Greeks of the Periclean age[25] – was saturated with the passion of homogenic comrade-love, must convince us that this passion cannot be lightly dismissed as of no account – must convince us that it has an important part to play in human affairs. On the one hand we have anathemas and execrations, on the other we have the sublime enthusiasm of a man like Plato – one of the leaders of the world's thought for all time – who puts, for example, into the mouth of Phaedrus (in the *Symposium*) such a passage as this:[22] 'I know not any greater blessing to a young man beginning life than a virtuous lover, or to the lover than a beloved youth. For the principle which ought to be the guide of men who would nobly live – that principle, I say, neither kindred, nor honour, nor wealth, nor any other motive is able to implant so well as love. Of what am I speaking? Of the sense of honour and dishonour, without which neither states nor individuals ever do any good or great work....For what lover would not choose rather to be seen of all mankind than by his beloved, either when abandoning his post or throwing away his arms? He would be ready to die a thousand deaths rather than endure this. Or who would desert his beloved or fail him in the hour of danger? The veriest coward would become an inspired hero, equal to the bravest, at such a time; love would inspire him. That courage which, as Homer says, the god breathes into the soul of heroes, love of his own nature inspires into the lover.' Or again in the *Phaedrus* Plato makes Socrates say:[23] – 'In like manner the followers of Apollo and of every other god, walking in the ways of their god, seek a love who is to be like their god, and when they have found him, they themselves imitate their god, and persuade their love to do the same, and bring him into harmony with the form and ways of the god as far as they can; for they have no feelings of envy or jealousy towards their beloved, but they do their utmost to create in him the greatest likeness of themselves and the god whom they honour. Thus fair and blissful to the beloved when he is taken, is the mysteries of true love, if their purpose is effected.' And yet Plato throughout his discourses never suggests for a moment that the love of which he is speaking is any other than the homogenic passion, nor glosses over or conceals its stronger physical substructure.

II

We have now I think said enough to show from the testimony of History, Literature, Art, and even of Modern Science, that the homogenic passion is capable of splendid developments; and that a love and capacity of love of so intimate, penetrating and inspiring a kind – and which has played so important a part in the life-histories of some of the great races and individuals – is well worthy of respectful and thoughtful consideration. And I think it has become obvious that to cast a slur upon this kind of love because it may in cases lead to aberrations and extravagances would be a most irrational thing to do – since exactly the same charges, of possible aberration and extravagance, might be brought, and the same conclusion enforced, against the ordinary sex-love.

It is however so often charged against the sentiment in question that it is essentially unnatural and *morbid* in character, that it may be worth while, though we have already touched on this point, to consider it here at greater length. I therefore propose to devote a few more pages to the examination of the scientific position on this subject, and then to pass on to a consideration of the general place and purpose of the homogenic or comrade-love (its sanity being granted) in human character and social life.

It might be thought that the testimonies of History, Literature and Art, above referred to, would be quite sufficient of themselves to dispose of the charge of essential morbidity. But as mankind in general is not in the habit of taking bird's eye views of History and Literature, and as it finds it easy to assume that anything a little exceptional is also morbid, so it is not difficult to see how this charge (in countries where the sentiment *is* exceptional) has arisen and maintained itself. Science, of course, is nothing but common observation organized and systemized, and so we naturally find that with regard to this subject it started on its investigations from the same general assumptions that possessed the public mind. It may safely be said that until the phenomena of homogenic Love began to be calmly discussed by the few scientific men already mentioned, the subject had never since classical times been once fairly faced in the arena of literature or public discussion, and had as a rule been simply dismissed with opprobrious epithets well suited to give an easy victory to prejudice and ignorance. But the history of even these few years of scientific investigation bears with it a memorable lesson. For while at the outset it was easily assumed that the homogenic instinct was thoroughly morbid in itself, and probably always associated with distinct disease, either physical or mental, the progress of the inquiry – as already pointed out – served more and more to dissipate this view; and it is noticeable that Krafft-Ebing and Moll – the latest of the purely scientific authorities – are the least disposed to insist upon the theory of morbidity. It is true that Krafft-Ebing clings to the opinion that there is generally some *neurosis*, or degeneration of a nerve-centre, or *inherited tendency in that direction*, associated with the instinct; see p. 190 (seventh ed.), also p. 227, where he speaks, rather vaguely, of 'an hereditary neuropathic or psychopathic tendency' – *neuro(psycho)pathische Belastung*. But it is an obvious criticism on this that there are few people in modern life, perhaps none, who could be pronounced absolutely free from such a *Belastung*! And whether the Dorian Greeks or the Polynesian Islanders or the Kelts (spoken of by Aristotle, *Politics*, ii. 7) or the Normans or the Albanian mountaineers, or any of the other notably hardy races among whom the passion has been developed, were particularly troubled by nervous degeneration we may well doubt![#24] As to Moll, though he speaks[#25] of the instinct as morbid (feeling perhaps in duty bound to do so), it is very noticeable that he abandons the ground of its association with other morbid symptoms – as this association, he says, is by no means always to be observed; and is fain to rest his judgement on the *dictum* that the mere failure of the instinct to propagate the species is itself pathological – a *dictum* which in its turn obviously springs from that pre-judgement of scientists that generation is the sole object of love,[#26] and which if pressed would involve the good doctor in awkward dilemmas, as for instance that every worker-bee is a pathological specimen.

With regard to the nerve-degeneration theory, while it may be allowed that sexual inversion is not uncommonly found in connection with the specially nervous temperament, it must be remembered that its occasional association with nervous troubles or disease is quite another matter; since such troubles ought perhaps to be looked upon as the *results* rather than the causes of the inversion. It is difficult of course for outsiders not personally experienced in the matter to realize the great strain and tension of nerves under which those persons grow up from boyhood to manhood – or from girl to womanhood – who find their deepest and strongest instincts under the ban of society around them; who before they clearly understand the drift of their own natures discover that they are somehow cut off from the sympathy and understanding of those nearest to them; and who know that they can never give expression to their tenderest yearnings of affection without exposing themselves to the possible charge of actions stigmatized as odious crimes.[#27] That such a strain, acting on one who is perhaps already of a nervous temperament, should tend to cause nervous prostration or even mental disturbance is of course obvious; and if such disturbances are really found to be commoner among homogenic lovers than among ordinary folk we have in these social causes probably a sufficient explanation of the fact.

Then again in this connection it must never be forgotten that the medico-scientific enquirer is bound on the whole to meet with those cases that *are* of a morbid character, rather than with those that are healthy in their manifestation, since indeed it is the former that he lays himself out for. And since the field of his research is usually a great modern city, there is little wonder if disease colours his conclusions. In the case of Dr. Moll, who carried out his researches largely under the guidance of the Berlin police (whose acquaintance with the subject would naturally be limited to its least satisfactory sides), the only marvel is that his verdict is so markedly favourable as it is. As Krafft-Ebing says in his own preface 'It is the sad privilege of Medicine, and especially of Psychiatry, to look always on the reverse side of life, on the weakness and wretchedness of man.'

Having regard then to the direction in which science has been steadily moving in this matter, it is not difficult to see that the epithet 'morbid' will probably before long be abandoned as descriptive of the homogenic bias – that is, of the general sentiment of love towards a person of the same sex. That there are excesses of the passion – cases, as in ordinary sex-love, where mere physical desire becomes a mania – we may freely admit; but as it would be unfair to judge of the purity of marriage by the evidence of the Divorce courts, so it would be monstrous to measure the truth and beauty of the attachment in question by those instances which stand most prominently perhaps in the eye of the modern public; and after all deductions there remains, we contend, the vast body of cases in which the manifestation of the instinct has on the whole the character of normality and healthfulness – sufficiently so in fact to constitute this *a distinct variety of the sexual passion*. The question, of course, not being whether the instinct is *capable* of morbid and extravagant manifestation – for this can easily be proved of any instinct – but whether it is capable of a healthy and sane expression. And this, we think, it has abundantly shown itself to be.

Anyhow the work that Science has practically done has been to destroy the dogmatic attitude of the former current opinion from which itself started, and to leave the whole subject freed from a great deal of misunderstanding, and much more open than before. Its labours – and they have been valuable in this way – have been chiefly of a negative character. While unable on the one hand to characterize the physical attraction in question as definitely morbid or the result of morbid tendencies, it is unable on the other hand to say positively at present what physiological or other purpose is attained by the instinct.

This question of the physiological basis of the homogenic love – to which we have more than once alluded – is a very important one; and it seems a strange oversight on the part of Science that it has hitherto taken so little notice of it. The desire for corporeal intimacy of some kind between persons of the same sex existing as it does in such force and so widely over the face of the earth, it would seem almost certain that there must be some physiological basis for the desire: but until we know more than we do at present as to what this basis may be, we are necessarily unable to understand the desire itself as well as we might wish. It may be hoped that this is a point to which attention will be given in the future. Meanwhile, though the problem is a complex one, it may not be amiss here to venture a suggestion or two.

In the first place it may be suggested that an important part of *all* love-union, mental or physical, is its influence personally on those concerned. This influence is, of course, subtle and hard to define; and one can hardly be surprised that Science, assuming hitherto in its consideration of ordinary sexual relations that the mutual actions and reactions were directly solely to the purpose of generation and the propagation of the species, has almost quite neglected the question of the direct influences on the lovers themselves. Yet everyone is sensible practically that there is much more in an intimacy with another person than the question of children alone; that even setting aside the effects of actual sex-intercourse there are subtle elements passing from one to another which are indispensable to personal well-being, and which make some such intimacy almost a necessary condition of health. It may be that there are some persons for whom these necessary reactions can only come from one of the same sex. In fact it is obvious there are such persons. 'Successful love,' says Moll (p. 125) 'exercises a helpful influence on the Urning. His mental and bodily conditions improves, and capacity of work increases – just as it often happens in the case of a normal youth with *his* love.' And further on (p. 173) in a letter from a man of this kind occur these words: 'The passion is I suppose so powerful, just because one looks for everything in the loved man – Love, Friendship, Ideal, and Sense-satisfaction....As it is at present I suffer the agonies of a deep unresponded passion, which wake me like a nightmare from sleep. And I am conscious of physical pain in the region of the heart.' In such cases the love, in some degree physically expressed, of another person of the same sex, is clearly as much a necessity and a condition of healthy life and activity, as in more ordinary cases is the love of a person of the opposite sex.

It has probably been the arbitrary limitation of the function of love to child-breeding which has (unconsciously) influenced the popular mind against the form of love which we are considering. That this kind of union was not concerned with the propagation of the race was in itself enough to make people look askance at it; that any kind of love-union could exist in which the sex-act might possibly *not* be the main object was an incredible proposition. And, in enforcing this view, no doubt the Hebraic and Christian tradition has exercised a powerful influence – dating, as it almost certainly does, from far-back times when the multiplication of the tribe was one of the very first duties of its members, and of the first necessities of corporate life; though nowadays when the need has swung round all the other way it is not unreasonable to suppose that a similar revolution will take place in people's views of the place and purpose of the non-child-bearing love. We find in some quarters that even the most naive attachments between youths are stigmatized as 'unnatural' (though, inconsistently enough, not those between girls) – and this can only well be from an assumption that all familiarities are meant by Nature to lead up to generation and race-propagation. Yet no one – if fairly confronted with the question – would seriously maintain that the mutual stimulus, physical, mental and moral, which flows from embrace and endearment is nothing, and that because these things do not lead to actual race propagation therefore they must be discountenanced. If so, must even the loving association between man and wife, more than necessary for the breeding of children, or after the period of fertility has passed, be also discountenanced? Such questions might be multiplied indefinitely. They only serve to show how very crude as yet are all our theories on these subjects, and how necessary it is in the absence of more certain knowledge to suspend our judgement.[#28]

Summarizing then some of our conclusions on this rather difficult question we may yet say that the homogenic love, as a distinct variety of the sex-passion, is in the main subject to the same laws as ordinary love; that it probably demands and requires some amount of physical intimacy; that a wise humanity will quite recognize this; but that the degree of intimacy, in default of a more certain physiological knowledge than we have, is a matter which can only be left to the good sense and feeling of those concerned; and that while we do not deny for a moment that excesses of physical appetite exist, these form no more reason for tabooing all expression of the sentiment than they do in the case of the more normal love. We may also say that if on the side of science much is obscure, there is no obscurity in the principles of healthy morality involved; that there is no exception here to the law that sensuality apart from love is degrading and something less than human; or to the law that love – true love – seeks nothing which is not consistent with the welfare of the loved one; and that here too the principle of Transmutation applies[#29] – the principle that Desire in man has its physical, emotional and spiritual sides, and that when its outlet is checked along one channel, it will, within limits, tend to flow with more vehemence along the other channels – and that reasonable beings, perceiving this, will (again within limits) check the sensual and tend to throw the centre of their love-attraction upwards.

Probably in this, as in all love, it will be felt in the end by those who devote themselves to each other and to the truth, to be wisest to concentrate on the *real thing*, on the enduring deep affection which is the real satisfaction and outcome of the relation, and which like a young sapling they would tend with loving care till it grows into a mighty tree which the storms of a thousand years cannot shake; and those who do so heartily and truly can leave the physical to take care of itself. This indeed is perhaps the only satisfactory touchstone of the rightness and fitness of human relations generally, in sexual matters. People, not unnaturally, seek for an absolute rule in such matters, and a *fixed* line between the right and the wrong; but may we not say that there is no rule except that of Love – Love making use, of course, of whatever certain knowledge Science may from time to time be able to provide?

And speaking of the law of Transmutation and its importance, it is clear, I think, that in the homosexual love – whether between man and man or between woman and woman – the physical side, from the very nature of the case, can never find expression quite so freely and perfectly as in the ordinary heterosexual love; and therefore that there is a 'natural' tendency for the former love to run rather more along emotional channels.[30] And this no doubt throws light on the fact that love of the homogenic type has inspired such a vast amount of heroism and romance – and is indeed only paralleled in this respect (as J. Addington Symonds has pointed out in his paper on 'Dantesque and Platonic ideals of love')[31] by the loves of Chivalry, which of course owing to their special character, were subject to a similar transmutation.

It is well-known that Plato in many passages in his dialogues gives expression to the opinion that the love which at that time was common among the Greek youths had, in its best form, a special function in educational social and heroic work. I have already quoted a passage from the *Symposium*, in which Phaedrus speaks of the inspiration which this love provides towards an honourable and heroic life. Pausanias in the same dialogue says:[32] 'In Ionia and other places, and generally in countries which are subject to the barbarians, the custom is held to be dishonourable; loves of youths share the evil repute of philosophy and gymnastics *because they are inimical to tyranny*, for the interests of rulers require that their subjects should be pure in spirit, and that there should be no strong bond of friendship or society between them – which love above all other motives, is likely to inspire, as our Athenian tyrants learned by experience.' This is a pretty strong statement of the political significance of this kind of love.

Richard Wagner in his pamphlet *The Art-work of the Future*[33] has some interesting passages to the same effect – showing how the conception of the beauty of manhood became the formative influence of the Spartan State. He says: 'This beauteous naked man is the kernel of all Spartanhood; from genuine delight in the beauty of the most perfect human body – that of the male – arose that spirit of comradeship which pervades and shapes the whole economy of the Spartan State. This love of man to man, in its primitive purity, proclaims itself as the noblest and least selfish utterance of man's sense of beauty, for it teaches man to sink and merge his entire self in the object of his affection;' and again: 'The higher element of that love of man to man consisted even in this: that it excluded the motive of egoistic[#34] physicalism. Nevertheless it not only included a purely spiritual bond of friendship, but this spiritual friendship was the blossom and the crown of the physical friendship. The latter sprang directly from delight in the beauty, aye in the material bodily beauty of the beloved comrade; yet this delight was no egoistic yearning, but a thorough stepping out of self into unreserved sympathy with the comrade's joy in himself; involuntarily betrayed by his life-glad beauty-prompted bearing. This love, which had its basis in the noblest pleasures of both eye and soul – not like our modern postal correspondence of sober friendship, half busi- nesslike, half sentimental – was the Spartan's only tutoress of youth, the never-aging instructress alike of boy and man, the ordainer of common feasts and valiant enterprises; nay the inspiring helpmeet on the battlefield. For this it was that knit the fellowship of love into battalions of war, and fore-wrote the tactics of death-daring, in rescue of the imperilled or vengeance for the slaugh- tered comrade, by the infrangible law of the soul's most natural necessity.'

The last sentence in this quotation is well illustrated by a passage from a 'privately printed' pamphlet entitled *A Problem in Greek Ethics*, in which the author[26] endeavours to reconstruct as it were the genesis of comrade-love among the Dorians in early Greek times. Thus: 'Without sufficiency of women, without the sanctities of established domestic life, inspired by the memory of Achilles and venerating their ancestor Herakles,[#35] the Dorian warriors had special opportunity for elevating comradeship to the rank of an enthusiasm. The incidents of emigration into a distant country – perils of the sea, passages of rivers and mountains, assaults of fortresses and cities, landings on a hostile shore, night vigils by the side of blazing beacons, foragings for food, picquet service in the front of watchful foes – involved adventures capable of shedding the lustre of romance on friendship. These circumstances, by bringing the virtues of sympathy with the weak, tenderness for the beautiful, protection for the young, together with corresponding qualities of gratitude, self-devotion, and admiring attachment into play, may have tended to cement unions between man and man no less firm than that of marriage. On such connections a wise captain would have relied for giving strength to his battalions, and for keeping alive the flames of enterprise and daring.' The author then goes on to suggest that though in such relations as those indicated the physical probably had its share, yet it did not at that time overbalance the emotional and spiritual elements, or lead to the corruption and effeminacy of a later age.

At Sparta the lover was called *Eispnelos*, the inspirer, and the younger beloved *Aites*, the hearer. This alone would show the partly educational aspects in which comradeship was conceived; and a hundred passages from classic literature might be quoted to prove how deeply it had entered into the Greek mind that this love was the cradle of social chivalry and heroic life. Finally it seems to have been Plato's favourite doctrine that the relation if properly conducted led up to the disclosure of true philosophy in the mind, to the divine vision or mania, and to the remembrance or rekindling within the soul of all the forms of celestial beauty. He speaks of this kind of love as causing a 'generation in the beautiful'[#36] within the souls of the lovers. The image of the beloved one passing into the mind of the lover and upward through its deepest recesses reaches and unites itself to the essential forms of divine beauty there long hidden – the originals as it were of all creation – and stirring them to life excites a kind of generative descent of noble thoughts and impulses, which thenceforward modify the whole cast of thought and life of the one so affected.

I have now said enough I think to show that though Science has not yet been able to give any decisive utterance on the import of the physical and physiological side of the homogenic passion (and it must be remembered that its real understanding of this side of the ordinary sex-love is very limited), yet on its ethical and social sides – which cannot of course, in the last resort, be separated from the physiological – the passion is pregnant with meaning, and has received at various times in history abundant justification. And in truth it seems the most natural thing in the world that just as the ordinary sex-love has a special function in the propagation of the race, so the other love should have its special function in social and heroic work, and in the generation – not of bodily children – but of those children of the mind, the philosophical conceptions and ideals which transform our lives and those of society. This without limiting too closely. In each case the main object may be said to be union. But as all love is also essentially creative, we naturally look for the creative activities of different kinds of love in different directions – and seem to find them so.

If there is any truth – even only a grain or two – in these speculations, it is easy to see that the love with which we are specially dealing is a very important factor in society, and that its neglect, or its repression, or its vulgar misapprehension, may be matters of considerable danger or damage to the common-weal. It is easy to see that while on the one hand the ordinary marriage is of indispensable importance to the State as providing the workshop as it were for the breeding and rearing of children, another form of union is almost equally indispensable to supply the basis for social activities of other kinds.

Every one is conscious that without a close affectional tie of some kind his life is not complete, his powers are crippled, and his energies are inadequately spent. Yet it is not be expected (though it may of course happen) that the man or woman who have dedicated themselves to each other and to family life should leave the care of their children and the work they to do at home in order to perform social duties of a remote and less obvious, though may-be more arduous, character. Nor is it to be expected that a man or woman single-handed, without the counsel of a helpmate in the hour of difficulty, or his or her love in the hour of need, should feel equal to these wider activities. If – to refer once more to classic story – the love of Harmodius had been for a wife and children at home, he would probably not have cared, and it would hardly have been his business, to slay the tyrant. And unless on the other hand each of the friends had had the love of his comrade to support him, the two could hardly have nerved themselves to this audacious and ever-memorable exploit. So it is difficult to believe that anything except that kind of comrade-union which satisfies and invigorates the two lovers and yet leaves them free from the responsibilities and *impedimenta*[27] of family life can supply the force and liberate the energies required for social and mental activities of the most necessary kind.

For if the slaughter of tyrants is not the chief social duty nowadays, we have with us hydra-headed monsters[28] at least as numerous as the tyrants of old, and more difficult to deal with, and requiring no little social courage to encounter. And beyond the extirpation of evils we have solid work waiting to be done in the patient and life-long building up of new forms of society, new orders of thought, and new institutions of human solidarity – all of which in their genesis will meet with opposition, ridicule, hatred, and even violence. Such campaigns as these – though different in kind from those of the Dorian mountaineers described above – will call for equal hardihood and courage and will stand in need of a comradeship as true and valiant. It may indeed be doubted whether the higher heroic and spiritual life of a nation is ever quite possible without the sanction of this attachment in its institutions; and it is not unlikely that the markedly materialistic and commercial character of the last age of European civilized life is largely to be connected with the fact that the *only* form of love and love-union that it has recognized has been one founded on the quite necessary but comparatively materialistic basis of matrimonial sex-intercourse and child-breeding.[#37] Walt Whitman, the inaugurator, it may almost be said, of a new world of democratic ideals and literature, and – as one of the best of our critics[#38] has remarked – the most Greek in spirit and in performance of modern writers, insists continually on this social function of 'intense and loving comradeship, the personal and passionate attachment of man to man.' 'I will make,' he says, 'the most splendid race the sun ever shone upon, I will make divine magnetic lands....I will make inseparable cities with their arms about each others necks, by the love of comrades.'[29] And again, in *Democratic Vistas*, 'It is to the development, identification, and general prevalence of that fervid comradeship (the adhesive love at least rivalling the amative love hitherto possessing imaginative literature, if not going beyond it), that I look for the counterbalance and offset of materialistic and vulgar American Democracy, and for the spiritualization thereof....I say Democracy infers such loving comradeship, as its most inevitable twin or counterpart, without which it will be incomplete, in vain, and incapable of perpetuating itself.'

Yet Whitman could not have spoken, as he did, with a kind of authority on this subject, if he had not been fully aware that through the masses of the people this attachment was already alive and working – though doubtless in a somewhat suppressed and unselfconscious form – and if he had not had ample knowledge of its effects and influence in himself and others around him. Like all great artists he could but give form and light to that which already existed dim and inchoate in the heart of the people. To those who have dived at all below the surface in this direction it will be familiar enough that the homogenic passion ramifies widely through all modern society, and that among the masses of the people as among the classes, below the stolid surface and reserve of British manners, letters pass and enduring attachments are formed, differing in no very obvious respect from those correspondences which persons of opposite sexes knit with each other under similar circumstances; but that hitherto while this passion has occasionally come into public notice through the police reports, etc., in its grosser and cruder forms, its more sane and spiritual manifestations – though really a moving force in the body politic – have remained unrecognized.

It is hardly needful in these days when the social questions loom so large upon us to emphasize the importance of a bond which by the most passionate and lasting compulsion may draw members of the different classes together, and (as it often seems to do) none the less strongly because they are members of different classes. A moment's consideration must convince us that such a comradeship may, as Whitman says, have 'deepest relations to general politics'. It is noticeable, too, in this deepest relation to politics that the movement among women towards their own liberation and emancipation which is taking place all over the civilized world has been accompanied by a marked development of the homogenic passion among the female sex. It may be said that a certain strain in the relations between the opposite sexes which has come about owing to a growing consciousness among women that they have been oppressed and unfairly treated by men,[#39] and a growing unwillingness to ally themselves unequally in marriage – that this strain has caused the womankind to draw more closely together and to cement alliances of their own. But whatever the cause may be it is pretty certain that such comrade-alliances – and of a quite passionate kind – are becoming increasingly common, and especially perhaps among the more cultured classes of women, who are working out the great cause of their sex's liberation; nor is it difficult to see the importance of such alliances in such a campaign. In the United States where the battle of women's independence has been fought more vehemently perhaps than here, the tendency mentioned is even more strongly marked.

In conclusion there are a few words to be said about the legal aspect of this important question. It has to be remarked that the present state of the Law – arising as it does partly out of some of the misapprehensions above alluded to, and partly out of the sheer unwillingness of legislators to discuss the question – is really quite impracticable and unjustifiable, and will no doubt have to be altered.

The Law, of course, can only deal, and can only be expected to deal, with the outward and visible. It cannot control feeling; but it tries – in those cases where it is concerned – to control the expression of feeling. It has been insisted on in this essay that the Homogenic Love is a valuable social force, and, in cases, an indispensable factor of the noblest human character; also that it has a necessary root in the physical and sexual organism. This last is the point where the Law steps in. 'We know nothing' – it says – 'of what may be valuable social forces or factors of character, or of what may be the relation of physical things to things spiritual; but when you speak of a sexual element being present in this kind of love, we can quite understand that; and that is just what we mean to suppress. That sexual element is nothing but gross indecency, *any form of which by our Act of 1885 we make criminal.*'

Whatever substantial ground the Law may have had for previous statutes on this subject – dealing with a specific act (sodomy) – it has surely quite lost it in passing so wide-sweeping a condemnation on all relations between male persons.[#40] It has undertaken a censorship over private morals (entirely apart from social results) which is beyond its province, and which – even if it were its province – it could not possibly fulfil; it has opened wider than ever before the door to a real social evil and crime – that of blackmailing; and it has thrown a shadow over even the simplest and most natural expression of an attachment which may, as we have seen, be of the greatest value in national life.[#41]

That the homosexual passion may be improperly indulged in, that it may lead, like the heterosexual, to public abuses of liberty and decency we of course do not deny; but as, in the case of persons of opposite sex, the law limits itself on the whole to the maintenance of public order, the protection of the weak from violence and insult[#42] and, of the young from their inexperience: so it should be here. Whatever teaching may be thought desirable on the general principles of morality concerned must be given – as it can only be given – by the spread of proper education and ideas, and not be the clumsy bludgeon of the statute-book.[#43]

We have shown the special functions and really indispensable import of the homogenic or comrade love, in some form, in national life, and it is high time now that the modern States should recognize this in their institutions – instead of (as is also done in schools and places of education) by repression and disallowance perverting the passion into its least satisfactory channels. If the dedication of love were a matter of mere choice or whim, it still would not be the business of the State to compel that choice; but since no amount of compulsion can ever change the homogenic instinct in a person, where it is innate, the State in trying to effect such a change is only kicking vainly against the pricks of its own advantage – and trying, in view perhaps of the conduct of a licentious few, to cripple and damage a respectable and valuable class of its own citizens.

Richard Burton, Section D, 'Pederasty', from the 'Terminal essay', *The Thousand Nights and a Night*, 1885[30]

Extracted here are three passages from Section D of the 'Terminal essay': the opening exposition of his own invention, the Sotadic Zone, where homosexuality is endemic, and a minute treatment of pederasty in Greece and Rome; the ending, where he answers his critics; and his commentary on the Sodom and Gomorrah story. Burton's erudition was astounding, epitomized by his speaking twenty-eight languages, and the 'Terminal essay' as a whole delivers an account of sexual peccadillos across the world and all history.

The 'execrabilis familia pathicorum'[31] first came before me by a chance of earlier life. In 1845, when Sir Charles Napier[32] had conquered and annexed Sind, despite a faction (mostly venal) which sought favour with the now defunct 'Court of Directors to the Honourable East India Company', the veteran began to consider his conquest with a curious eye. It was reported to him that Karàchi, a townlet of some two thousand souls and distant not more than a mile from camp, supported no less than three lupanars or bordels, in which not women but boys and eunuchs, the former demanding nearly a double price,[#44] lay for hire. Being then the only British officer who could speak Sindi, I was asked indirectly to make enquiries and to report upon the subject; and I undertook the task on express conditions that my report should not be forwarded to the Bombay Government, from whom supporters of the Conquerer's policy could expect scant favour, mercy or justice. Accompanied by a Munshi,[33] Mirza Mohammed Hosayn of Shiraz, and habited as a merchant, Mirza Abdullah the Bushiri[#45] passed many an evening in the townlet, visited all the porneia[34] and obtained the fullest details which were duly despatched to Government House. But the 'Devil's Brother' presently quitted Sind leaving in his office my unfortunate official: this found its way with sundry other reports[#46] to Bombay and produced the expected result. A friend in the Secretariat informed me that my summary dismissal from the service had been formally proposed by one of Sir Charles Napier's successors, whose decease compels me pacere sepulto.[35] But this excess of outraged modesty was not allowed.

Subsequent enquiries in many and distant countries enabled me to arrive at the following conclusions:

1   There exists what I shall call a 'Sotadic Zone,' bounded westwards by the northern shores of the Mediterranean (N. Lat. 43°) and by the southern (N. Lat. 30°). Thus the depth would be 780 to 800 miles including meridional France, the Iberian Peninsula, Italy and Greece, with the coast-regions of Africa from Marocco to Egypt.
2   Running eastward the Sotadic Zone narrows, embracing Asia Minor, Mesopotamia[36] and Chaldaea,[37] Afghanistan, Sind, the Punjab and Kashmir.
3   In Indo-China the belt begins to broaden, enfolding China, Japan and Turkistan.
4   It then embraces the South Sea Islands and the New World where, at the time of its discovery, Sotadic love was, with some exceptions, an established racial institution.
5   Within the Sotadic Zone the Vice is popular and endemic, held at the worst to be a mere peccadillo, whilst the races to the North and South of the limits here defined practise it only sporadically amid the opprobrium of their fellows who, as a rule, are physically incapable of performing the operation and look upon it with the liveliest disgust.

Before entering into topographical details concerning Pederasty, which I hold to be geographical and climatic, not racial, I must offer a few considerations of its cause and origin. We must not forget that the love of boys has its noble sentimental side. The Platonists and pupils of the Academy,[38] followed by the Sufis or Moslem Gnostics[39] held such affection, pure as ardent, to be the beau idéal which united in man's soul the creature with the Creator. Professing to regard youths as the most clearly and beautiful objects in this phenomenal world, they declared that by loving and extolling the chef-d'oeuvre, corporeal and intellectual, of the Demiurgus,[40] disinterestedly and without any admixture of carnal sensuality, they are paying the most fervent adoration to the Causa causans.[41] They add that such affection, passing as it does the love of women, is far less selfish than fondness for and admiration of the other sex which, however innocent, always suggest sexuality;[#47] and Easterns add that the devotion of the moth to the taper is purer and more fervent than the Bulbul's love for the Rose.[42] Amongst the Greeks of the best ages the system of boy-favourites was advocated on considerations of morals and politics. The lover undertook the education of the beloved through precept and example, while the two were conjoined by a tie stricter than the fraternal. Hieronymous the Peripatetic[43] strongly advocated it because the vigorous disposition of youths and the confidence engendered by their association often led to the overthrow of tyrannies. Socrates declared that 'a most valiant army might be composed of boys and their lovers; for that of all men they would be most ashamed to desert one another.'[44] And even Virgil, despite the foul flavour of Formosum pastor Corydon,[45] could write:

Nisus amore pio pueri.[46]

The only physical cause for the practice which suggests itself to me and that must be owned to be purely conjectural, is that within the Sotadic Zone there is a blending of the masculine and feminine temperaments, a crasis which elsewhere occurs only sporadically. Hence the male *féminisme* whereby the man becomes patiens[47] as well as agens,[48] and the woman a tribade,[49] a votary of mascula[50] Sappho,[#48] Queen of Fricatrices or Rubbers.[#49] Prof. Mantegazza[51] claims to have discovered the cause of this pathological love, this perversion of the erotic sense, one of the marvellous list of amorous vagaries which deserve, not prosecution but the pitiful care of the physician and the study of the psychologist. According to him the nerves of the rectum and the genitalia, in all cases closely connected, are abnormally so in the pathic[52] who obtains, by intromission, the venereal orgasm which is usually sought through the sexual organs. So amongst women there are tribads who can procure no pleasure except by foreign objects introduced a posteriori.[53] Hence his threefold distribution of sodomy; (1) Periphic[54] or anatomical, caused by an unusual distribution of the nerves and their hyperaesthesia;[55] (2) Luxurious, when love a tergo[56] is preferred on account of the narrowness of the passage; and (3) the Psychical. But this is evidently superficial: the question is what causes this neuropathy, this abnormal distribution and condition of the nerves.[#50]

As Prince Bismarck finds a moral difference between the male and female races of history,[57] so I suspect a mixed physical temperament effected by the manifold subtle influences massed together in the word climate. Something of the kind is necessary to explain the fact of this pathological love extending over the greater portion of the habitable world, without any apparent connection of race or media, from the polished Greek to the cannibal Tupi of the Brazil. Walt Whitman speaks of the ashen grey faces of onanists: the faded colours, the puffy features and the unwholesome complexion of the professed pederast with his peculiar cathectic expression, indescribable but once seen never forgotten, stamp the breed, and Dr. G. Adolph is justified in declaring 'Alle Gewohnneits-paederasten erkennen sich einander schnell, oft mit einen Blick.'[58] This has nothing in common with the féminisme which betrays itself in the pathic by womanly gait, regard and gesture: it is a something sui generis; and the same may be said of the colour and look of the young priest who honestly refrains from women and their substitutes. Dr. Tardieu, in his well-known work, 'Etude Medico-légale sur les Attentats aux Moeurs', and Dr. Adolph note a peculiar infundibuliform[59] disposition of the 'After' and a smoothness and want of folds even before any abuse has taken place, together with special forms of the male organs in confirmed pederasts.[60] But these observations have been rejected by Caspar, Hoffman, Brouardel and Dr. J. H. Henry Coutagne (Notes sur la Sodomie, Lyon, 1880), and it is a medical question whose discussion would here be out of place.

The origin of pederasty is lost in the night of ages; but its historique has been carefully traced by many writers, especially Virey,[#51] Rosenbaum[#52] and M. H. E. Meier.[#53] The ancient Greeks who, like the modern Germans, invented nothing but were great improvers of what other races invented, attributed the formal apostolate of Sotadism to Orpheus, whose stigmata were worn by the Thracian women;[61]

– Omnemque refugerat Orpheus
Foemineam venerum; –
Ille etiam Thracum populis fuit auctor, amorem
In teneres transferre mares: citraque juventum

Aetatis breve ver, et primos carpere flores.

Ovid Metamorphosis x. 79–85.[62]

Euripides proposed Laius father of Oedipus as the inaugurator, whereas Timaeus declared that the fashion of making favourites of boys was introduced into Greece from Crete, for Malthusian reasons said Aristotle (Pol. ii, 10) attributing it to Minos.[63] Herodotus, however, knew far better, having discovered (ii. c. 80) that the Orphic and Bacchic rites were originally Egyptian.[64] But the Father of History was a traveller and an annalist rather than an archaeologist and he tripped in the following passage (i. c. 135), 'As soon as they (the Persians) hear of any luxury, they instantly make it their own, and hence, among other matters, they have learned from the Hellenes a passion for boys' ('unnatural lust' says modest Rawlinson[65]). Plutarch (De Malig. Herod.[66] xiii.)[#54] asserts with much more probability that the Persians used eunuch boys according to the *Mos Graeciae*, long before they had seen the Grecian main.

In the Holy Books of the Hellenes, Homer and Hesiod, dealing with the heroic ages, there is no trace of pederasty, although, in a long subsequent generation, Lucian suspected Achilles and Patroclus as he did Orestes and Pylades, Theseus and Pirithous.[67] Homer's praises of beauty are reserved for the feminines, especially his favourite Helen. But the Dorians of Crete seem to have commended the abuse to Athens and Sparta and subsequently imported it into Tarentum, Agrigentum and other colonies. Ephorus in Strabo[68] (x. 4 § 21) gives a curious account of the violent abduction of beloved boys (παραστοθεντες) by the lover (εραστης); of the obligations of the ravisher (φιλητωρ) to the favourite (κιλεινος)[#55] and of the 'marriage-ceremonies' which lasted two months. See also Plato *Laws* i. c. 8.[69] Servius (Ad Aeneid. x. 325) informs us 'De Cretensibus accepimus, quod in amore puerorum intemperantes fuerunt, quod postea in Laconas et in totam Graeciam translatum est.'[70] The Cretans and afterwards their apt pupils the Chalcidians[71] held it disreputable for a beautiful boy to lack a lover. Hence Zeus the national Doric god of Crete loved Ganymede;[#56] Apollo, another Dorian deity, loved Hyacinth,[72] and Hercules, a Doric hero who grew to be a sun-god, loved Hylas[73] and a host of others: thus Crete sanctified the practice by the examples of the gods and demigods. But when legislation came, the subject had qualified itself for legal limitation and as such was undertaken by Lycurgus and Solon, according to Xenophon (*Lac.* ii. 13), who draws a broad distinction between the honest love of boys and dishonest (αιχιστος) lust.[74] They both approved of pure pederastia, like that of Harmodius and Aristogiton;[75] but forbade it with serviles because degrading to a free man. Hence the love of boys was spoken of like that of women

(Plato: *Phaedrus; Republic.* vi. c. 19 and Xenophon, *Synop.* iv. 10) *e.g.* 'There was once a boy, or rather a youth, of exceeding beauty and he had very many lovers'[76] – this is the language of Hafiz and Sa'adi. Aeschylus, Sophocles and Euripides were allowed to introduce it upon the stage, for 'many men were as fond of having boys for their favourites as women for their mistresses; and this was a frequent fashion in many well-regulated cities of Greece.'[77] Poets like Alcaeus, Anacreon, Agathon and Pindar affected it and Theognis sang of a 'beautiful boy in the flower of his youth'.[78] The statesmen Aristides and Themistocles[79] quarrelled over Stesileus of Teos; and Pisistratus loved Charmus who first built an altar to Puerile Eros, while Charmus loved Hippias son of Pisistratus. Demosthenes the Orator took into keeping a youth called Cnosion greatly to the indignation of his wife. Xenophon loved Clinias and Autolycus; Aristotle, Hermeas, Theodectes[#57] and others; Empedocles, Pausanias; Epicurus, Pytocles; Aristrippus, Eutichydes and Zeno with his Stoics had a philosophic disregard for women, affecting only pederastia. A man in Athenaeus (iv. c. 40) left in his will that certain youths he had loved should fight like gladiators at his funeral; and Charicles in Lucian abuses Callicratidas for his love of 'sterile pleasures'.[80] Lastly there was the notable affair of Alcibiades and Socrates, the 'sanctus paederasta'[#58] being violemment soupçonné when under the mantle: – non semper sine plagâ ab eo surrexit.[81] Athanaeus (v. c. 13) declares that Plato represents Socrates as absolutely intoxicated with his passion for Alcibiades.[#59] The ancients seem to have held the connection impure, or Juvenal would not have written –

Inter Socraticos notissima fossa cinaedos,[82]

followed by Furmicus (vii. 14) who speaks of 'Socratici paedicones'. It is the modern fashion to doubt the pederasty of the master of Hellenic Sophrosyne, the 'Christian before Christianity'; but such a world-wide term as Socratic love can hardly be explained by the lucus-a-non-lucendo[83] theory. We are overapt to apply our nineteenth century prejudices and prepossessions to the morality of the ancient Greeks who would have specimen'd such squeamishness in Attic salt.

The Spartans, according to Agnon the Academic (confirmed by Plato, Plutarch and Cicero), treated boys and girls in the same way before marriage: hence Juvenal (xi. 173) uses 'Lacedaemonius' for a pathic[84] and other writers apply it to a tribade. After the Peloponnesian War, which ended in 404 B.C., the use became merged in the abuse. Yet some purity must have survived, even amongst the Boeotians who produced the famous Narcissus,[#60] described by Ovid (*Met.* iii. 339):

Multi illum juvenes, multae cupiere puellae;
Nulli illum juvenes, nullae tetigere puellae:[#61] [85]

for Epaminondas, whose name is mentioned with three beloveds, established the Holy Regiment composed of mutual lovers, testifying the majesty of Eros and preferring to a discreditable life a glorious death.[86] Philip's reflections on the fatal field of Chaeroneia form their fittest epitaph.[87] At last the Athenians, according to Aeschines, officially punished sodomy with death; but the threat did not abolish bordels of boys, like those of Karachi; the Porneia and Pornobokskeia, where slaves and pueri venales[88] 'stood', as the term was, near the Pnyx, the city walls and a certain tower, also about Lycabettus (Aesch. contra Timarchus); and paid a fixed tax to the state. The pleasures of society in civilised Greece seem to have been sought chiefly in the heresies of love – Hetairesis[#62] and Sotadism....

Pederastia had in Greece, I have shown, its noble and ideal side: Rome, however, borrowed her malpractices, like her religion and polity, from those ultra-material Etruscans and debauched with a brazen face. Even under the Republic Plautus (*Casina* ii. 21) makes one of his characters exclaim, in the utmost sang-froid, 'Ultro te, amator, apage te a dorso meo!'[89] With increased luxury the evil grew and Livy notices (xxxix. 13), at the Bacchanalia, plura virorum inter sese quam foeminarum stupra.[90] There were individual protests; for instance, S. Q. Fabius Maximus Servilianus (Consul U. C. 612) punished his son for dubia castitas;[91] and a private soldier, C. Plotius, killed his military Tribune, Q. Luscius, for unchaste proposals. The Lex Scantinia (Scatinia?),[92] popularly derived from Scantinius the Tribune and of doubtful date (226 B. C.?), attempted to abate the scandal by fine and the Lex Julia by death;[93] but they were trifling obstacles to the flood of infamy which surged in with the Empire. No class seems then to have disdained these 'sterile pleasures': l'on n'attachoit point alors à cette espèce d'amour une note d'infamie, comme en pais de chrétienté, says Bayle under 'Anacreon'.[94] The great Caesar, the Cinaedus calvus[95] of Catullus,[96] was the husband of all the wives and the wife of all the husbands in Rome (Suetonius, cap. lii.);[97] and his soldiers sang in his praise Gallias Caesar subegit, Nicomedes Caesarem[98] (Suetonius. cies. xlix.); whence his sobriquet 'Fornix Bithynicus'.[99] Of Augustus the people chaunted

Videsne ut Cinaedus orbem digito temperet?[100]

Tiberius, with his pisciculi[101] and greges exoletorum,[102] invented the Symplegma[103] or nexus of Sellarii, agentes et patientes, in which the spinthriae (lit. women's bracelets) were connected in a chain by the bond of flesh[#63] (Seneca Quaest. Nat.).[104] Of this refinement, which in the earlier part of the nineteenth century was renewed by sundry Englishmen at Naples, Ausonius wrote (*Epigrammata*. cxix. 1)

Tres uno in lecto: stuprum duo perpetiuntur;[105]

And Martial had said (xii. 43)

Quo symplegmate quinque cupulentur;
Qua plures teneantur a catena; etc.[106]

Ausonius recounts of Caligula he so lost patience that he forcibly entered the priest M. Lepidus, before the sacrifice was completed.[107] The beautiful Nero was formally married to the Pythagoras (or Doryphoros) and afterwards took to wife Sporus who was first subjected to castration of a peculiar fashion; he was then named Sabina after the deceased spouse and claimed queenly honours. The 'Othonis et Trajani pathici'[108] were famed; the great Hadrian openly loved Antinoüs and the wild debaucheries of Heliogabalus[109] seem only to have amused, instead of disgusting, the Romans.

We find the earliest written notices of the Vice in the mythical destruction of the Pentapolis (Gen. xix.), Sodom, Gomorrah (= 'Amirah, the cultivated country'), Adama, Zeboim and Zoar or Bela. The legend has been amply embroidered by the Rabbis who make the sodomites do everything *à l'envers*: e.g. if man were wounded he was fined for bloodshed and was compelled to fee the offender; and if one cut off the ear of a neighbour's ass he was condemned to keep the animal till the ear grew again. The Jewish doctors declare the people to have been a race of sharpers with rogues for magistrates, and thus they justify the judgement which they read literally. But the traveller cannot accept it. I have carefully examined the lands at the North and at the South of that most beautiful lake, the so-called Dead Sea, whose tranquil loveliness, backed by the grand plateau of the Moab, is an object of admiration to all save patients suffering from the strange disease 'Holy Land on the Brain'.[#64] But I found no traces of craters in the neighbourhood, no signs of vulcanism, no remains of 'meteoric stones': the asphalt which named the water is a mineralized vegetable washed out of the limestones, and the sulphur and salt are brought down by the Jordan into a lake without issue. I must therefore look upon the history as a myth which may have served a double purpose. The first would be to deter the Jew from the Malthusian practices of his pagan predecessors, upon whom obloquy was thus cast, so far resembling the scandalous and absurd legend which explained the names of the children of Lot by Pheiné and Thamma as 'Moab' (Mu-ab) the water or semen of the father, and 'Ammon' as mother's son, that is, bastard. The fable would also account for the abnormal fissure containing the lower Jordan and the Dead Sea, which the late Sir R. I. Murchison used wrong-headedly to call a 'Volcano of Depression':[110] this geological feature, that cuts off the river-basin from its natural outlet the Gulf of Eloth (Akabah), must date from myriads of years before there were 'Cities of the Plains'. But the main object of the ancient lawgiver, Osarsiph, Moses or the Moseidae, was doubtless to discountenance a perversion prejudicial to the increase of a population. And he speaks with no uncertain voice, Whoso lieth with a beast shall surely be put to death (Exod. xxii. 19): If a man lieth with mankind as he lieth with a woman, both of them have committed an abomination: they shall surely be put to death; their blood shall be upon them (Levit. xx. 13; where vv. 15–16 threaten with death man and woman who lie with beasts). Again, There shall be no whore of the daughters of Israel nor a sodomite of the sons of Israel (Deut. xxii. 5).

The old commentators on the Sodom-myth are most unsatisfactory e.g. Parkhurst, s.v. Kadesh. 'From hence we may observe the peculiar propriety of this punishment of Sodom and of the neighbouring cities. By their sodomitical impurities they meant to acknowledge the Heavens as the cause of fruitfulness independently upon, and in opposition to Jehovah,[#65] therefore Jehovah, by raining upon them not genial showers but brimstone from heaven, not only destroyed the inhabitants, but also changed all that country, which was before as the garden of God, into brimstone and salt that is not sown nor beareth, neither any grass groweth therein.' It must be owned that to this Pentapolis was dealt very hard measure for religiously and diligently practising a popular rite which a host of cities even in the present day, as Naples and Shiraz, to mention no others, affect for simple luxury and affect with impunity. The myth may probably reduce itself to very small proportions, a few Fellah villages destroyed by a storm, like that which drove Brennus from Delphi.[111]

The pederasty of The Nights may briefly be distributed into three categories. The first is the funny form, as the unseemly practical joke of masterful Queen Budur (vol. iii. 300–306)[112] and the not less hardi jest of the slave-princess Zumurrud (vol. iv. 226).[113] The second is in the grimmest and most earnest phase of the perversion, for instance where Abu Nowas[#66] debauches the three youths (vol.

v. 64–69);[114] whilst in the third form it is wisely and learnedly discussed, to be severely blamed, by the Shaykhah or Reverend Woman (vol. v. 154).[115]

To conclude this part of my subject, the éclaircissement des obscénités.[116] Many readers will regret the absence from *The Nights* of that modesty which distinguishes *Amadis de Gaul*; whose author when leaving a man and maid together says, 'And nothing shall be here related; for these and suchlike things which are conformable neither to good conscience nor nature, man ought in reason lightly to pass over, holding them in slight esteem as they deserve.' Nor have we less respect for Palmerin of England who after a risqué scene declares, 'Herein is no offence offered to the wise by wanton speeches, or encouragement to the loose by lascivious matter.'[117] But these are not oriental ideas and we must e'en take the Eastern as we find him. He still holds 'Naturalia non sunt turpia', together with 'Mundis omnia munda'; and, as Bacon assures us the mixture of a lie doth add to pleasure, so the Arab enjoys the startling and lively contrast of extreme virtue and horrible vice placed in juxtaposition.

Those who have read through these ten volumes will agree with me that the proportion of offensive matter bears a very small ration to the mass of the work. In an age saturated with cant and hypocrisy, here and there a venal pen will mourn over the 'Pornography' of *The Nights*, dwell upon the 'Ethics of Dirt' and the 'Garbage of the Brothel'; and will lament the 'wanton dissemination (!) of ancient and filthy fiction'. This self-constituted Censor morum[118] reads Aristophanes and Plato, Horace and Virgil, perhaps even Martial and Petronius, because 'veiled in the decent obscurity of a learned language'; he allows men Latinè loqui;[119] but he is scandalized at stumbling-blocks much less important in plain English. To be consistent he must begin by bowdlerizing not only the classics, with which boys' and youths' minds and memories are soaked and saturated at schools and colleges, but also Boccaccio and Chaucer, Shakespeare and Rabelais; Burton, Sterne, Swift and a long list of works which are yearly reprinted and republished without a word of protest. Lastly, why does not this inconsistent puritan purge the Old Testament of its allusions to ordure and the pudenda; to carnal copulation and impudent whoredom, to adultery and fornication, to onanism, sodomy and bestiality? But this he will not do, the whited sepulchre! To the interested critic of the *Edinburgh Review* (No. 335 of July, 1886),[120] I return my warmest thanks for his direct and deliberate falsehoods: – lies are one-legged and short-lived, and venom evaporates.[#67] It appears to me that when I show to such men, so 'respectable' and so impure, a landscape of magnificent prospects whose vistas are adorned with every charm of nature and art, they point their unclean noses at a little heap of muck here and there lying in a field-corner.

Charles Kains-Jackson, 'The New Chivalry', *The Artist and Journal of Home Culture*, 2 April 1894

England has only now emerged into conditions favourable to a real civilisation and a high moral code. For 437 years at least there has been a necessity for increasing the population, a necessity on which the national existence depended. Necessity makes its own laws, and makes its own morals. It dictates what form religion shall assume and decides what classes of a religious code shall be enforced or left inoperative by the civil law. We accordingly find that any contract in restraint of marriage during this period of defective population as compared with our neighbours has been held invalid at law as 'contrary to public policy'. *Salus populi suprema lex.*[121] We find that second marriages have always been allowed, that a celibate priesthood has been legally discouraged, that marriages however much of affection, are null at law unless 'consummated', in other words that not love or fidelity, but a physical act is 'of the essence of the contract'. Yet the sense of humour always inherent in the English people has kept them from such curious exhibitions of nasty mindedness and truculence as marked the Jewish laws of family marriages and as express themselves in the Levitical books, in such passages as 'Habeo duas filias – vobis placuerit'. (Gen. xix., 8), and 'Ingredere – cum Dominus' (Gen. xxxviii., 8–10); Semitic influences however, continue to secure that the work containing these cold-blooded incitements to phallic filthiness is actually allowed to be published at the leading seats of learning, as well as in the metropolis. Even health and science when their teachings clashed with this desire for population have had to go to the wall, and despite the increase of insanity resulting, the marriage of first cousins is permitted – so jealous has the State been of any restraint, even that of hygiene, on marriage.

That the next century, at all events, will have to be lived for Englishmen under widely different circumstances than the last five have been is a point which hardly requires to be enforced. Time and circumstances have conspired to remove the dangers which affected the past. Even a hundred years ago either France or Germany would have conquered England twice over if valour were merely equal. We had frightful arrears of fighting strength to make up. Today even without our colonies we are too numerous for this to happen and it is probable that we should be assisted by England oversea. The problem therefore is shifted and from the dangers foreseen in the Middle Ages in England, from the dangers to which the Jews eventually succumbed, we have now to turn and confront the new series of perils involved in 'the people exceeding the means to live contentedly'.

Again, will necessity effect our laws, our morals, the enforcement or non-enforcement of different sections of a religious code. It will not be all gain; no change ever is. But we can at least make the best of it; as can the wise of all changes. Wherefore just as the flower of the early and imperfect civilization was in what we may call the Old Chivalry, or the exaltation of the youthful feminine ideal, so the flower of the adult and perfect civilization will be found in the New Chivalry or the exaltation of the youthful masculine ideal. The time has arrived when the eternal desire for Love which nature has implanted in the breast of man requires to be satisfied without such an increase in population as has characterized the past. The methods connected with the agreeable names of Bradlaugh, Besant and Drysdale need no notice here. We need not consider the degree of viciousness involved in what is known as 'French vice'. It will suffice for us that it is essentially bourgeois, that it is not only lacking in the aesthetic element but is directly antipathetic thereto. To the aesthete a smirched flower is worse than no flower at all, and the intrusion of chill precaution upon the heat of passion can only result in that lukewarm condition which aestheticism rejects as forcibly as ever orthodoxy did Laodicea.

The new ideal therefore will be one which unites true fancies and a lofty aspiration with a freedom from the two classes of evil already considered. The direction in which it is to be found is indicated by the natural tendencies which secure the survival of the fittest. The animal ideal is to secure immortality by influencing the body. The spiritual is that addition by which we are differentiated from the animal. And the law of evolution is addition, is change. Wherefore the human animal to which the spiritual has been added, will eventually find the line of proper and ultimate evolution is emphasizing that which has been added. The men of most influence on their fellows will be those who are the most spiritual, not those who are the most animal. At the same time the majority will always lag behind the more advanced type, a provision by which the perpetuation of the species is adequately secured. For five centuries in England the necessity that the race should increase and multiply has been paramount, but these five centuries of assistance have now secured their result, and we need at the present time no more than not to go back in numbers, at the same time that we greatly need to increase in the average of wealth. 'Il faut traffiquer de notre superflu.'

The New Chivalry then is also the new necessity. Happily it is already with us. The advanced – the more spiritual types of English manhood already to look to beauty first. In the past the beauty has been conditioned and confined to such beauty as could be found in some fair being *capable of increasing the population.* The condition italicized is now for the intelligent, removed. The New Chivalry therefore will not ask that very plain question of the Marriage Service. 'Will it lead to the procreation of children?' It will rest content with beauty – God's outward clue to the inward Paradise. No animal consideration of mere sex will be allowed to intrude on the higher fact. A beautiful girl will be desired before a plain lad, but a plain girl will not be considered in the presence of a handsome boy. Where boy and girl are of equal outward grace the spiritual ideal will prevail over the animal and the desire of influencing the higher mind, the boy's, will prevail over the old desire to add to the population. The higher form of influence will be chosen.

The gain in human happiness will be direct and immediate. It has been obvious in the past that the praiseworthy attempts of women to be beautiful have in the next generation been half abolished by the want of such attempt in their husbands. Thus the human animal in England got 'no forwarder' in physical beauty. But the New Chivalry inducing boys to be beautiful as well as girls, will remedy this. The whole species will move on, and a type of higher beauty will be evolved.

The gain in human intelligence will be direct, for love will impart with the eagerness of joy all its most treasured intellectual acquisitions, all its experiences of life. It will not fear to bare its errors to loving eyes and will not grudge even shame if so be it may save the beloved from the like. As in Sparta so once more, will the lover be the inbreather – eispnelos, the beloved 'this listener', – aites. A royal road to learning will be found. The gain in human physique will be direct. For the carelessness of fathers, the sexual impossibilities of mother and sisters, the more the indifference of brothers, the watchful and devoted discipline of the lover will be substituted. The boy will find exactly the words, the cautions, he requires, the incentives which best stimulate in the converse of the lover still young and strong enough to preach by act, and finding as in Sir Frederick Leighton's admirable canvas no greater glory than in guiding younger and well loved hands to the mark.

That comparisons are not popular has been affirmed by many authorities and in cases where evolution is working out its silent inevitable course they are also unnecessary. There are, however, two matters wherein the New Chivalry inspires us with a new hope. It is evident that in the Old Chivalry there was always a certain absence of freewill, in other words its essential element, a refusal to take by force and for ought than love, was at best imperfect. A married woman blessed with children is cajoled by nature itself, as it were, into tolerating the husband for the sake of the children even where but for the Baconian 'hostages to fortunes' no such tolerance would be possible. And the marriage contract adds for the same sake a proviso which is not of chivalry or even – except for the good of the community as expressed in increase of population – of common sense. 'Till death us do part' is the phrase. 'Till Love us do part' is the obvious logic of the situation. The New Chivalry imposes no irksome or fatuous ties. It is genuine or it is nothing. Where love upholds its banner the heathen may rage in vain; and it is

> So strong
> That should its own hands dig its grave
> The wide world's power and pity shall not save.

The chief drawback is that under the New Chivalry all the plots of the French dramatists would disappear. Lovers while loving would not care for the 'world outside' and when they ceased to love there would be neither incongruity or scandal in their going apart.

A gain to the world of a new nature, but all the more important in an age when poverty of purse, not of population, is the danger, exists in the decrease of idleness involved by the New ideal. No woman wants to work. Every girl of the least personal attractiveness nourishes the hope of being kept in idleness. Above a certain class the proviso 'by a husband' is added. But the new lovers will both work and will be the happier for both working. The newer and intenser love will see its way to avoid the separation of hours, of interests and of resources which is the inevitable destiny of ninety-nine married couples out of every hundred. The desire of the male to express itself in action, will be fully satisfied in each case, age will make no difference. The ideal partnership indeed will more frequently than not be accomplished, the elder having the greater power of physical endurance, the younger too having greater powers of physical endurance under due direction. Had it but this single recommendation, the new ideal would still be adding enormously to the wealth and happiness of the country.

This is at best a brief and superficial note on a vast subject. The stimulating experiences of ancient Hellas, the wisdom of Saadi and Omar Khayyam have not been drawn upon for a single analogy or argument; there are, however, two facts, one suggested by nature and one by religion, which in their direct and immediate bearing on the issues already raised, cannot possibly be overlooked.

The one is that of the unique aid to be rendered through unity of sex. This is Nature's witness to the New Chivalry. Be a man ever so devotedly attached to his wife there will always remain 'a great gulf fixed'. Were this gulf unbridgeable by humanity it were easy to bear it, but far from this being so it is a beaten highway trod by every other woman. The slatternly charwoman may tread it or the painted Lais[122] of the Haymarket, but the husband may not, the lover is shut out. Nature's most intimate and instructive bond of sympathy is denied to the old love; it is opened to the new.

Of companionship also there is much to be said. Here it is enough to ask how much do ordinary engaged couples, how much even do husband and wife see of each other? How much may not lovers see if man and youth, if youth and boy? The joys of palaestra,[123] of the river, of the hunt and of the moor, the evening tent-piching of campers out, and the exhilaration of the early morning swim, for one pleasure of life and physical delight in each other's presence, touch and voice which man and woman ordinarily share, it is not too much to say that the new chivalry has ten. Intimacy of constant companionship, of physical and personal knowledge is also a power of help and aid which cannot be put into words.

And the other fact which we have in mind as essential to what has been said is that of the highest Ideal of all. 'For man is still God's dearest minion' says Sylvester.[124] In the development of adolescent powers both of body and of soul the highest ideal is surely set. That the most beautiful is not always the most intellectual also is the fault of our negligence and misunderstanding in a past, when it was wholly by the intellectual that man made his way, and moral differences were not weighed against absolute cleverness. Canon Liddon[125] once said to a friend 'Well, the Devil is exceedingly clever, and beautiful people are sometimes quite stupid, but cleverness and beauty only come together when The Third, Goodness, is there also.'

The mind of adolescent manhood being the development stage of potentially greater powers, must needs be capable under stimulus and guidance, of sweeter and fuller flower than that of girlhood, sweet as is that flower, and while no woman wishes to be loved for her intellect, youth is proud to be helped to learn. Nor is handsome youth less disposed towards knowledge than youth which is not handsome.

The possiblity of having to fight life's intellectual and physical battles side by side and shoulder to shoulder is full of a new inspiration, an inspiration which the old ideal could not take to itself, which the Old Chivalry never knew. When Love enters, then Possibility will become Desire, and Like will be drawn to Like by each attempting to attain for the sake of greater worthiness, to that which in the other is the Best.

That the tenderness of the elder for the younger, of one who has endured for him that has yet to endure, of the strong for the weak, the developed for the developing, is retained in all fulness, while these other things are added, is perhaps that note which gives its highest value to the New Chivalry.

GREEK LOVE

William Cory, 'Desiderato', *Ionica*, 1858

Oh, lost and unforgotten friend,
    Whose presence change and chance deny;
    If angels turn your soft proud eye
To lines your cynic playmate penned,

Look on them, as you looked on me,
    When both were young; when, as we went
    Through crowds or forest ferns, you leant
On him who loved your staff to be;

And slouch your lazy length again
    On cushions fit for aching brow,
    (Yours always ache, you know) and now
As dainty languishing as then,

Give them but one fastidious look,
    And if you see a trace of him
    Who humoured you in every whim,
Seek for his heart within his book:

For though there be enough to mark
    The man's divergence from the boy,
    Yet shines my faith without alloy
For him who led me through that park;

And though a stranger throw aside,
Such grains of common sentiment;
Yet your haughty head be bent
To take the jetsom of the tide;

Because this brackish turbid sea
Throws toward thee things that pleased of yore,
And though it wash thy feet no more,
Its murmurs mean: 'I yearn for thee.'

Edward Cracroft Lefroy, 'A Palaestral[126] Study', *Echoes from Theocritus and Other Poems*, 1885

The curves of beauty are not softly wrought:
These quivering limbs by strong muscles held
In attitudes of wonder, and compelled
Through shapes more sinuous than a sculptor's thought,
Tell of dull matter splendidly distraught,
Whisper of mutinies divinely quelled, –
Weak indolence of flesh, that long rebelled,
The spirit's domination bravely taught.
And all man's loveliest works are cut with pain.
Beneath the perfect art we know the strain,
Intense, defined, how deep soe'er it lies.
From each high master-piece our souls refrain,
Not tired of gazing, but with stretched eyes
Made hot by radiant flames of sacrifice.

S.S. Saale, 'Sonnet', from *The Artist*, 1 September 1890

Upon the wall, of idling boys a row,
    The grimy barges not more dull than they
    When sudden in the midst of all their play
They strip and plunge into the stream below;
Changed by a miracle, they rise as though
    The youth of Greece burst on this latter day,
    As on their lithe young bodies many a ray
Of sunlight dallies with its blushing glow.

Flower of clear beauty, naked purity,
    With thy sweet presence olden days return,
    Like fragrant ashes from a classic urn,
Flashed into life anew once more we see
Narcissus[127] by the pool, or 'neath the tree

Young Daphnis,[128] and new pulses throb and burn.

John Addington Symonds, 'The Dantesque and Platonic Ideals of Love', *In the Key of Blue and Other Prose Essays*, 1893

Platonic love, in the true sense of that phrase, was the affection of a man for a man; and it grew out of antecedent customs which had obtained from very distant times in Hellas.[129] Homer excludes this emotion from his picture of society in the heroic age. The tale of Patroclus and Achilles[130] in the 'Iliad' does not suggest the interpretations put on it by later generations; and the legend of Ganymede[131] is related without a hint of personal desire. It has therefore been assumed that what is called Greek love was unknown at the time when the Homeric poems were composed. This argument, however, is not conclusive; for Homer, in his theology, suppressed the darker and cruder elements of Greek religion, which certainly survived from ancient savagery, and which prevailed long after the supposed age of those poems. An eclectic spirit of refinement presided over the redaction of the 'Iliad' and the 'Odyssey'; and the other omission I have mentioned may possibly be due to the same cause. The orator Æschines, in his critique of the Achilleian story, adopts this explanation. Unhappily for the science of comparative literature, we have lost the Cyclic poems.[132] But there is reason to believe that these contained direct allusions to the passion in question. Otherwise, Æschylus, the conservative, and Sophocles, the temperate, would hardly have written tragedies (the 'Myrmidons' and the 'Lovers of Achilles') which brought Greek love upon the Attic[133] stage. If the 'Iliad' had been his sole authority, Æschylus could not have made Achilles burst forth into that cry of 'unhusbanded grief' over the corpse of his dead comrade, which Lucian[134] and Athenaeus[135] have preserved for us.

However this may be, masculine love, as the Greeks called it, appeared at an early age in Hellas. We find it localised in several places, and consecrated by divers legends of the gods. Yet none of the later Greeks could give a distinct account of its origin or importation. There are critical grounds for supposing that the Dorians[136] developed this custom in their native mountains (the home of Achilles and the region where it still survives), and that they carried it upon

161

their migration to Peloponnesus. At any rate, in Crete and Sparta, it speedily became a social institution, regulated by definite laws and sanctioned by the State. In each country a youth who had no suitor lost in public estimation. The elder, in these unions of friends, received the name of 'inspirer' or 'lover', the younger that of 'hearer' or 'admired'. When the youth grew up and went to battle with his comrade, he assumed the title of bystander in the ranks. I have not space to dwell upon the minute laws and customs by which Dorian love was governed. Suffice it to say that in all of them we discern the intention of promoting a martial spirit in the population, securing a manly education for the young, and binding the male members of the nation together by bonds of mutual affection. In earlier times at least care was taken to secure the virtues of loyalty, self-respect, and permanence in these relations. In short, masculine love constituted the chivalry of primitive Hellas, the stimulating and exalting enthusiasm of her sons. It did not exclude marriage, nor had it the effect of lowering the position of women in society, since it is notorious that in those Dorian states where the love of comrades became an institution, women received more public honour and enjoyed fuller liberty and power over property that elsewhere.

The military and chivalrous nature of Greek love is proved by the myths and more or less historical legends which idealised its virtues. Herakles, the Dorian demigod, typified by his affection for young men and by his unselfish devotion to humanity what the Spartan and Cretan warriors demanded from this emotion. The friendships of Theseus and Peirithous,[137] of Orestes and Pylades,[138] of Damon and Pythias,[139] comrades in arms and faithful to each other to the death, embalmed the memory of lives ennobled by masculine affection. Nearly every city had some tale to tell of emancipation from tyranny, of prudent legislation, or of heroic achievements in war, inspired by the erotic enthusiasm. When Athens laboured under a grievous curse and pestilence, two lovers, Cratinus and Aristodemus, devoted their lives to the salvation of the city.[140] Two lovers, Harmodius and Aristogeiton, shook off the bondage of the Peisistratidæ.[141] Philolaus and Diocles gave laws to Thebes.[142] Another Diocles won everlasting glory in a fight at Megara.[143] Chariton and Melanippus resisted the tyranny of Phalaris at Agrigentum.[144] Cleomachus, inspired by passion, restored freedom to the town of Chalkis.[145] All these men were lovers of the Greek type. Tyrants, says an interlocutor in one of Plato's dialogues, tremble before lovers. Glorying in their emotion, the Greeks pronounced it to be the crowning virtue of free men, the source of gentle and heroic actions, the heirloom of Hellenic civilisation, in which barbarians and slaves had and could have no part or lot. The chivalry of which I am speaking powerfully influenced Greek history. All the Spartan kings and generals grew up under the institution of Dorian comradeship. Epameinondas[146] and Alexander were notable lovers; and the names of their comrades are recorded. When Greek liberty expired upon the Plain of Chæronea, the Sacred Band of Thebans, all of whom were lovers, fell dead to a man; and Philip wept as he beheld their corpses, crying aloud: 'Perish the man who thinks that these men either did or suffered what is shameful.'[147] It powerfully increased Greek art. Pindar[148] and Sophocles[149] were lovers; Pindar died in the arms of Theoxenos, whose praise he sang in the Skolion of which we have a characteristic fragment.[150] Pheidias carved the name of his beloved Pantarkes on the chryselephantine statue of the Olympian Zeus.[151] Æschylus, as we have seen, wrote one of his most popular tragedies upon the affection of Achilles for Patroclus. Solon, Demosthenes, Æschines, among statesmen and orators, made no secret of a feeling which they regarded as the highest joy in life and the source of exalted enthusiasm.

Greek love, as I have shown, was in its origin and essence masculine, military, chivalrous. However repugnant to modern taste may be the bare fact that this passion existed and flourished in the highest-gifted of all races, yet it was clearly neither an effeminate depravity nor a sensual vice. Still such an emotion, being abnormal, could not prevail and dominate the customs of a whole nation without grave drawbacks....Immorality was, not occasionally, but continually mixed up with Greek love, was the soil in which it flourished. Therefore in those States especially, like Athens, where the love in question had not been moralised by prescribed laws, did it tend to degenerate. And it was just here, at Athens, that it received the metaphysical idealisation which justifies us in comparing it to the Italian form of mediæval chivalry. Socrates, says Maximus Tyrius, pitying the state of young men, and wishing to raise their affections from the mire into which they were declining, opened a way for the salvation of their souls through the very love they then abused.[152] Whether Socrates was really actuated by these motives, cannot be affirmed with certainty. At any rate, he handled masculine love with robust originality, and prepared the path for Plato's philosophical conception of passion as an inspiration leading men to the divine idea.

I have observed that in Dorian chivalry the lover was called 'inspirer', and the beloved 'hearer'. It was the man's duty to instruct the lad in manners, feats of arms, trials of strength and music. This relation of the elder to the younger is still assumed to exist by Plato. But he modifies it in a way peculiar to himself....Socrates, as interpreted in the Platonic dialogues entitled 'Phædrus' and 'Symposium', sought to direct and elevate a moral force, an enthusiasm, an exaltation of the emotions, which already existed as the highest form of feeling in the Greek race. In the earlier of those dialogues he describes the love of man for youth as a madness, or divine frenzy, not different in quality from that which inspires prophets and poets. The soul he compares to a charioteer guiding a pair of winged horses, the one of noble, the other of ignoble breed.[153] Under this metaphor is veiled the psychological distinctions of reason, generous impulse, and carnal appetite.[154] Composed of these triple elements, the soul has shared in former lives the company of gods, and has gazed on beauty, wisdom, and goodness, the three most eminent manifestations of the divine, in their pure essence. But, sooner or later, during the course of her celestial wanderings, the soul is dragged to earth by the baseness of the carnal steed. She enters a form of flesh, and loses the pinions which enabled her to soar. Yet even in her mundane life (that obscure and confused state of existence which Plato elsewhere compares to a dark cave visited only by shadows of reality)[155] she may be reminded of the heavenly place from which she fell, and of the glorious visions of divinity she there enjoyed. No mortal senses, indeed, could bear the sight of truth or goodness or beauty in their undimmed splendour. Yet earthly things in which truth, goodness, and beauty are incarnate, touch the soul to adoration, stimulate the growth of her wings, and set her on the upward path whereby she will revert to God. The lover has this opportunity when he beholds the person who awakes his passion; for the human body is of all earthly things in which real beauty shines most clearly. When Plato proceeds to say that 'philosophy in combination with affection for young men'[156] is the surest method for attaining to the higher spiritual life, he takes for granted that reason, recognizing the divine essence of beauty, encouraging the generous impulses of the heart, curbing the carnal appetite, converts the mania of love into an instrument of edification. Passionate friends, bound together in the chains of close yet temperament comradeship, seeking always to advance in wisdom, self-restraint, and intellectual illumination, prepare themselves for the celestial journey. 'When the end comes, they are light and ready to fly away, having conquered in one of the three heavenly or truly Olympian victories. Nor can human discipline or divine inspiration confer any greater blessing on man than this.'[157] Moreover, even should they decline toward sensuality and taste those pleasures on which the vulgar set great store, they, too, will pass from life, 'unwinged indeed, but eager to soar, and this obtain no mean reward of love and madness'.

The doctrine of the 'Symposium' is not different, except that here Socrates, professing to report the teaching of a wise woman Diotima, assumes a loftier tone, and attempts a sublimer flight. Love, he says, is the child of Poverty and

Contrivance, deriving something from both his father and his mother. He lacks all things, and has the wit to gain all things. Love too, when touched by beauty, desires to procreate; and if the mortal lover be one whose body alone is creative, he betakes himself to woman and begets children; but if the soul be the chief creative principle in the lover's nature, then he turns to young men of 'fair and noble and well-nurtured spirit', and in them begets the immortal progeny of high thoughts and generous emotions.[158] The same divine frenzy of love, which forms the subject of the 'Phædrus', is here again treated as the motive force which starts the soul upon her journey towards the regions of essential truth. Attracted by what is beautiful, the lover first dedicates himself to one youth in whom beauty is apparent; next he is led to perceive that beauty in all fair forms is a single quality; he then passes to the conviction that intellectual is superior to physical beauty; and so by degrees he attains the vision of a single science, which is the science of beauty everywhere, or the worship of the divine under one of its three main attributes.

The lesson which both of these Socratic dialogues seem intended to inculcate, may be summed up thus. Love, like poetry and prophecy, is a divine gift, which diverts men from the common current of their earthly lives; and in the right use of the gift lies the secret of all human excellence. The passion which grovels in the filth of sensual grossness may be transformed into a glorious enthusiasm, a winged splendour, capable of rising to the contemplation of eternal verities and reuniting the soul of man to God. How strange will it be, when once those heights of intellectual intuition have been scaled, to look down again on earth and view the human being in whom the spirit first recognized the essence of beauty.

John Addington Symonds, from *A Problem in Greek Ethics*, private publication, 1883

VI

We find two separate forms of masculine passion clearly marked in early Hellas – a noble and a base, a spiritual and a sensual. To the distinction between them the Greek conscience was acutely sensitive; and this distinction, in theory at least, subsisted throughout their history. They worshipped Eros, as they worshipped Aphrodite, under the twofold titles of Ouranios (celestial) and Pandemos (vulgar, or *volvivaga*); and, while they regarded the one love with the highest approval, as the source of courage and greatness of soul, they never publicly approved the other. It is true, as will appear in the sequel of this essay, that boy-love in its grossest form was tolerated in historic Hellas with an indulgence which it never found in any Christian country, while heroic comradeship remained an ideal hard to realise, and scarcely possible beyond the limits of the strictest Dorian sect. Yet the language of philosophers, historians, poets and orators is unmistakable. All testify alike to the discrimination between vulgar and heroic love in the Greek mind. I purpose to devote a separate section of this inquiry to the investigation of these ethical distinctions. For the present, a quotation from one of the most eloquent of the later rhetoricians will sufficiently set forth the contrast, which the Greek race never wholly forgot:[#68] –

'The one love is mad for pleasure; the other loves beauty. The one is an involuntary sickness: the other is a sought enthusiasm. The one tends to the good of the beloved; the other to the ruin of both. The one is virtuous; the other incontinent in all its acts. The one has its end in friendship; the other in hate. The one is freely given; the other is bought and sold. The one brings praise; the other blame. The one is Greek; the other is barbarous. The one is virile; the other effeminate. The one is firm and constant; the other light and variable. The man who loves the one love is a friend of God, a friend of the law, fulfilled of modesty, and free of speech. He dares to court his friend in daylight, and rejoices in his love. He wrestles with him in the playground and runs with him in the race, goes afield with him to the hunt, and in battle fights for glory at his side. In his misfortune he suffers, and at his death he dies with him. He needs no gloom of night, no desert place, for this society. The other lover is a foe to heaven, for he is out of tune and criminal; a foe to law, for he transgresses law. Cowardly, despairing, shameless, haunting the dusk, lurking in desert places and secret dens, he would fain be never seen consorting with his friend, but shuns the light of day, and follows after night and darkness, which the shepherd hates, but the thief loves.'

And again, in the same dissertation, Maximus Tyrius speaks to like purpose, clothing his precepts in imagery: –

'You see a fair body in bloom and full of promise of fruit. Spoil not, defile not, touch not the blossom. Praise it, as some wayfarer may praise a plant – even so by Phoebus' altar have I seen a young palm shooting toward the sun. Refrain from Zeus' and Phoebus' tree; wait for the fruit-season, and thou shalt love more righteously.'[159]

With the baser form of paiderastia I shall have very little to do in this essay. Vice of this kind does not vary to any great extent, whether we observe it in Athens or in Rome, in Florence of the sixteenth or in Paris of the nineteenth century;[#69] nor in Hellas was it more noticeable than elsewhere, except for its comparative publicity. The nobler type of masculine love developed by the Greeks is, on the contrary, almost unique[#70] in the history of the human race. It is that which more than anything else distinguishes the Greeks from the barbarians of their own time, from the Romans, and modern men in all that appertains to the emotions. The immediate subject of the ensuing inquiry will, therefore, be that mixed form of paiderastia upon which the Greeks prided themselves, which had for its heroic ideal the friendship of Achilles and Patroclus, but which in historic times exhibited a sensuality unknown to Homer. In treating of this unique product of their civilisation I shall use the terms *Greek Love*, understanding thereby a passionate and enthusiastic attachment subsisting between man and youth, recognised by society and protected by opinion, which, though it was not free from sensuality, did not degenerate into mere licentiousness.

XIII

The Attic gymnasia and schools were regulated by strict laws. We have already seen that adults were not supposed to enter the palaestra; and the penalty for the infringement of the rule by the gymnasiarch was death. In the same way schools had to be shut at sunset and not opened again before daybreak; nor was a grown-up man allowed to frequent them. The public chorus-teachers of boys were obliged to be above the age of forty.[#71] Slaves who presumed to make advances to a free boy were subject to the severest penalties; in like manner they were prohibited from gymnastic exercises. Æschines, from whom we learn these facts, draws the correct conclusion that gymnastics and Greek Love were intended to be the special privilege of freemen. Still, in spite of all restrictions, the palaestra was the centre of Athenian profligacy, the place in which not only honourable attachments were formed, but disgraceful bargains were concluded;[#72] and it is not improbable that men like Taureas and Miccus, who opened such places of amusement as a private speculation, may have played the part of go-betweens and panders. Their walls and the plane-trees which grew along their open courts were inscribed by lovers with the names of the boys who had attracted them. To scrawl up, 'Fair is Dinomeneus, fair is the boy,' was a common custom, as we learn from Aristophanes and from this anonymous epigram in the *Anthology*:[73]

> 'I said and once again I said, "fair, fair"; but still will I go on repeating how fascinating with his eyes is Dositheus. Not upon an oak, nor on a pine-tree, nor yet upon a wall, will I inscribe this word; but love is smouldering in my heart of hearts.'

Another attention of the same kind from a lover to a boy was to have a vase or drinking-cup of baked clay made, with a portrait of the youth depicted on its surface, attended by winged genii of health and love. The word 'Fair' was inscribed beneath, and symbols of games were added – a hoop or a fighting-cock.[74] Nor must I here omit the custom which induced lovers of a literary turn to praise their friends in prose or verse. Hippothales, in the *Lysis* of Plato, is ridiculed by his friends for recording the great deeds of the boy's ancestors, and deafening his ears with odes and sonnets. A diatribe on love, written by Lysias with a view to winning Phaedrus, forms the starting-point of the dialogue between that youth and Socrates.[75] We have, besides, a curious panegyrical oration (called *Eroticos Logos*), falsely ascribed to Demosthenes, in honour of a youth, Epicrates, from which some information may be gathered concerning the topics usually developed in these compositions.

Presents were of course a common way of trying to win favour. It was reckoned shameful for boys to take money from their lovers, but fashion permitted them to accept gifts of quails and fighting cocks, pheasants, horses, dogs, and clothes.[76] There existed, therefore, at Athens frequent temptations for boys of wanton disposition, or for those who needed money to indulge expensive tastes. The speech of Æschines, from which I have already frequently quoted, affords a lively picture of the Greek rake's progress, in which Timarchus is described as having sold his person in order to gratify his gluttony and lust and love of gaming. The whole of this passage,[77] it may be observed in passing, reads like a description of Florentine manners in a sermon of Savonarola.

The shops, the barbers, surgeons, perfumers, and flower-sellers had an evil notoriety, and lads who frequented these resorts rendered themselves liable to suspicion. Thus Æschines accuses Timarchus of having exposed himself for hire in a surgeon's shop at the Peiraeus; while one of Straton's most beautiful epigrams[78] describes an assignation which he made with a boy who had attracted his attention in a garland-weaver's stall. In a fragment from the Pyraunos of Alexis a young man declares that he found thirty professors of the 'voluptuous life of pleasure', in the Cerameicus during a search of three days; while Cratinus and Theopompus might be quoted to prove the ill fame of the monument to Cimon and the hill of Lycabettus.[79]

The last step in the downward descent was when a youth abandoned the roof of his parents or guardians and accepted the hospitality of a lover.[80] If he did this, he was lost.

In connection with this portion of the subject it may be well to state that the Athenian law recognized contracts made between a man and boy, even if the latter were of free birth, whereby the one agreed to render up his person for a certain period and purpose, and the other to pay a fixed sum of money.[81] The phrase 'a boy who has been a prostitute', occurs quite naturally in Aristophanes;[82] nor was it thought disreputable for men to engage in these *liaisons*. Disgrace only attached to the free youth who gained a living by prostitution; and he was liable, as we shall see, at law to loss of civil rights.

Public brothels for males were kept in Athens, from which the state derived a portion of its revenues. It was in one these bad places that Socrates first saw Phaedo.[83] This unfortunate youth was a native of Elis. Taken prisoner in war, he was sold in the public market to a slave-dealer, who then acquired the right by Attic law to prostitute his person and engross his earnings for his own pocket. A friend of Socrates, perhaps Cebes, bought him from his master, and he became one of the chief members of the Socratic circle. His name is given to the Platonic dialogue on immortality, and he lived to found what is called the Eleo-Socratic School. No reader of Plato forgets how the sage, on the eve of his death, stroked the beautiful long hair of Phaedo,[84] and prophesied that he would soon have to cut it short in mourning for his teacher.

Agathocles, the tyrant of Syracuse, is said to have spent his youth in brothels of this sort – by inclination, however, if the reports of his biographers are not calumnious.

From what has been collected on this topic, it will be understood that boys in Athens not infrequently caused quarrels and street-brawls, and that cases for recovery of damages or breach of contract were brought before the Attic law-courts. The Peiraeus was especially noted for such scenes of violence. The oration of Lysias against Simon is a notable example of the pleadings in a cause of this description.[85] Simon the defendant and Lysias the plaintiff (or some one for whom Lysias had composed the speech) were both of them attached to Theodotus, a boy from Plataea. Theodotus was living with the plaintiff; but the defendant asserted that the boy had signed an agreement to consort with him for the consideration of three hundred drachmae, and, relying on this contract, he had attempted more than once to carry off the boy by force. Violent altercations, stone-throwings, house-breakings, and encounters of various kinds having ensued, the plaintiff brought an action for assault and battery against Simon. A modern reader is struck with the fact that he is not at all ashamed of his own relation toward Theodotus. It may be noted that the details of this action throw light upon the historic brawl at Corinth in which a boy was killed, and which led to the foundation of Syracuse by Archias the Bacchiad.[86]

XIX

Sexual inversion among Greek women offers more difficulties than we met with in the study of paiderastia. This is due, not to the absence of the phenomenon, but to the fact that feminine homosexual passions were never worked into the social system, never became educational and military agents. The Greeks accepted the fact that certain females are congenitally indifferent to the male sex, and appetitive of their own sex. This appears from the myth of Aristophanes in Plato's *Symposium*, which expresses in comic form their theory of sexual differentiation. There were originally human beings of three sexes: men, the offspring of the sun; women, the offspring of the earth; hermaphrodites, the offspring of the moon. They were round with two faces, four hands, four feet, and two sets of reproductive organs apiece. In the case of the third (hermaphroditic or lunar) sex, one set of reproductive organs was male, the other female. Zeus, on account of the insolence and vigour of these primitive human creatures, sliced them into halves. Since that time the halves of each sort have always striven to unite with their corresponding halves, and have found some satisfaction in carnal congress – males with males, females with females, and (in the case of the lunar or hermaphroditic creatures) males and females with one another. Philosophically, then, the homosexual passion of female for female, and of male for male, was placed upon exactly the same footing as the heterosexual passion of each sex for its opposite. Greek logic admitted the homosexual female to equal rights with the homosexual male, and both to the same natural freedom as heterosexual individuals of either species.

Although this was the position assumed by philosophers, Lesbian passion, as the Greeks called it, never obtained the same social sanction as boy-love. It is significant that Greek mythology offers no legends of the goddesses parallel to those which consecrated paiderastia among the male deities. Again, we have no recorded example, so far as I can remember, of noble friendship between women rising into political and historical prominence. There are no female analogies to Harmodius and Aristogeiton, Cratinus and Aristodemus. It is true that Sappho and the Lesbian poetess gave this female passion an eminent place in Greek literature. But the Æolian women did not find a glorious tradition corresponding to that of the Dorian men. If homosexual love between females assumed the form of an institution at one moment in Æolia, this failed to strike roots deep into the subsoil of the nation. Later Greeks, while tolerating, regarded it rather as an eccentricity of nature, or a vice, than as an honourable and socially useful emotion. The condition of women in ancient Hellas sufficiently accounts for the result. There was no opportunity in the harem or the zenana of raising homosexual passion to the same moral and spiritual efficiency as it obtained in the camp, the palaestra, and the schools of the philosophers. Consequently, while the Greeks utilised and ennobled boy-love, they left Lesbian love to follow the same course of degeneracy as it pursues in modern times.

In order to see how similar the type of Lesbian love in ancient Greece was to the form which it assumed in modern Europe, we have only to compare Lucian's Dialogues with Parisian tales by Catulle Mendes or Guy de Maupassant. The woman who seduces the girl she loves, is, in the girl's phrase, 'overmasculine', 'androgynous'. The Megilla of Lucian insists upon being called Megillos. The girl is a weaker vessel, pliant, submissive to the virago's sexual energy, selected from the class of meretricious *ingénues*.

There is an important passage in the *Amores* of Lucian[160] which proves that the Greeks felt an abhorrence of sexual inversion among women similar to that which moderns feel for its manifestation among men. Charicles, who supports the cause of normal heterosexual passion, argues after this wise:

'If you concede homosexual love to males, you must in justice grant the same to females; you will have to sanction carnal intercourse between them; monstrous instruments of lust will have to be permitted, in order that their sexual congress may be carried out; that obscene vocable, tribad, which so rarely offends our ears – I blush to utter it – will become rampant, and Philaenis will spread androgynous orgies throughout our harems.'

What these monstrous instruments of lust were may be gathered from the sixth mime of Herodas, where one of them is described in detail.[161] Philaenis may, perhaps, be the poetess of an obscene book on sexual refinements, to whom Athanaeus alludes (*Deipnosophistae*, viii, 335). It is also possible that Philaenis had become the common designation of a Lesbian lover, a tribad. In the later periods of Greek literature, as I have elsewhere shown, certain fixed masks of Attic comedy (corresponding to the masks of the Italian *Commedia dell' Arte*) created types of character under conventional names – so that, for example, Cerdo became a cobbler, Myrtalë a common whore, and possibly Philaenis a Lesbian invert.

The upshot of this parenthetical investigation is to demonstrate that, while the love of males for males in Greece obtained moralisation, and reached the high position of a recognised social function, the love of female for female remained undeveloped and unhonoured, on the same level as both forms of homosexual passion in the modern European world are.

XX

Greece merged in Rome; but, though the Romans aped the arts and manners of the Greeks, they never truly caught the Hellenic spirit. Even Virgil only trod the court of the Gentiles of Greek culture. It was not, therefore, possible that any social custom so peculiar as paiderastia should flourish on Latin soil. Instead of Cleomenes and Epameinondas, we find at Rome Nero the bride of Sporus and Commodus the public prostitute. Alcibiades is replaced by the Mark Antony of Cicero's *Philippic*.[162] Corydon, with artificial notes, takes up the song of Ageanax. The melodies of Meleager are drowned in the harsh discords of Martial. Instead of love, lust was the deity of the boy-lover on the shores of Tiber.

In the first century of the Roman Empire Christianity began its work of reformation. When we estimate the effect of Christanity, we must bear in mind that the early Christians found Paganism disorganised and humanity rushing to a precipice of ruin. Their first efforts were directed toward checking the sensuality of Corinth, Athens, Rome, the capitals of Syria and Egypt. Christian asceticism, in the corruption of the Pagan systems, led logically to the cloister and the hermitage. The component elements of society had been disintegrated by the Greeks in their decadence, and by the Romans in their insolence of material prosperity. To the impassioned followers of Christ nothing was left but separation from nature, which had become incurable in its monstrosity of vices. But the convent was a virtual abandonment of social problems.

From this policy of despair, this helplessness to cope with evil and this hopelessness of good on earth, emerged a new and nobler synthesis, the merit of which belongs in no small measure to the Teutonic converts to the Christian faith. The Middle Ages proclaimed through chivalry the truth, then for the first time fully apprehended, that woman is the mediating and ennobling element in human life. Not in escape from the cloister, not in the self-abandonment to vice, but in the fellow-service of free men and women must be found the solution of social problems. The mythology of Mary gave religious sanction to the chivalrous enthusiasm; and a cult of woman sprang into being to which, although it was romantic and visionary, we owe the spiritual basis of our domestic and civil life. The *modus vivendi* of the modern world was found.

John Addington Symonds, 'The legend of Apollo', from *The Biography of John Addington Symonds*, 1895

Symonds's *Biography* was 'compiled from his papers and correspondence' by his friend and literary executor, Horatio F. Brown, with the approval of Symonds's widow. The existence of the biography is only odd in so far as Symonds had completed his autobiography some time before his death, a text which was not published until 1984,[163] and the biography is composed in large part of passages lifted verbatim from the manuscript of the memoirs. Brown bequeathed the manuscript of the memoirs to the London Library on his death in 1926, with instructions that it must not be published for fifty years. In the Preface to the first edition of the *Biography*, Brown celebrates the involvement of Symonds's family in revising his book, saying 'I can never sufficiently thank them for the patience and pains with which they have assisted me, in a task which I might otherwise have found to be even more difficult than it has proved', a suitably ambiguous acknowledgement of the pressures under which the text was created.

Walking to and fro between Clifton Hill and Wetherell Place, I used to tell myself long classic stories, and to improvise nonsense verses on interminable themes. The vehicle I used was chiefly blank verse or trochaics. I delighted my sense of rhythm with the current of murmured sound. The subject I chose for these peripatetic rhapsodies was the episode of young Apollo, in his sojourn among mortals, as the hind of King Admetus. What befell him there, I expanded into nebulous epics of suffering and love, and sorrow-dimmed deity involved with human sympathies. I declaimed the verse *sotto voce* as I walked. But now I can recall no incidents in the long poem, which, like a river, flowed daily, and might for ever have flowed on. The kernel of my inspiration was that radiant figure of the young Apollo, doomed to pass his time with shepherds, serving them, and loving them. A luminous haze of yearning emotion surrounded the god. His divine beauty penetrated my soul and marrow. I stretched out my arms to him in worship. It was I alone who knew him to be Olympian, and I loved him because he was a hind who went about the stables milking cows. I was, in fact, reading myself into this fable of Apollo, and quite unconsciously, as I perceive now, my day-dreams assumed an objective and idealised form. Indeed, this preoccupation with the legend of the discovered Phoebus casts vivid light upon my dumbly growing nature.

It is singular that a boy should have selected any legend so dim and subtle for treatment in the way I have described. But, what is far more curious, it seems, that I was led by an unerring instinct to choose a myth foreshadowing my peculiar temperament and distant future. I have lived to realise that obscure vision of my boyhood. Man loves man, and Nature; the pulse of human life, the contact with the genial earth are the real things. Art must ever be but a shadow for truly puissant individualities. In this way I have grown to think and feel. And just for this reason, my boyish preoccupation with the legend of Apollo in the stables of Admetus has psychological significance. It shows how early and instinctively I apprehended the truth, by the light of which I still live, that a disguised god, communing with mortals, loving mortals and beloved by them, is more beautiful, more desirable, more enviable, than the same god uplifted on the snow-wreaths of Olympus, or the twin peaks of muse-haunted Parnassus.

Rightly or wrongly, the principles involved in that boyish vision of Phœbus, the divine spirit serving and loving in plain ways of pastoral toil, have ended by fashioning my course. It has become my object to assimilate culture to the simplest things in man's life, and to assume from human sympathy of the crudest kind of fuel and fire for the vivifying of ideas. By means of this philosophy I have been enabled to revive from mortal sickness, and what is perhaps more, to apprehend the religious doctrine of democracy, the equality and homogeneity of human beings, the divinity enclosed in all. It was not, therefore, by accident, I think, that the prolonged daydreams of Apollo in exile haunted me during my somnambulistic boyhood. Temperaments of my stamp come to themselves by broodings upon fancies which prefigure the destiny in store for them, and are in fact the symbols of their soul.

Edward Cracroft Lefroy, 'Hylas',[164] from *Echoes from Theocritus and Other Poems*, 1885

What pool is this by galingale[165] surrounded,
With parsley and tall iris overgrown?
It is the pool whose wayward nymphs confounded
The quest of Heracles to glut their own
Desire of love. Its depths hath no man sounded
Save the young Mysian argonaut alone,
When round his drooping neck he felt, astounded,
The cruel grasp that sank him like a stone.
Through all the land the Hero wandered, crying
'Hylas!' and 'Hylas!' till the close of day,
And thrice there came a feeble voice replying
From watery caverns where the prisoner lay;
Yet to his ear it seemed but as the sighing
Of zephyrs[166] through the forest far away.

Roden Noel, 'Ganymede',[167] from *Beatrice and Other Poems*, 1868

Azure the heaven with rare a feathery cloud;
Azure the sea, far-scintillating light,
Soft rich like velvet yielding to the eye;
Horizons haunted with some dream-like sails;
A temple hypaethral[168] open to sweet air
Nigh on the height, columned with solid flame,
Of flutings and acanthus-work[169] instinct
With lithe green lizards and the shadows sharp
Slant barring golden floor and inner wall.

A locust-tree condensing all the light
On glossy leaves, and flaky spilling some
Sparkling among cool umbrage underneath;
There magically sobered mellow soft

At unaware beholding gently laid
A youth barelimbed the loveliest in the world,
Gloatingly falling on his lily side,
Smoothing one rounded arm and dainty hand
Whereon his head conscious and conquering
All chestnut-curled rests listless and superb;
Near him and leaning on the chequered bole
Sits his companion gazing on him fond,
A goat-herd whose rough hand on bulky knee
Holds a rude hollow reeden pipe of Pan,
Tanned clad with goatskin rudely-moulded huge;
While yonder, browsing in the rosemary
And cytisus, you hear a bearded goat,
Hear a fly humming with a droning bee
In yon wild thyme and in the myrtles low
That breathe in every feebly-blowing air;
Whose foamy bloom fair Ganymede anon
Plucks with a royal motion and an aim
Toward his comrade's tolerant fond face.
Far off cicada shrills among the pine,
And one may hear low tinkling where a stream
Yonder in planes and willows, from the beam
Of day coy hiding, runs with many a pool
Where the twain bathe how often in the cool!

    And so they know not of the gradual cloud
That stains the zenith with a little stain,
Then grows expansive, nearing one would say
The happy earth – until at last a noise
As of a rushing wind invades the ear,
Gathering volume, and the shepherd sees,
Amazed forth-peering, dusking closing all
Startled and tremulous rock-roses nigh,
Portentous shadow; and before he may
Rise to explore the open, like a bolt
From heaven a prodigy descends at hand,
Absorbing daylight; some tremendous bird,
An eagle, yet in plumage as in form
And stature far transcending any bird

Imperial inhabiting lone clefts
And piny crags of the Idaean range.

But lo! the supernatural dred thing,
Creating wind from cavernous vast vans,
Now slanting swoops toward them, hovering
Over the fair boy smitten dumb with awe.
A moment more, and how no mortal knows,
The bird hath seized him, if it be a bird,
And he though wildered hardly seems afraid,
So lightly lovingly those eagle talons
Lock the soft yielding flesh of either flank,
His back so tender, thigh and shoulder pillowed
How warmly whitely in the tawny down
Of that imperial eagle amorous!
Whose beaked head with eyes of burning flame
Nestles along the tremulous sweet heave
Of his fair bosom budding with a blush,
So that one arm droops pensile all aglow
Over the neck immense, and hangs a hand
Frail like a shell, pink like an apple bloom;
While shadowy wings expansive waving wind
Jealously hide some beauty from the sun.

Poor hind! he fancied as the pinions clanged
In their ascent, he looking open-mouthed
Distraught yet passive, that the boy's blue eye
Sought him in soaring; his own gaze be sure
Wearied not famished feeding upon all
The youth's dear charms for ever vanishing
From his poor longing, hungered for in heaven –
Took his last fill of delicate flushed face,
And swelling leg and rose-depending foot,
Slim ankle, dimpling body rich and full.
Behold! he fades receding evermore
From straining vision misting dim with tears,
Gleaming aloft swanwhite into the blue
Relieved upon the dusky ravisher,
Deeper and deeper glutting amorous light,
That cruel swallows him for evermore.

Michael Field, *Long Ago* XXVII, 1889

Mnasidica in form and gait
Eclipses her ill-favoured mate
   Gyrinna; when I call,
I tremble lest the girl appear
Whose very shadow on the wall
Repulses me, and when I hear
Her rude, slow step I shake with fear.

Her gesture has no rhythmic law;
She knows not how her dress to draw
   About her ankles thin;
And let the luckless child take care
Firmly her chiton-brooch[170] to pin,
For, oh, she must not ever dare
To leave her flabby shoulder bare!

But when Mnasidica doth raise
Her arm to feed the lamp I gaze
   Glad at the lovely curve;
And when her pitcher at the spring
She fills, I watch her tresses swerve
And drip, then pause to see her wring
Her hair, and back the bright drops fling.

And now she leaves my maiden train!
Those whom I love most give me pain;
   Why should I love her so?
Gyrinna hath a gentle face,
And a harmonious soul, I know,
Not very long can lack the trace,
O Aphrodite, of thy grace.

Oscar Wilde, 'The Disciple', from *Poems in Prose*, 1905

When Narcissus[171] died the pool of his pleasure changed from a cup of sweet waters into a cup of salt tears, and the Oreads[172] came weeping through the woodland that they might sing to the pool and give it comfort.

And when they saw that the pool had changed from a cup of sweet waters into a cup of salt tears, they loosened the green tresses of their hair and cried to the pool and said, 'We do not wonder that you should mourn in this manner for Narcissus, so beautiful was he.'

'But was Narcissus beautiful?' said the pool.

'Who should know that better than you?' answered the Oreads. 'Us did he ever pass by, but you he sought for, and would lie on your banks and look down at you, and in the mirror of your waters he would mirror his own beauty.'

And the pool answered, 'But I loved Narcissus because, as he lay on my banks and looked down at me, in the mirror of his eyes I saw ever my own beauty mirrored.'

Edmund Gosse, 'Greece and England', n.d.[173]

Would this sunshine be completer,
Or these violets smell sweeter,
Or the birds sing more in metre,
   If it all were years ago,
   When the melted mountain-snow
   Heard in Enna[174] all the woe
Of the poor forlorn Demeter?[175]

Would a stronger life pulse o'er us
If a panther-chariot bore us,
If we saw enthroned before us,
   Ride the leopard-footed god,
   With a fir-cone tip the rod,
   Whirl the thyrsus round, and nod
To a drunken Maenad-chorus?[176]

Bloomed there richer, redder roses
Where the Lesbian earth encloses
All of Sappho? where reposes
   Meleager,[177] laid to sleep
   By the olive-girdled deep?

Where the Syrian maidens weep,
Bringing serpolet[178] in posies?

Ah! it may be! Greece had leisure
For a world of faded pleasure;
We must tread a tamer measure,
    To a milder, homelier lyre;
    We must tend a paler fire,
    Lay less perfume on the pyre,
Be content with poorer treasure!

Were the brown-limbed lovers bolder?
Venus younger, Cupid older?
Down the wood-nymph's warm white shoulder
    Trailed a purpler, madder vine?
    Were the poets more divine?
    Brew we no such golden wine
Here, where summer suns are colder?

Yet for us too life has flowers,
Time a glass of joyous hours,
Interchange of sun and showers,
    And a wealth of leafy glades,
    Meant for loving men and maids,
    Full of warm green lights and shades,
Trellis-work of wild-wood bowers.

So while English suns are keeping
Count of sowing-time and reaping,
We've no need to waste our weeping,
    Though the glad Greeks lounged at ease
    Underneath their olive-trees,
    And the Sophoclean bees
Swarmed on lips of poets sleeping![179]

A. C. Swinburne, 'Sapphics', from *Poems and Ballads I*, 1866

All the night sleep came not upon my eyelids,

Shed not dew, nor shook nor unclosed a feather,
Yet with lips shut close and with eyes of iron
   Stood and beheld me.

Then to me so lying awake a vision
Came without sleep over the seas and touched me,
Softly touched mine eyelids and lips; and I too,
   Full of the vision,

Saw the white implacable Aphrodite,
Saw the hair unbound and the feet unsandalled
Shine as fire of sunset on western waters;
   Saw the reluctant

Feet, the straining plumes of the doves that drew her,
Looking always, looking with necks reverted,
Back to Lesbos, back to the hills whereunder
   Shone Mitylene;[180]

Heard the flying feet of the Loves behind her
Make a sudden thunder upon the waters,
As the thunder flung from the strong unclosing
   Wings of a great wind.

So the goddess fled from her place, with awful
Sound of feet and thunder of wings around her;
While behind a clamour of singing women
   Severed the twilight.

Ah the singing, ah the delight, the passion!
All the Loves wept, listening; sick with anguish,
Stood the crowned nine Muses about Apollo;
   Fear was upon them,

While the tenth sang wonderful things they knew not.
Ah the tenth, the Lesbian! the nine were silent,
None endured the sound of her song for weeping;
   Laurel by laurel,

Faded all their crowns; but about her forehead,
Round her woven tresses and ashen temples
White as dead snow, paler than grass in summer,
   Ravaged with kisses,

Shone a light of fire as a crown for ever.
Yea, almost the implacable Aphrodite
Paused, and almost wept; such a song was that song.
    Yea, by her name too

Called her, saying, 'Turn to me, O my Sappho';
Yet she turned her face from the Loves, she saw not
Tears for laughter darken immortal eyelids,
    Heard not about her

Fearful fitful wings of the doves departing,
Saw not how the bosom of Aphrodite
Shook with weeping, saw not her shaken raiment,
    Saw not her hands wrung;

Saw the Lesbians kissing across their smitten
Lutes with lips more sweet than the sound of lute-strings,
Mouth to moth and hand upon hand, her chosen,
    Fairer than all men;

Only saw the beautiful lips and fingers,
Full of songs and kisses and little whispers,
Full of music; only beheld among them
    Soar, as a bird soars

Newly fledged, her visible song, a marvel,
Made of perfect sound and exceeding passion,
Sweetly shapen, terrible, full of thunders,
    Clothed with the wind's wings.

Then rejoiced she, laughing with love, and scattered
Roses, awful roses of holy blossom;
Then the Loves thronged sadly with hidden faces
    Round Aphrodite,

Then the Muses, stricken at heart, were silent;
Yea, the gods waxed pale; such a song was that song.
All reluctant, all with a fresh repulsion,
    Fled from before her.

All withdrew long since, and the land was barren,
Full of fruitless women and music only.
Now perchance, when winds are assuaged at sunset,

Lulled at the dewfall,

By the grey sea-side, unassuaged, unheard of,
Unbeloved, unseen in the ebb of twilight,
Ghosts of outcast women return lamenting,
  Purged not in Lethe,[181]

Clothed about with flame and with tears, and singing
Songs that move the heart of the shaken heaven,
Songs that break the heart of the earth with pity,
  Hearing, to hear them.

GAVESTON AND MR W. H.

Walter Pater, 'Conclusion',[87]
The Renaissance, 1888

To regard all things and principles of things as inconstant modes of fashions has more and more become the tendency of modern thought. Let us begin with that which is without – our physical life. Fix upon it in one of its more exquisite intervals, the moment, for instance, of delicious recoil from the flood of water in summer heat. What is the whole physical life in that moment but a combination of natural elements to which science gives their names? But those elements, phosphorus and lime and delicate fibres, are present not in the human body alone: we detect them in places most remote from it. Our physical life is a perpetual motion of them – the passage of the blood, the waste and repairing of the lenses of the eye, the modification of the tissues of the brain under every ray of light and sound – processes which science reduces to simpler and more elementary forces. Like the elements of which we are composed, the action of these forces extends beyond us: it rusts iron and ripens corn. Far out on every side of us those elements are broadcast, driven in many currents; and birth and gesture and death and the springing of violets from the grave are but a few out of ten thousand resultant combinations. That clear, perpetual outline of face and limb is but an image of ours, under which we group them – a design in a web, the actual threads of which pass out beyond it. This at least of flame-like our life has, that it is but the concurrence, renewed from moment to moment, of forces parting sooner or later on their ways.

Or if we begin with the inward world of thought and feeling, the whirlpool is still more rapid, the flame more eager and devouring. There it is no longer the gradual darkening of the eye, the gradual fading of colour from the wall – movements of the shore-side, where the water flows down indeed, though in apparent rest – but the race of the mid-stream, a drift of momentary acts of sight and passion and thought. At first sight experience seems to bury us under a flood of external objects, pressing upon us with a sharp and importunate reality, calling us out of ourselves in a thousand forms of action. But when reflexion begins to play upon those objects they are dissipated under its influence; the cohesive force seems suspended like some trick of magic; each object is loosed into a group of impressions – colour, odour, texture – in the mind of the observer. And if we continue to dwell in thought on this world, not of objects in the solidity with which language invests them, but of impressions, unstable, flickering, inconsistent, which burn and are extinguished with our consciousness of them, it contracts still further: the whole scope of observation is dwarfed into the narrow chamber of the individual mind. Experience, already reduced to a group of impressions, is ringed round for each one of us by that thick wall of personality through which no real voice has ever pierced on its way to us, or from us to that which we can only conjecture to be without. Every one of those impressions is the impression of the individual in his isolation, each mind keeping as a solitary prisoner its own dream of a world. Analysis goes a step further still, and assures us that those impressions of the individual mind to which, for each one of us, experience dwindles down, are in perpetual flight; that each of them is limited by time, and that as time is infinitely divisible, each of them is infinitely divisible also; all that is actual in it being a single moment, gone while we try to apprehend it, of which it may ever be more truly said that it has ceased to be than that it is. To such a tremulous wisp constantly re-forming itself on the stream, to a single sharp impression, with a sense in it, a relic more or less fleeting, of such moments gone by, what is real in our life fines itself down. It is with this movement, with the passage and dissolution of impressions, images, sensations, that analysis leaves off – that continual vanishing away, that strange, perpetual, weaving and unweaving of ourselves.

Philosophiren, says Novalis, *ist dephlegmatisiren, vivificiren.* The service of philosophy, of speculative culture, towards the human spirit, is to rouse, to startle it to a life of constant and eager observation. Every moment some form grows perfect in hand or face; some tone on the hills or the sea is choicer than the rest; some mood of passion or insight or intellectual excitement is irresistibly real and attractive to us, – for that moment only. Not the fruit of experience, but experience itself, is the end. A counted number of pulses only is given to us of a variegated, dramatic life. How may we see in them all that is to be seen in them by the finest senses? How shall we pass most swiftly from point to point, and be present always at the focus where the greatest number of vital forces unite in their purest energy?

To burn always with this hard, gem-like flame, to maintain this ecstasy, is success in life. In a sense it might even be said that our failure is to form habits: for, after all, habit is relative to a stereotyped world, and meantime it is only the roughness of the eye that makes any two persons, things, situations, seem alike. While all melts under our feet, we may well grasp at any exquisite passion, or any contribution to knowledge that seems by a lifted horizon to set the spirit free for a moment, or any stirring of the senses, strange dyes, strange colours, and curious odours, or work of the artist's hands, or the face of one's friend. Not to discriminate every moment some passionate attitude in those about us, and in the very brilliancy of their gifts some tragic dividing of forces on their ways, is, on this short day of frost and sun, to sleep before evening. With this sense of the splendour of our experience and of its awful brevity, gathering all we are into one desperate effort to see and touch, we shall hardly have time to make theories about the things we see and touch. What we have to do is to be for ever curiously testing new opinions and courting new impressions, never acquiescing in a facile orthodoxy, of Comte, or of Hegel, or of our own. Philosophical theories or ideas, as points of view, instruments of criticism, may help is to gather up what might otherwise pass unregarded by us. 'Philosophy is the microscope of thought.' The theory or idea or system which requires of us the sacrifice of any part of this experience, in consideration of some interest into which we cannot enter, or some abstract theory we have not identified with ourselves, or of what is only conventional, has no real claim upon us.

One of the most beautiful passages of Rousseau is that in the sixth book of the *Confessions*, where he describes the awakening in him of the literary sense. An undefinable taint of death had clung always about him, and now in early manhood he believed himself smitten by mortal disease. He asked himself how he might make as much as possible of the interval that remained; and he was not biassed by anything in his previous life when he decided that it must be by intellectual excitement, which he found just then in the clear, fresh writings of Voltaire. Well! we are all *condamnés,* as Victor Hugo says: we are all under sentence of death but with a sort of indefinite reprieve – *les hommes sont tous condamnés à mort avec des sursis indéfinis*: we have an interval, and then our place knows us no more. Some spend this interval in listlessness, some in high passions, the wisest, at least among 'the children of this world', in art and song. For our one chance lies in expanding that interval, in getting as many pulsations as possible into the given time. Great passions may give us this quickened sense of life, ecstasy and sorrow of love, the various forms of enthusiastic activity, disinterested or otherwise, which come naturally to many of us. Only be sure it is passion – that it does yield you this fruit of a quickened, multiplied consciousness. Of such wisdom, the poetic passion, the desire of beauty, the love of art for its own sake, has most. For art comes to you proposing frankly to give nothing but the highest quality to your moments as they pass, and simply for those moments' sake.

A. C. Benson, from 'Early Writings', *Walter Pater*, 1906

We come to the 'Conclusion', a most elaborate texture of writing made obscure by its compression, by its effort to catch and render the most complicated effects of thought. This 'Conclusion' was omitted in the second edition of the book. Pater says that he excluded it, 'as I conceived it might possibly mislead some of those young men into whose hands it might fall'. He adds that he made a few changes which brought it closer to his original meaning, and that he had dealt more fully with the subject in *Marius the Epicurean*.

The only substantial alterations in the essay are as follows. Pater originally wrote:

'High passions give one this quickened sense of life, ecstasy and sorrow of love, political or religious enthusiasm, or the "enthusiasm of humanity."'

This sentence became:

'Great passions may give us this quickened sense of life, ecstasy and sorrow of love, the various forms of enthusiastic activity, disinterested or otherwise, which come naturally to many of us.'

Again, in a passage dealing with the various ways of using life, so as to fill it full of beautiful energy, he says that 'the wisest' spend it 'in art and song'. In the later version he qualifies the words 'the wisest' by the addition of the phrase 'at least among "the children of this world"'.

The alterations do not appear at first sight to have any very great significance; but Pater says that they brought out his original meaning more clearly; and the very minuteness of the changes serves at least to show his sense of the momentousness of phrases.

He traces, in a passage of rich and subtle complexity, the bewildering effect upon the mind of the flood of external impressions; and compares it with the thought that gradually emerges, as the spirit deals with these impressions, of the loneliness, the solitude of personality; and with the mystery of the movement of time, the flight of the actual moment which is gone even while we try to apprehend it. He compares the perception to 'a tremulous wisp constantly re-forming itself on the stream' of sense; and goes on to indicate that the aim of the perceptive mind should be to make the most of these fleeting moments, to 'be present always at the focus where the greatest number of vital forces unite in their purest energy'. 'To burn always with this hard, gemlike flame, to maintain this ecstasy, is success in life.' 'Not to discriminate every moment some passionate attitude in those about us, is, on the short day of frost and sun, to sleep before evening.'

He goes on to say that to get as many pulsations into the brief interval of life, is the one chance which is open to a man; and art, he says, gives most of these, 'for art comes to you professing frankly to give nothing but the highest quality to your moments as they pass, and simply for those moments' sake'.

The 'Conclusion', then, is a presentment of the purest and highest Epicureanism, the Epicureanism that is a kind of creed, and realises the duty and necessity of activity and energy, but in a world of thought rather than of action. The peril of such a creed, of which Pater became aware, is that it is in the first place purely self-regarding, and in the second place that, stated in the form of abstract principles, it affords no bulwark against the temptation to sink from a pure and passionate beauty of perception into a grosser indulgence in sensuous delights. The difficulty in the artistic, as in the ethical scale, is to discern at what point the spirit begins to yield to the lower impulse....Pater felt, no doubt, that having struck a sensuous note in his essays, this statement of principles of artistic axioms lent itself to misrepresentations; and nothing could more clearly prove the affectionate considerateness of his nature, his desire for sympathy and relationship, his tender care for those whom he loved in spirit, than his fear of giving a wrong bias to their outlook. And thus the omission has a biographical interest, as showing the first shadow of disapproval falling on the sensitive mind, that disapproval which sometimes hung like a cloud over Pater's enjoyment of the world, though it never for a moment diverted his from his serious and sustained purpose, as a prophet of mysteries.

John Addington Symonds, from *The Sonnets of Michael Angelo Buonarroti and Tommaso Campanella*, 1878

Nearly all Michael Angelo's sonnets express personal feelings, and by far the greater of them were composed after his sixtieth year....Vittoria Colorina and Tommaso de' Cavalieri, the two most intimate friends of his old age in Rome, received from him some of the most pathetically beautiful of his love-poems. But to suppose that either one or other was the object of more than a few well authenticated sonnets would be hazardous. Nothing is more clear than that Michael Angelo worshipped Beauty in the Platonic spirit, passing beyond its personal and specific manifestations to the universal and impersonal....If we bear in mind that he habitually regarded the loveliness of man or woman as a sign and symbol of eternal and immutable beauty, we shall feel it of less importance to discover who it was that prompted him to this or that poetic utterance. That the loves of his youth were not so tranquil as those of his old age, appears not only from the regrets expressed in his religious verses, but also from one or two of the rare sonnets referable to his manhood.

Sonnet xxx, 'To Tommaso de' Cavalieri'

With your fair eyes a charming light I see,
   For which my own blind eyes would peer in vain;
   Stayed by your feet the burden I sustain
   Which my lame feet find all too strong for me;
Wingless upon your pinions forth I fly;
   Heavenward your spirit stirreth me to strain;
   E'en as you will, I blush and blanch again,
   Freeze in the sun, burn 'neath a frosty sky.

Your will includes and is the lord of mine;
   Life to my thoughts within your heart is given;
   My words begin to breathe upon your breath:
Like to the moon am I, that cannot shine
   Alone; for lo! our eyes see nought in heaven
   Save what the living sun illumineth.

Edward Dowden, from *Shakspere: His Mind and Art*, 1909

Were there in the life of Shakspere certain events which compelled him to a bitter yet precious gain of experience in the matter of the wrongs of man to man, and from which he procured instruction in the difficult art of bearing oneself justly towards one's wrongers? If the Sonnets of Shakspere, written many years before the close of Shakspere's career as a dramatist, be auto-biographical, we may perhaps discover the sorrow which first roused his heart and imagination to their long inquisition of evil and grief, and which, sinking down into his great soul, and remaining there until all bitterness had passed away, bore fruit in the most mature of Shakspere's writings, distinguished as they are by serene pathetic strength and stern yet tender beauty.[88]

The Sonnets of Shakspere were probably written during those years when as dramatist he was engaged upon the substantial material of English history, and when he was accumulating those resources which were to make him a wealthy burgher of Stratford. This practical, successful man, who had now arrived at middle age, and was growing rich, who had never found delight, as Marlowe, Nash, Greene, and other wild livers had, in the flimsy idealism of knocking his head against the solid laws of the world, was yet not altogether that self-possessed, cheerful, prudent person, who has stood with some writers for the veritable Shakspere. In the Sonnets we recognise three things – that Shakspere was capable of measureless personal devotion; that he was tenderly sensitive, sensitive above all to every diminution or alteration of that love his heart so eagerly craved; and that when wronged, although he suffered anguish, he transcended his private injury, and learned to forgive. There are lovers of Shakspere so jealous of his honour that they are unable to suppose that any grave moral flaw could have impaired the nobility of his life and manhood. Shakspere, as he is discovered in his poems and his plays, appears rather to have been a man who by strenuous effort, and with the aid of the good powers of the world, was saved, so as by fire. Before Shakspere zealots demand our attention to ingenious theories which help us to credit the immaculateness of Shakspere's life, let them prove to us that his writings never offend. When they have shown that Shakspere's poetry possesses the proud virginity of Milton's poetry, they may go on to show that Shakspere's youth was devoted, like the youth of Milton, to an ideal of moral elevation and purity. When we have been convinced that the same moral and spiritual temper which gave rise to the 'Comus' gave rise to the 'Venus and Adonis', we shall think it probable that

Shakspere could have uttered the proud words about his unspotted life that Milton uttered.

Assuredly the inference from Shakspere's writings is not that he held himself with virginal strength and pride remote from the blameful pleasures of the world. What no reader will find anywhere in the plays of poems of Shakspere is a cold-blooded, hard, or selfish line; all is warm, senstive, vital, radiant with delight, or a-thrill with pain. And what we may dare to affirm of Shakspere's life is that whatever its sins may have been, they were not hard, selfish, deliberate, cold-blooded sins. The errors of his heart originated in his sensitiveness, in his imagination (not at first inured to the hardness of the fidelity to the fact), in his quick consciousness of existence, and in the self-abandoning devotion of his heart. There are some noble lines by Chapman, in which he pictures to himself the life of great energy, enthusiasms, and passions, which for ever stands upon the edge of utmost danger, and yet for ever remains in absolute security:–

Give me the spirit that on this life's rough sea
Loves to have his sails fill'd with a lusty wind
Even till his sail-yards tremble, his masts crack,
And his rapt ship run on her side so low
That she drinks water, and her keel ploughs air;
There is no danger to a man that knows
What life and death is, – there's not any law
Exceeds his knowledge; neither is it lawful
That he should stoop to any other law.[#89]

Such a master-spirit, pressing forward under strained canvas, was Shakspere. If the ship dipped and drank water, she rose again; and at length we behold her within view of her haven, sailing under a large, calm wind, not without tokens of stress of weather, but if battered, yet unbroken by the waves. It is to dull, lethargic natures that a moral accident is fatal, because they are tending nowhither, and lack energy and momentum to right themselves again. To say anything against decent, lethargic vices, and timid virtues, anything to the advantage of the strenuous life of bold action and eager emotion, which necessarily incurs risks, and sometimes, is, we shall be told, 'dangerous'. Well, then, be it so; it is dangerous.

The Shakspere whom we discern in the Sonnets had certainly not attained the broad mastery of life which the Stratford bust asserts to have been Shakspere's in his closing years. Life had been found good by him who owned those lips, and whose spirit declares itself in the massive animation of the total outlook of that face.[#90] When the greater number of these Sonnets were written Shakspere could have understood Romeo; he could have understood Hamlet; he could not have conceived Duke Prospero. Under the joyous exterior of those days lay a craving, sensitive, unsatisfied heart, which had not entire possession of itself, which could misplace its affections, and resort to all those pathetic frauds, by which misplaced affections strive to conceal an error from themselves. The friend in whose personality Shakspere found a source of measureless delight – high-born, beautiful, young, clever, accomplished, ardent – wronged him. The woman from whom Shakspere for a time received a joyous quickening of his life, which was half pain – a woman of stained character, and the reverse of beautiful, but a strong nature, intellectual, a lover of art, and possessed of curious magnetic attraction, with her dark eyes which illuminated a pale face – wronged him also. Shakspere bitterly felt the wrong – felt most bitterly the wrong which was least to be expected, that of his friend. It has been held to be an additional baseness that Shakspere could forgive, that he could rescue himself from indignant resentment, and adjust his nature to the altered circumstances. Possibly Shakspere may not have subscribed to all the items in the code of honour; he may not have regarded as inviolable the prohibited degrees of forgiveness. He may have seen that the wrong done to him was human, natural, almost inevitable. He certainly saw that the chief wrong was not that done to him, but committed by his friend against his own better nature. Delivering his heart from the prepossessions of wounded personal feeling, and looking at the circumstances as they actually were, he may have found it very natural and necessary not to banish from his heart the man he loved. However this may have been, his own sanity and strength, and the purity of his work as artist depended on his ultimately delivering his soul from all bitterness. Besides, life was not exhausted. The ship righted itself, and went ploughing forward across a broad sea. Shakspere found ever more and more in life to afford adequate sustenance for man's highest needs of intellect and of heart. Life became ever more encircled with presences of beauty, of goodness, and of terror; and Shakspere's fortitude of heart increased. Nevertheless, such experiences as those recorded in the Sonnets could not pass out of life, and in the imaginative recurrence of past moods might at any subsequent time become motives of his art. Passion had been purified; and at last the truth of things stood out clear and calm.[#91]

The Sonnets tell more of Shakspere's sensitiveness than of Shakspere's strength. In the earlier poems of the collection, his delight in human beauty, intellect, grace, expresses itself with endless variation. Nothing seems to him more admirable than manhood. But this joy is controlled and saddened by a sense of the transitoriness of all things, the ruin of time, the inevitable progress of decay. The love expressed in the early Sonnets is love which has known no sorrow, no change, no wrong; it is an ecstasy which the sensitive heart is as yet unable to control:

As an imperfect actor on the stage
Who with his fear is put beside his part,
Or some fierce thing replete with too much rage,
Whose strength's abundance weakens his own heart,
So I, for fear of trust, forget to say
The perfect ceremony of love's rite,
And in my own love's strength seem to decay,
O'ercharged with burden of mine own love's might.

The prudent and sober Shakspere – was it he who bore this burden of too much love, he whose heart was made weak by the abundance of its strength? He cannot sleep; he lies awake, haunted in the darkness by the face that is dear to him. He falls into sudden moods of despondency, when his own gifts seem narrow and of little worth, when his poems, which yield him his keenest enjoyment, seem wretchedly remote from what he had dreamed, and in the midst of his depression he almost despises himself because he is depressed:

Wishing me like to one more rich in hope,
Featured like him, like him with friends possessed,
Desiring this man's art, and that man's scope,
With what I most enjoy contented least.

He weeps for the loss of precious friends, for 'love's long-since-cancelled woe'; but out of all these clouds and damps the thought of one human soul, which he believes beautiful, can deliver him:

Haply I think on thee, and then my state,
Like to the lark at break of day arising
From sullen earth, sings hymns at heaven's gate.

Then comes the bitter discovery, – a change in love that had seemed to be made for eternity; coldness, estrangement, wrongs upon both sides; and at the same time external trials and troubles arise, and the injurious life of actor and

playwright – injurious to the delicate harmony and purity of the poet's nature
– becomes more irksome:

And almost thence my nature is subdued
To what it works in, like the dyer's hand.

He pathetically begs, not now for love, but for pity. Yet at the worst, and
through all the suffering, he believes in love:

Let me not the marriage of true minds
Admit impediments. Love is not love
Which alters when it alteration finds.

It can accept its object even though imperfect, and still love on. It is not in
the common acceptation of the word prudential – but the *infinite* prudence of
the heart is indeed no other than love:

It fears not Policy, that heretic
Which works on leases of short-numbered hours,
But all alone stands hugely politic,
That it nor glows with heat, nor drowns with showers.

He has learnt his lesson; his romantic attachment, which attributed an impossible perfection to his friend, has become the stronger love which accepts his
friend and knows the fact; knows the fact of fraility and imperfection; knows also
the greater and infinitely precious fact of central and surviving loyalty and goodness; and this new love is better than the old, because more real:

Oh benefit of ill! now I find true
That better is by evil still made better;
And ruined love, when it is built anew,
Grows fairer than at first, more strong, far greater.

And thus he possesses his soul once more; he 'returns to his content'.
Such, briefly and imperfectly hinted, is the spirit of Shakspere's Sonnets. A
great living poet, who has dedicated to the subject of friendship one division of
his collected works, has written these words:

Recorders ages hence?

Come, I will take you down underneath this impassive exterior, –
I will tell you what to say of me;
Publish my name, and hang up my picture as that of the tenderest lover.

And, elsewhere of these Calamus poems, the poems of tender and hardy friendship, he says:

Here the frailest leaves of me, and my strongest-lasting:
Here I shade and hide my thoughts – I myself do not expose them,
And yet they expose me more than all my other poems.

These words of Whitman may be taken as a motto of the Sonnets of Shakspere. In these poems Shakspere has hid himself and is exposed.

Oscar Wilde, from 'The Portrait of Mr. W. H.', 1895

One day I got a letter from Cyril asking me to come round to his rooms that evening. He had charming chambers in Piccadilly overlooking the Green Park, and as I used to go and see him every day, I was rather surprised at his taking the trouble to write. Of course I went, and when I arrived I found him in a state of great excitement. He told me that he had at last discovered the true secret of Shakespeare's Sonnets; that all the scholars and critics had been entirely on the wrong tack; and that he was the first who, working purely by internal evidence, had found out who Mr. W. H. really was. He was perfectly wild with delight, and for a long time would not tell me his theory. Finally, he produced a bundle of notes, took his copy of the Sonnets off the mantelpiece, and sat down and gave me a long lecture on the whole subject.

He began by pointing out that the young man to whom Shakespeare addressed these strangely passionate poems must have been somebody who was a really vital factor in the development of his dramatic art, and that this could not be said either of Lord Pembroke or Lord Southampton. Indeed, whoever he was, he could not have been anybody of high birth, as was shown clearly by the 25th Sonnet, in which Shakespeare contrasts himself with those who are 'great princes' favourites'; says quite frankly –

'Let those who are in favour with their stars
Of public honour and proud titles boast,
Whilst I, whom fortune of such triumph bars,
Unlook'd for joy in that I honour most.'

and ends the sonnet by congratulating himself on the mean state of him he so adored.

'Then happy I, that loved and am beloved
Where I may not remove nor be removed.'

This sonnet Cyril declared would be quite unintelligible if we fancied that it was addressed to either the Earl of Pembroke or the Earl of Southampton, both of whom were men of the highest position in England and fully entitled to be called 'great princes'; and he in corroboration of his view read me Sonnets cxxiv. and cxxv., in which Shakespeare tells us that his love is not 'the child of state', that it 'suffers not in smiling pomp', but is 'builded far from accident'. I listened with a good deal of interest, for I don't think the point had ever been made before; but what followed was still more curious, and seemed to me at the time to entirely dispose of Pembroke's claim. We know from Meres that the Sonnets had been written before 1598, and Sonnet civ. informs us that Shakespeare's friendship for Mr. W. H. had been already in existence for three years. Now Lord Pembroke, who was born in 1580, did not come to London, till he was eighteen years of age, that is to say till 1598, and Shakespeare's acquaintance with Mr. W. H. must have begun in 1594, or at latest 1595. Shakespeare, accordingly, could not have known Lord Pembroke till after the Sonnets had been written.

Cyril pointed out also that Pembroke's father did not die till 1601; whereas it was evident from the line,

'You had a father, let your son say so,'

that the father of Mr. W. H. was dead in 1598. Besides it was absurd to imagine that any publisher of the time, and the preface is from the publisher's hand, would have ventured to address William Herbert, Earl of Pembroke, as Mr. W. H.; the case of Lord Buckhurst being spoken of as Mr. Sackville being not really a parallel instance, as Lord Buckhurst was not a peer, but merely the younger son of a peer, with a courtesy title, and the passage in *England's Parnassus*, where he is so spoken of, is not a formal and stately dedication, but simply a casual allusion. So far for Lord Pembroke, whose supposed claims Cyril easily demolished while I sat by in wonder. With Lord Southampton Cyril had even less difficulty. Southampton became at a very early age the lover of Elizabeth Vernon, so he needed no entreaties to marry; he was not beautiful; he did not resemble his mother, as Mr. W. H. did –

'Thou art thy mother's glass, and she in thee
   Calls back the lovely April of her prime';

and, above all, his Christian name was Henry, whereas the punning sonnets (cxxxv. and cxliii.) show that the Christian name of Shakespeare's friend was the same as his own – *Will*.

As for the other suggestions of unfortunate commentators, that Mr. W. H., is a misprint for Mr. W. S., meaning Mr. William Shakespeare; that 'Mr. W. H. all' should be read 'Mr. W. Hall'; that Mr. W. H. is Mr. William Hathaway; and that a full stop should be placed after 'wisheth', making Mr. W. H. the writer and not the subject of the dedication, – Cyril got rid of them in a very short time; and it is not worth while to mention his reasons, though I remember he sent me off into a fit of laughter by reading to me, I am glad to say not in the original, some extracts from a German commentator called Barnstorff, who insisted that Mr. W. H. was no less a person than 'Mr. William Himself'. Nor would he allow for a moment that the Sonnets are mere satires on the work of Drayton and John Davies of Hereford. To him, as indeed to me, they were poems of serious and tragic import, wrung out of the bitterness of Shakespeare's heart and made sweet by the honey of his lips. Still less would he admit that they were merely a philosophical allegory, and that in them Shakespeare is addressing his Ideal Self, or Ideal Manhood, or the Spirit of Beauty, or the Reason, or the Divine Logos, or the Catholic Church. He felt, as indeed I think we all must feel, that the Sonnets are addressed to an individual, – to a particular young man whose personality for some reason seems to have filled the soul of Shakespeare with terrible joy and no less terrible despair.

Having in this manner cleared the way, as it were, Cyril asked me to dismiss from my mind any preconceived ideas I might have formed on the subject, and to give a fair and unbiased hearing to his own theory. The problem he pointed out was this: Who was that young man of Shakespeare's day who, without being of noble birth or even of noble nature, was addressed by him in terms of such passionate adoration that we can but wonder at the strange worship, and are almost afraid to turn the key that unlocks the mystery of the poet's heart? Who was he whose physical beauty was such that it became the very corner-stone of

Shakespeare's art; the very source of Shakespeare's inspiration; the very incarnation of Shakespeare's dreams? To look upon him as simply the object of certain love poems is to miss the whole meaning of the poems: for the art of which Shakespeare talks in the Sonnets is not the art of the Sonnets themselves, which indeed were to him but slight and secret things – it is the art of the dramatist to which he is always alluding; and he to whom Shakespeare said –

'Thou art all my art, and dost advance
As high as learning my rude ignorance,'

he to whom he promised immortality,

'Where breath most breathes, even in the mouth of men,' –

was surely none other than the boy-actor for whom he created Viola and Imogen, Juliet and Rosalind, Portia and Desdemona, and Cleopatra herself. This was Cyril Graham's theory, evolved as you see purely from the Sonnets themselves, and depending for its acceptance not so much on demonstrable proof or formal evidence, but on a kind of spiritual and artistic sense, by which alone he claimed could the true meaning of the poems be discerned. I remember his reading to me that very fine sonnet –

'How can my Muse want subject to invent,
While thou dost breathe, that pour'st into my verse
Thine own sweet argument, too excellent
For every vulgar paper to rehearse?
O, give thyself the thanks, if aught in me
Worthy perusal stand against thy sight;
For who's so dumb that cannot write to thee,
When thou thyself dost give invention light?
Be thou the tenth Muse, ten times more in worth
Than those old nine which rhymers invocate;
And he that on thee, let him bring forth
Eternal numbers to outlive long date'

– and pointing out how completely it corroborated his theory; and indeed he went through all the Sonnets carefully, and showed, or fancied that he showed that, according to this new explanation of their meaning, things that had seemed obscure, or evil, or exaggerated, became clear and rational, and of high artistic import, illustrating Shakespeare's conception of the true relations between the art of the actor and the art of the dramatist.

It is of course evident that there must have been in Shakespeare's company some wonderful boy-actor of great beauty, to whom he intrusted the presentation of his noble heroines; for Shakespeare was a practical theatre manager as well as an imaginative poet, and Cyril Graham had actually discovered the boy-actor's name. He was Will, or, as he preferred to call him, Willie Hughes. The Christian name he found, of course, in the punning sonnets, cxxxv. and cxliii.; the surname was, according to him, hidden in the eighth line of the 20th Sonnet, where Mr. W. H. is described as –

'A man in hew, all *Hews* in his controwling.'

In the original edition of the Sonnets 'Hews' is printed with a capital letter and in italics, and this, he claimed, showed clearly that a play on words was intended, his view receiving a good deal of corroboration from those sonnets in which curious puns are made on the words 'use' and 'usury'. Of course I was converted at once, and Willie Hughes became to me as real a person as Shakespeare. The only objection I made to the theory was that the name of Willie Hughes does not occur in the list of the actors of Shakespeare's company as it is printed in the first folio. Cyril, however, pointed out that the absence of Willie Hughes's name from this list really corroborated the theory, as it was evident from Sonnet lxxxvi. that Willie Hughes had abandoned Shakespeare's company to play at a rival theatre, probably in some of Chapman's plays. It is in reference to this that in the great sonnet on Chapman, Shakespeare said to Willie Hughes –

'But when your countenance filled up his line,
Then lacked I matter; that enfeebled mine' –

the expression 'when your contenance filled up his line' referring obviously to the beauty of the young actor giving life and reality and added charm to Chapman's verse, the same idea being also put forward in the 79th Sonnet –

'Whilst I alone did call upon thy aid,
My verse alone had all thy gentle grace,
But now my gracious numbers are decayed,
And my sick Muse does give another place';

198

and in the immediately preceding sonnet, where Shakespeare says –

'Every alien pen has got my *use*
And under thee their poesy disperse,'

the play upon words (use = Hughes) being of course obvious, and the phrase 'under thee their poesy disperse', meaning 'by your assistance as an actor bring their plays before the people'.

It was a wonderful evening, and we sat up almost till dawn reading and re-reading the Sonnets. After some time, however, I began to see that before the theory could be placed before the world in a really perfected form it was necessary to get some independent evidence about the existence of this young actor, WIllie Hughes. If this could be once established, there could be no possible doubt about his identity with Mr. W. H.; but otherwise the theory would fall to the ground.

I took down from the bookshelf my copy of Shakespeare's Sonnets, and began to go carefully through them. Every poem seemed to me to corroborate Cyril Graham's theory. I felt as if I had my hand upon Shakespeare's heart, and was counting each separate throb and pulse of passion. I thought of the wonderful boy-actor and saw his face in every line.

Two sonnets, I remember, struck me particularly: they were the 53rd and the 67th. In the first of these, Shakespeare, complimenting Willie Hughes on the versatility of his acting, on his wide range of parts, a range extending from Rosalind to Juliet, and from Beatrice to Ophelia, says to him –

'What is your substance, whereof are you made,
That millions of strange shadows on you tend?
Since every one hath, every one, one shade,
And you, but one, can every shadow lend' –

lines that would be unintelligible if they were not addressed to an actor, for the word 'shadow' had in Shakespeare's day a technical meaning connected with the stage. 'The best in this kind are but shadows', says Theseus of the actors in the *Midsummer Night's Dream*, and there are many similar allusions in the literature of the day. These sonnets evidently belonged to the series in which Shakespeare discusses the nature of the actor's art, and of the strange and rare temperament that is essential to the perfect stage-player. 'How is it,' says Shakespeare to Willie Hughes, 'that you have so many personalities?' and then he goes on to point out that his beauty is such that it seems to realise every form and phase of fancy, to embody each dream of the creative imagination – an idea that is still further expanded in the sonnet that immediately follows, where, beginning with the fine thought,

'O, how much more doth beauty beauteous seem
By that sweet ornament which *truth* doth give!'

Shakespeare invites us to notice how the truth of acting, the truth of visible presentation on the stage, adds to the wonder of poetry, giving life to its loveliness, and actual reality to its ideal form. And yet, in the 67th Sonnet, Shakespeare calls upon Willie Hughes to abandon the stage with its artificiality, its false mimic life of painted face and unreal costume, its immoral influences and suggestions, its remoteness from the true world of noble action and sincere utterance....One point puzzled me immensely as I read the Sonnets, and it was days before I struck on the true interpretation, which indeed Cyril Graham himself seems to have missed. I could not understand how it was that Shakespeare set so high a value on his young friend marrying. He himself had married young, and the result had been unhappiness, and it was not likely that he would have asked Willie Hughes to commit the same error. The boy-player of Rosalind had nothing to gain from marriage, or from the passions of real life. The early sonnets, with their strange entreaties to have children, seemed to me a jarring note. The explanation of the mystery came on me quite suddenly, and I found it in the curious dedication. It will be remembered that the dedication runs as follows: –

TO. THE. ONLIE. BEGGETER. OF.

THESE. INSUING. SONNETS.

MR W.H. ALL. HAPPINESSE

   AND. THAT. ETERNITE.

      PROMISED.

        BY.

OUR. EVER-LIVING. POET

      WISHETH.

THE. WELL-WISHING.

ADVENTURER. IN.

     SETTING.

     FORTH.

        T.T.

Some scholars have supposed that the word 'begetter' in this dedication means simply the procurer of the Sonnets for Thomas Thorpe the publisher; but this view is now generally abandoned, and the highest authorities are quite agreed that it is to be taken in the sense of inspirer, the metaphor being drawn from the analogy of physical life. Now I saw that the same metaphor was used by Shakespeare himself all through the poems, and this set me on the right track. Finally I made my great discovery. The marriage that Shakespeare proposes for Willie Hughes is the 'marriage with his Muse', an expression which is definitely put forward in the 82nd Sonnet, where, in bitterness of his heart at the defection of the boy-actor for whom he had written his greatest parts, and whose beauty had indeed suggested them, he opens his complaint by saying –

'I'll grant thou wert not married to my Muse.'

The children he begs him to beget are no children of flesh and blood, but more immortal children of undying fame. The whole cycle of the early sonnets is simply Shakespeare's invitation to go upon the stage and become a player. How barren and profitless a thing, he says, is this beauty of yours if it be not used: –

'When forty winters shall besiege thy brow,
And dig deep trenches in thy beauty's field,
Thy youth's proud livery, so gazed on now,
Will be a tattered weed, of small worth held:
Then being asked where all thy beauty lies,
Where all the treasure of thy lusty days,
To say within thine own deep sunken eyes,
Were an all-eating shame and thriftless praise.'

You must create something in art: my verse 'is thine, and *born* of thee'; only listen to me, and I will '*bring forth* eternal numbers to outlive long date', and you shall people with forms of your own image the imaginary world of the stage. These children that you beget, he continues, will not wither away, as mortal children do, but you shall live in them and in my plays: do but –

'Make thee another self, for love of me,
That beauty still may live in thine or thee!'

I collected all the passages that seemed to corroborate this view, and they produced a strong impression on me, and showed me how complete Cyril

Graham's theory really was. I also saw that it was quite easy to separate those lines in which he speaks of the Sonnets themselves from those in which he speaks of his great dramatic work. This was a point that had been entirely overlooked by all critics up to Cyril Graham's day. And yet it was one of the most important points in the whole series of poems. To the Sonnets Shakespeare was more or less indifferent. He did not wish to rest his fame on them. They were to him his 'slight Muse', as he calls them, and intended, as Meres tells us, for private circulation only among a few, a very few, friends. Upon the other hand he was extremely conscious of the high artistic value of his plays, and shows a noble self-reliance upon his dramatic genius. When he says to Willie Hughes:

'But thy eternal summer shall not fade,
Nor lose possession of that fair thou owest;
Nor shall Death brag thou wander'st in his shade,
When in *eternal lines* to time thou growest;
So long as men can breathe or eyes can see,
So long lives this and this gives life to thee' –

The expression 'eternal lines' clearly alludes to one of his plays that he was sending him at the time, just as the concluding couplet points to his confidence in the probability of his plays being always acted. In his address to the Dramatic Muse (Sonnets c. and ci.), we find the same feeling.

'Where art thou, Muse, that thou forget'st so long
To speak of that which gives thee all thy might?
Spends thou thy fury on some worthless song,
Darkening thy power to lend base subjects light?'

he cries, and he then proceeds to reproach the mistress of Tragedy and Comedy for her 'neglect of Truth in Beauty dyed', and says –

'Because he needs no praise, wilt thou be dumb?
Excuse not silence so; for't lies in thee
To make him much outlive a gilded tomb,
And to be praised of ages yet to be.
    Then do thy office, Muse; I teach thee how
    To make him seem long hence as he shows now.'

It is, however, perhaps in the 55th Sonnet that Shakespeare gives to this idea its fullest expression. To imagine that the 'powerful rhyme' of the second line refers to the sonnet itself is to entirely mistake Shakespeare's meaning. It seemed to me that it was extremely likely, from the general character of the sonnet, that a particular play was meant, and that the play was none other but *Romeo and Juliet.*

'Not marble, nor the gilded monuments
Of princes, shall outlive this powerful rhyme;
But you shall shine more bright in these contents
That unswept stone besmeared with sluttish time.
When wasteful wars shall statues overturn,
And broils root out the work of masonry,
Not Mars his sword nor war's quick fire shall burn
The living record of your memory.
'Gainst death and all-oblivious enmity
Shall you pace forth; your poise shall still find room
Even in the eyes of all posterity
That wear this world out to the ending doom.
    So, till the judgement that yourself arise,
    You live in this, and dwell in lovers' eyes.'

It was extremely suggestive to note how here as elsewhere Shakespeare promised Willie Hughes immortality in a form that appealed to men's eyes – that is to say, in a spectacular form, in a play that is to be looked at.

For two weeks I worked hard at the Sonnets, hardly ever going out, and refusing all invitations. Every day I seemed to be discovering something new, and Willie Hughes became to me a kind of spiritual presence, an ever-dominant personality. I could almost fancy that I saw him standing in the shadow of my room, so well had Shakespeare drawn him, with his golden hair, his tender flower-like grace, his dreamy deep sulken eyes, his delicate mobile limbs, and his white lily hands. His very name fascinated me. Willie Hughes! Willie Hughes! How musically it sounded! Yes; who else but he could have been the master-mistress of Shakespeare's passion,[92] the lord of his love to whom he was bound in vassalage,[93] the delicate minion of pleasure,[94] the rose of the whole world,[95] the herald of the spring[96] decked in proud livery of youth,[97] the lovely boy whom it was sweet music to hear,[98] and whose beauty was the very raiment of Shakespeare's heart,[99] as it was the keystone of his dramatic power? How bitter now seemed the whole tragedy of his desertion and his shame! – shame that he made sweet and lovely#100 by the mere magic of his personality, but that was none the less shame. Yet as Shakespeare forgave him, should not we forgive him also? I did not care to pry into the mystery of his sin….How well, too, had Shakespeare drawn the temperament of the stage-player! Willie Hughes was one of those

'That do not do the thing they most do show,
Who, moving others, are themselves as stone.'

He could act love, but could not feel it, could mimic passion without realising it.

'In many's looks the false heart's history
Is writ in moods and frowns and wrinkles strange,'

But with Willie Hughes it was not so. 'Heaven', says Shakespeare, in a sonnet of mad idolatry –

'Heaven in thy creation did decree
That in thy face sweet love should ever dwell;
Whate'er thy thoughts or thy heart's workings be,
Thy looks should nothing thence but sweetness tell.'

In his 'inconstant mind' and his 'false heart', it was easy to recognise the insincerity and treachery that somehow seemed inseparable from the artistic nature, as in his love of praise that desire for immediate recognition that characterises all actors. And yet, more fortunate in this than other actors, Willie Hughes was to know something of immortality.

Once I thought that I had really found Willie Hughes in Elizabethan literature. In a wonderfully graphic account of the last days of the great Earl of Essex, his chaplain, Thomas Knell, tells us that the night before the Earl died, 'he called William Hewes, which was his musician, to play upon the virginals and sing. "Play", said he, "my song, Will Hewes, and I will sing it to myself." So he did it most joyfully, not as a howling swan, which, still looking down, waileth her end, but as a sweet lark, lifting up his hands and casting up his eyes to his God, with this mounted the crystal skies, and reached with his unwearied tongue the top of the highest heavens.' Surely the boy who played the virginals to the dying father of Sidney's Stella was none other but the Willie Hughes to whom Shakespeare dedicated the Sonnets, and whom he tells us was himself sweet 'music to hear'. Yet Lord Essex died in 1576, when Shakespeare himself was but twelve years of age. It was impossible that his musician could have been the Mr. W. H. of the Sonnets. Perhaps Shakespeare's young friend was the son of the player upon the virginals? It was at least something to have discovered that Will Hews was an Elizabethan name. Indeed the name Hews seemed to have been closely connected with music and the stage. The first English actress was the lovely Margaret Hews, whom Prince Rupert so madly loved. What more probable than that between her and Lord Essex's musician had come the boy-actor of Shakespeare's plays? But the proofs, the links – where were they? Alas! I could not find them. It seemed to me that I was always on the brink of absolute verification, but that I could never really attain to it.

From Willie Hughes's life I soon passed to thoughts of his death. I used to wonder what had been his end.

Perhaps he had been one of those English actors who in 1604 went across the sea to Germany and played before the great Duke Henry Julius of Brunswick, himself a dramatist of no mean order, and at the Court of that strange Elector of Brandenburg, who was so enamoured of beauty that he was said to have bought for his weight in amber the young son of a travelling Greek merchant, and to have given pageants in honour of his slave through that dreadful famine year of 1606–7, when the people died of hunger in the very streets of the town, and for the space of seven months there was no rain. We know at any rate that *Romeo and Juliet* was brought out at Dresden in 1613, along with *Hamlet* and *King Lear*, and it was surely to none other than Willie Hughes that in 1615 the death-mask of Shakespeare was brought by the hand of one of the suite of the English ambassador, pale token of the passing away of the great poet who had so dearly loved him. Indeed there would have been something peculiarly fitting in the idea that the boy-actor, whose beauty had been so vital an element in the realism and romance of Shakespeare's art, should have been the first to have brought to Germany the seed of the new culture, and was in his way the precursor of that Aufklärung or Illumination of the eighteenth century, that splendid movement which, though begun by Lessing and Herder, and brought to its full and perfect issue by Goethe, was in no small part helped on by another actor – Friedrich Schroeder – who awoke the popular consciousness, and by means of feigned passions and mimetic methods of the stage showed the intimate, the vital, connection between life and literature. If this was so – and there was certainly no evidence against it – it was not improbable that Willie Hughes was one of those English comedians (*mimae quidam ex Britannia*,[182] as the old chronicle calls them), who were slain at Nuremburg in a sudden uprising of the people, and were secretly buried in a little vineyard outside the city by some young men 'who had found pleasure in their performances, and of whom some had sought to be instructed in the mysteries of the new art'. Certainly no more fitting place could there be for him to whom Shakespeare said, 'thou art all my art', than this little vineyard outside the city walls. For was it not from the sorrows of Dionysus that Tragedy sprang? Was not the light laughter of Comedy, with its careless merriment and quick replies, first heard on the lips of the Sicilian vine-dressers? Nay, did not the purple and red stain of the wine-froth on face and limbs give the first suggestion of the charm and fascination of disguise – the desire for self-concealment, the sense of the value of objectivity thus showing itself in the rude beginnings of the art? At any rate, wherever he lay – whether in the little vineyard at the gate of the Gothic town, or in some dim London Churchyard amidst the roar and bustle of our great city – no gorgeous monument marked his resting-place. His true tomb, as Shakespeare saw, was the poet's verse, his true monument the permanence of the drama. So it had been with others whose beauty had given a new creative impulse to their age. The ivory body of the Bithynian slave rots in the green ooze of the Nile, and on the yellow hills of the Cerameicus is strewn the dust of the young Athenian; but Antinous lived in sculpture, and Charmides in philosophy.

After three weeks had elapsed, I determined to make a strong appeal to Erskine to do justice to the memory of Cyril Graham, and to give to the world his marvellous interpretation of the Sonnets – the only interpretation that thoroughly explained the problem. I have not any copy of my letter, I regret to say, nor have I been able to lay my hand upon the original; but I remember that I went over the whole ground, and covered sheets of paper with passionate reiteration of the arguments and proofs that my study had suggested to me. It seemed to me that I was not merely restoring Cyril Graham to his proper place in literary history, but rescuing the honour of Shakespeare himself from the tedious memory of a commonplace intrigue. I put into the letter all my enthusiasm. I put into the letter all my faith.

No sooner, in fact, had I sent it off than a curious reaction came over me. It seemed to me that I had given away my capacity for belief in the Willie Hughes theory of the Sonnets, that something had gone out of me, as it were, and I was perfectly indifferent to the whole subject. What was it that had happened? It is difficult to say. Perhaps, by finding perfect expression for a passion, I had exhausted the passion itself. Emotional forces, like the forces of physical life, have their positive limitations. Perhaps the mere effort to convert any one to a theory involves some form of renunciation of the power of credence. Perhaps I was simply tired of the whole thing, and, my enthusiasm having burnt out, my reason was left to its own unimpassioned judgement. However it came about, and I cannot pretend to explain it, there was no doubt that Willie Hughes suddenly became to me a mere myth, an idle dream, the boyish fancy of a young man who, like most ardent spirits, was more anxious to convince others than to be himself convinced.

As I had said some very unjust and bitter things to Erskine in my letter, I determined to go and see him at once, and to make my apologies to him for my behaviour. Accordingly the next morning I drove down to Birdcage Walk, and found Erskine sitting in his library, with the forged picture of Willie Hughes in front of him.

'My dear Erskine!' I cried, 'I have come to apologise to you.'

'To apologise to me?' he said. 'What for?'

'For my letter,' I answered.

'You have nothing to regret in your letter,' he said. 'On the contrary, you have done me the greatest service in your power. You have shown me that Cyril Graham's theory is perfectly sound.'

'You don't mean to say that you believe in Willie Hughes?' I exclaimed.

'Why not?' he rejoined. 'You have proved the thing to me. Do you think I cannot estimate the value of evidence?'

'But there is no evidence at all,' I groaned, sinking into a chair. 'When I wrote to you I was under the influence of a perfectly silly enthusiasm. I had been touched by the story of Cyril Graham's death, fascinated by his romantic theory, enthralled by the wonder and novelty of the whole idea. I see now that the theory is based on a delusion. The only evidence for the existence of Willie Hughes is that picture in front of you, and the picture is a forgery. Don't be carried away by mere sentiment in this matter. Whatever romance may have to say about the Willie Hughes theory, reason is dead against it.'

'I don't understand you,' said Erskine, looking at me in amazement. 'Why, you yourself have convinced me by your letter that Willie Hughes is an absolute reality. Why have you changed your mind? Or is all that you have been saying to me merely a joke?'

'I cannot explain it to you,' I rejoined, 'but I see now that there is nothing to be said in favour of Cyril Graham's interpretation. The Sonnets are addressed to Lord Pembroke. For heaven's sake don't waste your time in a foolish attempt to discover a young Elizabethan actor who never existed, and to make a phantom puppet the centre of the great cycle of Shakespeare's Sonnets.'

'I see that you don't understand the theory,' he replied.

'My dear Erskine,' I cried, 'not understand it! Why, I feel as if I had invented it.'

J. A. Nicklin, 'Marlowe's "Gaveston"', *The Free Review*, 1895

In [Marlowe's] poetry may be found every token by which we recognize the genuine Renaissance spirit. The 'repugnance to touch images of physical ugliness'...'the intense feeling for the imaginative show and color of things', the attitude of delightful curiosity before relics of antiquity and memories of old-world cities: the keenest sense – and this was the most intimate trait of all – of physical loveliness, of the charm of shapely men and beautiful women – such things one might say *elemented* the genius of Marlowe.

The play of 'Edward the Second' was written in a mood dominated by disillusion. Here, for a marvel, grey tones prevail in the scheme of colour. It is only in the character of the handsome, haughty, dissolute favourite that the joyous licence of the Pagan world asserts itself again. If research could recover for us, with adequate fulness, the outward and inward life of that marvellous Earl of Cornwall, we surely should find, whatever else the result might be, a character very different from Marlowe's creation. The favourite at a rude feudal court, even though his origin were from a more humanised district of France, was never, we may be sure, formed in this mould, nor could he have won his place in the king's affections by such arts as Marlowe imagines. The conception of Gaveston, and his relation to Edward is entirely Pagan. When the elder Mortimer, in palliation of Edward's fondness is made to speak in this fashion:

'The mightiest kings have had their minions:
Great Alexander loved Hephestion,
The conquering Hercules for Hylas wept,
And for Patroclus stern Achilles drooped' –

Marlowe only makes a disclosure of his own standpoint. To put such language – and such a sentiment – into the mouth of that grim old war dog was a glaring breach of dramatic propriety. 'Minion', a word used so often throughout the play to describe Gaveston, gives the key to his position. Marlowe is thinking of the *mignons* of the last of the Valois; Gaveston, as he lived for Marlowe, is the pet and darling of another Henri Trois. He is the counterpart of the brilliant and dissolute young men who shared the monarch's orgies; the forerunner, in a measure, of such artificial creatures as Carr, Earl of Somerset, and Villiers, Duke of Buckingham....Piers Gaveston knew far better than the English Barons, with their barbaric tastes, what can be obtained from outward show. The limits of dramatic writing do not allow of direct portraiture, but, by one happy, lucid touch, we receive a distinct impression of the brilliant exterior, and the scornful air, which distinguished Edward's 'minion'. Young Mortimer breaks out into railing at the fantastic attire of the favourite.

'He wears a short Italian hooded cloak,
Larded with pearl, and in his Tuscan cap
A jewel of more value than the crown.
While others walk below, the king and he
From out a window laugh at such as we,
And flout our train and jest at our attire.'

It is indeed for externals that Gaveston gives most thought, and it is through them that he sways 'the pliant king'. He has only the greatest contempt for 'the multitude that are but sparks raked up in embers of their poverty'. He is brave, and skilful in warlike exercises, but at heart he cares nothing for military fame; he only wishes to shine at court, and to stand first in the king's regards. A suitor who looks for encouragement, in virtue of being 'a soldier that hath served against the Scot', is met with the retort, 'Why, there are hospitals of such as you. I have no war, and therefore, sir, begone. 'These are not men for me,' he exclaims, 'I must have wanton poets, pleasant wits, musicians.'

It is a certain feminine quality, perhaps, in Gaveston, that inclines his thoughts to linger so much on the surface of things. And it is this feminine quality that makes his power over the king. He is endowed with something much more effectual than the mere skill to contrive a pleasant and luxurious environment: he has a strange capacity for intensely feeling certain kinds of emotion – such kinds as would be strange in a mind of more manly fibre. Edward answers the contemptuous question, 'Why should you love him whom the world hates so?' with 'Because he loves me more than all the world.' There is something of poetry in the *abandon* of Gaveston's friendship, as well as in his keen sensitiveness to things of luxury that are lovely to look on. When he receives the king's letter to announce the death of the aged Edward and call him back to England, he breaks forth with a southern impetuosity of passion: –

'Sweet prince, I come; these, these my amorous lines
Might have enforced me to have swum from France
And, like Leander, gasped upon the sand
So thou wouldst smile and take me in thy arms.'

…We cannot understand the sentiment which made the *droit de seigneur* both natural and just. But we need not, therefore, discredit the historic fact. Gaveston's love for Edward is not unlike in its nature to the love which the Stuarts inspired in their mistresses. Like Beatrix Esmond, Gaveston is dazzled by the monarch's isolated pre-eminence, overtopping all men. Just as many women of those times lost sight of the point where deference to lawful sovereign ended and sexual love began, Gaveston's friendship is inextricably mixed up with an overpowering apprehension of the splendour of royalty: –

'What greater bliss can hap to Gaveston,
Than live and be the favourite of a king?'
''Tis something to be pitied of a king.'

Marlowe's treatment of the love-passages between Gaveston and the heiress of Gloucester is most suggestive. It would not fall in with the rest of Marlowe's conception, that the bond of affection between Edward and his Gaveston should be severed or relaxed by a new passion, and yet he did not wish to represent his hero as a laggard in love. With consummate skill Marlowe has set before us only the impression that Gaveston has made on the heart of his mistress. We find that nothing is wanting to the fulness of that impression; Gaveston has been found capable of satisfying the demands of the most exacting tenderness, and yet we feel no clashing with the central interest, the King's friendship. That collision of interests would have been inevitable if Gaveston had been brought on, in person, as the lover of Gloucester's daughter. As it is, we are most artfully given to feel that he is possessed of such a large-heartedness of passion, that he can, as we might say, take this lesser love in his stride. Yet none the less it is made clear that with all his depth of passionate feeling, he is one to be loved more than to love.

Other notable qualities Gaveston has, not so prominent, yet as clearly marked, qualities that harmonise with and go to complete the outlines of this unique conception. The facile wit, playing so lightly, yet often so scathingly; the profound scorn of those things which are opposed to, or outside of, his own scheme of life; the craving for what is *intense* in action and in environment; without these things the Gaveston of this play would be only half himself.

It is easy to fix the prominent features, to catalogue them, to offer some superficial explanation, but Marlowe's imagination, even when one has toiled honestly, still preserves to itself unfathomed deeps. The ultimate reality, the whole essence of what the poet had chosen for presentation in the person of Gaveston, still baffles any attempt to reproduce it. Perhaps one comes nearest to success in the simple statement that Marlowe has set himself to accomplish, in the world of psychological fact, something of the same miracle as the artist of the *statue enigmatique* of the Louvre, in bodily form. Piers Gaveston is, in truth, the Hermaphrodite in soul.

'Chimère ardente, effort suprême
　　De l'art et de la volupté,
Monstre charmant, comme je t'aime
　　Avec ta multiple beauté.'[183]

WHITMANIA[184]

John Addington Symonds to Walt Whitman, 3 August 1890

My dear Master...I want next to ask you a question about a very important portion of your teaching, which has puzzled a great many of your disciples and admirers. To tell the truth, I have always felt unable to deal, as I wish to do, comprehensively with your philosophy of life, because I do not even yet understand the whole drift of 'Calamus'. If you have read Mr Havelock Ellis' 'New Spirit', which contains a study of your work in thought and speculation, you may have noticed on p. 108 that he expresses some perplexity about the doctrine of 'manly love', and again on p. 121 he uses this phrase 'the intimate and physical love of comrades and lovers'.

This reference to Havelock Ellis helps me to explain what it is I want to ask you. In your conception of Comradeship, do you contemplate the possible intrusion of those semi-sexual emotions and actions which no doubt do occur between men? I do not ask, whether you approve of them, or regard them as a necessary part of the relation? But I should much like to know whether *you are prepared to leave them to the inclinations and the conscience of the individuals concerned?*

For my own part, after mature deliberation, I hold that the present laws of

France and Italy are right upon this topic of morality. They place the personal relations of adults of both sexes upon the same foundation: that is to say, they protect minors, punish violence, and guard against outrages of public decency. Within these limitations, they leave individuals to do what they think fit. But, as you know, these principles are in open contradiction with the principles of English (and I believe American) legislation.

It has not infrequently occurred to me among my English friends to hear your 'Calamus' objected to, as praising and propagating a passionate affection between men, which (in the language of the objectors) has 'a very dangerous side', and might 'bring people into criminality'.

Now: it is of the utmost importance to me as your disciple, and as one who wants sooner or later to diffuse a further knowledge of your life-philosophy by criticism; it is most important to me to know what you really think about all this.

I agree with the objectors I have mentioned that, human nature being what it is, and some men having a strong natural bias towards persons of their own sex, the enthusiasm of 'Calamus' is calculated to encourage ardent and *physical* intimacies.

But I do not agree with them in thinking that such a result would be absolutely prejudicial to Social interests, while I am certain that you are right in expecting a new Chivalry (if I may so speak) from one of the main and hitherto imperfectly developed factors of the human emotional nature. This, I take it, is the spiritual outcome of your doctrine in Calamus.

And, as I have said, I prefer the line adopted by French and Italian legislature to that of the English penal code.

Finally, what I earnestly desire to know is whether you are content to leave the ethical problems regarding the private behaviour of comrades toward each other, to the persons' own sense of what is right and fit – or whether, on the other hand, you have never contemplated while uttering the Gospel of Comradeship, the possibility of any such delicate difficulties occurring.

Will you enlighten me on this? If I am not allowed to hear from yourself or from some one who will communicate your views, I fear I shall never be able to utter what I want to tell the world about your teaching, with the confidence and the thorough sense of not misinterpreting you in one way or the other which are inseparable from truly sympathetic and powerful exposition.

The precise drift of 'Whoever you are' – what the one indispensable thing is – I cannot get at; and I am not sure what the drift of 'Earth my likeness' is. – Ah, if I could only once have spoken to you, you would certainly have let me know – Lieber Mann, geehrter Meister, das fehlt mir doch![185]

It is perhaps strange that a man within two months of completing his 50th year should care at all about this ethical bearing of Calamus. Of course I do not care much about it, except that ignorance on the subject prevents me from forming a complete view of your life-philosophy.

Believe me truly gratefully and affectionately yours

John Addington Symonds

John Addington Symonds to Edward Carpenter, 13 February 1893

Dear Carpenter

I wrote in the Summer of 1890 to Whitman asking him what his real feeling about masculine love was, & saying that I knew people in England who had a strong sexual bias in such passions, felt themselves supported & encouraged by Calamus. Unluckily I have not got a copy of my letter.

He replied (Aug. 19, ' 90)

'About the questions on Calamus etc: they quite daze me. L[eaves] of G[rass] is only to be rightly construed by & within its own atmosphere & essential character – all of its pages & pieces so coming strictly under –: that the Calamus part has even allowed the possibility of such construction as mentioned is terrible – I am fain to hope that the pp themselves are not to be even mentioned for such gratuitous & quite at the time undreamed & unrecked possibility of morbid inferences – wh are disavowed by me & seem damnable.'

That is all that is to the point. He rambles on about his being less 'restrained' by temperament & theory than I (J.A.S.) am – 'I at certain moments let the spirit impulse (female) rage its utmost wildest damnedest (I feel I do so sometimes in L. of G. & I do so).'

That last passage seems meant to qualify the first. But if it does so, it implies that these inferences are not so gratuitous morbid & damnable as supposed.

At the end of the letter (wh is a long one) he resumes:

'My life, young manhood, mid-age times South, etc, have been jolly bodily & doubtless open to criticism. Though unmarried I have had six children – two are dead – one living Southern grandchild fine boy writes to me occasionally – circumstances (connected with their benefit & fortune) have separated me from intimate relations.'

It struck me when I first read this p.s. that W.W. wanted to obviate 'damnable inferences' about himself by asserting his paternity....I fear that the blind idolators of W.W. will not wholly like [my 'Study of W.W.'].

213

Yours affcly

J.A.S.

John Addington Symonds, from *Walt Whitman: A Study*, 1893

To bear the yoke of universal law is the plain destiny of human beings. If we could learn to bear that yoke with gladness, to thrill with vibrant fibres to the pulses of the machine we constitute...then we might stand where Whitman stood with 'feet tenoned and mortised in granite'. I do not think it is a religion only for the rich, the powerful, the wise, the healthy. For my own part I may confess that it shone upon me when my life was broken, when I was weak, sickly, and of no account; and that I have ever lived thenceforward in the light and warmth of it. In bounden duty towards Whitman, I make this personal statement; for had it not been for the contact of his fervent spirit with my own, the pyre ready to be lighted, the combustible materials of modern thought awaiting the touch of the fire-bringer, might never have leapt up into flame of life-long faith and consolation. During my darkest hours, it comforted me with the conviction that I too played my part in the illimitable symphony of cosmic life. When I sinned, repined, sorrowed, suffered, it touched me a gentle hand of sympathy and understanding, sustained me with the strong hand of assurance that in the end I could not go amiss (for I was part, an integrating part of the great whole); and when strength revived in me, it stirred a healthy pride and courage to effectuate myself, to bear the brunt of spiritual foes, the slings and arrows of outrageous fortune. For this reason, in duty to my master Whitman, and in the hope that my experience may encourage others to seek the same source of inspiration, I have exceeded the bounds of an analytical essay by pouring forth my personal confession....Studying his works by their own light, and by the light of their author's character, interpreting each part by reference to the whole, an impartial critic will, I think, be drawn to the conclusion that what he calls the 'adhesiveness' of comradeship is meant to have no interblending with the 'amativeness' of sexual love. Personally, it is undeniable that Whitman possessed a specially keen sense of the fine restraint and continence, the cleanliness and chastity, that are inseparable from the perfectly virile and physically complete nature of healthy manhood. Still we have the right to predicate the same ground-qualities in the early Dorians, those founders of the martial institution of Greek love; and yet it is notorious to students of Greek civilisation that the lofty sentiment of their masculine chivalry was intertwined with much that is repulsive to modern sentiment.

Whitman does not appear to have taken some of the phenomena of contemporary morals into due account, although he must have been aware of them. Else he would have foreseen that, human nature being what it is, we cannot expect to eliminate all sensual alloy from emotions raised to a high pitch of passionate intensity, and that permanent elements within the midst of our society will imperil the absolute purity of the ideal he attempts to establish. It is obvious that those unenviable mortals who are the inheritors of sexual anomalies, will recognise their own emotion in Whitman's 'superb friendship, exalté, previously unknown', which 'waits, and has always been waiting, latent in all men', the 'something fierce in me, eligible to burst forth', 'ethereal comradeship', 'the last athletic reality'. Had I not the strongest proof in Whitman's private correspondence with myself that he repudiated any such deductions from his 'Calamus', I admit that I should have regarded them as justified; and I am not certain whether his own feelings upon this delicate topic may not have altered since the time when 'Calamus' was first composed....The manliness of the emotion which is thus expressed so shyly, allegorically indicated, appears in the magnificent address to soldiers at the close of the great war: 'Over Carnage rose Prophetic a Voice.'[101] Its tenderness emerges in the elegy on a slain comrade:[102]

Vigil for boy of responding kisses (never again on earth responding):
Vigil for comrades swiftly slain – vigil I never forget, how as day brightened,
I rose from the chill ground, and folded my soldier well in his blanket,
And buried him where he fell.

Its pathos and clinging intensity transpire through the last lines of the following piece, which may have been suggested by the legends of David and Jonathan, Achilles and Patroclus, Orestes and Pylades:[103]

When I peruse the conquered fame of heroes, and the victories of mighty
    generals,
I do not envy the generals,
Nor the President in his Presidency, nor the rich in his great house;
But when I read of the brotherhood of lovers, how it was with them,
How through life, through dangers, odium, unchanging, long and long,
Through youth, and through middle and old age, how unfaltering, how
    affectionate and faithful they were,

Then I am pensive – I hastily put down the book, and walk away, filled with
the bitterest envy.

But Whitman does not conceive of comradeship as a merely personal possession,
delightful to the friends it links in bonds of amity. He regards it eventually as a
social and political virtue. This human emotion is destined to cement society
and to render commonwealths inviolable. Reading some of his poems we are
carried back to ancient Greece, – to Plato's *Symposium*, to Philip gazing on the
sacred band of Thebans after the fight at Chaeronea....We may return from
this analysis to the inquiry whether anything like a new chivalry is to be
expected from the doctrines of *Calamus*, which shall in the future utilize some
of those unhappy instincts which at present run to waste in vice and shame. It
may be asked what these passions have in common with the topic of
Whitman's prophecy? They have this in common with it. Whitman recognizes
among the sacred emotions and social virtues, destined to regenerate political
life and to cement nations, an intense, jealous, throbbing, sensitive, expectant
love of man for man: a love which yearns in absence, droops under the sense
of neglect, revives at the return of the beloved: a love that finds honest delight
in hand-touch, meeting lips, hours of privacy, close personal contact. He
proclaims this love to be not only a daily fact in the present, but also a saving
and ennobling aspiration. While he expressly repudiates, disowns and brands
as damnable all 'morbid inferences' which may be drawn by malevolence or
vicious cunning from his doctrine, he is prepared to extend the gospel of
comradeship to the whole human race. He expects democracy, the new religious ideal of mankind to develop and extend 'that fervid comradeship', and
by its means to counterbalance and to spiritualize what is vulgar and materialistic in the modern world. 'Democracy', he maintains, 'infers such loving
comradeship, as its most inevitable twin or counterpart, without which it will
be incomplete, in vain, and incapable of perpetuating itself.'

If this is not to be a dream, if he is right in believing that 'threads of manly
friendship, fond and loving, pure and sweet, strong and life-long, carried to
degrees hitherto unknown', will penetrate the organism of society, 'not only
giving tone to individual character, and making it unprecedentedly emotional,
muscular, heroic, and refined, but having deepest relations to general politics'
– then are we perhaps justified in foreseeing here the advent of an enthusiasm
which shall rehabilitate those outcast instincts, by giving them a spiritual
atmosphere, an environment of recognised and healthy emotions, wherein to
expand at liberty and purge away the grossness and the madness of their pariah-
dom? This prospect, like all ideals, until they are realized in experience, may

seem fantastically visionary. Moreover, the substance of human nature is so mixed that it would perhaps be fanatical to expect from Whitman's chivalry of 'adhesiveness', a more immaculate purity than was attained by the mediaeval chivalry of 'amativeness'. Nevertheless, that mediæval chivalry, the greatest emotional product of feudalism, though it fell short of its own aspiration, bequeathed incalculable good to modern society by refining and clarifying the crudest male appetites. In like manner, this democratic chivalry, announced by Whitman, may be destined to absorb, control, and elevate those darker more mysterious, apparently abnormal appetites, which we know to be widely diffused and ineradicable in the ground-work of human nature.

Returning from the dream, the vision of a future possibility, it will, at any rate, be conceded that Whitman has founded comradeship, the enthusiasm which binds man to man in fervent love, upon a natural basis. Eliminating classical associations of corruption, ignoring the question of a guilty passion doomed by law and popular antipathy to failure, he begins anew with sound and primitive humanity. There he discovers 'a superb friendship, exalté, previously unknown'. He perceives that 'it waits, and has always been waiting, latent in all men'. His method of treatment fearless, and uncowed by any thought of evil, his touch upon the matter, chaste and wholesome and inspiring, reveal the possibility of restoring in all innocence to human life a portion of its alienated or unclaimed moral birthright.

It were as well to close upon this note. The half, as the Greeks said, is more than the whole; and the time has not yet come to raise the question whether the love of man for man shall be elevated through a hitherto unapprehended chivalry to nobler powers, even as the barbarous love of man for woman once was. This question at the present moment is deficient in actuality. The world cannot be invited to entertain it....He helped to free me from many conceits and pettinesses to which academical culture is liable. He opened my eyes to the beauty, goodness and greatness which may be found in all worthy human beings, the humblest and the highest. He made me respect personality more than attainments or position in the world. Through him, I stripped my soul of social prejudices. Through him, I have been able to fraternize in comradeship with men of all classes and several races, irrespective of their caste, creed, occupation and special training. To him I owe some of the best friends I now can claim – sons of the soil, hard workers, 'natural and nonchalant', 'powerful uneducated' persons....What he has done for me, I feel he will do for others – for each and all if those who take counsel with him, and seek from him a solution of difficulties differing in kind according to the temper of the individual – if only they approach him in the right spirit of confidence and openmindedness.

The Eagle Street College

John Johnston (1852–1927), a Scottish GP who practised in Bolton from the 1870s, and who was actively involved in the development of the St John's Ambulance Brigade, was a key member of an informal reading group which met at 14 Eagle Street, Bolton, the home of another member, J. W. Wallace. From 1885 onwards those meetings became regular and formal and the members termed themselves the Eagle Street College. The original spur for the reading group was a shared passion for the writings and philosophy of Walt Whitman, which persisted with the more formal establishment of the group. The College was described by Edward Carpenter in *My Days and Dreams* (1916) as 'the ardent little coterie of Bolton, Lancashire, who for many years celebrated [Whitman's] birthday with decorations of lilac boughs and blossoms, songs, speeches and recitations and the passing of loving cups to his memory'. Amongst the surviving documents relating to the Eagle Street coterie are a mass of diaries, manuscripts and published poetry by Johnston, accounts of many of the birthday celebrations and copies of poems recited at them, and a number of objects sent by Whitman to his Bolton fan club, including his stuffed canary. The fervour with which the coterie, who were mainly but not exclusively male, write about and to Whitman, is markedly lacking in any restraint or sense of the need for restraint, and their ideas and works were not in any way intended to be private, but rather demonstrate a proselytizing zeal. Johnston's diaries, indeed, seem not to be a purely private matter since they show considerable evidence of editing (improvements in expression, corrections etc.) and also signs of being addressed to an audience, and while they were never published, he did donate them to the Reference Department of Bolton Public Library in 1924. They now reside in the Archives and Local Studies Department of Bolton Central Library.

John Johnston

From the Manuscript Diaries, Monday 5 May 1890

During the last two years the greatest satisfaction of my life has been the existence of the College & what it has been able to do. These weekly meetings have been reunions of old friends – & there are no friends like old friends – some of them life-long friends but all of long standing. Our meetings have not

218

only been merely for the purpose of general converse & pleasant intercourse but they have been spent profitably I think. Not only have they cemented the ties of a friendship which in the case of some of us will last until life's end but they have been profitable to us intellectually & more especially spiritually. We have discussed some of the deepest problems of life and thought & being on such an intimate footing we have been able to speak our minds freely & sympathetically without fear of misconceptions on the part of those who differed from us & who could not see eye to eye with us....One great lesson we must all have acquired is a large hearted toleration for the opinions of others wh. differed from our own & wh. were held by men for whom we could not but hold the highest respect and esteem.[186]

From the Manuscript Diaries, Tuesday 26 August 1890

More communications from Walt Whitman! Today JWW has received two newspapers, a newspaper cutting and a post card from him – the latter as follows.

'Aug 15 '90
As I write am getting a little uneasy at not hearing of my Dr J. no doubt he is all right & back there. Send me a word <u>immediately</u> on getting this – he did not visit Dr Bucke, Canada (wh. Dr B regrets much). I send you my last screed in <u>Critic</u> NY (have sent other papers too). Am getting along fairly considering – memories and best respects to you & all

Walt Whitman.'

JWW came specially down from Adlington at night to shew me this & the papers & to tell me he had sent a cablegram to Walt acknowledging ~~the papers~~ their receipt & to assure him of my welfare & to tell him that letters were en route. He was in a very excited condition – the effect of Whitmans communications – and was full of admiration for the deep interest the post card shewed he had in me. 'Nothing' he said 'could be more tenderly touching & beautiful than the ~~fatherly~~ paternal concern it evinced. Your own father could not have been more lovingly solicitous about you & it is just another proof of how much he must have enjoyed your visit. I know of nothing more beautiful. The more I think of it the more deeply am I impressed with your wonderful good fortune & with the splendid manner in which you were treated. It far surpassed anything I ever dreamt of. I can think of nothing but Whitman until my ~~head~~ brain which is teter enough at the best is in a whirl. He's <u>killing</u> me!'

219

Nothing that has ever happened to me has given me greater pleasure than that post card. It shews that Walt must have regarded me as something ~~far~~ more than an ordinary visitor for he says that he is getting uneasy at not hearing from me and asks JWW to send him word <u>immediately</u>.

The dear old man! How I love & honour him for that & all the other kindnesses which he lavished upon me. As day after day goes on I am the more deeply impressed with the magnificent & at the same time homely hearty & spontaneous reception he gave & emptying of himself as it were into me, loading me with gifts & messages for me & my friend until my portmanteau fairly overflowed & filling my heart with his great love.

Truly has he acted up to his own words 'When I give I give myself.'

He has given me <u>himself</u> & enriched my life with treasures.

From 'A week-end visit to Edward Carpenter Aug 28th–30th 1915'

To my suggestion that the two [Walt Whitman and Mrs Gilchrist] were in love with each other, EC said it might have been so in the case of Mrs Gilchrist & that Walt entertained a very high admiration & regard for her.

In a letter he (EC) had read from Mrs Calder – formerly Mrs O'Connor – she confirmed the story as to Whitman's paternity; but she doubted the existence of more than one child – his statement as to his having had 'six children' being probably exaggeration, through his calling possible grandchildren 'children' – there being no sufficient time in that obscure period of his to allow for the truth of so many children. 'And said EC 'at the time he made the statement – in his letter to Symonds – he was faced with the desirability of the charge – which he characterised as 'damnable' – then being brought against L of G. 'In addition to this the old man's memory was probably none of the best – and we know what tricks memory can play upon us all at times.'[187]

W.T. Hawkins, read at Walt Whitman's birthday celebration, 31 May 1906, from *Annandale Observer*, 15 June 1906

Once more we meet – as pilgrims at a shrine,
  To reassert our Comradeship sincere;
Around the Master's head a wreath t'entwine,

Then lay it lovingly upon his bier.

To dear, dead Walt, who, being dead, yet speaks,
    In us and through us with the same old tone;
Breathing his message, as the ripple breaks
    Upon the shingle, kissing sand and stone.

That message, which the world has scarcely heard,
    Or having heard it, has not understood;
His life-thought centred in one sacred word,
    The password of true Comrades – 'Brotherhood!'

We leave behind the traffic of the mart,
    We steal away from busy, bustling street;
As Comrades, Brothers, standing heart to heart,
    Breathing the fragrance of his presence sweet.

His birthday! The one day of all the year
    Kept in remembrance by his comrades true;
We chant no mournful dirge, we shed no tear,
    But joy that we our spirits thus renew.

'Joy shipmate, joy!' There sounds his cheery hail!
    No longer troubles vex, or cares annoy;
Do riches flee us? Do we fear to fail?
    List to the good, glad cry – 'Joy, shipmate, joy!'

Have men betrayed us? He will not betray!
    Have Comrades let us in the hour of need?
They were no Comrades, let them pass away;
    The slaves of passion, prejudice, or greed.

Hark to the glad old cry that greets us still!
    Sounding above the ocean's mighty roar;
What other message can our bosoms thrill
    Like that grand greeting from Paumanok's shore?

Comrades, join hands! So shall we symbolise
    The love that binds us with its golden chain.
True Comrades; linked in love! Though all else dies,
    Let this sweet bond of Comradeship remain.

Amid the turmoil of the striving days,
    One night each year at least we'll call a halt,

And to his memory our glasses raise,
   And drink the same old toast – 'Here's to you, Walt!'

John Addington Symonds to J. W. Wallace, 19 December 1892

Dear Mr Wallace

I returned a short while since from my long absence in England & Italy. Here[188] I found the note-books of your American journey, which are full of a deep & pathetic interest. I am reading them with care, & will return them duly registered.

I have nearly finished writing a 'Study of Walt Whitman', the thinker & poet, not the man. It is an attempt to know the relations of Religion, Science, Personality, Sex, Comradeship, Democracy, Literature, in his writings. I think I shall have to publish it separately as a little book.

I am still perplexed about the real drift of 'Calamus'. Whitman once wrote me a very emphatic letter, repudiating the idea that under any circumstances the passionate attachment between friend and friend could pass into physical relations. Yet there are certainly a large number of men born with 'homosexual' tendencies, who could not fail, while reading 'Calamus', to think their own emotions justified by Whitman.

The subject is of considerable interest & importance for students of W. W. I have lately been obliged to read the most recent French, German, & Italian researches into the phenomenon, in course of writing my new life of Michelangelo, who was certainly born with innate sexual inversion. I had not any idea what a large part this anomaly plays in modern life.

By the way, I have noticed in some newspapers that a prosecution was going on at Bolton under what is called 'Labouchere's Clause'. Do you think that you or Dr Johnston could give me any exact information regarding it?[189] Whatever view the psychologist may take of homosexual passions, every citizen of a free country must feel that Labouchere's Clause is a disgrace to legislation, because of its vague terminology & plain incitement to false accusations.

This of course is not a matter of great moment. Still, if you can send me a report, you would oblige me.

Pray give my kindest regards to Dr Johnston, & believe me very sincerely yours

John Addington Symonds

If you have any advice to give me regarding the publication of my 'Study of W. Whitman', or any suggestions to make about 'Calamus', I shall be grateful to you for them.

P. S. Since writing the enclosed, I spent the whole morning reading through your notes, & now I want to tell you what a profound & genial impression they have made on me. I seem to feel the whole of the Camden circle quite as old friends, & to have gained a vivid presentment of them to the inner eye. But what is even more, I am immersed in a definite atmosphere of friendliness, essential kindness, fine brotherly benevolence. Of course some of Whitman's own spoken words are very pregnant, & throw to a certain extent fresh light upon his works. I have been so free as to jot down a few phrases: & these, if you gave permission, might, I think, be used with profit to authorize the views I have taken in my 'Study of W. W.' on certain points. But I will most assuredly not do so without sanction from yourself.

It seems to me that you & other friends, to whom I feel linked in bonds of sympathy with W. W., must regard me as cold, irresponsive, apathetic. About him to some extent – & also about the kindness you have shown me.

But you must remember in what a huge mass of study & literature this matter of Whitman is for me of necessity embedded. Also, I am alone, quite alone here, in all that concerns him. I have as yet nowhere found men of my own pursuits & condition who sympathized with me upon this point – I mean, found through personal society and contact.

So make excuses for me, & believe that my belief in Whitman is very permanent & real, if possibly less enthusiastic & exclusive than some of his younger disciples might desire.

Edward Carpenter, from *Some Friends of Walt Whitman: A Study in Sex Psychology*, c. 1898

In the 1860 edition of *Leaves of Grass* there is a poem (p. 355, of that edition) written on the occasion of his desertion or betrayal by someone whom he loved very dearly, which is almost painful to read on account of the weight of feeling with which it is charged. In later editions this and one other similar poem are excised and omitted – probably, I should say, on account of that very weight of feeling which they reveal (for Whitman – great artist that he was –

could never bear to have anything excessive or unbalanced in his work), though to us that weight of feeling makes them all the more indispensable and precious. Who that 'someone' was to whom Walt Whitman was, for the time being, so devoted, we do not know; but the internal evidence points conclusively to a *man* friend; and some of the points to which I shall refer presently make the situation easier to understand.

The poem in question is as follows: –

Hours continuing long, sore and heavy-hearted,
Hours of the dusk, when I withdraw to a lonesome and unfrequented spot,
seating myself, leaning my face in my hands;
Hours sleepless, deep in the night, when I go forth, speeding swiftly the
country roads or through the city streets, or pacing miles and miles, stifling
plaintive cries;
Hours discouraged, distracted – for the one I cannot content myself without,
soon I saw him, content himself without me;
Hours when I am forgotten (O weeks and months are passing, but I believe I
am never to forget!)
Sullen and suffering hours! (I am ashamed – but it is useless – I am what I am);
Hours of my torment – I wonder if other men have the like, out of the like
feelings?
Is there even one like me – distracted – his friend, his lover lost to him?
Is he, too, as I am now? Does he still rise in the morning, dejected, thinking
who is lost to him? and at night awaking, thinking who is lost?
Does he, too, harbor his friendship silent and endless? harbor his anguish and
passion?
Does some stray reminder, or the casual mention of a name, bring the fit back
upon him, taciturn and deprest?
Does he see himself reflected in me? In these hours does he see the face of his
hours reflected?

No one can doubt the intensity of feeling and the anguish of mind from which that poem sprang. But in this case we see that that flood of emotion was roused by what some folk would call an unusual passion – the passion namely for another *man*. We in this Society,[190] who have studied the by-ways of Sex-psychology, are not surprised at this. We know now that although love between persons of opposite sex is as a rule the most powerful and absorbing, it is by no means always so, and that there are cases of overwhelming passion between those of the same sex. The whole of that section of *Leaves of Grass* which is called *Calamus* illustrates this fact, and it would seem that Whitman by collecting out of the great mass of his poems just this group was able to illustrate and give expression to what we should now call homo sexual passion – which passion, though at that time ignored and unacknowledged by the world, was burning fiercely within him and pressing for deliverance.

The whole section *Calamus* is, as I say, occupied with this subject, and to those who wish to gain an insight into Whitman's inner nature I strongly recommend a reading through of that section. At the present moment it may suffice to quote two or three of the poems contained in it. Here, for instance, is one entitled *A Glimpse*: –

A glimpse through an interstice caught,
Of a crowd of workmen and drivers in a bar-room around the stove late of a winter night, and I unremark'd seated in a corner,
Of a youth who loves me and whom I love, silently approaching and seating himself near, that he may hold me by the hand,
A long while amid the noises of coming and going, of drinking and oath and smutty jest,
There we are, content, happy in being together, speaking little, perhaps not a word.

Or this: –

Earth, my likeness,
Though you look so impassive, ample and spheric there,
I now suspect that is not all;
I now suspect there is something fierce in you eligible to burst forth.
For an athlete is enamour'd of me, and I of him,
But towards him there is something fierce and terrible in me eligible to burst forth,
I dare not tell it in words, not even in these songs.

John Addington Symonds, as we all know, wrote a great deal about Whitman, and about the homo sexual temperament generally, manifested both in the Greek world and in modern times, and his work has been most valuable, though it has been somewhat vitiated – and its value decreased – by a certain lack of solidity and self-reliance in Symonds's nature. Symonds's visits to England were but rare, and for myself I actually met him only once – though we corresponded occasionally; but I have no doubt at all about his attitude to homo sexuality. He shared the temperament completely, and every-thing which threw light on the subject interested him. But in his expressions about it he vacillated somewhat. (We must remember that he wrote at a time when people were more hesitating and less outspoken on such subjects than they are now.) And while sometimes he wrote with ardour as almost a propa-gandist of the faith, at other times he hedged and went backwards on himself as one alarmed at his own temerity. This change of attitude is for instance very conspicuous in the last pages of his *A Problem in Greek Ethics*, for while throughout the body of that *brochure* he handles the question magnificently and lays out his description of the Greek customs like one intent on arriving at an accurate statement of them and with no *parti pris* on either side, in those last pages he almost runs away from himself, and might be accused by an unfriendly critic of throwing dust in the eyes of the reader and deliberately causing the latter to mistake his real meaning. When I say this I am sure my audience will not charge me with unfriendly sentiments towards Symonds, for whose memory I have the greatest respect; but this is a case in which absolute truthfulness must not be dispensed with, and I feel sure that by his occasional vacillation and timidity Symonds did as a matter of fact do a certain amount of injury to the cause which really lay so close to his heart – the investigation of homo sexuality, not as a sin or a crime, but as a natural phenomenon.

The same trouble may be observed in Symonds's dealing through corre-spondence with Whitman himself and (consequently) in his book about Whitman.[104] After reading and studying for some time the group of poems entitled *Calamus*, Symonds felt uncertain (as no doubt many other people have felt uncertain) how far the natural inferences from these poems about physical relationships among men were distinctly contemplated and envisaged by the author. He therefore wrote to Whitman – not once only but several times – posing this question. I think most people will admit that this was a very foolish and mistaken thing to do. No one cares to be pinned down to a state-ment in black and white of his views on a difficult and complex subject. Least of all was Whitman open to such treatment. He hated snap questions and snip answers generally, knowing how seldom such things arrive anywhere near the real truth. But here was Symonds putting him in a very awkward position. He, Whitman, could hardly with any truthfulness deny any knowledge or contem-plation of such inferences; but if on the other hand he took what we might call the reasonable line, and said that, while not *advocating* abnormal relations in any way, he of course made allowance for possibilities in that direction and the occasional development of such relations, why, he knew that the moment he said such a thing he would have the whole American Press at his heels, snarling and slandering, and distorting his words in every possible way. Things are pretty bad here in this country; but in the States (in such matters) they are ten times worse. Symonds ought to have known and allowed for this, but apparently did not do so. In the end Whitman wrote a letter (which is quoted in part by Symonds) in which he expressly repudiates, disowns, and brands as damnable all 'morbid inferences' which may be drawn from the gospel of comradeship. That of course was a perfectly safe and correct line to take, but it does not bring us much further on our way, as it still leaves open the question what inferences *are* really morbid and what are not so. It is evident that this ill-judged letter annoyed and irritated the poet – and very naturally – and I (for one) can only regret Symonds ever wrote it; for the incident has given a handle to the reactionary folk and a push in the direction of Comstock and all his crew. We must remember too, how different the atmosphere on all these matters was then (especially in the U.S.A.) from what it is now in the centres of modern culture, and in places like Oxford and Cambridge and London, where you can nowadays talk as freely as you like, and where sex variations and even abnormalities are almost a stock subject of conversation.

Personally, having known Whitman fairly intimately, I do not lay great stress on that letter. Whitman was in his real disposition the most candid, but also the most cautious of men. An attempt was made on this occasion to drive him into some sort of confession of his real nature; and it may be that that very effort aroused all his resistance and caused him to hedge more than ever....I say he was a passionate lover of mankind. But although I have just used the word (mankind) in its more general and vague application as to the human race at large I must now explain that I mean it also and particularly in its application to one section of the race. There is no doubt in my mind that Walt Whitman was before all a lover of the Male. His thoughts turned towards Men first and foremost, and it is no good disguising that fact. A thousand passages in his poems might be quoted in support of that contention – passages in which the male, perfectly naturally and without affectation, figures as the main object of attention, and as the ideal to which his thoughts are directed. These passages are convincing, I think, in their scope, their power and their sincerity. In such a case as that it is useless to rush in with some tag of warning or talk about propriety or morality. What we have to do first is to establish a *fact*, and then afterwards to analyse and discuss that fact; and it seems to me – though of course I may be wrong – that the plain fact is his preoccupation, throughout his poems, with the male rather than with the female....Thousands of people date from their first reading of them *a new era in their lives* just as decidedly as they might date a similar era from the arrival of their first child. Thousands date from the reading of them a new inspiration and an extraordinary access of vitality carrying their activities and energies into new channels. How *far* this process may go we hardly yet know, but that it is one of the factors of future evolution we can hardly doubt. I mean that the loves of men towards each other – and similarly the loves of women for each other – may become factors of future human evolution just as necessary and well-recognised as the ordinary loves which lead to the birth of children and the propagation of the race.

Textual footnotes

1 'Homosexual', generally used in scientific works, is of course a bastard word. 'Homogenic' has been suggested, as being from two roots, both Greek, *i.e., homos* 'same', and *genos* 'sex'.

2 *Athenaeus*, xiii., c. 78.

3 See Plutarch *Eroticus,* xvii.

4 See *Natural History of Man* by J. G. Wood. Vol: 'Africa', p. 419.

5 See also Livingstone's *Expedition to the Zambesi*, Murray, 1865, p. 148.

6 Though these two plays, except for some quotations, are lost.

7 Mantagazza and Lombroso. See Albert Moll, *Conträre Sexualempfinding,* second ed., p. 36.

8 Though in translations this fact is often by pious fraudulence disguised.

9 W. Pater's *Renaissance*, pp. 8–16.

10 Among *prose* writers of this period Montaigne, whose treatment of the subject is enthusiastic and unequivocal, should not be overlooked. See Hazlitt's *Montaigne*, ch. xxvii.

11 I may be excused for quoting here the sonnet No. 54, from J. A. Symonds' translation of the sonnets of Michel Angelo:

> From thy fair face I learn, O my loved lord,
> That which no mortal tongue can rightly say;
> The soul imprisoned in her house of clay,
> Holpen by Thee to God hath often soared:
> And though the vulgar, vain, malignant horde
> Attribute what their grosser wills obey,
> Yet shall this fervent homage that I pay,
> This love, this faith, pure joys for us afford.
> Lo, all the lovely things we find on earth,
> Resemble for the soul that rightly sees,
> That source of bliss divine which gave us birth;
> Nor have we first-fruits or remembrances
> Of heaven elsewhere. Thus, loving loyally,
> I rise to God, and make death sweet by thee.

The labours of von Scheffler, followed by J. A. Symonds, have now pretty conclusively established the pious frauds of the nephew, and the fact that the love-poems of the elder Michel Angelo were, for the most part, written to male friends.

12 See an interesting paper in W. Pater's *Renaissance*.

13 See pamphlet, *Sex-Love,* p. 7 [by Edward Carpenter].

14 As indeed the majority of people have a difficulty in appreciating the inner feeling of most love.

15 From Uranos – because the celestial love was the daughter of Uranos (see Plato's *Symposium*, speech of Pausanias).

16 With regard to the number of these *quite exclusive* homosexuals (supposably born so) estimates vary, from one man in every 50 to one in every 500. See Moll. *Conträre Sexual-empfinding,* second edn., p. 75.

17 Though there is no doubt a general *tendency* towards femininity of type in the male Urning, and towards masculinity in the female.

18 *Gli amori degli uomini.*

19 *Psychopathia Sexualis*, seventh ed., p. 227.

20 *Ibid*: pp. 229 and 258.

21 'How deep congenital sex-inversion roots may be gathered from the fact that the pleasure-dream of the male Urning has to do with male persons, and of the female with females.' (Krafft-Ebing *P. S.* seventh ed., p. 228.)

22 Jowett's *Plato* (second ed.) Vol. II., p. 30.

23 Jowett, op. cit., Vol II., p. 130.

24 It is interesting, too, to find that Walt Whitman, who certainly had the homogenic instinct highly developed, was characterized by his doctor, W. B. Drinkard, as having 'the most natural habits, bases, and organization he had ever met with or ever seen' in any man. *In re Walt Whitman*, p. 115.

25 *Conträre Sexual-empfinding*, second ed., p. 269.

26 See *Sex-Love*, p. 23.

27 'Though then before my own conscience I cannot reproach myself, and though I must certainly reject the judgement of the world about us, yet I suffer greatly. In very truth I have injured no one, and I hold my love in its nobler activity for just as holy as that of normally disposed men, but under the unhappy fate that allows us neither sufferance nor recognition I suffer often more than my life can bear.' – (Extract from a letter given by Krafft-Ebing.)

28 'The truth is that we can no more explain the inverted sex-feeling than we can the normal impulse; all the attempts at explanation of these things, and of Love, are defective.' (Moll, second ed. p. 253.)

29 See *Sex-Love*, p. 8.

30 See *Marriage*, p. 7.

31 See *In the Key of Blue* by J. A. Symonds (Published by Elkin Matthews, 1893).

32 Jowett's *Plato*, second ed. vol. ii. p. 33.

33 Prose-works of Richard Wagner, translated by W. A. Ellis.

34 The emphasis is on the word *egoistic.*

35 Whose tomb on account of his attachment to Iolaus was a place where Comrades swore troth to each other (Plutarch on *Love*, section xvii).

36 *Symposium*: speech of Socrates.

37 It is interesting in this connection to notice the extreme fervour, almost of romance, of the bond which often unites lovers of like sex over a long period of years, in an unfailing tenderness of treatment and consideration towards each other, equal to that shown in the most successful marriages. The love of many such men, says Moll (p. 119), 'developed in youth lasts at times the whole life through. I know of such men, who had not seen their first love for years, even decades, and who yet on meeting showed the old fire of their first passion. In other cases a close love-intimacy will last unbroken for many years.'

38 J. A. Symonds.

39 See *Woman*, p. 11, etc.

40 Though, inconsistently enough, making no mention of females.

41 Dr. Moll maintains (second ed., pp. 314, 315) that if familiarities between those of the same sex are made illegal, as immoral, self-abuse ought to much more to be so made.

42 Though it is doubtful whether the marriage-laws even do this!

43 In France since the adoption of the Code Napoleon, sexual inversion is tolerated under the same restrictions as normal sexuality; and according to Carlier, formerly Chief of the French Police, Paris is not more depraved in this matter than London. Italy in 1889 also adopted the principles of the Code Napoleon on this point.

44 This detail especially excited the veteran's curiosity. The reason proved to be that the scrotum of the unmutilated boy could be used as a kind of bridle for directing the movements of the animal. I find nothing of the kind mentioned in the Sotadical literature of Greece and Rome, although the same cause might be expected everywhere to have the same effect. But in Mirabeau (Kadhesch) a grand seigneur moderne, when his valet-de-chambre de confiance proposes to provide him with women instead of boys, exclaims, 'Des femmes! eh! c'est comme si tu me servais un gigot sans manche' [*Oeuvres érotiques*: 'Women! It's as if you served me a leg of mutton without a neck']. See also infra for 'Les poids du tisserand' [lit. the weight of the weaver].

45 See *Falconry in the Valley of the Indus*, London, John Van Voorst, 1852.

46 Submitted to Government on Dec. 31, '47 and March 2, '48, they were printed in *Selections from the Records of the Government of India*, Bombay, New Series, No. xvii, Part 2, 1855. These are (1) Notes on the Population of Sind, etc., and (2) Brief Notes on the Modes of Intoxication, etc., written in collaboration with my late friend Assistant-Surgeon John E. Stocks, whose early death was a sore loss to scientific botany.

47 Glycon the Courtesan in *Athenaeus*. xiii. 84 declares that 'boys are handsome only when they resemble women;' and so the Learned Lady in *The Nights* (vol. v, 160) declares 'Boys are likened to girls because folks say, Yonder boy is like a girl.' For the superior physical beauty of the human male compared with the female, see *The Nights*, vol. iv. 15; and the boy's voice before it breaks excels that of any diva.

48 'Mascula' from the priapiscus, the over-development of clitoris (the veretrum muliebre, in Arabic Abu Tartur, habens cristam [the womanly parts have a cocks-comb]) which enabled her to play the man. Sappho (nat. 612 B.C.) has been retoillée like Mary Stuart, La Brinvilliers, Marie Antoinette and a host of feminine names which have a savour not of sanctity. Maximus of Tyre (Dissertations. xxiv.) declares that the Eros of Sappho was Socratic and the Gyrinna and Atthis were as Alcibiades and Charmides to Socrates: Ovid, who could consult documents now lost, takes the same view in the Letter of Sappho to Phaon and in Tristia ii. 365 [actually ii. 265].

Lesbia quid docuit Sappho nisi amare puellas? [What did Lesbian Sappho teach except the love of girls?]

Suidas supports Ovid. Longinus eulogises the ερωτικη μανια [erotic mania] (a term applied only to carnal love) of the far-famed Ode to Atthis:

Ille mi par esse Deo videtur...
Heureux! qui près de toi pour toi seule soupire...
(Blest as th' immortal gods is he, etc.)

By its love symptoms, suggesting that possession is the sole cure for passion, Erasistratus discovered the love of Antiochus for Stratonice. Mure (*History of Greek Literature*, 1850) speaks of the Ode to Aphrodite (Frag. 1) as 'one in which the whole volume of Greek literature offers the most powerful concentration into one brilliant focus of the modes in which amatory concupiscence can display itself'. But Bernhardy, Bode, Richter, K.O. Müller and esp. Welcker have made Sappho a model of purity, much like some of our dull wits who have converted Shakespeare, that most debauched genius, into a good British bourgeois.

49 The Arabic Sahhakah, the Tractatrix of Subigitatrix, who has been noticed in vol. iv. 134. Hence to Lesbianise (λεσβιζειν) and tribassare (τριβεσθαι); the former applied to the love of woman for woman and the latter to its mécanique: this is either natural, as friction of the labia and insertion of the clitoris when unusually developed; or artificial by means of the fascinum, the artificial penis (the Persian 'Maya jang'); the patte de chat [cat's paw], the banana-fruit and a multitude of other succedanea [positions, movements]. As this feminine perversion is only glanced at in *The Nights* I need hardly enlarge upon the subject.

50 Plato (*Symposium*) is probably mystical when he accounts for such passions by there being in the beginning three species of humanity, men, women, and men-women or androgynes. When the latter were destroyed by Zeus for rebellion, the two others were individually divided into equal parts. Hence each division seeks its other half in the same sex; the primitive man prefers men and the primitive woman women. C'est beau, but – is it true? The idea was probably derived from Egypt which supplied the Hebrews with androgynic humanity; and thence it passed to extreme India, where Shiva as Ardhanari was male on one side and female on the other side of the body, combining paternal and maternal qualities and functions. The first creation of humans (Genesis i. 27) was hermaphrodite (= Hermes and Venus) masculum et foeminam creavit eos – male and female created He them – on the sixth day, with the command to increase and multiply (ibid. v. 28) while Eve the woman was created subsequently. Meanwhile, say certain Talmudists, Adam carnally copulated with all races of animals. See L'Anandryne in Mirabeau's *Erotika Biblion*, where Antoinette Bourgnon laments the undoubling which disfigured the work of God, producing monsters incapable of independent self-reproduction like the vegetable kingdom.

51 *De la Femme*, Paris, 1827.

52 *Die Lustseuche des Alterhum's*, Halle, 1839.

53 See his exhaustive article on (Grecian) 'Paederastie' in the *Allgemeine Encyclopaedie* of Ersch and Gruber, Leipzig, Brockhaus, 1837. He carefully traces it through the several states, Dorians, Aeolians, Ionians, the Attic cities and those of Asia Minor. For these details I must refer my readers to M. Meier; a full account of these would fill a volume not the section of an essay.

54 Against which see Henri Estienne, *Apologie pour Hérodote*, a society satire of xvith century, lately reprinted by Liseux.

55 In Sparta the lover was called εισπνηλας or εισπνηλος and the beloved as in Thessaly αιτας or αιτης.

56 The more I study religions the more I am convinced that man never worshipped anything but himself. Zeus, who became Jupiter, was an ancient king, according to the Cretans, who were entitled liars because they showed his burial-place. From a deified ancestor he would become a local god, like the Hebrew Jehovah as opposed to Chemosh of Moab; the name would gain amplitude by long time and distant travel and the old island chieftain would end in becoming the Demiurgus. Ganymede (who possibly gave rise to the old Lat. 'Catamitus') was probably some fair Phrygian boy ('son of Tros') who in process of time became a symbol of the wise man seized by the eagle (perspicacity) to be raised among the Immortals; and the chaste myth simply signified that only the prudent are loved by the gods. But it rotted with age as do all things human. For the Pederastia of the Gods see Bayle [Pierre Bayle, *Dictionary*] under Chrysippe.

57 See *Dissertation sur les idées morales des Grecs et sur les danger de lire Platon*. Par M. Audé, Bibliophile, Rouen, Lemonnyer, 1879. This is the pseudonym of the late Octave Delepierre, who published with Gay, but not the Editio Princeps – which, if I remember rightly, contains much more matter.

58 The phrase of J. Matthias Gesner, *Comm. Reg. Soc. Gottingen* i. 1–32. It was founded upon Erasmus' 'Sancte Socrate, ora pro nobis', and the article was translated by M. Alcide Bonmaire, Paris, Liseux, 1877.

59 The subject has employed many a pen, *e.g. Alcibiade Fanciullo a Scola*, D. P. A. (supposed to be Pietro Aretino – ad captandum?), Oranges par Juann VVart, 1652: small square 8vo. of pp. 102, including 3 preliminary pp. and at end an unpaged leaf with 4 sonnets, almost Venetian, by V. M. There is a re-impression of the same date, a small 12mo. of longer format, pp. 124 with pp. 2 for sonnets: in 1682 the Imprimerie Raçon printed 102 copies in 8vo. of pp. iv.-108, and in 1863 it was condemned by the police as a liber spurcissimus atque execrandus de criminis sodomici laude et arte [a very dirty and detestable book for its praise and knowledge of the crime of sodomy]. This work produced *Alcibiade Enfant à l'école*, traduit pour le première fois de l'Italien de Ferrante Pallavicini, Amsterdam, chez l'Ancien Pierre Marteau, mdcclxvi. Pallavicini (nat. 1618), who wrote against Rome, was beheaded, aet. 26 (March 5, 1644) at Avignon in 1644 by the vengeance of the Barberini: he was a bel esprit déréglé, nourri d'études antiques [an immoderate wit, nourished by ancient studies] and a Member of the Academia Degl' Incognito. His peculiarities are shown by his *Opere Scelte*, 2 vols.12mo, Villafranca, mdclxiii.; these do not include *Alcibiade Fanciullo*, a dialogue between Philotimus and Alcibiades which seems to be a mere skit at the Jesuits and their Péché philosophique [philosophical sin]. Then came the *Dissertation sur l'Alcibiade fanciullo a scola*, traduit de l'Italien de Giambattista Baseggio et accompagnée de notes et d'une post-face par un bibliophile français (M. Gustave Brunet, Librarian of Bordeaux), Paris. J. Gay, 1861 – an octavo of pp. 78 (paged), 254 copies. The same Baseggio printed in 1850 his *Disquisizioni* (23 copies) and claims for F. Pallavicini the authorship of *Alcibiades* which the Manuel du Libraire wrongly attributes to M. Girol. Adda in 1859. I have heard of but not seen the *Amator fornaceus, amator ineptus* (Palladii, 1633) supposed by some to be the origin of *Alcibiade Fanciullo*; but most critics consider it a poor and insipid production.

60 The word is from ναρκη, numbness, torpor, narcotism: the flowers, being loved by the infernal gods, were offered to the Furies. Narcissus and Hippolytus are often assumed as types of morosa voluptas [hard to please in sexual intercourse], masturbation and clitorisation for nymphomania: certain mediaeval writers found in the former a type of the Saviour; and Mirabeau a representation of the androgynous or first Adam: to me Narcissus suggests the Hindu Vishnu absorbed in the contemplation of his own perfections.

61 The verse of Ovid is parallel'd by the song of Al-Zahir al-Jazari (*Ibn Khall*. iii. 720).

Illium impuberum amaverunt mares; puberum feminae.
Gloria Deo! nunquam amatoribus carebit.

['Men loved him when he was a boy, girls when he was a man. Glory be to God! He shall never lack lovers'; I have been unable to trace this quotation.]

62 The venerable society of prostitutes contained three chief classes. The first and lowest were the Dicteriads, so called from Diete (Crete) who imitated Pasiphaë, wife of Minos, in preferring a bull to a husband; above them was the middle class, the Aleutridae who were the Almahs or professional musicians, and the aristocracy were represented by the Hetairai, whose wit and learning enabled them to adorn more than one page of Grecian history. The grave Solon, who had studied in Egypt, established a vast Dicterion (Philemon in his Delphica), or bordel, whose proceeds swelled the revenue of the Republic.

63 This and Saint Paul (Romans i. 27) suggested to Caravaggio his picture of St Rosario (in the museum of the Grand Duke of Tuscany), showing a circle of thirty men turpiter

ligati ['foully joined'; no such painting appears in any catalogue of the works of Caravaggio or of his school].

64 See the marvellously absurd description of the glorious 'Dead Sea' in the Purchas v. 84.

65 Jehovah here is made to play an evil part by destroying men instead of teaching them better. But, 'Nous faisons les Dieux à notre image et nous portons dans le ciel ce que nous voyons sur la terre' [We make the gods in our own image and we carry to the heavens that which we see on earth]. The idea of Yahweh, or Yah is palpably Egyptian, the Ankh or ever-living One: the etymon, however, was learned at Babylon and is still found among the cuneiforms.

66 Of this peculiar character Ibn Khallikan remarks (ii. 43), 'There were four poets whose works clearly contraried their character. Abu al-Atahiyah wrote pious poems himself being an atheist; Abu Hukayma's verses proved his impotence, yet he was more salacious than a he-goat; Mohammed ibn Hazim praised contentment, yet he was greedier than a dog; and Abu Nowas hymned the joys of sodomy, yet he was more passionate for women than a baboon.'

67 A virulently and unjustly abusive critique never yet injured its object: in fact it is generally the greatest favour an author's unfriends can bestow upon him. But to notice in a popular Review books which have been printed and not published is hardly in accordance with the established courtesies of literature. At the end of my work I propose to write a paper 'The Reviewer Reviewed' which will, amongst other things, explain the motif of the writer of the critique and the editor of the Edinburgh.

68 Maximus of Tyre, *Dissertations.*, ix.

69 See Sismondi, vol. ii. p. 324; Symonds, *Renaissance in Italy, Age of the Despots*, p. 435; Tardieu, *Attentats aux Moeurs. Les Ordures de Paris*; Sir R. Burton's *Terminal Essay* to the 'Arabian Nights'; Carlier, *Les Deux Prostitutions*, etc.

70 I say almost, because something of the same sort appeared in Persia at the time of Saadi.

71 See the law on these points in *Æschines. adv. Timarchum.*

72 Thus Aristophanes quoted above.

73 Aristophanes, *Acharnae*, 144, and *Mousa Paidiki*, 130

74 See Sir William Hamilton's *Vases*.

75 Lysias, according to Suidas, was the author of five erotic epistles addressed to young men.

76 See Aristophanes, *Plutus*, 153–159; *Birds*, 704–707. Cp. *Mousa Paidiké*, 44 239, 237. The boys made extraordinary demands upon their lovers' generosity. The curious tale told about Alcibiades points in this direction. In Crete they did the like, but also set their lovers to execute difficult tasks as Eurystheus imposed the twelve labours on Herakles.

77 Page 29.

78 *Mousa Paidiké*, 8: cp. a fragment of Crates, *Poetae Comici*, Didot, p. 83.

79 *Comici Graeci*, Didot, pp. 562, 31, 308.

80 It is curious to compare the passage in the second *Philippic* about the youth of Mark Antony with the story told by Plutarch about Alcibiades, who left the custody of his guardians for the house of Democrates.

81 See both *Lysias against Simon* and *Æschines against Timarchus.*

82 *Peace,* line 11; compare the word *Pallakion* in Plato, *Comici Graeci*, p. 261.

83 Diogones Laertius, ii. 105.

84 Plato's *Phaedo*, p. 89.

85 *Oratationes Attici*, vol. ii. p. 223.

86 See Herodotus. Maximus of Tyre tells the story (*Dissertations*, xxiv. 1) in detail. The boy's name was Actaeon, wherefore he may be compared, he says, to that other Actaeon who was torn to death by his own dogs.

87 This brief 'Conclusion' was omitted in the second edition of this book, as I conceived it might possibly mislead some of those young men into whose hands it might fall. On the whole, I have thought it best to reprint it here, with some slight changes which bring it closer to my original meaning. I have dealt more fully in *Marius the Epicurean* with the thoughts suggested by it.

88 I shall not enter into the controversy as to the interpretation of the Sonnets. The principal theories held with respect to them may be classified as follows: I. They are poems about an imaginary friendship and love; Dyce, Delius, H. Morley. II. They are partly imaginary, partly autobiographical; C. Knight, H. von Friesen, R. Simpson (On the Italian love-philosophy see Simpson's interesting 'Philosophy of Shakspere's Sonnets', Trübner, 1868.) III. They form a great allegory; Dr Barnstorff ('Schlüssel zu Shakspere's Sonnetten', 1860. Mr W. H. = Mr William Himself!), Mr Heraud ('Shakspere's Inner Life'. The young friend = Ideal Manhood), Carl Karpf. IV. They are autobiographical; (a) Mr W. H. = Henry Wriothesley (the initials reversed), Earl of Southampton: – Drake, Gervinus, Kreyssig, and others; (b) Mr W. H. = William Herbert, Earl of Pembroke: – Bright, Boaden, A. Brown, Hallam, H. Brown. V. They were partly addressed to Southampton; other sonnets were written in his name to Elizabeth Vernon; other some, to Southampton in E. Vernon's name; and subsequently the Earl of Pembroke engaged Shakspere to write sonnets on his behalf to the dark woman, Lady Rich. Of part of this theory the first suggestion was given by Mrs Jameson. It was elaborated by Mr Gerald Massey in the *Quarterly Review*, April 1864, and in his large volume 'Shakspere's Sonnets, and his Private Friends'. The peculiarity of Mr Henry Brown's interpretation ('The Sonnets of Shakspere Solved'. J. R. Smith, 1870) is, that he discovers in the sonnets an intention of Shakspere to parody or jest at the fashionable love-poetry and love-philosophy of the day. See on this subject the articles by Delius and by H. von Friesen in Shakspere Jahrbücher, vols. i and iv.; the chapter 'Shakspere's episch-lyrische Gedichte und Sonnette' in H. von. Friesen's 'Altengand und WIlliam Shakspere' (1874); and 'Der Mythus von William Shakspere', by N. Delius (Bonn, 1851), pp. 29–31. Critics whose minds are of the business-like, matter-of-fact, prosaic type cannot conceive how the poems could be autobiographical. Coleridge, on the other hand, found no difficulty in believing them to be such; and Wordsworth emphatically declares them to express Shakspere's 'own feelings in his own person.'

89 Byron's Conspiracy, *Act iii, Scene 1* (last lines).

90 This is the more remarkable, because the original of the bust was almost certainly a mask taken after death; and the bust betrays the presence of physical death, over which however life triumphs.

91 All that refers in the above paragraph to the supposed facts which underlie the Sonnets, may be taken with reserve. Only, if this portion of 'the mythus of Shakspere' be no myth but a reality, the interpretation of events in their moral aspect given above is the one borne out by the sonnets and by Shakspere's subsequent life.

92 Sonnet xx. 2.

93 Sonnet xxvi. 1.

94 Sonnet cxxvi. 9.

95 Sonnet cix. 14.

96 Sonnet i. 10.

97 Sonnet ii. 3.

98 Sonnet viii. 1.

99 Sonnet xxii. 6.

100 Sonnet xcv. 1.

101 'Drum Taps', Complete Poems, p. 247.

102 *ibid*, p. 238.

103 'Leaves of Grass', Complete Poems, p. 107. Since writing the above, I have been privileged to read a series of letters addressed by Whitman to a young man, whom I will call

P., and who was tenderly beloved by him. They throw a flood of life upon 'Calamus', and are superior to any commentary. It is greatly to be hoped that they may be published. Whitman, it seems, met P. at Washington not long before the year 1869, when the lad was about eighteen years of age. They soon became attached, Whitman's friendship being returned with at least equal warmth by P. The letters breathe a purity and simplicity of affection, a *naïveté* and reasonableness, which are very remarkable considering the unmistakable intensity of the emotion. Throughout them Whitman shows the tenderest and wisest care for his young friend's welfare, helps him in material ways, and bestows upon him the best advice, the heartiest encouragement, without betraying any sign of patronage or preaching. Illness soon attacked Walt. He retired to Camden, and P., who was employed as 'baggage-master on the freight-trains' of a railway, was for long unable to visit him. There is something very wistful in the words addressed from a distance by the ageing poet to this 'son of responding kisses'. I regret that we do not possess P.'s answers. Yet, probably, to most readers, they would not appear highly interesting; for it is clear he was only an artless and uncultured workman.

104 *Walt Whitman: a Study*, by John Addington Symonds. London: George Routledge & Sons. (No date.)

5 LOVE

From Tennyson's *In Memoriam* of 1850 to Edward Carpenter's *Towards Democracy* of 1905, there is a language for love between men which appears in the form of intense, emotional friendship that can fulfil the individual. It is often mysterious, spiritual, almost always non-sexual, but often with strong elements of muscular sensualism, a celebration of the physical presence of the beloved object, whether a hiking companion or a goalkeeper. These works are most seemingly straightforward where they name the object of the love as 'friend' or 'Friend', an entirely legitimate relationship being implied by that label, which has no overtones of anything untoward. The slightly more hearty 'comrade' (or 'Comrade'), with its overtones of socialistic labouring-together, permits an element of physical camaraderie, since it is used literally or by association in relation to work and sport. Thus comrades are men doing manly things with other men, and no reference need be made to absent women. Friends are honourable, loyal, thoroughly English, engaged in non-domestic endeavour and extra-domestic duties. An interesting exception to the non-appearance of heterosexuality in these texts is the very late friendship poem 'Alec', where the relationship between the men will be ended with their inevitable marriages, a thing to be mourned.

But the love poems written between men generally depict either relationships that have failed or are about to fail, or relationships that can never be. Most commonly this takes the form of non-communication and non-mutuality of desires. The poet looks on from afar, expressing voyeuristic longing that can never be satisfied, because the beloved object does not know or cannot know what they feel. Alternatively, there are the poems which refer to the friend as strange, unknown, unfamiliar, as someone either not yet met with, or when met, is encountered as a stranger. Such texts seem an expression of a fantasy, a moment of mutual recognition and mutual desire, in a world where the desire is not publicly speakable, and therefore such recognition has a magical quality, that around the next corner is that one strange, unknown friend, so longed for.

But even these poetic fantasies bear the marks of the culture's judgement on the unnaturalness of such relationships. There is an oft-repeated trope through many of these texts of this love as sterile (unproductive of human life) and, concomitantly, corrupt. This is most fulsomely played out in the allegorical poem 'The Valley of Vain Desires', where such desires seem to condemn their owner to the pit of decay and despair. And whether there is a sense of unnaturalness explicitly in the text or not, the speaker of the poem is almost always the victim of the other, either because they cannot know the speaker's true feelings, or, in a world with no solid underpinnings to such relationships, no cultural validity, because there is only rejection, sooner or later.

Yet the tendency to infantilize or feminize the male beloved is a clear sign that these works share the dominant cultural conception of how a relationship is constructed. There is an inequality of some kind or another in-built into each relationship, with the exception of the 'Comrade' poems, which premise themselves on a Whitmanian doctrine of democracy. Sometimes the inequality is age, sometimes power, sometimes simply who has knowledge of the fact of the desire.

Commentaries and treatments of love, emotional and sensual, between women, tend to be franker, less tentative, more freely expressed than that between men. In part this is due to the clearly defined and maintained gender roles at work in dominant culture, which, while they condemned any weakness, effeminacy or limpness in men, gave permission to women to be loving, nurturing and needy in relation to any other adult, and women writing about love for other women turn this to their advantage. It has become a dogma of modern lesbian-feminist theory that these women meant nothing sexual by their passionate declarations of love and appreciation of one another's bodies, and that it is only due to the influence of sexology and male prurience that a twentieth-century reader, coming to these texts, sees in them expressions of genital sexuality. In this, these critics seem to concur with the apocryphal tale of Queen Victoria refusing to sign any legislation outlawing sex between women because it was something she could not imagine.[1] Since no critic was actually present in any of their bedrooms, it is impossible to know whether or not they actually 'did' anything. But that is not the point. Rather, the texts by women depict a vivid, varied set of ideas and experiences about loving and/or desiring other women, so it is not possible to make sweeping generalizations about 'romantic friendship'.

The largest body of work belongs to the poet Michael Field, a joint *nom de plume* of Katherine Bradley and Edith Cooper, who lived and wrote together for thirty years, who write in their poetry and their journals of their love, and who produced works which seem frankly sexual, if couched in somewhat coded or idiosyncratic language. A range of their poetic output and two small extracts from their jointly made journals are included below, and their language of love seems strikingly more complex and developed than that of their contemporaries. The works of Adah Isaacs Menken and Amy Levy express sentiments comparable to those of the male authors, of longing, of unrequited desire, of the lover's cruelty. But it is perhaps Levy who strikes the key note in relation to the representation of women's love for one another, in the final poem in this chapter, where, with a degree of smugness, she writes:

It is our secret, only ours,
Since all the world is blind.

Women are protected from any legal or social penalty for loving one another. In fact, it would make them unnatural women if they did not love one another, a point implicitly made by the arch-conservative Eliza Lynn Linton in her essay 'The Epicene Sex' (see Chapter 1 above). But, while they were granted permission to love, their own or any woman's sexuality was too much the object of ideological training and restraint for it to be possible to conceive of their physical relationships in any comparable fashion to that of their male peers, whose sexuality was as much an object of scrutiny as their emotions.

MEN

Alan Stanley, 'To G—', *Love Lyrics*, 1894

These poems are all of love, and you
Inspired them, sweet.
Your beauty thrilled me through and through;
As melody to viola
So was I tuned to you.
What else, fond lover, can I do
But lay these offerings at your feet –
These poor, frail flowers at your feet.

Frederick Faber, 'XL', *Poems*, 1856
Keswick, August 3, 1838

Some fall in love with voices, some with eyes,

Some men are linked together by a tear;
Others by smiles; many who cannot tell
What time the spirit passed who left the spell.
It comes to us among the winds that rise
Scattering their gifts on all things far and near.
The fields of unripe corn, the mountain lake,
And the great-hearted sea – all objects take
Their glory and their witchery from winds:
All save the few black pools the woodman finds
Far in the depths of some unsunny place,
Which stand, albeit the happy winds are out
In all the tossing branches round about,
As silent and as fearful as a dead man's face.

Frederick Faber, 'Admonition', *Poems*, 1856

I know thee not, bright friend! but that thy looks
Do draw me to thee, with thy boyhood rushing,
As a sweet fever through thy veins, and gushing
From thy clear eyes in merry falls, like brooks
Leaping, clear crystal things, from their stone fountains,
And waking echoes in the noonday mountains.
This is no place for thee; be warned in time.
Thou must go haunt some free and breezy knoll,
Ere this grey city come with spell sublime,
Freezing her heartless state into thy soul.
Thou hast surely been cradled out of doors,
And the great forms that nursed thee are the truest;
And, though these courts were Heaven's own azure floors,
Yet days are coldest when the skies are bluest.

Frederick Faber, 'To a Friend', *Poems*, 1856

Oh by the love which unto thee I bear,
By the tall trees and streams, and everything
In the white-clouded sky or woodland air,

Whether of sight or sound, that here may bring
The joyous freshness of the grassy spring –
Fain would I warn thee; for too well I know,
Be what thou wilt, thou must be dear to me.
And lo! thou art in utter bondage now,
Whence I would have thy manly spirit free.
Among the hills we two did never mar
The moss about the springs, but learnt to spare
Pale flowers which rude hands would not leave to grow;
And if thou wert so wisely gentle there –
Thy soul hath better flowers – oh! be as guiltless now.

Alfred, Lord Tennyson, from *In Memoriam*, 1850

CXXIX

Dear friend, far off, my lost desire,
    So far, so near in woe and weal;
    O loved the most, when most I feel
There is a lower and a higher;

Known and unknown; human, divine;
    Sweet human hand and lips and eye;
    Dear heavenly friend that canst not die,
Mine, mine, for ever, ever mine.

Strange friend, past, present, and to be;
    Loved deeplier, darklier understood;
    Behold, I dream a dream of good,
And mingle all the world with thee.

Edmund Gosse, 'Prelude', *On Viol and Flute*, 1873

Take hands with me, dear unknown friend, and find

Some downy hollow, sheltered from the wind,
    Where summer meadows overlook the sea;
There let us, in the grass at length reclined,

Hold converse, while the melting air around
Is full of golden light and murmuring sound,
    And let your soul shine frankly upon me,
And I will tell you the best my heart has found.

But first hold up against the light your wrist,
Where blue veins hide like unhewn amethyst,
    So shall I know that you have bodily fire,
And purple that the sacred sun hath kissed.

Else, if your blood be chilly, go your way, –
I have no songs to sing to you to-day;
    The goal to which our lyric hearts aspire
Must be the very core of life in May.

Edward Cracroft Lefroy, 'A Disciple Secretly I', 1897²

One glance upon the dead face, – only one.
You think it strange; but he can never know;
Or with a spirit's knowledge would he shun
Last look from any friend who loved him so
As I have loved: in happy mood and low,
In hours of grave content, in hours of fun,
In mind's debate, in full-heart's overflow,
Through all his course, till all his course was done.
What if I spake but little, – did not tell
The wealth of reverence ever waxing more
As he grew worthier worship? Is it well
To pluck a secret from the heart's kind core, –
Play thief where Self-Respect as sentinel
Keeps watch upon a still unopened door?

Edward Cracroft Lefroy, 'A Football-Player', *Echoes from Theocritus and Other Poems*, 1885

If I could paint you, friend, as you stand there,
Guard of the goal, defensive, open-eyed,
Watching the tortured bladder slide and glide
Under the twinkling feet; arms bare, head bare,
The breeze a-tremble through crow-tufts of hair;
Red-brown in face, and ruddier having spied
A wily foeman breaking from the side,
Aware of him, – of all else unaware:
If I could limn[3] you, as you leap and fling
Your weight against his passage, like a wall;
Clutch him and collar him, and rudely cling
For one brief moment till he falls – you fall:
My sketch would have what Art can never give,
Sinew and breath and body; it would live.

A. C. Benson, 'The Gift', *The Poems of Arthur Christopher Benson*, 1908

Friend, of my intimate dreams
    Little enough endures;
Little howe'er it seems,
    It is yours, all yours.

Fame hath a fleeting breath,
    Hopes may be frail or fond;
But Love shall be Love till death,
    And perhaps beyond!

Roden Noel, 'To —', *My Sea and Other Poems*, 1896

Comrade beloved, and helpful soulfellow,
I fear lest that fine pallor I admire,
Wherefrom by twilight of the rosy fire.
Your eyes, like stars in limpid water, glow,
From pain and frequent weariness may flow!
Ah! more than one who loved me and my lyre
Hath left me darkling, and hath risen higher;
I pray thee, comrade, to abide below!

With tuneful voice, and with the Poet's heart
You sing to heal and gladden our sad time.
With Mary you have chosen the better part,
Shedding soul-rays upon our weary clime;
Neither your friend will yield you, nor your Art;
He needs yourself, and she requires your rhyme.

Edmund John, 'Dream', *The Flute of Sardonyx*, 1913

For thy sake youth is fallen and grown cold,
And there is blood upon Love's wings of gold,
And hope is mockery, and passed is pride of pain;
For thy sake I am grey and lost and old,
Broken because I dreamed awhile in vain.
For thy sake, and for the wild words I said
When I cursed God, and for the stain of red
Upon my fingers when I slew my soul,
I am cast out alive among the dead.

A. C. Swinburne, 'Song', *Poems and Ballads, Series II*, 1878

Love laid his sleepless head
On a thorny rosy bed;
And his eyes with tears were red,
And pale his lips as the dead.

And fear and sorrow and scorn
Kept watch by his head forlorn,
Till the night was overworn
And the world was merry with morn.

And Joy came up with the day
And kissed Love's lips as he lay,
And the watchers ghostly and grey
Sped from his pillow away.

And his eyes as the dawn grew bright,
And his lips waxed ruddy as light:
Sorrow may reign for a night,
But day shall bring back delight.

A. C. Swinburne, 'Fragoletta', *Poems and Ballads, Series I*, 1866

O Love! what shall be said of thee?
The son of grief begot by joy?
Being sightless, wilt thou see?
Being sexless, wilt thou be
Maiden or boy?

I dreamed of strange lips yesterday
And cheeks wherein the ambiguous blood
Was like a rose's – yea,
A rose's when it lay
Within the bud.

What fields have bred thee, or what groves

244

Concealed thee, O mysterious flower,
O double rose of Love's,
With leaves that lure the doves
From bud to bower?

I dare not kiss it, lest my lip
Press harder than an indrawn breath,
And all the sweet life slip
Forth, and the sweet leaves drip,
Bloodlike, in death.

O sole desire of my delight!
O sole delight of my desire!
Mine eyelids and eyesight
Feed on thee day and night
Like lips of fire.

Lean back thy throat of carven pearl,
Let thy mouth murmur like the dove's;
Say, Venus hath no girl,
No front of female curl,
Among her Loves.

Thy sweet low bosom, thy close hair,
Thy strait soft flanks and slenderer feet,
Thy virginal strange air,
Are these not over fair
For Love to greet?

How should he greet thee? what new name,
Fit to move all men's hearts, could move
Thee, deaf to love or shame,
Love's sister, by the same
Mother as Love?

Ah sweet, the maiden's mouth is cold,
Her breast-blossoms are simply red,
Her hair mere brown or gold,
Fold over simple fold
Binding her head.

Thy mouth is made of fire and wine,
Thy barren bosom takes my kiss

And turns my soul to thine
And turns thy lip to mine,
And mine it is.

Thou hast a serpent in thine hair,
In all the curls that close and cling;
And ah, thy breast-flower!
Ah love, thy mouth too fair
To kiss and sting!

Cleave to me, love me, kiss mine eyes,
Satiate thy lips with loving me;
Nay, for thou shalt not rise;
Lie still as Love that dies
For love of thee.

Mine arms are close about thine head,
My lips are fervent on thy face.
And where my kiss hath fed
Thy flower-like blood leaps red
To the kissed place.

O bitterness of things too sweet!
O broken singing of the dove!
Love's wings are over fleet,
And like the panther's feet
The feet of Love.

Oscar Wilde, 'Quia Multum Amavi',[4]
Poems, 1881

Dear Heart, I think the young impassioned priest
　　When first he takes from out the hidden shrine
His god imprisoned in the Eucharist,
　　And eats the bread, and drinks the dreadful wine,

Feels not such awful wonder as I felt
　　When first my smitten eyes beat full on thee,
And all night long before thy feet I knelt
　　Till thou wert wearied of Idolatry.

Ah! hadst thou liked me less and loved me more,
    Through all those summer days of joy and rain,
I had not now been sorrow's heritor,
    Or stood a lackey in the House of Pain.

Yet, though remorse, youth's white-faced seneschal,
    Tread on my heels with all his retinue,
I am most glad I loved thee – think of all
    The suns that go to make one speedwell blue!

Edward Carpenter, 'Little heart within thy cage', *Towards Democracy*, 1905

Beating, still beating, so tenderly yearning
For Comrade love, the love which is to come:
Often near stopping, or wounded like a bird, so full of pain – thy thread of life
almost snapt –
    Yet with joy so wonderful over all and through all continuing:

Soon together shalt thou stop, little heart, and the beating and the pain here shall
cease;
    But out of thee that life breathed into the lips of others shall never stop nor
    cease.
Through a thousand beautiful forms – so beautiful! – through the gates of a
thousand hearts – emancipated freed we will pass on:
    I and my joy will surely pass on.
    Little heart within thy cage so many years – year after year –

Edward Carpenter, 'When I am near you', *Towards Democracy*, 1905

Now when I am near to you, dear friend,
Passing out of myself, being delivered –
Through those eyes and lips and hands, so loved, so ardently loved,
I am become free;
In the sound of your voice I dwell

As in a world defended from evil.

When I am accounted by the world to be – all that I leave behind;
It is nothing to me any longer.
Like one who leaves a house with all its mouldy old furniture and pitches
    his camp under heaven's blue,
    So I take up my abode in your presence –
I find my deliverance in you.

John Gambril Nicholson, from 'A Chaplet of Southernwood', *A Chaplet of Southernwood*, 1896

III

I love him wisely if I love him well,
    And so I let him keep his innocence;
    I veil my adoration with pretence
Since he knows nothing of Love's mystic spell;
I dare not for his sake my passion tell
    Though strong desire upbraid my diffidence; –
    To buy my happiness at his expense
Were folly blind and loss unspeakable.

Suspicious of my simplest acts I grow;
    I doubt my passing words, however brief;
    I catch his glances feeling like a thief.
Perchance he wonders why I shun him so, –
It would be strange indeed if he should know
    I love him, love him, love him past belief!

John Gambril Nicholson, 'Our Secret', *A Chaplet of Southernwood*, 1896

He has given himself to me,
    And he calls me his at last.

All's well that is to be,
　　And all is well that is past.

Long we counted the cost,
　　We tested well the ground,
And when all for Love was lost
　　Then all in Love was found.

Goodbye to days of doubt
　　And nights on a mental rack;
We blot their memory out,
　　We bid them ne'er come back.

The bitter under my kiss
　　He tastes no longer there;
I look in his eyes and miss
　　The mask they were wont to wear.

Just a touch of the hand,
　　And there's nothing left to say,
For lovers understand
　　When barriers melt away.

Moray Stuart-Young, 'Alec', *Out of Hours*, 1909[5]

Your face is not divine; but softly wrought
　　Are your white shoulders which strong muscles hide.
　　I like you thus and am most satisfied
That you have posed as in a sculptor's thought.
Watching your sinuous breasts makes me distraught
　　In memory of the time we defied
　　The indolence of flesh; and magic taught
Each to the other, and no thrill denied!
Man's loveliest labours are conceived in pain –
　　The charms of woman-nature meet in you,
　　Intense, defined, exquisite; and I knew
Both poles of feeling in your love's refrain.
Years hurry each to marriage – but the strain

Of the sweet past shall haunt us, old yet new!

John Addington Symonds, 'Love in Dreams', *New and Old: A Volume of Verse*, 1880

Love hath his poppy-wreath,
   Not Night alone.
I laid my head beneath
   Love's lilied throne:
Then to my sleep he brought
   This anodyne –
The flower of many a thought
   And fancy fine:
A form, a face, no more;
   Fairer than truth;
A dream from death's pale shore;
   The soul of youth:
A dream so dear, so deep,
   All dreams above,
That still I pray to sleep –
   Bring Love back, Love!

John Addington Symonds, 'A Lieder Kreis IV', *Fragilia Labilia: written mostly between 1860 and 1862*, 25 copies printed for the author's use, 1884

Love sat like a boy by my pillow,
   And murmured a song in mine ears
Of death on the breasts of the billow
   And darkness and desolate years.

His sweet eyes were streaming with sorrow,

His tresses were tangled and torn;
On his fair brows the fear of to-morrow
    Was fixed like the tooth of a thorn.

He smiled at the close of his singing;
    He kissed me with kisses of air:
When I woke in the dawn, I was wringing
    Vain hands in a passion of prayer.

John Addington Symonds, 'From Friend to Friend', *Pamphlet VI*, private publication, n.d.

Dear Friend, I know not if such aching nights
Of sweet strange comradeship as we have spent,
    Or if twin minds with equal ardour spent,
To search the world's unspeakable delights
    Or if long days passed on Parnassian heights
Together in rapt interminglement
    Of heart with heart on hope sublime intent,
Or if the tide of turbulent appetites
    That sway both breasts in harmony, have wrought
Our spirits to communion:[6] but I swear
    That neither chance or change nor time nor aught
That makes the future of our lives less fair,
    Shall sunder us who once have breathed this air
Of soul-commingling friendship passion-wrought.

John Addington Symonds, 'The Valley of Vain Desires', *New and Old*, 1880[#1]

There lurks a chasm, embedded, deep and drear,
Ringed round with jags and ragged teeth sublime
Of heights Himâlyan; where the hills uprear

Their hideous circuit to far snows, and climb

By barren cliff and scaur and splintered stair
Funereal. Never since the birth of time

Fell dew upon the valley-basement bare;
Nor light of day direct, nor starry spear
Shot earthward; but the opaque lurid air,

Unsunned and lustreless, like a salt mere,
Breeds exhalations. Here the craggy spines,
Converging from dimmed summits, build a bier,

Hollow and hateful, merging their sharp lines
In dismal flatness; and the floor is scarred
With seams and furrows: withered roots of pines

Grapple the fleshless granite: pits are barred
With broken branches, age-old skeletons
Of what were trees: and, horror! on the hard

Face of the grey stone skulls that grin, and bones
That bleach and wither in the windless gloom,
Dry-rot to dust by bleak battalions.

What hosts are these? Hounded by what fell doom,
Lured by what livid glamour, down the walls
Of this foul cauldron crept they? Doth the tomb

With plague-fierce phosphorescent festivals
Entice the languor of their dream-led feet?
Or sought they yon pale fruit that ripes and falls

From boughs aerial? Lo! how sickly sweet
The clammy spheres in clusters, green as dates,
As o'er-ripe plaintains blue, in the faint heat

Fester upon the tree that glooms and grates
Scant twilight with lean branches! Far or nigh
In the whole circle of the hills no mates

Frown upon its bulk mysterious; nor doth eye
Of dragon guard from pirate hands the fruit
Of its death-damned Hesperides;[7] but dry

And doleful round the poison-fibred root
Spring agarics[8] with fleshly shapes obscene.

Here never wheels the bat nor screech-owls hoot;

But all is silence; and no change is seen
Of noon or night, save when the shivering morn
Walks forth upon the silver-cinctured[9] screen

Of unapproachable faint peaks forlorn
Far in the zenith, or an errant star
Haunts for awhile perchance some glimmering horn.

All winding ways, circling from near or far,
Dive to this centre; and upon them all
Lie wrecks and ruins of remorseless war

Waged against life by one grim cannibal. –
What place is this, whereof in dreams the dread
Curdles my soul with spells tyrannical?

Yea, but I dreamed: and lo! my feet were led
Down the slow spirals of those deadly stairs:
And I too in my inmost spirit bred

Desire of that fell fruit; and through the lairs
Of poison-fretted charnels crept, and came,
With quivering flesh and horror-stiffened hairs,

Beneath those dismal branches. There a flame
Burned blue about the blossoms; and I stood,
And caught the falling juices; and, though shame

Shook in my shivering pulse, I snuffed the lewd
Scent of those corpse-cold clusters; and I fell
Amid the dying, dead, delirious brood,

Sweltering upon that altar-stone of Hell. –
What next my dream disclosed, in faltering speech
And feeble let my parched tongue strive to tell.

Far as these faint and swooning eyes could reach,
There, lying lapped in loathsomeness, I spied,
Coming and going, men who yearned; and each

Knew what his fellow's thin and shuddering side
Concealed of heart-ache, and of fear, and fire –
Of fierce forth-stretchings after joys denied,

And horrible, unquenchable desire.
Each forehead throbbed with fever; and each eye,
Gleaming 'neath hollow temples, seemed a pyre

For some slow flame to feed on. Silently
They stole adown the craggy stairs, and strained
Lean hand toward the branches: loathingly,

Yet with a terrible strange longing, gained
The gangrened fruit, and ate, and, as they chewed,
Pain that was pleasure filled them. Then they waned

Even where they stayed; for that fierce poison brewed
Despair within their spirit. Yet, once more,
Athirst they rose and ate; till lassitude

Of what the soul loathes and the veins abhor,
Possessed them, and they perished, and dust grew
Year after year upon the granite floor.

O ye, whoe'er ye are, that never knew
The achings of the ague fits of sin!
Who never from foul founts delusive drew

Flesh-parching poison; nor heaped lively in
With open eyes, where lakes of molten brass
Made a delirious mirage, and the green

Margent[10] of crusted bronze-rust fairer was
To your strained senses than all delicate
Dim tresses of the swaying summer grass! –

How can I teach you by what fearful fate
Foredoomed, dogged downsward by what pangs, enticed
By what pale cravings, lured alike by hate

And love, these guilty things, of God despised,
Of man rejected, moaning crept beneath
The treacherous tree, and fed, and cursing Christ,

Dragged the slow torture of plague-stricken breath
Onward through days or weeks or months or years
To fade at last in horror-shrouded death?

Yet such my dream was: and no gentle tears

Assuaged its anguish: for the founts were quenched
Of pity by strange loathing and wild fears.

I saw – yea, even now my cheeks are blenched
With thinking of the sorrow of that sight –
A youth Phoebean,[11] whose fair brows, entrenched

With scars untimely, bore the branded blight
Of shame 'neath withered bay-leaves: his long hair,
Once crisped in curls that mocked the morning light

For lustre, clung dishevelled, sere and rare,
Around his shuddering shoulders: as he ran,
His feet upon the grisly granite stair

Dropped dew, wherewith the dusk obsidian[12]
Blushed into bloodstone;[13] and so pure and fine
Was that fierce chrism[14] that, methought, flowers wan

Struggled to spring therefrom, but straight did pine,
Seeing that nought with life in it might linger
Beneath those scathing branches serpentine.

A broken lute he held, with crazy finger
Fumbling the voiceless chords; and ever sighed
His inarticulate throat, as though some singer

Divine, Olympian, on his lips had died. –
What woe was mine to feel that loveliness
Stretched in the leprous desert by my side!

To know that tender bosoms longed to press
Those delicate limbs, wherein the life decayed!
That maiden lips, mid the forsaken bliss

Of peaceful homes, might yesternight have laid
Poor cooling kisses on those cheeks whereon
Now fed the poison of the fearful glade!

Let one tale speak for all! – the Upas[15] shone
Above his glistening eyeballs; and its scent
Stank in his nostrils like the carrion

Mid jasmines festering by some Indian tent;
So that he loathed and loved it. Then he ate.

255

Sleep swallowed shame. But oh! the ravishment

Of that next waking, ere his eyes were set
To scan the horrors of the hopeless vale! –
Beneath his feet thick grass spread dewy wet

(So fancy fooled him) in a pleasant dale;
And he, a boy, uprising, fain would go
Forth to green crofts of golden galingale,

Daylong to muse and watch the murmuring flow
Of alder-shaded streams – Ah God! – Alas! –
Tigerlike on his soul the sudden woe

Leapt in one moment of the awful place;
And rising – as Eve rose, what time she broke
The fatal bough – upon his shrivelled face

The face of Never, Nevermore! awoke
Thenceforth to feed undying. Then he turned
Breast-downward, smitten with sharp throes that shook

The putrid air. Nathless[16] keen fever burned
Yet in his veins: then he would crawl and lean
Weak limbs against the trunk: – at times he spurned,

At times he clutched the mellow fruit that green
And rank bent downward to his panting lip;
And ever and anon the heavens serene

Disclosed above his eyes; and stars would slip
Through the clear azure on the edge of snow;
Or dawning's tremulous pure fingertip

Of rose would glide along the horns, or glow
A little downward, ever out of reach,
Delusive, taunting him midmost his woe.

Sweet thoughts swam through him of the leafy beech
Broad by his father's houseroof, where he played,
Or spread at eventide with plum and peach

The rustic board, a free child, ere sin laid
Her loathly finger on his luminous hair.
In dreams the angel of that old life made

Music most eloquent, till all things fair
Once more bloomed round him; yet he might not seize
The blossom of their beauty: for despair

Shrivelled his spirit with foul phantasies:
And this of all his torment was the worst,
That knowing purity and joy and peace,

He might not even yearn for them, accurst
With the one hunger of the hideous tree. –
Thus in my dream I watched that devilish thirst

Consume and rot and wreck him utterly,
Till he too perished. In what dark abyss
Of Thy deep counsel dwells the black decree

Whereby, O God, such shapes of blessedness
Must sink beneath the scurf and barren spume
Of lust unlovely, loathed and lustreless?

* * *

Even as I wailed and wrung wild hands, the gloom
Lightened, and lo! around me like thin flowers
Of clouds that on the brows of sunset bloom,

Blazed angel choirs innumerous – Thrones and Powers,
Princes, Archangels, flame-tongued Seraphim,[17]
Shrilling through all their cohort: He is ours!

Then gazing on the ash-white corse[18] of him
Who erewhile sank soul-smitten by fierce pain,
I saw a little dust, pure, white, and dim;

Kind earth's true substance. But amid that train
Flamed one intense keen orb of living light,
That throbbed and shouted; and the purple grain

Of heaven grew pale around it – with such white
Wild radiance pierced its splendour through and through
The fabric of God's infinite delight.

Therewith the love within my spirit drew

Me upward with those angels; yea, I went,
Last of their choir, through fields of trackless blue:

For faith and hope and yearning in me lent
Wings to my weakness; and I heard the singer,
Divine, Olympian, in free ravishment

Flood the waste skies with living strains, that linger
Yet in these tingling ears and eager heart.
No more about his lute the restless finger

Strayed; for he needed neither hand nor art
Nor voice nor throat, since joy alone and life
Made music through his lustre. Yea, the smart

Of that past passion and all its sinful strife
Bloomed into bliss triumphant. Then I turned
My gaze 'mid stars, wherewith the way was rife,

Downward, and lo! a little spark that burned,
Serenely stationed amid sister spheres:
And is that Earth? my wistful spirit yearned:

Yea, Earth it is; but here where neither years,
Nor place, nor change, nor forms are, but all's One –
One light, one joy, one life, – thy world appears

E'en what she is, pure splendour! There was none
In all that luminous band, but flamed and shed
Smiles like the arrows of the orient sun,

While from the singer's soul the new lore sped
Striking my dizzied senses. Then – for now
The tents of very heaven disclosed o'erhead,

And scathing glory smote my aching brow –
Sleep fell apart, and waking I was ware
How that above me in the golden glow

Of the dawning all the Alpine summits fair,
Unbarred of midnight blackness, row by row
Blazed in the brilliance of the August air.

       * * *

Yea, Lord! one thing alone of truth we know –
That Thou art good and gracious! Could but we
Behold the rivers of Thy wisdom flow

From the first fount of Thy felicity,
Through all the ocean where those myriad streams
Commingle, 'twere an easy task to see
Concorde above the discord of our dreams.

Marc-André Raffalovich

Raffalovich was a Russian émigré who came to London, via Paris, in the 1880s, attended by his childhood nurse, Miss Gribble. He is reputed to have been despised by Wilde, who accused him of coming to London to open a salon, and succeeding in opening a saloon, an antipathy he answered in his 'scientific' book, *Uranisme et unisexualité* (see p. 69 above), where he describes Wilde as 'having neither a sense of life, nor a talent for it', as well as castigating his physical appearance and morals:

> One could not see him speak without noticing his sensual lips, his discoloured teeth, and his tongue which seemed to lick his words.... His egotism, it is true, was imperturbable. He addressed himself to the youngest and tried to turn their heads with flattery and make them his disciples. He gossiped, gossiped inexhaustibly, and smoked cigarettes.... He took an interest then in all sexual perversions, he feared them, dreaded them for himself. He loved talking about them. He knew the little histories of the whole of London. Great tribades fascinated him like courageous or loving sodomites. He prowled around the neighbour-hood. He was innocent, he said, but he followed the lead of others.

While on the margins of the circle of writers and artists surrounding Wilde, which included the two women who comprised Michael Field, and the designers and illustrators Charles Ricketts and Charles Shannon, Raffalovich formed a relationship with the poet John Gray, who is supposed to be the original of Dorian Gray in Wilde's novel of that name. Whatever the nature of that relationship, it lasted for the rest of Raffalovich's life, continuing when Gray became a Roman Catholic priest. They both moved to Edinburgh, Raffalovich built his friend a church and they had tea together every afternoon.

Raffalovich published a number of volumes of poetry during the 1880s and 1890s. Included here are four from a range of those volumes, where he writes about love and sensuality between men.

Marc-André Raffalovich 'Love, Vice, Crime, and Sin', *The Thread and the Path*, 1895

The lips of Vice were painted,
    The face of Vice was white,
Love passed on unacquainted,
    Intent on Love's delight.

And though Love's heart beat faster
    Beneath the eyes of Crime,
His breath he strove to master,
    And hummed a foolish rhyme.

But when the sun was shining
    Love reached a shadowy place,
And there at last reclining
    Sin had his true love's face.

Marc-André Raffalovich 'Hyde Park – November', *The Thread and the Path*, 1895

Pale love, sweet sufferer whose cold hands I chafe,
To whom my show of courage courage lends,
How do they love whose love is always safe,
Sure of the base approval of their friends?
Slaves, masters of their poor world's poor delight,
Obedient, popular and prosperous,
Who in warm rooms are sheltered from the night,
The bitter, foggy night that comforts us –

How do they love? Not better than we do.
I would not change our happiness for theirs,
Or our unhappiness. My dear, would you?
Your arms around my neck! And great love tears
Great clouds from Heaven and heaps bare trees above
For us to feel each other's kiss and love.

Marc-André Raffalovich 'To One of My Readers', *Cyril and Lionel and Other Poems: A Volume of Sentimental Verse*, 1884

O fair as those I love, and sweet and fair
As those whose sweetness is so fair to me,
O dearer than the love my love does dare
Hardly to greet when sight grows ecstasy,
As strange as any idol of the past
Whose youth mine worshipped in a youthful trance,
Are not thine tenderness and strength? And hast
Thou not a mouth controlling all romance?
Is love more meaningful than are thy frowns?
Hast not thou shyness for a rosy shroud,
And curls of misty gold that clings and crowns
A breathing fairness and a marble cloud?
    O mayest thou take this volume in thy hand,
    And turn the leaves, and read, and understand!

Marc-André Raffalovich 'The World Well Lost IV', *In Fancy Dress*, 1886

The cheat deceives the cheat, the vain the vain, the blind the blind, the weak
the weak.

Because our world has music, and we dance;
Because our world has colour, and They gaze;
Because our speech is tuned, and schooled our glance,
And we have roseleaf nights and roseleaf days,
And we have leisure, work to do, and rest;
Because They see us laughing when we meet,
And hear our words and voices, see us dressed
With skill, and pass us and our flowers smell sweet:–
They think that we know friendship, passion, love!
Our peacock, Pride! And Art our nightingale!
And Pleasure's hand upon our dogskin glove!
And if they see our faces burn or pale,
    It is the sunlight, think They, or the gas.
    – Our lives are wired like our gardenias.

Digby Mackworth Dolben and John Addington Symonds, 'Tema con Variazioni'[19], n.d.

'Tema' by Digby Mackworth Dolben

The World is young today;
Forget the gods are old;
Forget the years of gold,
When all the months were May.

A little flower of Love
Is ours, without a root,
Without the end of fruit;
Yet take the scent thereof.

There may be hope above;
There may be rest beneath;
I know not; only Death
Is palpable and Love.

'Variazioni' by John Addington Symonds

Came Love, and in his hand
A blood-red rose he bare:
The morning breezes fanned
Bright blossoms in his hair.

Came Death, and on the sod
He set a lily white,
A lily pale as night,
Before the laughing god.

Love's red red roses fell;
They had nor root nor fruit:
O'er leaf and lusty shoot
Death's lily reared her bell.

Love wept, but Death was kind,
When all Love's flowers were shed,
He bade Love pluck and bind
Death's lily round his head.

Walter Headlam, 'Life's Lesson', *His Letters and Poems*, 1910

Long taught now by the loves I have endured,
Eyes open, and the sane mind well assured
Beforehand of the inevitable pain,
Here stand with the sea beneath my feet.

As, were the choice mine, I would choose again
To live the whole life through, that I have found
So bitter, for the all-transcending sweet;
So, though I know you, so though I know me,
I love you, and borne high, though I be drowned,

At least for all my full tide will reign
Upon the splendid, uncompassionate sea.

WOMEN

Michael Field, from *The Tragedy of Pardon*, Act III, scene iii, 1911

There is love
Of woman unto woman, in its fibre
Stronger than knits a mother to her child.
There is no lack in it, and no defect;
It looks nor up nor down,
But loves from plenitude to plenitude,
With level eyes, as in the Trinity
God looks across and worships. O my dear,
To keep you moving in and out my days!

E. F. Benson, from *Mother*, 1925[20]

My mother, throughout her life, like all very intellectual women, formed strong emotional attachments to those of her own sex. It was through friendship, she says somewhere, that love first came to her, and just at this [great spiritual] crisis there entered into her environment a woman with whom she instantly made one of those intimate and noble friendships, not knowing, as she records, that she was the messenger. 'I played with the human love I had for her, and she for me, and all the time Thou hadst sent her...'. As the intimacy deepened, she found that her friend knew the road which she instinctively felt must be her own, and, as by some splendid illumination, long groped for in dimness, came the light. Surely no one had ever lived a sweeter and more unselfish life than she, but all that appeared to her now to have been but a blind stumbling of steps, a haphazard goalless wandering, and it was with something of the inspired vision of the mystic that she then that which never afterwards, even in the darkest places (and many were dark) through which her way led her, ceased to enlighten her. 'Only this I know,' she wrote now, 'that it is this innermost ultimate self that is filled with consuming hunger and thirst for the living Saviour. It seemed first a famine for God, simply; now I find I need a Way to Him. I linger in the holy place, and so once, for all mankind, Thou rentest the veil, so surely for each individual there comes a rending, and seeing Thee at last for their Saviour, they find that a Holy of Holies is open, yes, even to the mercy-seat of God. Therefore, Jesu, my joy, I have burned the incense of prayer before the veil dimly, with eager longing. Surely the Day of Atonement is near, even is it not here? And is not the veil even now rending, and the glory of the Lord filling the house of my heart?...'

Charlotte Brontë to Ellen Nussey, 20 February 1837[21]

I read your letter with dismay, Ellen – what shall I do without you? Why are we so to be denied each other's society? It is an inscrutable fatality. I long to be with you because it seems as if two or three days or weeks spent in your company would beyond measure strengthen me in the enjoyment of those feelings which I have so lately begun to cherish. You first pointed out to me that way in which I am so feebly endeavouring to travel, and now I cannot keep you by my side, I must proceed sorrowfully alone.

Why are we to be divided? Surely, Ellen, it must be because we are in danger of loving each other too well – of losing sight of the *Creator* in idolatry of the *creature*. At first I could not say, 'Thy will be done.' I felt rebellious; but I know it was wrong to feel so. Being left a moment alone this morning, I prayed fervently to be enabled to resign myself to *every* decree of God's will – though it should be dealt forth with a far severer hand than the present disappointment. Since then, I have felt calmer and humbler – and consequently happier....

I have written this note at a venture. When it will reach you I know not, but I was determined not to let slip an opportunity for want of being prepared to embrace it. Farewell; may God bestow on you all His blessings. My darling – Farewell. Perhaps you may return before midsummer – do you think you possibly can? I wish your brother John knew how unhappy I am; he would almost pity me.

A note on Michael Field

'Michael Field' (see p. 237) was the joint pen-name of aunt and niece Katherine Bradley and Edith Cooper, who lived and wrote together from the 1870s to their deaths in 1914 and 1913 respectively. The name was less a pseudonym than a means of marking their identity as 'Poet', a persona that was greater than the sum of its parts. Whether or not their relationship was sexual in any way is impossible to know. But they produced a vast corpus of work, encompassing poetry, plays and the jointly kept journals, all of which are full of depictions and celebrations of female beauty and sensualism. They name each other 'Love' and 'lover' in those works which are evidently about themselves and each other, as in the first poem included here, 'To E[dith] C[ooper]'. One of their most ambitious productions is *Long Ago*, a volume which completes all of Sappho's fragments, under the inspiration of the poet and Aphrodite, and which depicts a world of Lesbian love between women, complete with jealousy, rejection of women on the basis of their personal appearance, and the destructive effects of heterosexuality. They were not modest about their talents, bridling at Robert Browning's injunction that they should 'wait fifty years' for fame.[22] Their paganism was eventually succeeded by joint conversion to Roman Catholicism, in part under the influence of John Gray (see p. 259 above), and their later work is characterized by a cultish worship of the Virgin Mary and a belief that they will continue to be 'poets and lovers' in the next world too.

Arran Leigh,[23] 'To E. C.', *The New Minnesinger and Other Poems*, 1875

My deep need of thy love, its mast'ring power,
   I scarce can fathom, thou wilt never know;
   My lighter passions into rhythm may glow;
This is for ever voiceless. Could the flower
Open its petall'd thought, and praise the dower
   Of sunlight, or the fresh gift of dew,
   The bounteous air that daily round it blew,
Blessing unweariedly in sun and shower,
   Methinks would miss its praises: so I drink
My life of thee; and put to poet's use

Whatever crosses it of strange and fair,
Thou hast fore-fashioned all I do and think;
And to my seeming it were words' abuse
    To boast a wealth of which I am the heir.

Michael Field, From 'Works and days', the manuscript journals, 1913

Edith Cooper:
I am moved to read to Francis [Brookes] (I believe it is only to him I could read what is so thrilling & sacred to my heart) I am moved to read Michael's poems to me. 'Old Ivories' – 'The dear temptation of her face' with 'Atthis, my darling' of <u>Long Ago</u> added – the loveliest nocturne ever created, <u>Palimpsest</u> – to say by heart

'A girl
Her soul a deep wave pearl.'

I am moved to show him my triumph & joy in this lovely praise & in showing him my so often-shaded mood before my glory I also let my Beloved realise what her poet's gift has been to me – her poet-lover's gift. Think of it! She has often read these lovely poems to me. She has never heard them, tender but high-voiced, from my lips. It is Paradise between us. When we're together eternally our spirits will be interpenetrated with our love & our Art under the benison of the Vision of God. For it wants <u>another</u>. There was need of Francis to listen to <u>Wild Honey</u>.

October 27th
Edith:
It is the early morning of my own love's birthday. How dear she is to me – how the sweetness & clench of love grow pain & joy as I look at her, touch her, & receive her little wreath of kisses in my withered hour.
    We have had the bond of our Art, precious, precious: we have had the Bond of Race, with the delicious adventure of the stranger nature, introduced by the beloved father: we have had the Bond of Life, deep set in the years – & now we have the Bond of Faith & the Bond – different from any other Bond – of

threatened Death....Above all she has to face the possibility of dying before I die. But there have been such prayers about <u>that</u>. I believe in God Almighty it will not happen. Michael has been <u>all life</u> to me; & now there are moments when she brushes my doomed earthly being with the flap & tragic presence of nearness to Death.

Michael Field, From *Long Ago*, 1889

XXII

Atthis, my darling, thou dids't stray
A few feet to the rushy bed,
When a great fear and passion shook
My heart lest haply thou wert dead;
It grew so still about the brook,
As if a soul were drawn away.

Anon thy clear eyes, silver-blue,
Shone through the tamarisk branches fine;
To pluck me iris thou hads't sprung
Through galingale and celandine;
Away, away the flowers I flung
And thee down to my breast I drew.

My darling! Nay, our very breath
Nor light nor darkness shall divide;
Queen Dawn shall find us in one bed,
Nor must thou flutter from my side
An instant, lest I feel the dread,
Atthis, the immanence of death.

Michael Field, 'A Palimpsest', *Wild Honey from Various Thyme*, 1908

...The rest[24]
Of our life must be a palimpsest –
The old writing written there the best.

In the parchment hoary
Lies a golden story,
As 'mid secret feathers of a dove,
As 'mid moonbeams shifted through a cloud;

Let us write it over,
O my lover,
From the far Time to discover,
As 'mid secret feathers of a dove,
As 'mid moonbeams shifted through a cloud!

Michael Field, 'A Girl', *Underneath the Bough: A Book of Verses*, 1893

A girl
   Her soul a deep-wave pearl
Dim, lucent of all lovely mysteries;
   A face flowered for heart's ease,
   A brow's grace soft as seas
   See through faint forest-trees;
   A mouth, the lips apart,
Like aspen-leaflets trembling in the breeze
   From her tempestuous heart,
   Such: and her soul's so knit,
   I leave the page half-writ –
   The work begun
Will be to heaven's conception done,
   If she come to it.

Michael Field, 'Prologue', *Underneath the Bough: A Book of Verses*, 1893

It was deep April, and the morn
   Shakespeare was born;
The world was on us, pressing sore;
My love and I took hands and swore,

Against the world, to be
Poets and lovers evermore,
To laugh and dream on Lethe's shore,
To sing to Charon in his boat,
Heartening the timid souls afloat;
Of judgement never to take heed,
But to those fast-locked souls to speed,
Who never from Apollo fled,
Who spend no hour among the dead;
Continually
With them to dwell.
Indifferent to heaven and hell.

Michael Field 'Lo, my Loved is Dying', 1913[25]

Lo, my loved is dying, and the call
Is come that I must die,
All the leaves are dying, all
Dying, drifting by.
Every leaf is lonely in its fall,
Every flower has its speck and stain;
The birds from hedge and tree
Lisp mournfully,
And the great reconciliation of this pain
Lies in the full, soft rain.

Oct., 1913

Michael Field, 'Lovers', 1913

Lovers, fresh plighting lovers in our age
Lovers in Christ – so tender at the heart
The pull about the strings as they engage –
One thing is plain: – that we can never part.
O Child, thou hauntest me in every room;
Not for an instant can we separate;
And thou or I, if absent in a tomb

Must keep unqualified our soul's debate.
Death came to me but just twelve months ago
Threatening thy life; I counted thee as dead –
Christ by thy bier took pity of my woe
And lifted thee and on my bosom spread;
And did not then retire and leave us twain:
Together for a little while we stood
And looked on Him, and chronicled His pain,
The wounds for is that started in their blood –
We, with one care, our common days shall spend,
As on that noble sorrow we attend.

Michael Field, 'Your Rose is Dead', n.d.[26]

Your *rose* is *dead*,
They said,
The Grand Mogul – for so her splendour
Exceeded, masterful, it seemed her due
By dominant male titles to commend her;
But I, her lover, knew
That myriad-coloured blackness, wrought with fire,
Was woman to the rage of my desire.
My rose was dead? She lay
Against the sulphur, lemon and blush-gray
Of younger blooms, transformed, morose,
Her shrivelling petals gathered round her close,
And where before
Coils twisted thickest at her core
A round, black hollow: it had come to pass
Hints of tobacco, leather, brass,
Confounded, gave her texture and her colour.
I watched her, as I watched her, growing duller,
Majestic in recession
From flesh to mould.
My rose is dead – I echo the confession,
And they pass to pluck another;
While I, drawn on to vague, prodigious pleasure,
Fondle my treasure.

O sweet, let death prevail
Upon you, as your nervous outlines thicken
And totter, as your crimsons stale,
I feel fresh rhythms quicken,
Fresh music follows you. Corrupt, grow old,
Drop inwardly to ashes, smother
Your burning spices, and entoil
My senses till you sink a clod of fragrant soil!

Adah Isaacs Menken

Menken was an actress, a model, a circus performer and the author of one volume of poetry. She was a sometime friend of Swinburne (who wrote for her and then repeatedly repudiated an eight-line poem, 'Dolorida'), and a long-time associate of the novelist George Sand, with whom she frequently dined and went out in public, both attired in men's clothing. Of Sand she wrote to Theophile Gautier: 'She so infuses me with the spirit of life that I cannot bear to spend an evening apart from her.'[27] Most of the poems in *Infelicia* are concerned with painful, unrequited love for men, but a small number treat of love between women, of which two are included here.

Adah Isaacs Menken 'A Memory', *Infelicia*, 1868

I see her yet, that dark-eyed one,
    Whose bounding heart God folded up
In His, as shuts when day is done,
    Upon the elf the blossom's cup.
On many an hour like this we met,
    And as my lips did fondly greet her,
I blessed her as love's amulet:
    Earth hath no treasure, dearer, sweeter.

The stars that look upon the hill,
    And beckon from their homes at night,
Are soft and beautiful, yet still
    Not equal to her eyes of light.

They have the liquid glow of earth,
The sweetness of a summer even,
   As if some angel at their birth
Had dipped them in the hues of Heaven.

They may not seem to others sweet,
   Nor radiant with the beams above,
When first their soft sad glances meet
   The eyes of those not born for love;
Yet when on me their tender beams
   Are turned, beneath love's wide control,
Each soft, sad orb of beauty seems
   To look through mine into my soul.

I see her now that dark-eyed one,
   Whose bounding heart God folded up
In His, as shuts when day is done,
   Upon the elf the blossom's cup.
Too late we met, the burning brain,
   The aching heart alone can tell,
How filled our souls of death and pain
   When came the last, sad word, *Farewell!*

Adah Isaacs Menken, 'Infelix', *Infelicia*, 1868

Where is the promise of my years;
   Once written on my brow?
Ere errors, agonies and fears
   Brought with them all that speaks in tears,
Ere I had sunk beneath my peers;
   Where sleeps that promise now?

Naught lingers to redeem those hours,
   Still, still to memory sweet!
The flowers that bloomed in sunny bowers
   Are withered all; and Evil towers
Supreme above her sister powers
   Of Sorrow and Deceit.

I look along the columned years,
　　And see life's riven fane,
Just where it fell, amid the jeers
　　Of scornful lips, whose mocking sneers,
Forever hiss within mine ears
　　To break the sleep of pain.

I can but own my life is vain,
　　A desert void of peace;
I missed the goal I sought to gain,
　　I missed the measure of the strain
That kills Fame's fever in the brain,
　　And bids earth's tumult cease.

Myself! alas for theme so poor
　　A theme but rich in fear;
I stand a wreck on Error's shore,
　　A spectre not within the door,
A houseless shadow ever more,
　　An exile lingering here.

Havelock Ellis, from *My Life*, 1916[28]

Being alone, Edith was joined by an old friend of nearly her own age whom she had known from girlhood, a woman brought up in a luxurious home but of simple wholesome hearty nature, affectionate but unsentimental, made to be a staunch friend rather than a lover of either man or woman. But in the fermentation now working in Edith to a new experience of freedom and joy her heart went out with exuberant emotion to the friend whom chance had thrown close to her. I knew, for she had told me everything, of the sentimental and sometimes passionate attraction which from early school life up to a few years before marriage she had experienced for girl friends. I knew that when a schoolgirl the resulting relationships had sometimes possessed a slight but definite sensuous character, though it had not found that experience in later adult friendships with women. I knew that such feelings were common in young girls. But at that time I had no real practical knowledge of inborn sexual inversion of character. In the essay I had written on Walt Whitman in *The New Spirit* I had passed over the homosexual strain in Whitman, in a deprecatory footnote, as negligible.[29] I am sure that if I ever asked myself whether there was a homosexual strain in

Edith I answered it similarly. I was not yet able to detect all those subtle traits of an opposite sexual temperament as surely planted in her from the beginning as in Whitman, and really the roots not only of the disharmonies which tortured her but of much of the beauty and strength of her character. The masculine traits were indeed not obvious in Edith any more than the feminine traits in Whitman; most people, I believe, failed to see them, and I cannot too often repeat than she was not really man at all in any degree, but always woman, boy, and child, and these three, it seemed, in almost equal measure.

As soon as she perceived this new emotional outflow towards her old friend Claire (as I will call her) she wrote to tell me of it with all her native trustful confidence, simple, direct and spontaneous. If I remember right, she wrote with a misgiving hesitation at first. There was, as I now look back, a pathetic wonder and beauty in that appeal to my comprehending love, as though addressed to a divine being superior to the weaknesses of a human husband. The response, as her letters show, was the response she desired and expected. But it by no means came from a godhead, but from a human and suffering heart. It was true that – though I cannot now be sure – I do not think my pain was immediate. My emotions work slowly....I had tried to conquer, and given little or no sign that the conquest was not complete, or even that there had been any need of conquest. But, after all, I was human. There remained beneath the surface the consciousness of a flaw in the ideal of married love I had so far cherished, and a secret wound of the heart 'not so deep as a well nor so wide as a church door',[30] but enough to kill that conception of mutual devotion in marriage which all my purely intellectual interest in Hinton's doctrines[31] had never destroyed as a personal aim. We were destined to work out a larger and deeper conception of love, but that beautiful conventional conception had for us been killed. Even my strong sense of justice could scarcely have long tolerated so one-sided a sexual freedom in marriage. It might be true that I was exclusively heterosexual and she was not, and that therefore there was no demand on me to go outside marriage for love. But it was also true that the very qualities in her nature which made her largely homosexual were qualities which, fortifying as they might be to our comrade-ship, were inimical to the purely feminine qualities of sweetness and repose which a man seeks in a woman, and therefore opposed in our case a strict conjugal fidelity. And so it proved....There was always a place in Edith's heart, a sacred and beautiful place, only to be filled by a woman who must be more than a friend in the conventional sense, a woman on whom she would expand a love which was like passion, even if an etherealised passion, and lavish those tender refinements and protective cares of which she so well knew the secrets.

It was Lily who occupied this place in her heart, during the brief period she knew her, more securely than any other woman before or after, and at her death was worshipped as Edith never worshipped anyone else, not even her mother, who had never been a real living person for her.

Lily was a St. Ives artist who lived with an elder sister, by whom she was jealously tended and guarded, in a little home of refined culture....She was a creature of fascinating charm that was felt alike by men and women, by rich and poor. She possessed, moreover, that artistic temperament which at this time so appealed to Edith. Much as Edith always admired the clean, honest, reliable Englishwoman, there was yet, as I have already indicated, something in that type that was apt to jar on her in intimate intercourse; she craved something more gracious, less prudish, pure by natural instinct rather than by moral principle. In Lily she found the ideal embodiment of all her cravings....Edith and Lily came to know each other slowly. Circumstances – especially the circumstance of the elder sister ever watchful over Lily like a mother – seldom permitted more than occasional and difficult private meetings. Sometimes these were stolen and took place in a quiet little wood between St. Ives and Carbis. But they often met more openly in Lily's studio at Porthminster. On one occasion I gave up my studio at Hawkes Point for the day, to enable them to picnic quietly there. It was but rarely indeed that they could spend the night together and that Lily would run to Carbis[32] with her little nightdress at a late hour when she had almost been given up. Of all those meetings there was only one which stood for ever after in Edith's memory in a halo of beauty, an October night which always lingered in her memory. In what the special beauty of that night lay it was not for her to tell, or for me to ask, only to divine, but I know that she always recalled the anniversary of it as one of the sacred days of her life. She was indefatigable, as she always was, in her devotion, and endlessly inventive in a lover's attentions. At such times she had all the air and spirit of an eager boy, even the deliberate poses and gestures of a boy, never of a man, and on one side of her, deeply woman-hearted as she was, it was more than a pose, with her restless activity and her mischeviousness and her merry ringing laugh, which suited so well with her well-shaped compact head with her short curly hair. To Lily this boyish ardour was certainly delightful, as delightful as was Lily's ethereal fragility to Edith. For notwithstanding that element of wholesome grossness in her love of the earth and even sometimes in her humour, Edith felt an intense repugnance to all grossness in love; even a trace of its presence, or a suggestion of viciousness, more than once brought to nought her nascent attraction to a woman.[#2] Lily's purity, with its brightness and its reserve – a reserve that seemed to both of them deeper than the more superficial reserve of the

English – and its flashes of audacity, together with her charming wit, and the touch of the instinctive artist in all her actions, suited Edith perfectly. Throughout her life she had numerous intimate relationships with women, but no woman, before or after, ever appealed to her so deeply, or satisfied her so utterly, as Lily. I think she more or less clearly realised that fragility which was a note of Lily's character as well as of her physical constitution, and knew that they could never be mates in soul, for Lily had no soul, but she knew that there is a sphere of love in which that counts for nothing (there was doubtless the thought of Lily in her mind when many years later she wrote a little play called *The Pixy*), and it was precisely because Lily embodied something that was entirely unlike and outside herself that the fascination she exerted was so strong. They were never sufficiently long together for Lily's weakness of character to grow into a barrier between them.

I can see that after she began to know Lily there was in Edith's love for me a subtle change which had not been produced by her affection for Claire. She no longer called me 'sweetheart' or said that I was both woman and man to her. I remained her 'boy', her 'child', always her 'comrade', and 'the one person in the world who understands me'. I am sure she realised that Lily was not only ethereal but fragile, the last person in the world to rely upon. I never felt the slightest twinge of jealousy, for Lily so clearly represented something with which I could not compete. I would as soon have been jealous of the beauty of a star. Lily was for Edith a star, a star to which for all the rest of her life the chariot of her spirit was attached.

Amy Levy

Levy (1861–89) was a protégée of Oscar Wilde, and the author of a number of poetry volumes, before her suicide in September 1889. She attended Newnham College, Cambridge, and in her lifetime achieved some success and notoriety for *Reuben Sachs* (1888), a satire on Jewish society.

Amy Levy, 'Sinfonia Eroica (to Sylvia)', *A Minor Poet and Other Verse*, 1884

My Love, my Love, it was a day in June,
A mellow, drowsy, golden afternoon;

And all the eager people thronging came
To that great hall, drawn by the magic name
Of one, a high magician, who can raise
The spirits of the past and future days,
And draw the dreams from out the secret breast,
Giving them life and shape.
    I, with the rest,
Sat there athirst, atremble for the sound;
And as my aimless glances wandered round,
Far off, across the hush'd expectant throng,
I saw your face that fac'd mine.
     Clear and strong
Rush'd forth the sound, a mighty mountain stream;
Across the clust'ring heads mine eyes did seem
By subtle forces drawn, your eyes to meet.
Then you, the melody, the summer heat,
Mingled in all my blood and made it wine.
Straight I forgot the world's great woe and mine;
My spirit's murky lead grew molten fire;
Despair itself was rapture.
     Ever higher,
Stronger and clearer rose the mighty strain;
Then sudden fell; then all was still again,
And I sank back, quivering as one in pain,
Brief was the pause; then, 'mid a hush profound,
Slow on the waiting air swell'd forth a sound
So wondrous sweet that each man held his breath;
A measur'd, mystic melody of death.
Then back you lean'd your head, and I could note
The upward outline of your perfect throat;
And ever, as the music smote the air,
Mine eyes from far held fast your body fair.
And in that wondrous moment seem'd to fade
My life's great woe, and grow an empty shade
Which had not been, nor was not.
     And I knew
Not which was sound, and which, O Love, was you.

Amy Levy, 'To Sylvia', *A Minor Poet and Other Verse*, 1884

'O Love, lean thou thy cheek to mine,
And let the tears together flow' –
Such was the song you sang to me
      Once, long ago.

Such was the song you sang; and yet
(O be not wroth!) I scarcely knew
What sounds flow'd forth; I only felt
      That you were you.

I scarcely knew your hair was gold,
Nor of the heaven's own blue your eyes.
Sylvia and song, divinely mixt,
      Made Paradise.

These things I scarcely knew; to-day,
When love is lost and hope is fled,
The song you sang so long ago
      Rings in my head.

Clear comes each note and true; to-day,
As in a picture I behold
Your turn'd-up chin, and small, sweet head
      Misty with gold.

I see how your dear eyes grew deep,
How your lithe body thrilled and swayed,
And how were whiter than the keys
      Your hands that played...[33]

Ah, sweetest! cruel have you been,
And robbed my life of many things.
I will not chide; ere this I knew
      That Love had wings.

You've robbed my life of many things –
Of love and hope, of fame and pow'r.
So be it, sweet. You cannot steal
      One golden hour.

Amy Levy, 'In the Mile End Road', *A London Plane Tree and Other Verse*, 1889

How like her! But 't is she herself,
    Comes up the crowded street,
How little did I think, the morn,
    My only love to meet!

Who else that motion and that mien?
    Whose else that airy tread?
For one strange moment I forgot
    My only love was dead.

Amy Levy, 'At a Dinner Party', *A London Plane Tree and Other Verse*, 1889

With fruit and flowers the board is deckt.
    The wine and laughter flow;
I'll not complain – could one expect
    So dull a world to know?

You look across the fruit and flowers,
    My glance your glances find. –
It is our secret, only ours,
    Since all the world is blind.

Textual footnotes

1 This is an attempt to describe by way of allegory the attraction of vice that fascinates and is intolerable; with its punishment of spiritual extinction or madness in this life. I have often doubted whether the nightmare horror which I tried to adumbrate, is a fit subject for poetic treatment. I content myself, however, by reflecting that the sense or the presentiment of sin, when sternly realized, involves this horror, and that, as it is a frequent phase of spiritual experience, we are not bound to shrink from even its most poignant presentation.

2 It was significant that never, even at her fiercest moments, did Edith bring out the vulgar swear words which so easily come to women of rather similar temperament. But she could on occasion cut or crush ruthlessly with her own more original and pungent speech.

6 SEX

This chapter is composed of texts which deal explicitly with sex between men, drawn from diverse genres, including letters, an edition of classical erotica, anonymous pornography and published poetry. The chapter is divided into three sections. The first deals with sodomy and sadomasochism (primarily birching, known on the continent then as the English vice), the second with texts which have boys and youths as their objects of desire, and the third with the fetishistic conceptualization of working-class youths and foreign boys.

These texts cannot be seen to represent an accurate picture of what men may have been doing sexually with one another in the nineteenth century. They are a selection of what has survived, was written down in the first place or is available for the twentieth-century reader. And, as with twentieth-century pornography and erotica, the ordinary, the commonplace acts may never be recorded for others' titillation. It is, however, a significant representation of the presence of resistance to the edicts of the state and the law. Such people were not supposed to exist, let alone catalogue and describe their pleasures.

SODOMY AND OTHER ACTS

Any sexual act between two or more men was criminalized for the whole of the period covered in this book. The minimum sentence handed out between 1820 and 1895 was nine months in prison, the maximum, death. In the context of this, however, it was possible not only to conceptualize pleasure in those acts, but to record them. These texts often show the pressures exerted by their production in such a social and legal context. Sex between men, in which the seed, intended by nature for propagation of the species, is diverted into other orifices and used for other purposes, is conceptualized, even by homosexuals defending their desires, as having marked effects on the male body. John Addington Symonds notes such effects in two letters to Edward Carpenter:

> I have no doubt myself that the absorption of semen implies a real modification of the physique of the person who absorbs it, & that, in these homosexual relations, this constitutes an important basis for subsequent condition – both spiritual and corporeal.

[Silvio Venturi][1] experimented upon patients by the injection in them of bestial & human semen, with results which (if one may trust his report), show that semen received into the system is a powerful nervous agent.[2]

Such a notion makes sense in a culture which views the choice of sex act and sex object as determining thoroughly the nature and identity of the individual, a framework inevitably taken up, and then re-made in almost infinitely varied forms, by those with a vested interest. Those texts which deal with sodomy and flagellation do so with a vigorous and lively pleasure, even when the price paid seems almost gratuitously severe, and a commentary on the necessary secrecy of the acts.

Perhaps the most remarkable text which deals with the eroticization of the male body is Simeon Solomon's *A Vision of Love Revealed in Sleep*, a prolonged dream or fantasy of an allegorical country where Love is sorely wounded by the injuries done to him by prejudice, condemnation and rejection. It is the only prose work by a man known otherwise for his artwork, and for his disreputable conduct. He was depicted as indulging in naked revels with Algernon Swinburne at the latter's house, he was arrested for an act of indecency in a public lavatory and jailed, and ended his life homeless and impoverished, despite the best efforts of his would-be patrons. *A Vision of Love* is an extraordinary document and quite unlike anything else from the period.

Richard Burton and Leonard Smithers, from *Priapeia, or Sportive Epigrams on Priapus by Divers Poets in English Verse and Prose*, 1890

From the 'Introduction'

The *Priapeia*, for the first time literally and completely translated into English verse and prose, is a collection of short Latin poems in the shape of jocose epigrams affixed to the statues of the god Priapus. These were often rude carvings from a tree-trunk, human-shaped, with a huge phallus which could at need be used as a cudgel against robbers, and they were placed in the gardens of wealthy Romans, for the twofold process of promoting fertility and of preventing depredations on the produce.

Most of these *facetiae*[3] are by unknown authors....The general opinion is that they are the collective work of a group of *beaux esprits*[4] who formed a reunion at the house of Maecenas (the well-known patron of Horace), and who amused themselves by writing these verses in a garden-temple consecrated to Priapus. Subsequently Martial and Petronius added several imitative epigrams, and eventually the whole was collected in one volume by the writer of the opening verses. Catullus, Tibullus, Cinna and Anser are also credited with a share in the work. The cento[5] consists chiefly of laudatory monologues by Priapus himself, jocosely and satirically written, in praise of his most prominent part – the *mentule*[6] – and of fearful warnings to thieves not to infringe upon the Garden God's domains under pain of certain penalties and punishments, obscene and facetious. At times a witty epigram sparkles from the pages, notably numbers 2, 14, 25, 37, 47, 69 and 84, the Homeric burlesque in number 69 being *merum sal*,[7] whilst numbers 46 and 70 show a degree of pornography difficult to parallel.

That the *Priapeia* has not hitherto been translated into the English tongue is to be expected: the nature of the work is such that it cannot be included in a popular edition of the classics. But to the philological and anthropological student this collection is most valuable, and the reason for omitting it from the list of translations is not applicable to a version produced for private circulation and limited to an edition of five hundred copies. Putting aside conventionalities, the translators have endeavoured to produce a faithful reflection of the original Latin, shirking no passages, but rendering all the formidably plain-spoken expressions in a translation as close as the idioms of the two languages allow....Although the value of the work in illustrating the customs of the old Romans may be small *per se*, yet when read in conjunction with the legacies of certain writers (Catullus, Petronius, Martial, Juvenal and Ausonius, for example), it explains and corroborates their notices of sundry esoteric practices, and thus becomes a supplement to their writings. With the view of making the work an explanatory guide to the erotic *dicta*[8] of the authors above-mentioned, the bulk of the notes and the excursus[9] explaining and illustrating the text and exceeding its length by some five times is devoted to articles on pederasty with both sexes, irrumation,[10] the *cunnilinges*, masturbation, bestiality, various *figurae Veneris* (modes and postures of coition, particularly that in which the man lies supine under the woman); excerpts from the Latin erotic vocabulary, including exhaustive lists of Latin terms designating the sexual organs, male and female; a list of classical amatory writers, and a host of miscellaneous matters, e.g. the habits of the Roman dancing-girls, eunuchism, tribadism of the Roman matrons, the use of phalli, religious prostitution, aphrodisiacs, the 'infamous' finger, *tabellae* or licentious paintings, the *fibula*[11] as a preventative of coition, the *crepitus ventris,*[12] etc. etc., illustrated by poetical versions of many of the epigrams culled from various sources, by parallel elucidatory passages (many hitherto untranslated) from classical writers, and by quotations from authors, ancient and modern.

English literary students have good reason to congratulate themselves on the collaboration of a certain talented *littérateur*, the mere mention of whose name would be a sufficient guarantee for the quality of the work. He has most kindly enriched the volume with a complete metrical version of the epigrams, and this is, indeed, the principal *raison d'être* of this issue. I have also gratefully to acknowledge obligations of no small weight, not only for his careful and thorough revision of the prose portion of the translation, but also for the liberal manner in which I have availed myself of his previous labours in the preparation of my notes and excursus. The name of Sir Richard F. Burton, translator of *The Book of the Thousand Nights and a Night*, has been inadvertently connected with the present work. It is, however, only fair to state that under the circumstances he distinctly disclaims having taken any part in the issue.
July 1890

64

Priapus

One than a goose's marrow softer far,
Comes hither stealing for its penalty's sake:
Steal he as pleases him: I will see him not.

A certain one, more tender than the marrow of a goose, comes hither thieving for love of the punishment.[#1] He may steal when he lists, I shall not see him.

67

Priapus

PEnelope's first syllable followed by firstling of DIdo
Take, and of CAmus the front also of REmus the head.
Whatso thou makest of these unto me when caught in my orchard
Thief! thou shalt give, such pain for thy thieving atone.

284

Let the first syllable of PEnelope be followed by the first of DIdo, the first of CAmus by that of REmus.[#2] What is made from these thou to me, when caught in my garden, O thief, shalt give; by this punishment thy fault is atoned for.

70

Priapus

When the fig's honied sweet thy taste shall catch
And hither tempt the hand of thee to stretch;
Glance at my nature, Thief! and estimate
The mentule thou must cack and what's its weight.

When the sweetness of the fig shall come into thy mind and thou shalt long to stretch forth thine hand hither, glance mindfully on me, O thief, and calculate what weight of mentule will be voided by thee.

From *Teleny*, by various authors, 1893

Teleny, or the Reverse of the Medal was first published in 1893 by Leonard Smithers, under the fictitious Cosmopoli imprint, in a limited run of 200 copies. It has been attributed in part to Oscar Wilde, although there is no evidence for this, and appears to have been written in a kind of relay by a number of anonymous authors, who delivered and collected the manuscript from a bookshop called the Librairie Parisienne in Coventry Street, London, owned by Charles Hirsch, a notable importer of pornography from Europe. The varying quality of the writing and the diversity of sexual interests represented in the text certainly support this. How it passed from Hirsch to Smithers is not known, but they themselves may also have had a hand in the writing.[13] The extract below is taken from the description of an orgy, attended only by men, at the house of a nobleman called Briancourt.

'Ah!' said the Spahi,[14] quietly lighting a cigarette, 'what pleasures can be compared with those of the Cities of the Plain?[15] The Arabs were right. They are our masters in this art; for there, if every man is not passive in his manhood, he is always so in early youth and in old age, when he cannot be active any longer. They – unlike ourselves – know by long practice how to prolong this pleasure for an everlasting time. Their instruments are not huge, but they swell out to goodly proportions. They are skilled in enhancing their own pleasure by the satisfaction they afford to others. They do not flood you with watery sperm, they squirt on you a few thick drops that burn you like fire. How smooth and glossy their skin is! What a lava is bubbling in their veins! They are not men, they are lions; and they roar to lusty purpose.'

'You must have tried a good many, I suppose?'

'Scores of them: I enlisted for that, and I must say I did enjoy myself. Why, Viscount, your implement would only tickle me agreeably, if you could only keep it stiff long enough.'

Then pointing to a broad flask that stood on the table – 'Why, that bottle there could, I think, be easily thrust in me, and only give me pleasure.'

'Will you try?' said many voices.

'Why not?'

'No, you had better not,' quoth Dr. Charles, who had kept by my side.

'Why, what is there to be afraid of?'

'It is a crime against nature,' said the physician smiling.

'In fact, it would be worse than buggery, it would be bottlery,' quoth Briancourt.

For all answer the Spahi threw himself face upwards on the ledge of the couch, with his bum uplifted towards us. Then two men went and sat on either side, so that he might rest his legs on their shoulders, after which he took hold of his buttocks, which were as voluminous as those of a fat old harlot's, and opened them with his two hands. As he did so, we not only had a full view of the dark parting line, of the brown halo and the hair, but also of the thousand wrinkles, crests – or gill-like appendages – and swellings all around the hole, and judging by them and by the excessive dilatation of the anus, and the laxity of the sphincter, we could understand that what he had said was no boast.

'Who will have the goodness to moisten and lubricate the edges a little?'

Many seemed anxious to give themselves that pleasure, but it was allotted to one who had modestly introduced himself as a maître de langues,[16] 'although with my proficiency' – he added – 'I might well call myself professor in the noble art.' He was indeed a man who bore the weight of a great name, not only of old lineage – never sullied by any plebeian blood – but also famous in war, statesmanship, in literature and in science. He went on his knees before that mass of flesh, usually called an arse, pointed his tongue like a lance-head, and darted it in the hole as far as it could go, then, flattening it out like a spatula, he began spreading the spittle all around most dextrously.

'Now,' said he, with the pride of an artist who has just finished his work, 'my task is done.'

Another person who had taken the bottle, and had rubbed it over with the grease of a *pâté de foie gras*, then he began to press it in. At first it did not seem to be able to enter; but the Spahi, stretching the edges with his fingers, and the operator turning and manipulating the bottle, and pressing it slowly and steadily, it as last began to slide in.

'Aïe, aïe!' said the Spahi, biting his lips; 'it is a tight fit, but it's in at last.'

'Am I hurting you?'

'It did pain a little, but now it's all over;' and he began to groan with pleasure.

All the wrinkles and swellings had disappeared, and the flesh of the edges was now clasping the bottle tightly.

The Spahi's face expressed a mixture of acute pain and intense lechery; all the nerves of his body seemed stretched and quivering, as if under the action of a strong battery; his eyes were half closed, and the pupils had almost disappeared, his clenched teeth were gnashed, as the bottle was, every now and then, thrust a little further in. His phallus, which had been limp and lifeless when he had felt nothing but pain, was again acquiring its full proportions; then all the veins in it began to swell, the nerves to stiffen themselves to their utmost.

'Do you want to be kissed?' asked someone, seeing how the rod was shaking.

'Thanks,' said he, 'I feel enough as it is.'

'What is it like?'

'A sharp and yet an agreeable irritation from my bum up to my brain.'

In fact his whole body was convulsed, as the bottle went slowly in and out, ripping and almost quartering him. All at once the penis was mightily shaken, then it became turgidly rigid, the tiny lips opened themselves, a sparkling drop of colourless liquid appeared on their edges.

'Quicker – further in – let me feel – let me feel!'

Thereupon he began to cry, to laugh hysterically; then to neigh like a stallion at the sight of a mare. The phallus squirted out a few drops of thick, white, viscid sperm.

'Thrust it in – thrust it in!' he groaned, with a dying voice.

The hand of the manipulator was convulsed. He gave the bottle a strong shake.

We were all breathless with excitement, seeing the intense pleasure the Spahi was feeling, when all at once, amidst the perfect silence that followed each of the soldier's groans, a slight shivering sound was heard, which was at once succeeded by a loud scream of pain and terror from the prostrate man, of horror from the other. The bottle had broken; the handle and part of it came out, cutting all the edges that pressed against it, the other part remained engulfed within the anus....At first there was a general *sauve qui peut*[17] from Briancourt's. Dr. Charles sent for his instruments and extracted the pieces of glass, and I was told that the poor young man suffered the most excruciating pain like a Stoic without uttering a cry or a groan; his courage was indeed worthy of a better cause. The operation finished, Dr. Charles told the sufferer that he ought to be transported to the hospital, for he was afraid that an inflammation might take place in the pierced parts of the intestines.

'What!' said he; 'go to the hospital, and expose myself to the sneers of all the nurses and the doctors – never!'

'But,' said his friend, 'should inflammation set in –'

'It would be all up with me?'

'I am afraid so.'

'And is it likely that the inflammation will take place?'

'Alas! more than likely.'

'And if it does –'

Dr. Charles looked serious, but gave no answer.

'It might be fatal?'

'Yes.'

'Well, I'll think it over. Anyhow, I must go home – that is, to my lodgings, to put some things to rights.'

In fact, he was accompanied home, and there he begged to be left alone for half an hour.

As soon as he was by himself, he locked the door of the room, took a revolver and shot himself. The cause of the suicide remained a mystery to everybody except ourselves.

Theodore Wratislaw, 'L'Éternal Féminin', *Caprices*, 1893[18]

Lilith or Eve, I was before the flood,
And Eden grew the palace of my sin
Wherewith I stirred the lust that slumbered in
The then unquickened furnace of man's blood;

Kissing my mouth he saw that ill was good,
Lust was Love's brother, Vice to Virtue kin;
God gave into my hand all things to win;
Between him and man's captive soul I stood.

So still I reign, for still I weave a snare
With the hot snakes of my lascivious hair,
Chain with my arms his body and fulfil
His soul with poison that my lips distil;
For God is with me, God who for my right
Of old took arms against the Sodomite!

Simeon Solomon, *A Vision of Love Revealed in Sleep*, 1871

Until the day break
And the shadows flee away
Song of Songs

IN MEMORIAM DDD

Upon the waning of the night, at that time when the stars are pale, and when dreams wrap us about more closely, when a brighter radiance is shed upon our spirits, three sayings, of the wise King came unto me. These are they: – *I sleep, but my heart waketh*;[19] also, *Many waters cannot quench love*;[20] and again, *Until the day break, and the shadows flee away*;[21] and I fell to musing and thinking much upon them. Then there came upon me a vision, and behold, I walked in a land that I knew not, filled with a strange light I had not seen before; and I was clad as a traveller. In one hand I carried a staff, and I hid the other in the heavy folds of a colourless garment; I went forward with my eyes cast upon the earth, pondering, and dazed as one who sets forth upon a journey, but who knows not yet its goal. Then I besought my spirit to make itself clearer before me, and to show me, as in a glass, what I sought; then knowledge came upon me, and I looked within my spirit, and I saw my yearning visibly manifested, and great desire was born, and sprang forth and strengthened my feet and quickened my steps. Now I stood among olive-trees, whose boughs and leaves lay still upon the air, and no light was cast upon them. Then the deep silence was broken by the stirring of the spirit within me;

my frame appeared to be rent, and a faintness fell upon me, and for a little space I knew nothing, so powerfully the spirit wrought within me. Then afterwards, as when one who works miracle lays his healing fingers upon another who is maimed, and makes him whole, so my strength was renewed, and I lifted up my eyes; and behold, the form of one stood by me, unclothed, save for a fillet binding his head, whereof the ends lay upon either side his neck; also upon his left shoulder hung a narrow vestment; in his right hand he bore a branch of dark foliage, starred with no blossoms; his face had on it the shadow of glad things unattained, as of one who has long sought but not found, upon whom the burden of humanity lies heavy; his eyes, half shaded by their lashes, gave forth no light.

I knew that my Soul stood by me, and he and I went forth together; and I also knew that the visible images of those things which we knew only by name were about to be manifested unto me. When I gazed into the lampless eyes of my Soul, I felt that I saw into the depths of my own spirit, shadow meeting shadow. Then my Soul first spoke, and said unto me, *Thou hast looked upon me, and thou knowest me well, for in me thou but seest thyself, not hidden and obscured by the cruel veil of flesh. I am come forth of thee for thy well-doing, therefore see to it that thou do me no injury. By me shalt thou attain unto the end I know thou seekest, for he whom we go forth to find may only in his fullness be manifested by my aid; for when he appears to those who, with damned eyes, grope in the waking darkness of the world, I am put aside, and he is not fully known. By me alone shalt thou behold him as he absolutely is; but in visions shall he be seen of thee many times before his full light be shed upon thee, and thy spirit shall be chastened and saddened because of them, but it shall not utterly faint. Look upon me, and I will support thee, and in thy need I will bear thee up. Looking upon me thou shalt read thine inmost self, as upon a scroll, and in my aspect shall thy spirit be made clear. Come.*

Then we went forth towards a dim sea at ebb, lying under the veil of the mysterious twilight of dawn. On its grey sands sat one whom I knew for Memory. Over her face passed the changeful alternations of sun and cloud, shade and shine; the voice of the shell which she held to her ear unburied the dead cycles of the soul; it sang to her of good and evil things gone by, and her introverted eyes looked upon them as when one looks in a mirror upon all save oneself. My Soul turned his dusky eyes upon me, and then I too heard the voice of the shell; and the ocean cast up my dead before my eyes, and all was unto me as though it had not gone by. Memory bore upon her head and breast a light rain of faded autumn leaves and blossoms, and upon her raiment small flecks of foam had already dried; her lips trembled with the unuttered voices of the past, but she did not weep.

Then I was carried back in the spirit to the time past, and as I walked forth by my Soul, my gaze was drawn inward, and I beheld myself in one of the sunny places of the world; and there was a mist arising from the joy of nature, and my spirit seemed to dance within me. And I beheld, after a space, that the mist formed itself into many visible objects, which all gave me a delight such as one feels in looking upon the golden circles which play within the depths of a sun-lighted pool; and beyond the mist I discerned the forms of many whom Memory brought back to me: they had no radiance about their heads, but their countenances bore no shadow upon them, and the light in the air wherein they moved made a music which was very pleasant unto me. As the heart sits enthroned within the body, and its pulses inform it, so sat one in their midst whose spirit made their feet to dance and their mouths to sing; she rested beneath the shade of an autumn apple-tree, and the sun had kissed her body as it had kissed the fruit of the tree and made it glow: she was naked, but guile was removed from her, therefore she knew it not: the aspect of her face was as that of the face of a child who hears new things, and holds its breath, lest the one who relates them should make too quick an end; her grey eyes looked forth without fear, and in their soft depths were mirrored the things about her that she loved so well; by her side sported all joyous, simple creatures, and she was of them and one with them; the shadow of the burden of consciousness had not fallen upon her; she had not known the sickness of the soul, for within the ark of her body the soul had found no resting-place. Looking upon her, I saw that she was good, but I knew that there was that about her which left me not content; she was even as sweet notes heard once and lost for ever.

Then I withdrew my gaze from my spirit, and raised my eyes and looked upon my Soul, and he spoke these words unto me: *It is well that thou hast thus looked upon Pleasure which is past, for with the greater ardour dost thou now desire him whom we go forth to seek: canst thou bear to look forward?* Then, as we went along, while the shallow wave drew back from the grey beach, my spirit took upon itself a great sadness; and lifting my eyes I beheld one, whom I then knew not, seeking shelter in the cleft of a rock. The shame that had been done him had made dim those thrones of Charity – his eyes; and as the wings of a dove, beaten against a wall, fall weak and frayed, so his wings fell about his perfect body; his locks, matted with the sharp moisture of the sea, hung upon his brow, and the fair garland on his head was broken, and its leaves and blossoms fluttered to the earth in the chill air. He held about him a sombre mantle, in whose folds the fallen autumn leaves had rested: and now he came forth of his sheltering place, and as he went along the light upon his head was blown about in thin flames by the cold breath of the sea; and I saw moving beside him in the grey air the spirits of those who had brought him to this pass, and the sound of their mockings fell upon my ears. Then my spirit sighed very heavily within me, and I could look no longer, for I discerned in that company the image of myself; and then all this vision passed away.

I held my regard upon the earth and marvelled at what I had seen; and I communed in sadness with my spirit, for I then knew the part I had taken to hold Love in contumely, and how I had been one of those who plant rue, thinking to behold myrtles spring therefrom; and my spirit being chastened, I lifted my eyes to my Soul, and I saw upon his face the pale light of sorrow; yet I remembered how he spoke to me at the first, and told me that he would uphold me, and that my spirit should not faint utterly. Then he and I went on gradually ascending a sandy slope, patched here and there with scanty grass; and against the pale blue sky we saw one, for whom, looking upon him, my Soul dissolved in tears, so stricken with unavailing sorrow was he, so wounded beyond the hope of healing, bound hand and foot, languishing under the weight of his humanity, crushed with the burden of his so great tenderness. I looked upon the face of my Soul, and I knew that he, in whose presence we now stood, was Love, dethroned and captive, bound and wounded, bereft of the natural light of his presence; his wings drooping, broken and torn, his hands made fast to the barren and leafless tree; the myrtles upon his brow withered and falling; and upon that heart, from whose living depths should proceed the voice of the revolving spheres, there was a wound flowing with blood, but changing into roses of the divinest odour as it fell. I stood motionless, my eyes refusing to look longer upon my stricken lord, then drawn unto my Soul, from whom I had no comfort; the voice of the shell of Memory yet sounded in my ears, and I knew that the divine captive read my spirit's inmost thoughts; from his lips proceeded inaudibly the words, *Thou hast wounded my heart.*

After a moment of mystical agony, I raised my eyes: and behold, the vision of Love was gone. Yea, and upon my own heart the words of Love became engraven, and ringed it about with flame; and then I knew to the full how my hands had been among those which had bound and wounded Love thus. Albeit my spirit found how unworthy it was to receive the odour of the roses which came forth of his heart, yet it clung about me, and became as it were a crown to my head, and I was even lifted up because of my humiliation. Then I turned unto my Soul, and saw that his gaze was bent upon me with pity, and

292

he spoke these words: *Alas! look well into thy spirit, search thy heart and pluck from it its dead garlands, cast them from thee and make it clean, and prepare it for him who shall hereafter enter therein; thou art even puffed up because the wound thou hast been one of those to deal sends forth divine fragrance; rather lament that thou hast not left whole the temple whence it comes forth: of thee and of thy like is its destruction: let us go upon our way.* Then we set forward, and silence was between us; the burden upon my spirit lay very heavy, and I knew not how to raise up my eyes.

And now a sound of great lamentation clove the dull air; it was as the wail the mother lifts up when the last of the fruit of her body is wrested from her; it was as the cry of one whose anguish may know no respite, whose soul is rent and cast abroad; it entered deep into my spirit. Then he who walked by me spake these words: *Canst thou lift thy gaze upon her who comes across the sea, upon her who is ravening like it, and is one with it? Look well upon her, for thou shalt behold in her one who would dash thee aside from the path which thou hast chosen. Look well unto thy heart, lest her breath dry up its springs. Behold.* Then I looked out to sea, and there came towards us one whose name I knew was Passion, she who had wounded and had sought to slay Love, but who, in her turn, was grievously wounded and tormented in strange, self-devised ways. The glory of her head was changed into the abiding-place of serpents whose malice knew no lull; her wasted beauty preyed upon itself; her face was whitened with pale fires, a hollow image of unappeased desire; her eyes flowed with unavailing tears; in her right hand she bore a self-wrought sword of flame, and in her left the goodly fruits and flowers she held were scorched and withered, and crawled upon by evil things; her feet were bound in inextricable folds; she was borne forth she knew not whither; her breath was as the breath of the hungry sea, and rest shall not be given unto her. And then the gentle voice of Memory spoke to me, and told me how she who was thus tormented had been at the first like unto her whom I saw in the spirit beneath the shade of the apple-tree, lying in the light of peace; and how the sun had also shone upon her, and made her face to shine; but she looked beyond the fair and happy things that were about her, and lusted after she knew not what; and then the pleasant place wherein she abode with her happy fellows was taken from her, and, as one who hungers after what he wittingly lost unto himself, so she craved and was not satisfied; she set at naught the gracious things that had been given unto her, and became the paramour of Hate; then she went about seeking to woo Love to her evil ends, and she fared to him as one humble and poorly clad; and Love had pity upon her, and bent his ear to her supplications, for he knew her not; but anon her aspect waxed

293

cruel, and fierce, deceitful flames went forth of her eyes, and dreadful things clung about her, and shamed the air that he made holy, and with her fiery breath she well-nigh slew him; and when I looked upon her and knew that she would have slain Love, pity was congealed in my heart. Then the voice of the shell spoke to me by the spirit, and said, *Thou hast no pity on thyself.* And this vision also passed from us.

Then my Soul spoke unto me these words: *It is even so, thou hast no pity on thyself, for thou too hast essayed to slay Love, as it has been shown to thee, thou hast wounded him: let us set forth, and I will show thee a vision of that which may yet be averted.* Then we fared along by the sea, and its hollow breath fell sore upon my spirit: and anon we came upon a crowd who all bore different aspects, and again among these I chose forth one who was myself; some were mocking, and some carried an air of scorn upon them, and others of deceit; some feigned mourning, and others were not moved by what they saw. Then I approached, bent down by a great awe of sorrow; and through my tear-dulled lashes I looked upon him who had been bound and wounded. He lay as one without life; the voice of his heart was dead within him; looking upon his face it seemed as if the end of all had come, and the air about him was laden with lamentations; upon his pallid brow one had thrown a spray of yew, but his body lay untended, and none had clothed him with his last garment; a thin flame rose from his heart and hovered upon it; and the cords wherewith he had been bound to the tree yet confined his hands, his feet, and his shattered wings; the light about his head had gone, and in its place the sea-froth made a crown; they who were gathered about him when we drew near had left him one by one. For myself a burning shame wrapped me round, and I sank upon the earth, and utterly abased my spirit for a space; then I heard the voice of my Soul speaking to me, and I lifted my eyes, and behold, the dolorous vision was gone. And, my heart laden with weeping, I turned unto my Soul, and he said these words unto me: *Did I not tell thee at the first that whilst thou hadst me by thy side, and didst me no injury, thy spirit should not utterly faint; therefore be not cast down at the grievous vision we go forth from beholding, but lay it as a sign upon thy heart; so shalt thou be warned in good time. We now bend our steps towards one who is mighty indeed, and it is given to man to overcome him; yet when thou shalt look upon him, thou shalt see of how a mild an aspect he is, and so thou shalt put terror away from thee. Come.*

And we yet went forth by the sea, until we came upon a temple standing alone; and the breath from the heart of the sea came up as the litanies of the dead who lay beneath it, and girt it about and fell close upon my spirit, and well-nigh made the pulses of my life to cease; but my Soul, faithful as when he first bent his eyes upon me by the olive-trees, supported me; and the door of the temple being touched by the branch which he bore, opened of itself, and my spirit yearned for the further and dreadful mystery that was to be shown me. It was well for me that there abode one beside me who would hold me up, or my heart, frozen within my breast, would have refused to support me, fainting as I was. I raised my eyes, whereof the light had gone out in the black air about us, and sought help of my Soul. He bent towards me, and said, *Cast fear from thee. Behold, thou shalt not fail.*

Before us and over us was a shadow as of the darkness before all things were; Hope was removed from the midst of it, and, looking upon it, Despair seemed to be enthroned therein; and the spirit wholly forgot that light had ever sprung forth upon the universe. Again I sought succour of him who stood beside me, and again it was vouchsafed to me: then, essaying to strengthen my eyes, I looked forward, and I beheld, slowly revealing himself in the heart of the thick darkness, one seated upon a dim and awful throne; he was wrapt about with sighs for raiment, and cypress, heavy with the tears of ages, was the crown upon his head; although his face was hidden in his potent hands when first he was manifested to my sight, yet I knew he wept, and his weeping was as the gathered-up lamentations of all time; how sore it fell upon my heart I may not say; and a great pity was begotten within me, which went forth upon my spirit, towards his throne. Anon he lifted his face, and the sadness and mourning which go forth of the hearts of all men seemed transfigured upon it, and I saw that it was overshadowed with the dark mystery of life: it appeared to me as the face of one who dwells for ever without the Holy Place, upon whose brow the highest radiance may never fall. Then I thought upon the words my Soul had spoken to me, before we entered herein, when he told me how mild of aspect was the face I should look upon. For I saw that his mien had in it an exceeding gentleness, as of a creature that desires to caress and to be caressed, but who dares not approach, lest he bring terror with him – as of one who throughout all eternity bears upon him a loveless burden, whereof he may not rid himself: his was the pallor of one who had wrestled with another strong as himself, and had prevailed, but whose own dominion was as gall to him, the knowledge of whose hateful might gnawed his own spirit through and through with an unquenchable fire, whose power was his humiliation, whose strength his weakness. For a moment's space I could not look upon him, for the memories of his prowess crowded within my heart, and surged up in a bitter stream into my eyes. Then I sought the face of my Soul, and I saw upon its darkness the answer to my unuttered question, and I knew that I stood in the presence of him who had done battle with Love, Death, who would love us did he dare, whom we would love did we dare; for, when he folds us about with the chill white raiment, he sets the seal of his love upon us; and, as the bridegroom and the bride stand linked together, overshadowed by the mystic saffron-coloured veil, and one spirit makes them one; so, at that hour when time slips from us, are we wedded to him before whom I stood, and with the sacrament of his kiss he signs us unto himself, and makes us of one flesh with him.

Then I lifted my eyes and looked yet again, and I saw that one stood by the throne, who held his finger upon his lip; he bore in one hand a crystal globe wherefrom the eyes of Death were ever averted, for he might not look therein; upon his head there bloomed a lotos flower, and lotos flowers hid his feet; the fathomless silence of the tomb came up and clothed him as with a pall, and he was girdled round with mystery, and mystery was written upon the air about him; his eyes were fixed upon the globe he held, and made dim because of what he saw therein; and the secrets of the tomb came forth and racked his face, and his face sweated with the pallid fires that rose from the dead he looked upon. And now my spirit welled up beseechingly within me, and looked forth of my eyes, and I turned them upon my Soul's face, as if suppli-cating; and his face was towards mine, and he knew the question that rested upon my lips, and he spoke and said, *Seek not to look upon the globe, for thou assuredly knowest it is given to no man to search its depths and live. He who bears it is Eternal Silence. Behold how his face is seared and furrowed with the things he knows, with the secrets that are laid bare to him. Let his name be a sign unto thee.* He ceased to speak, and my spirit was drawn inward, and I pondered upon what he who brooded upon the throne before me had wrought; and I marvelled the more at his might when I had seen how humble of demeanour he was; and these thoughts came upon me:- When he had rent asunder those newly come together and made one, when he had set at nought the bitter desire of years and the late-found joy, did he wear upon his countenance that great sadness, well-nigh sweet? When the shriek of the mother shattered the night, because the sole one left of her withered blossoms had been plucked by him, and she was left as an uprooted plant cast upon the wave, was he then crowned with humility? When I thought upon those who had made the face of her that bare them to shine, and were as the sun's kiss to her, and how he had wrapt them in his chill raiment one by one in his sight, and I looked upon his eyes whence the tears ceased not to flow, my heart failed within me, and my marvelling became too hard for me. Then I turned towards my Soul and sought his gaze; he fixed it upon me, and spoke these words: *I have read thine inmost thoughts, and they are hard indeed. Of the thing whereon thou hast pondered thou canst, of thy nature, know nothing, but only this: – When he, before whom we stands, bends his face over those whose spirits wing them away, he takes upon it the exceeding gentleness those hast seen, albeit it is not beheld of them who stand by sorrowing; for they have not looked upon his face; therefore they know it not until he lays his finger upon their lips, and touches them with his own. Let us go forth upon our way.* And he led me as who should lead one lately risen from the couch of disease, weak, and before whom the earth seems to spin, and darkness was upon us.

And my Soul said, *Raise thine eyes and behold somewhat which shall gladden them, as it hath gladdened all men before. Let the balm of this vision sink into thy spirit; so shall it make thee whole of the sickness that came upon thee in the house of Death.* I lifted my eyes, and I saw coming towards us what had the appearance of a bird moving softly along the still, grey air. As it approached us, I perceived two presences, one reclining upon the other who gently fanned the air with great wings. And now a deep calm fell upon my spirit, such as one feels when the burden of a sharp trouble is averted, and my Soul and I wept when we saw him who was being thus carried towards us; he lay lightly across the breast of his supporter, cheek reposing against cheek; upon his head were two small fair wings, and round his brow were bound the flowers and buds of poppies; upon his face there shone a distant light of child-hood; his parted lips breathed forth peace; the one who bore him smiled upon him, and rejoiced because of his burden. I knew that he who was winged was called Divine Charity, and his charge Sleep.

When we went forth out of the temple wherein abode Death, we came to a strange land stretching far out towards the wan sea, and inland the earth was overgrown with rank weeds; and ever the voice of the shell of Memory sounded in my ears, and the land to right and left of me seemed to image my past years; the comfort which I had had of Sleep departed from me, and when I sought the eyes of my Soul no rays of consolation came forth therefrom, no blossoms of golden light yet starred the dull branch he bore: the shadow of the house of Death lay heavy upon him.

Albeit the burden of great bitterness that was shed upon my spirit by him I saw upon the gloomy throne had choked up the springs of my heart, yet within my breast the flame of yearning towards him who should be the end and crown of my journeying burst forth and impelled me onward; and my spirit told me that in a short space I should look upon him, in what guise I knew not. Therefore I turned my questioning eyes upon my Soul, and a light of sadness fell upon me from his face, and he spoke and said these words:

Alas! not yet shall it be vouchsafed unto thee to behold him in his sovereign glory, clad in radiance, but thou shalt see him as he has been carried forth whence we last looked upon him with grief-dulled eyes, when he was as one bereft of life. He, whose bliss it was to make his burden Love, is a supreme spring of pity, and men laving themselves in the streams that go forth of him, account them blessed; the hurt that has been done them passes by; in his arms the broken of spirit are cherished; and when he holds the hearts that are cleft to his breast, they are once more bound together. And I raised my eyes after he had spoken these words, and sought to gather strength to look upon the coming vision.

Now again two came towards us, one bearing the other, and treading down the dark growth of weeds that thickened about us. When I saw him who reposed in the other's arms, a trembling seized me, and an awe came upon me – the awe which is begotten of exceeding pity: around his head shone a faint and flickering light, his white and perfect body was flecked here and there with blood, and, as when we saw him by the sea, betrayed, wounded, and helpless. He who supported him was ravaged with the storms of ages; in his eyes there shone a light of infinite memories; in his ears there rang the voices of unnumbered years; his mien had in it the great tenderness of one unconquerable; as a mother encircles with her arms a beloved and sorrowing child, and softly murmurs to him the songs of his infancy, so he pressed his bruised and smitten charge to his breast, comforting him with the universal voice.

And when this vision was fulfilled, the shell of Memory again sang in my ears, and I knew that what had past was the image of somewhat long gone by; and I humbled my spirit when I knew that I had been among those who consign Love to the arms of Time; casting the potent lord upon the earth, and taking no heed of him; leaving the bruises wherewith he had been buffeted to be tended perchance of none. The earth was now covered with poppies, and the air was heavy with their odours, and I would fain have sought Sleep, but that I knew it was forbidden unto me; moreover, it was given me to know by my Soul, through the spirit, that another vision was shortly to be vouchsafed unto me. The air was murmurous with faint sounds borne on the odour of the poppies: these were the echoes of the voices of my past years. I again sought the eyes of him who walked beside me, and, by the pale light of the first stars, I saw reflected in their depths the vague image of something which stamped a calm upon them; yet, as we set forth along that mystic land, our hearts were still burdened with the weariness of sorrow hard to cast away from us. Then, as my Soul turned towards me, I saw, in the shadows that gained strength about us, that a great presence was gathering itself, and, as we gazed upward, our vision rested upon one seated; around her head burned the light of the new-born stars, whose harmony made glad the pulses of the air; from her wide brow went forth a healing balm; in her aspect all men seek their rest and hide them in her shadow. She bore upon her knees one still beautiful, but pallid with woes, riven with wasting troubles, weary and dying; within her heart she hid his passing spirit; the waning golden light about him faded in the gloom of her hair, the falling blossoms of his head lightly strewed her dusky raiment wherewith she wholly enfolded him; he sank beneath her sacramental kiss, and Day was lulled to death in the all-embracing arms of Night.

And now we went forth upon our dimly lighted path, where the red and purple of the poppies faded into sombre grey beneath the faint rays of the lately risen stars, and the depths of the still pools which lay to right and left of us sent up their pale reflections, and ever the utterances of the sea of my life spoke to me by the voice of the shell of Memory: and this night seemed to be a figure of my years gone by.

After my spirit had bent itself to the pondering of these things, I turned towards my Soul, and I saw that his eyes were heavy with the sense of what was to come; also my spirit leapt up, for albeit I was yet ignorant of what was yet to be shown forth, a voice within me told me that it should be of much import; and I bent towards him who was with me and gazed earnestly upon him, as one importunate, and who sought to be prepared and made ready to receive what would be to his great benefit. And my Soul, seeing my urgency, spoke and said, *Look well upon this shortly to befall us, and take great heed unto it, for it will be of weight to thee; and it shall be, as it were, the opening of the scroll whereon we may read the rest. He, whom we relax not in seeking, shall again be revealed unto thee; but, alas, again the pulses of thy heart shall fail when thou seest him; and by the lesson of the vision shalt thou learn that thou art yet unready to behold him in his fullness; yea, and this shall not be the last trial put upon thee. Now shall be set forth before thee somewhat of the history of his shame whom we shall seek, and, how, as one who brushes not away the cobwebs that have gathered themselves together upon the fair sculpture of one divine, and has even said Ha, ha, at the spiders busy upon it; so have men laid upon him the darkness of the earth, as a thick veil wherethrough his light shall not come. I cease; the vision will unfold itself clearly in thine eyes.* Then I looked forward, and I saw that we approached what appeared to be a temple in ruin, long forsaken and not remembered; its crumbling marble walls and pillars, worn by time and storms, glimmered dimly beneath the stars; about it lay the decayed fragments of its dead beauty, and its entrances were choked up with poppies and clinging weeds, but to my spiritual vision there appeared a radiance about it that made me know that the light of him whom I sought penetrated the depths of its enduring gloom. Our heads bowed, and in silence we approached the entrance; we put aside the rank growths which sought to hinder our going in, and stood on its grass-grown threshold; then the silence of my heart was broken by its weeping, and a faintness fell upon me when I lifted up my eyes to the vision now revealed to me. Before us was an altar-like monument carved with the legend of old time, whereon the joyful creatures who sported in procession across it were wasting in decay, time-discoloured and riven; upon it he lay, whom, when we stood in the presence of Death, we saw borne to earth by Divine Charity; he was wrapped about with the slumber of those upon whom no shadow has fallen, upon his face there lay that far-off light of childhood; the mildness of his half-formed smile drew the spirit unto itself, his lashes were yet moist with late-shed tears, born not of sorrow but of tenderness; looking upon him, our wave-tossed spirits found their haven, and rest fell upon us.

Before I dared to look upon him who was present with Sleep, and whom I have not wearied of seeking, I saw by the spirit that one rose impalpably from the heart of the poppies, and hovered upon them, lapped in his half-shut wings; his eyes were not covered by their lids, yet it seemed as if slumber had fallen upon them; he fixed his mystic gaze upon a crystal globe he held in both his hands, wherein I knew by the spirit he saw pass the dreams of those who sleep beneath the stars; his locks were softly lifted by the air, and his lips trembled with the weight of the myriads of visions he called forth; his bent face was over-shadowed by the exceeding sadness of one who knows the thoughts of men.

Again I raised my eyes, and I saw her who had been lately been revealed to us receiving the passing breath of day; with unrelaxing gaze, and eyes from whose depths comes forth all gentleness, she watched Sleep, her beloved son; and she, to whom all was as an open scroll, wept when she looked upon him whose heart was as the heart of a little child; her dusky locks flowed forth upon the air, and from their shade the stars sent down their beams; their garments were fragrant with the blossoms begotten of Day's death, and hymns proceeded from the silence that was about her; upon her all-supporting arms, and hidden in her raiment, she bore those who slept and dreamed, and those who watched; she whispered peace unto those who know it not when she is not; she put away from them the sword, and healed the wounds that gape and bleed when she is not by to close them; she drew the spirit of the mother to her child who dwells in far-of lands, and in her arms the long-separated were brought together; beneath her shadow the lost little one yet again nestled upon her mother's breast; she hid the stricken in her heart, by her forsaken were taken back to the hearts of the forsakers; she brooded over the uncared-for with the soft care of her wings, and by her the forgotten were brought to remembrance.

Then I sought my Soul in trembling, for I knew that there was one present on whom I had not yet dared to look, and my Soul said to me by the spirit, *Behold him whom we seek, but we are not yet prepared.* Then I turned my gaze upon him; in the gloom of the unremembered temple he sat in all lowliness upon the fragment of a broken frieze, whereon the sculptured histories of his ancient glory crumbled and fell away, forgotten and uncared for, blighted by the breath of ages, stained with the rust of storms that know no mercy; his red and golden raiment hung loose about his limbs, and the blossoms from his hair had fallen crisped and dead upon his shoulders; the tears of a divine agony yet lay upon his cheek; the radiance which I had seen by my spirit, before my feet had gained the threshold of the temple, sprang from the wound upon his heart; and when I looked upon and saw it illumine the dim eyes of my Soul, my spirit abased itself, and my gaze fell upon the earth. Then I knew that this vision had been fulfilled, and my heart, ringing with the inner voices of the things that had been revealed to us, and my eyes laden with their images, I again turned unto my Soul, and saw that upon his countenance rested the light that came forth of Love's wound, and made it shine; and, as we departed from the temple, I rejoiced secretly at this; also I felt strengthened and gladdened at heart because of Sleep; and my spirit was softened by reason of his smile. And we turned our steps towards the waning stars.

And the awe which comes upon man at the passing away of night fell upon us, and I bethought me again of the words of the wise king, *Until the day break, and the shadows flee away.* And a strong yearning was begotten within me, and a sob burst forth from my mouth up out of my heart, and my lips said inaudibly, *Ah, that the day would break, and the shadows verily and indeed flee away;* and the spirit essayed to escape, and in travail I sought help of my Soul, and it was given unto me, and he spoke these words: *Put thy sorrowing away from thee, for the sword shall not again cruelly cleave thy spirit; yet, as I told thee before we stood upon the threshold of the ruined temple we have erewhile left, another trial shall be laid upon thee, and the spirit must needs crouch beneath the weight of it; but, albeit sorrow shall go up as a mist before thee, when thou beholdest what is at hand, thou shalt see, as behind a thick cloud, the presence of light; in the coming vision shall be dimly heralded his effulgence; it shall appear in thine eyes as it were the strong weeping that goes before joy; and as the springing forth of hope from despair: it shall not be seen of thee as a dark mystery; thy spirit will look into it and know it.* He made an end of speaking, and by the pale beams of the sinking stars I saw an image dimly mirrored in his eyes. I removed my gaze from his face, and looked abroad, and beheld, dark against the wan air of the dying night, Love seated upon a throne lowly and poor, and not worthy to bear him, – no longer, indeed, wounded and bleeding, but still bereft of his perfect glory; in his eyes there shone a soft light of suffering not yet past, but on his brow, where poppies were mingled with the myrtles, there lay the shadow which falls upon one not remembered; upon his parted lips hovered the half-formed smile of a child who halts between weeping and laughter; he was fully clothed in raiment of dim and sullied red and gold; in one hand he bore a poppy branch bound about the myrtle, from which the stars had fallen one by one, and in the other a golden globe whose brightness was obscured and shamed by dust; his feet were wholly hidden in the thick growth of weeds and poppies that crowded round his throne; he spoke no word, only the faint sounds in the air about him and the grief-dimmed eyes of my Soul told me he was Love imprisoned in an alien land of oblivion – forgotten, put away.

Again my heart sank, and the flowing of its streams waxed dull, and the words of him bound by the sea burned upon it with a more ardent flame, and the vision we passed from filled my eyes, and came forth of them in bitter tears; yet I forgot not the saying of my Soul, that this should be as the darkly revealed sign of the joy to come, for was not Love enthroned – poorly indeed – and had not the shadow of suffering well-nigh lifted, albeit indeed its sear remained, and looked upon the countenance of him beside me; and behold, upon it, despite the eyelids drooping with foregone grief, I saw the longed-for smile, and I took content upon me.

Our course now lay along an upward slope, whereon the poppies waxed scantier, and the weeds less rank; a soft mossy grass soothed our wayworn feet, and I could see by the light of the dying stars that small golden blossoms lay in a pattern upon the sward. As we neared the brow of the hill, I knew that a yet unseen and mysterious presence was about to be revealed to us; soft breezes bore his light to us upon their wings, and voices from the passing Night spoke to us of him; he was half-seated, half-lying, upon a height beyond which was stretched out the faintly glimmering sea; there lay upon him yet the shadow of Night, but his face had upon it the radiance of an expected glory, the light of glad things to come; his eyes were yet soft with the balm of Sleep, but his lips were parted with desire; his breath was as that of blossoms that awake and lift up their heads and give forth their odours; his dusky limbs were drawn up as if in readiness to depart, and his great and goodly wings softly

302

beat the air; with one hand he cast away his dim and dewy mantle from him, and with the other he put aside the poppies that had clustered thickly about him; as he turned his head to the East, the poppies fell from his hair, and the light rested upon his face: the smile it kindled made the East to glow, and Dawn spread forth his wings to meet the new-born Day. And when the Day was seated on his throne, we passed along a pleasant land that lay beneath the light of a great content; and the radiance yet lingered on the countenance of my Soul, and the sadness that had made the curves of his mouth heavy, and had dimmed his eye, now gradually departed, and there came upon him an aspect of calm, as of one certain of a good thing shortly to befall, although he knows not fully what it may be; and when I looked upon his eyes my spirit took heart, and I girded myself and set forth with my head no more bent; and we were met by many who had been shown me in my former dreams, and who all bore the reflection of a light upon their faces.

Also I saw with great joy many whom I knew by name, and who were dear to me, and they were clad in garments of beauty, so that it joyed my eyes to behold them. And it appeared to me as though I felt beating upon my breast the warmth that came from theirs towards me; and youth was set a crown upon their heads, and they bore branches blossoming from the breath of youth, and its divine essence coloured all the air about them; and I discerned one face in that company beloved of me beyond the rest; a northern sun had set a ruddy sweetness upon it, and southern suns had kissed it into perfect bloom; from the depths of the grey eyes welled up and sprang forth the spirit of Love, and, most loath to depart, yet brooded upon them as the dove in early time upon the waters; a sacred light, as of the guileless dreams of childhood, looked out from them and gladdened my own, and the softness of Sleep was bound upon the head. When I looked upon the face, I felt, indeed, that my travail was well-nigh over, and as it passed from me, and was lost to me, my spirit bathed its dusty wings in the warm, glad tears that bubbled from my heart, and was refreshed. And when the throne of day was set well-nigh above our heads, and there was that in the air which moves the heart of nature, we rested ourselves beside a running stream, whose waters brought joyous sounds from afar, as it were the long-forgotten songs and gentle voices of our childhood, yet laden with a heavier and fuller harmony from a source we knew not yet; and as we journeyed on in the dawn of the evening, an awe fell upon me, as when one enters upon a new and unknown way, and all the air about teemed with the echoes of things past and the vague intimations of things to come.

Then my Soul turned towards me and spoke these words: *Lay upon thy spirit a glad humility, and essay to strengthen thine eyes, that they may bear to behold the things which shall shortly be brought before thee to thy comfort and solace. As thou hast hitherto only seen him we see sinking beneath the burdens that have been laid upon him by thee and by the like of thee; as thou hast seen the glory about him shattered and made dull be reason of the wounds and weakness the bitter darkness of the world has inflicted, so shalt thou now behold him gathering his natural power about him, and clothed with light; but not yet shall it be given to thee to see him in the plenitude of his glory. I will support thee. Look up.*

And now I raised my eyes and looked upon the stream, and it seemed to me as though the waters were cleft apart, and there was a hollow in their midst; and lo, the air about it appeared changed, and its pulses stood still, and the sounds I had heard borne on its wave collected themselves and took form; and the form was of the colour of the sun-lighted sea, and within it I saw one borne gently upward, naked, and glowing exceedingly; the stars of the living myrtles burned fresh upon his hair, and his countenance was as the supreme excellence of youth transfigured, the wound upon his heart was healed, and on its place I saw burning a ruddy flame, whereof the tongues came forth to me and touched my own, whereon were engraven the words which I heard Love speak when we saw him bound to the tree, and in their stead the flame wrought this saying, letter by letter, *Many waters cannot quench Love, neither can the floods drown it*; and now the radiant mist wherein he was lifted up rose and enfolded him, and hid his aspect from me, and its form was dispersed, and it was changed to gentle sounds in the stream, and all the air about became as it was before.

Then I turned my eyes upon my Soul and saw that he appeared well pleased, and the sparkling light sent up from the ripples of the stream whereby we sat played across his brow and illuminated his dusky hair. Then I knew that I should be gladdened by what he was going to tell me. He spoke and said, *Thou hast well seen that the travail of Love is past and gone by, and content and joy are spread over the whole air because of it. Now there will arise upon thy vision a mystery which thou wilt, of thy nature, comprehend but dimly; yet fail not to look well upon it, for by it the springs of the heart of the universe are fed and made glad; and because Love is thus gone up from the wave in thy sight, it is given to thee to look upon it.*

He ceased to speak, and I turned my gaze in the direction where I had seen the last vision; and behold, again the air seemed changed, and I saw a happy light gathering itself there, and it seemed, as it were, to be formed of the warmth which makes the earth bring forth its fruit; and there appeared to me within the light an inner living glow, and the glow divided itself in twain, and

304

became two Holy Ones, each having six wings; their limbs moved not, but the ardour wherewith their spirits were endued bore them along. As one sees in a soft air two flower-laden branches bend one towards the other, and, mingling, send forth a two-fold fragrance, so I saw one of these impelled towards his fellow and lightly touch him, and a living pulse seemed to beat in the flame that went forth from them, and a form was given to it, and a heart informed it, and all the fire-coloured air about it breathed hymns at this marvellous birth. Albeit, my spirit had not yet been fully purified, so that I should clearly know what this mystery showed forth; yet I was greatly rejoiced in that it was given to me to see it. And now my Soul turned towards me and spoke these words, *What thou hast just beheld it is vouchsafed to no man to comprehend, save he see the glory that comes forth of the Holy Place; therefore gird up thy spirit that thou be ready for the call of him who shall lead thee thereunto. What thou hast seen it was given to the three Holy Ones to know fully when they were cast into the furnace; for as the serpent-rod which the prophet threw forth swallowed its fellows, the greater eating the lesser, so did the fiercer flames of that Charity which thou hast erewhile seen wonderfully and mystically begotten go forth of the righteous children's heart, and devour and utterly dry up the heat that burned about them.*

He ceased to speak, and then I turned my gaze upon his eyes, and rejoiced greatly through my spirit to see a brighter glow upon them, as from the expected coming of the long-desired; and when I cast my eyes upon the earth I discerned there many happy creatures, joyous and beautiful, and such as have no existence in the neighbourhood of evil. After a space, and when my eyes had been gladdened by reason of these things, I again turned them upon my Soul, and I knew that what we sought would now shortly be revealed to us. A weakness fell upon me, but my Soul supported me; we looked forward, and saw one approaching clothed about with a soft light; he moved towards us, gently lifted by the spirit from the ground, neither flying nor running. Ever and again his feet, wherefrom sprang glowing wings, touched the earth and caused it to bring forth flowers; his head was bound with a fillet of violet, and violet blossoms breathed upon by Love; he carried a mystic veil of saffron colour, which depended from his head upon his shoulders even to the ground, and his shining body was half girt with fawn-skin; in his hand he carried a staff, which was as the rod of the high priest, for as I looked upon it its barrenness burst forth in almond bloom; and, as when the prophet put away his shoes off his feet before the Holy Place, and beheld the bush burning with fire but not consumed, even so I saw upon the staff the dancing tongues of flame cling round the wood, but leave it scatheless; and this thing appeared marvellous in my eyes, and I thought upon the words my Soul had spoken to me concerning the three Holy Ones, and how the fires which wrapped them about did but make their stronger and fairer than before.

And now, looking upon the face of him who came towards us, it appeared as the face of one dwelling in the Holy Place, glowing with the perfect peace which is shed of Love, for he had borne the Very Love within his hands, therefore upon him the shadow of the burden of humanity had not rested; and now, encouraged by his gentle mien, and by the strengthened light upon the eyes of my Soul, I went forward until I set myself in front of him who bore the saffron veil; the waves of Love that moved about him laved my face, they refreshed me, and loosened me from the grip of my humanity, but it was not yet vouchsafed to me to cast it from me.

As the holy seer prayed to be purged of his transgressions by the burning coal of Charity, so I too desired that my lips should be touched, and my eyes made clear and worthy to behold those things whence flow the springs of life. When the aspect of him who bore the blossoming staff fell full upon me it generated a stronger yearning towards the Beatific Vision, and the distant harmonies of the spheres became clearer unto me; I then first felt conscious that a faint light hovered about my own head, like that upon the head of my Soul, and the voice of him who bore the mystic veil spoke to me by my spirit, and I heard these words, *Before thou art worthy to behold Him whom thou hast so long sought in the perfect fullness of His glory, thou must be purged of all grossness, thou must be clothed utterly with change of raiment, and the dead fruit of thy heart and of thy lips must be put away from thee; and when these things shall have been done, yea, even then thou shalt not see His full effulgence with none between it and thee, but through the veil of Sleep shall it be revealed unto thee. Follow me.* Then, chastened by these words, I again bent my head, and my Soul led me forward.

Then I turned unto me and bent a look upon him as of one questioning, and, seeing my aspect, he turned towards me and spoke these words: *Wouldst thou learn who is this thus leading us on towards Him we seek; thou sawest his name upon his brow, but the lingering darkness of thy spirit forbade thee to decipher it aright; he it is whom thou hast known since first thou camest away from thy mother's breast, for with what thou receivedst therefore, thou acceptedst him; looking upon him thou lookest upon what has ever dwelt within thy heart of hearts, for by him shall the Very Love be revealed unto thee; he has no beginning, for throughout all ages has he stood by and ministered to Him we seek and shown Him forth: it has been desired of many from the first years unto this day to put him aside and even to slay him, but, like the flame-girt, unconsumed staff he bears, he passes through the fire, and even in these latter days gives forth the light that has first been shed upon him. The violets upon his brow are those of young time, yet the dew is fresh upon them; and though it was believed of many that his staff was sapless and withered, behold how the air about it is made fragrant by the blossoms that it bears. Faithful is he through all; he holds on high his lamp so that those who look above the high fogs that cling about the earth may be led of it, and the flames about him penetrate the thick darkness of the waking world. Many have sought to tear the wings from off his feet that they may not see the light that springs forth from them; yet still the radiance of Him who he shows forth makes his feet shed light abroad, and still the earth yields flowers at his approach. Let us follow him.*

He who bore the flame-girt staff floated lightly along his path of flowers, and the glow about his winged feet made their petals to expand. And now in all humility I stood upon the threshold of a glowing temple; the air about it was moved by the breath of Him who dwelt within, its waves were heavy with the odours that came forth of His presence, and its pulses echoed with the voices of the worlds that revolve because of Him. Within the court of the temple I heard the sounds of wings that ceased not to beat the air; then a tremor came upon my hands and feet, for remembrance brought to me the image of him we saw by the grey sea, bound hand and foot, and the voice from his heart sounded yet in my ears. Then one came unto me, having six wings, which overshadowed my Soul and me, and, though I looked not upon his face, I knew he touched my forehead and lips with it, and they were purified by fire, but not seared with its sting. Then his fellow came unto me, and put away my traveller's garb from off me, and clothed me with a vestment in colour like the heart of an opal, and over my left shoulder he laid a stole tinted like a flame seen through water, and he placed upon my head a veil which covered my eyes, but did not dim my spiritual vision; and now again the words which came from Love's mouth, when I saw him bound by the sea, rang in my ears, *Thou hast wounded my heart*, and a deeper humility fell upon me. Then I heard him of the winged feet say unto my Soul, *He is prepared, come*; and I was borne along by the spirit through the outer court and toward the Holy Place, and ever the rushing sound of the wings became louder and louder, and I knew that the temple was filled with seraphim, for the veil which hung over my eyes but shielded them from a light which, when it should fall upon them, would blind them; also I knew that he whose head was bound with violets had left us, and consigned me to the care of my Soul.

Now there arose before me the image of him whom we had seen sleeping in the ruined temple; his arms were wound about his head, which lay back upon them; he was naked, but his form was wrapped about with the soft star-lighted air; his lashes were no longer moist with tears, but his face shone as became one through whom the Very Love was to be revealed. And now I felt the heart of the universe beat, and its inner voices were made manifest unto me, the knowledge of the coming presence of the Very Love informed the air, and its waves echoed with the full voices of the revolving spheres. Then my Soul spoke to me and said, *In the beginning of time the universe and all that was therein was grey, and its springs were without life, as a fair body, joyless and lacking beauty, because no spirit stirs it; light had not come upon it; and, as when one is in a trance, the pulses are dead, and await the aid of that which shall enter them and make the dead alive; even so, there sprang forth, of its own power and holy ardour, a light over the face of all things, and the heat of it made them glow, and the grey became green: the golden air sang over all, and an universal hymn arose and went up, and its voice yet gladdens the circling worlds. As the prophet saw in the dark valley the dead bones come together and take life upon them, even so Love, who was the light, smiled upon the uninformed countenance of things, and it was kindled because of it; and there went from him a two-fold essence, whereof the streams have flowed for ever, and cease not to flow; and by them are we upheld, and our spirits replenished; and, as the priest holds the flower-starred crown over the heads of the bridegroom and the bride, so now and again do the streams unite within us, and Love, whence they go forth, is the crown over us and the light about us. But through the thick veil of the darkness of the world this is not seen or known of men, but only through the spirit may it be made clear unto us; and the spirit soars aloft rejoicing, and is girt about with delight because of it.*

And now the image of Sleep filled the orbit of my sight, and through the veil of his form I saw him who bore the mystic saffron raiment wherewith he had covered his hands. My spirit well-nigh fainting, I turned unto my Soul, and knew by the increasing glow upon him that strength was given me yet again to lift my eyes. Well was it for me that what came was revealed to me through the veil of Sleep, else I could not have borne to look upon it.

From out the uplifted hands of him who stood within the Holy Place there sprang forth a radiance of a degree so dazzling that what else of glory there was within the temple was utterly obscured; as one seeing a thin black vapour resting before the face of the mid-day sun, so I saw upon the radiance the brooding cherubim, their wings meeting, their faces hidden; I saw within the glory, one who seemed of pure snow and of pure fire, the Very Love, the Divine Type of Absolute Beauty, primaeval and eternal, compact of the white flame of youth, burning in ineffable perfection.

For a moment's space I shielded my eyes from the blinding glow, then once more raised them upon the Beatific Vision. It seemed to me as though my spirit were drawn forth from its abiding place, and dissolved in unspeakable ardours; anon fiercely whirled round in a sphere of fire, and swiftly borne along a sea of throbbing light into the Very Heart. Ah, how may words shew forth what it was then vouchsafed to me to know? As when the thin, warm tears upon the cheek of the sleeping bride are kissed away by him who knows that she is wholly his, and one with him; as softly as his trembling lips are set upon the face transfigured on his soul, even so fell upon my heart, made one with the Heart of Love, its inmost, secret flame: my spirit was wholly swallowed up, and I knew no more.

Then all this wondrous vision was fulfilled, and looking upon the sky, I saw that the stars had set and the dawn had spread his wings over the world; and again the words of the sage King, *Until the day break and the shadows flee away*, came into my mind.

Algernon Charles Swinburne to
D. G. Rossetti, 22 December 1869[22]

As for Tennyson's Pelleas,[23] you flatter him by calling him a schoolboy who misses the birch – the generic schoolboy is precociously excitable 'with all (such) *appliances* and means to boot'[24] – but the very birch could hardly have drawn human blood – the blood of 'a brother and boy' from that biped. Unlike a young cousin of mine to whom at his earnest prayer I gave a copy of my Poems (hoping they might be truly blessed to him through Jesus our Saviour and His redeeming Blood), but his tutor confiscated the book under penalties, and the boy of course cribbed it, and was (I am happy to say) caught, as he deserved, studying a most appropriately named and especially prohibited poem – and had what he calls 'such a jolly good swishing' that his elder brother tells me he came out of his tutor's study with his clothes readjusted but the blood visibly soaking through his shirt and the seat of his breeches (these being, providentially, very light) in patches and stripes – to the wild delight of the junior male members of the household, who received him with acclamations. I wished *mon vieux*[25] had been by to hear – it would have made him wriggle and bubble with enjoyment till his teeth came out – a sight profitable for admonition....Well, I did think my poems had not much of ideal infamy to teach a public schoolboy of four or five years' standing, and he might have read them in holiday time 'unwhipped of justice', saying to his tutor, 'Hide thee, thou bloody hand'[26] (in a double sense of the adjective). I must confess though he asked me one day lately to explain one or two points in Anactoria[27] which perplexed his young intelligence; but I declined to coach him in Sapphics,[28] and referred him to his tutor for a construe of Catullus 'in Priapum'[29] – but somehow he didn't seem to see it quite. I must say though I was sorry for him I was much tickled (otherwise tickled than he was, and elsewhere) at the idea of a young disciple having already watered the roots of the Church planted by me; and we know that '*Sanguis martyrum semen* (so to speak) *ecclesiae*'.[30] Not that I *enjoyed* it – for 'oh! monsieur – il est donc possible qu'on puisse prendre du plaisir à voir suffrir – à voir conter le sang? – Tu le vois, bougresse, lui répond cet homme immoral; oui, putain, tu le vois!'[31] Vide the Marquis passim. Now if the boy had been reading the classic work of that immortal man there might have been some call for birch – if yet of any use. However I hope that like Justine he 'offered his flogging to God' – though I'm sure I don't see what God could do with it; but that young woman you know always prayed thus after flagellation or other infliction – 'Reçois, Être Supreme, la triste offrande de mes souffrances!'[32] So I suppose it is the right thing.

'Etonensis', from 'Arthur's Flogging', 1888[33]

And over him in front stood Philip Shirley
    And Edward Beauchamp, holding up his shirt;
And if he plucked it from them, they looked surly,
    As they drew up again the blood-stained skirt,
And shook their fists aside at Arthur's curly
    Head, or else grinned, and whispered, 'Does it hurt?'
And only held the spotted shirt up higher,
Till the birch seemed to set his bum on fire.

He clapped his hands behind – the birch twigs caught 'em
    Across, and made them tingle too and bleed;
And harder still the birch fell on his bottom,
    And left some fresh red letters there to read;
Weeks passed before the part inscribed forgot 'em,
    The fleshy tablets, where the master's creed

Is written on a boy's skin with birchen pen,
At each re-issue copied fair again.

This was the third edition, not the first,
    Printed on Arthur's bottom in red text
That very week, with comments interspersed,
And cuts that left the student's eye perplexed,
Though in the lore of flagellation versed,
    You hardly could tell one cut from the next;
All the smooth creamy paper, white and pink,
Was crossed and scored and blotted with red ink.

The fair full page of white and warm young flesh
    Was ruled across with long thick lines of red,
And lettered on the engraved backside with fresh
    Large characters, by all boys to be read,
In hieroglyphs fine as a spider's mesh,
    With copious coloured cuts illustrated,
Warm from the hand that begot 'em,
To adorn the bare blank page of Arthur's bottom.

All down the cream white margins, line on line,
    Ran the red tracery of the engraver's tool,
With many a capital and flourish fine,
    And ere the characters had time to cool
The well-soaked birch, still supple from the brine,
    Made a fresh score in sight of the whole school,
Who saw the inscription on the bare flesh scored,
While Arthur writhed in agony, and roared.

Just where the broad bare bottom, smooth and plump,
    Flaked with red drops like rose leaf fallen on snow,
Sloped towards the tender thighs, – there, worn to a stump,
    The frayed birch dealt its last and sharpest blow;
On either swelling cheek the whipped boy's rump
    Had fresh red lines and starting blood to show,
Even where the round cheeks gradually divide,
The specks of blood sprang forth on either side.

'That's all for this time; now get up, boy.' As
    These words fell from the master's lips at last,
And Arthur heard, and rose, his bottom was

A map of bloody line, where lashes past
Had left the fair flesh one red and quivering mass
    Of stripes and cuts and sores; so hard and fast
The birch had laid its strokes on, that his bottom
Not for a fortnight or a month forgot 'em.

He rose, and drew his trousers up, and turned
    Back to his place; tears on his face were yet,
And still his smarting bottom throbbed and burned,
    As he sat down with cheeks all flushed and wet,
And flinched, and then tried to seem unconcerned
    As far as pain would let him, when he met
The next boy's laughing eyes, and felt him jogging
His arm, 'Well, Arthur, how d'ye like your flogging?'

Aleister Crowley, from *White Stains: The Literary Remains of George Archibald Bishop, a Neuropath*[34] *of the Second Empire*, private publication, 1898

Crowley's Preface to *White Stains* presents the text as the literary output of George Archibald Bishop, and its publication as fulfilling their author's request that his manuscripts not be printed until thirty years after his death. That this is a fiction is indicated by Crowley's account of the reason for writing *White Stains*, in his *Confessions* (see p. 316 below), in which he describes it as a highly moral book designed to explore the psychology of sexual vice. The poems are a literary account of the sexual activities of Bishop, but the 'biography' of Bishop offered by Crowley contains many elements not referred to in the poems. Bishop was born a bastard, a product of adultery, but believed by his mother's husband to be the second coming of the Messiah who took the baby to Russia to escape Herod and to present him to Gog and Magog[35] as the Antichrist. After the husband's death the nurse brought Bishop back to England. As an adult he went mad 'with absinthe and satyriasis'. The asylum he was sent to burnt down and he died.

   The poems are presented chronologically, and chart Bishop's progress from romantic heterosexuality, through bestiality and pederasty, to sado-masochism and necrophilic cannibalism. Included here are two of the pederastic poems. A third, on a more refined fetish object, will be found later in this chapter (p. 340 below).

From the Preface

The Editor hopes that Mental Pathologists, for whose eyes alone this treatise is intended, will spare no precaution to prevent it falling into other hands.

The present collection of verses will hardly be popular; if the lost works turn up, of course it may be that there may be found 'shelter for songs that recede'. Still, even here, one is, on the whole, more attracted than repelled; the author has enormous power, and he never scruples to use it, to drive us half mad with horror, or, in his earlier more exquisite works, to move us to the noblest thoughts and deeds. True, his debt to contemporary writers is a little obvious here and there; but these are small blemishes on a series of poems whose originality is always striking, and often dreadful, in its broader features....The Works of George Archibald Bishop will speak for themselves; it would be both impertinent and superfluous in me to point out in detail their many and varied excellences, or their obvious faults. The raison d'être, though, of their publication is worthy of especial notice. I refer to their psychological sequence, which agrees with their chronological order. His life-history, as well as his literary remains, give us an idea of the progression of diabolism as it really is; not as it is painted. Note also, (1) the increase of selfishness in pleasure, (2) the diminution of his sensibility to physical charms. Pure and Sane is his early work; then he is carried into the outer current of the great vortex of Sin, and whirls lazily through the sleepy waters of mere sensualism; the pace quickens, he grows fierce in the mysteries of Sapphism and the cult of Venus Aversa[36] with women; later of the same forms of vice with men, all mingled with wild talk of religious dogma and a general exaltation of Priapism at the expense, in particular, of Christianity, in which religion however, he is undoubtedly a believer till the last; then the full swing of the tide catches him, the mysteries of death become more and more an obsession, and he is flung headlong into Sadism, Necrophilia, all the maddest, fiercest vices that the minds of fiends ever brought up from the pit. But always to the very end his power is unexhausted, immense, terrible. His delirium does not amuse; it appals! A man who could conceive as he did must have had some glorious chord in his heart vibrating to the eternal principle of Boundless Love. That this love was wrecked is for me, in some sort a relative of his, a real and bitter sorrow. He might have been so great! He missed Heaven! Think kindly of him!

Dédicace[37]

You crown me king and queen. There is a name
    For whose soft sound I would abandon all
    This pomp. I liefer would have had you call
Some soft sweet title of belovéd shame.
Gold coronets be seemly, but bright flame
    I choose for diadem; I would let fall
    All crowns, all kingdoms, for one rhythmical
Caress of thine, one kiss my soul to tame.

You crown me king and queen: I crown thee lover!
I bid thee hasten, nay, I plead with thee,
    Come in the thick dear darkness to my bed.
Heed not my sighs, but eagerly uncover,
    As our mouths mingle, my sweet infamy,
    And rob thy lover of his maidenhead.

Lie close; no pity, but a little love.
    Kiss me but once and all my pain is paid.
Hurt me or soothe, stretch out one limb above
    Like a strong man who would constrain a maid.
Touch me; I shudder and my lips turn back
    Over my shoulder if so be that thus
My mouth may find thy mouth, if aught there lack
    To thy desire, till love is one with us.

God! I shall faint with pain, I hide my face
    For shame. I am disturbed, I cannot rise,
I breathe hard with thy breath; thy quick embrace
    Crushes; thy teeth are agony – pain dies
In deadly passion. Ah! you come – you kill me!
Christ! God! Bite! Bite! Ah Bite! Love's fountains fill me.

A Ballad of Passive Paederasty

Of man's delight and man's desire
    In one thing is no weariness –
To feel the fury of the fire,
    And writhe within the close caress

Of fierce embrace, and wanton kiss,
And fine nuptial done aright.
　　How sweet a passion, shame, is this,
A strong man's love is my delight!

Free women cast a lustful eye
　　On my gigantic charms, and seek
By word and touch with me to lie,
　　And vainly proffer cunt and cheek;
　　Then angry they miscall me weak,
Till one, divining me aright,
　　Points to her buttocks, whispers 'Greek'! –
A strong man's love is my delight!

Boys tempt my lips to wanton use,
　　And show their tongues, and smile awry,
And wonder why I should refuse
　　To feel their buttocks on the sly,
　　And kiss their genitals, and cry:
'Ah! Ganymede, grant me one night!'
　　This is the one sweet mystery:
A strong man's love is my delight!

To feel him clamber on me, laid
　　Prone on the couch of lust and shame,
To feel him force me like a maid,
　　And his great sword within me flame,
　　His breath as hot and quick as fame;
To kiss him and to clasp him tight;
　　This is my joy without a name,
A strong man's love is my delight!

To feel again his love grow grand
　　Touched by the languor of my kiss;
To suck the hot blood from my gland
　　Mingled with fierce spunk that doth hiss,
And boils in sudden spurted bliss;
Ah! God! the long-drawn lusty fight!
　　Grant me eternity of this!
A strong man's love is my delight!

Envoi
Husband, come early to my bed,
  And stay beyond the dawn of light
In mighty deeds of lustihead.
  A strong man's love is my delight!

Aleister Crowley, from *The Confessions of Aleister Crowley*,[38] 1929

My essential spirituality is made manifest by yet another publication, which stands as a testimony of my praeterhuman innocence. The book is called *White Stains* and is commonly quoted by my admirers as evidence of my addiction to every kind of unmentionable vice. Asses! It is, indeed, technically, an obscene book, and yet the fact that I wrote it proves the purity of my heart and mind in the most extraordinary fashion.

The facts are as follows: In the course of my reading I had come across von Krafft-Ebing's *Psychopathia Sexualis*. The professor tries to prove that sexual aberrations are the result of disease. I did not agree. I thought that I was able to understand the psychology involved; I thought that the acts were mere magical affirmations of perfectly intelligible points of view. I said to myself that I must confute the professor. I could only do this by employing the one form at my disposal: the artistic form. I therefore invented a poet who went wrong, who began with normal and innocent enthusiasms, and gradually developed various vices. He ends by being stricken with disease and madness, culminating in murder. In each of his poems he describes his downfall, always explaining the psychology of each act.

The conclusions of the book might therefore be approved in any Sunday School, and its metaphysics is orthodox from the point of view of the theologian. I wrote the book in absolute seriousness and in all innocence. It never occurred to me that a demonstration of the terrible results of misguided passion might be mistaken for pornography. Indeed, now that I do understand that vile minds think it a vile book, I recognize with grim satisfaction that *Psychopathia Sexualis* itself has attained its enormous popularity because people love to gloat over such things. Its scientific form has not protected it from abuse, any more than the artistic form of my own reply to it.

BOY-LOVE

> I feel my strongest, purest desire in the sight of charming, boyish features....The only thing that disturbs my illusion is, when the beautiful boy grows older, and a beard develops....Only quite young, tender, shy, girlish boys attract me, not strong and robust ones, and indeed only those with decent and pure hearts.[39]

Works which deploy the figure of the young boy or youth as the object of desire may seem to late twentieth-century eyes to be bordering on the paedophilic. Sex is not the automatic, explicit or implicit, goal of these narrators. The fetishistic elements of these texts are focused not on acts, but on the type of boy, his purity and passivity, and his fidelity to the adult. Sex and the flesh are there to be negotiated, but it is thus that the double bind arises. Sex might be nice, but if the boy should actively choose it, then sex is no longer wanted because the precondition of the desire for sex has gone. The boy who appears in these texts is consistently slim, sexually seductive, sexually innocent, physically vigorous, generalized and depersonalized. They are depicted in environments where nudity and physical activity are normal, and one of the principle sub-genres of the boy-love literature is the bathing-boy poem. Swimming was, at this time, properly a single-sex activity, and offered a legitimate reason to represent a group of naked young males. The narrators cast themselves as mere observers of the scene, or identify themselves with the water embracing the bodies of the boys. In either case authority rests with the voyeur, who constructs the boys as the object of desire, while ostensibly reporting on real-life episodes, as in Rolfe's 'Ballade of Boys Bathing', or commenting on works produced by others, such as the poems based on paintings. In this way, culpability is mitigated, without any need to alter the text or its images for publication.

The inequalities attendant on age difference structure the relationship between adult and child, but the adult is frequently cast as the victim of the child's beauty. The adult may have a father-like responsibility for the child,[40] but he is vulnerable to the caprices and whims of childhood, exemplified in Bertram Lawrence's 'A Summer Hour', and he mourns the transitoriness of youthfulness, and the corruption that comes with adulthood. The declared aim of several of the bathing-boy poems, and the implicit aim of others, is to fix in words the transience of masculine adolescence or childhood, to keep available to the reader a vivid representation of the body of perfect boyhood, and the possibility of bodily contact with such a boy.

Bertram Lawrence,[41] 'A Summer Hour', *The Artist and Journal of Home Culture*, October 1894

Love tarried for a moment on his way,
Against my cheek his curly head he lay;
He said that he would never leave my breast
If I would give him what I valued best.
Mine arms went out to greet him then and there,
What heart had I to cast out one so fair?

He whispered that his little feet were sore,
He was so weary that he could go no more,
He showed the wounds upon his tender flesh,
And, as he whispered, bound me in his mesh.
He whispered in mine ear his piteous tale,
What heart had I to cast out one so frail?

I kissed his little hands, his lips, his hair,
And kissing gave my soul into his care,
Love laughed a little, like a child at play, –
'Regretted that he could no longer stay,
He had so many things to do today', –
Another moment Love was far away.

Percy Osborn, 'Heartsease and Orchid', *The Spirit Lamp*, vol. 3, 17 February 1893

Heartsease it was from his dear hand I took,
A dainty flower that loves the garden air,
Breathing the freshness of his boyhood fair.
So it was treasured in a golden book.
There came another with a far-off look,
His hand an orchid gave; 'twas strange and rare,
And caught my senses in a beauteous snare,
Till sunlight for the furnace I forsook.

My heart grew drowsy with a sweet disease;
And fluttered in a cage of fantasy;
And I remembered how his face was pale,
Yet by its very paleness more did please;
Now hath the orchid grown a part of me,
But still the heartsease tells its olden tale.

E. F. Benson, from *Mother* (Chapter XII), 1925

I had long wanted to write some kind of chronicle concerning a boy's adolescence, when for a time, shy and impressionable and vastly sentimental, he belongs to neither of the two sexes, and does not melt into his own sex for a year or two yet. Some boys, rather rare exceptions, are thoroughly male throughout this period, but most are of some strange third sex, lively but quite indeterminate. Just at that age everything is fiery; the proper human boy, who is on the way to become a man with stuff in him, whether for the building of empire or the amelioration of slums or the more ascetic devotion to art, touches life with a burning finger. His affections and friendships, like his cricket or butterfly-collecting, are passions to him. With girls the same general principle holds good, but with this difference, that a girl is far more a little woman than a boy of corresponding age is a little man. Her sex has more definitely declared itself than his, and though the normal girl makes passionate friendships with those of her own sex, she is always imagining herself a woman with marriage and wife-hood and child-bearing dimly in front of her. Two girls, in fact, will confide to each other, in virgin intimacy and innocence, the glories of a boy, but two boys of fifteen or sixteen, in similar circumstances, will not so often rave over the wonder of a girl. The riddle of sex bothers them less, the expression of it more, but they have a compensation in the greater outlets for energy that they enjoy. Boys (the energy of the sexes being taken as equal) can blow off their steam over games, which to girls are more a recreation than a game. There is, though boys are just as sentimental as girls, a larger sluice, the joy of running and hitting.

In both boys and girls then about the time of adolescence, there occur these signs and signals of love: an adoration, that is to say, and a devotion wholly transcending the normal limits of friendships. In an adult they would rightly be termed abnormal, but at an earlier age they are so common that we must regard them as a stage in ordinary natural development. But the whole subject from the male point of view was somehow tainted with beastliness, or guttered away into mere tallowy slosh; if rash people wrote a story about school-boys and touched on their affections, they seemed at the most to set their climax at the school-concert, where the small boy (treble) sang 'Oh, for the wings of a dove', and felt that he was singing at the captain of the school cricket eleven, who, eighteen years old, blue-eyed and golden-haired, had made a century that day, and was sitting next to the headmaster's daughter, whom he married afterwards. Sometimes the younger boy contracted consumption, and, as in *Tim* was carefully kissed by the elder shortly before he died.[42] Otherwise, school stories, if more discreet, were even more blatantly unreal: there were cheats and bullies (Group I) and cricketers and noble young people (Group II), and the cheats were detected and degraded to lower forms, and the bullies were birched, and all the cricketers made immense scores, and all the noble young people got scholarships at Balliol.

But why not try, so I had long thought to myself (and probably fail), to write a school story not about cheats and bullies and sopranos, to deal with affairs that conceivably might have happened: to imagine a boy clean-minded and instinctively revolting from sentiment, who is yet absorbed in such passionate friendship as is characteristic of the fiery age? There was no need to get rid of the captain of the eleven, for he invariably occurs in real life, nor of normal boys madly keen on cricket and friendship, who, though loathing the expression of sentimentality, were, nevertheless, profoundly sentimental. All this had churned in my head for years past, and now, just now, what completer escape from the tragedy and boredom could a scribbler find? It was to be boyhood again before the war was invented or sex manifested, when four copper coins would infallibly produce a pound of sugar, when perfect bliss could be enjoyed with half-a-dozen racket balls and friends and when anyone over the age of twenty seemed already ripe for the winding-sheet.[43]

Algernon Charles Swinburne, 'Erotion', *Poems and Ballads, First Series*, 1865

Sweet for a little even to fear, and sweet,
O love, to lay down fear at love's fair feet;
Shall not some fiery memory of his breath
Lie sweet on lips that touch the lips of death?
Yet leave me not: yet, if thou wilt, be free;
Love me no more, but love my love of thee.

Love where thou wilt, and live thy life; and I,
One thing I can, and one love cannot – die.
Pass from me; yet thine arms, thine eyes, thine hair
Feed my desire and deaden my despair.
Yet once more ere time change us, ere my cheek
Whiten, ere hope be dumb or sorrow speak,
Yet once more ere thou hate me, one full kiss;
Keep other hours for others, save me this.
Yea, and I will not (if it please thee) weep,
Lest thou be sad; I will but sigh, and sleep.
Sweet, does death hurt? thou canst not do me wrong:
I shall not lack thee, as I loved thee, long.
Hast thou not given me above all that live
Joy, and a little sorrow shalt not give?
What even though fairer fingers of strange girls
Pass nestling through thy beautiful boy's curls
As mine did, or those curled lithe lips of thine
Meet theirs as these, all theirs come after mine;
And though I were not, though I be not, best,
I have loved and love thee more than all the rest.
O love, O lover, loose or hold me fast,
I had thee first, whoever have thee last;
Fairer or not, what need I know, what care?
To thy fair bud my blossom once seemed fair.
Why am I fair at all before thee, why
At all desired? seeing thou art fair, not I.
I shall be glad of thee, O fairest head,
Alive, alone, without thee, with thee, dead;
I shall remember while the light lives yet,
And in the night-time I shall not forget.
Though (as thou wilt) thou leave me ere life leave,
I will not, for thy love I will not, grieve;
Not as they use who love not more than I,
Who love not as I love thee though I die;
And though thy lips, once mine, be oftener prest
To many another brow and balmier breast,
And sweeter arms, or sweeter to thy mind,
Lull thee or lure, more fond thou wilt not find.

John Gambril Nicholson, 'A Fresh Chance', *Love in Earnest: Sonnets, Ballades, and Lyrics*, 1892

When I lie in the darkness, pondering
   The problems of Wrong and Right,
A soft little hand comes wandering
   Out of the wakeful night.

An arm in slumber straying
   Around my neck is thrown,
Its rhythmic pulses saying
   That a heart beats close to my own.

He will rescue all my to-morrows, –
   This boy who condescends
In spite of my sins and sorrrows
   To be my friend of friends.

And his arm about me lingers
   Till to dreamland I depart,
Clasping the warm little fingers
   And blessing the warm little heart.

'Saloninus', 'By the Aegean', *The Artist and Journal of Home Culture*, 2 January 1893

Beauty long sought for, incarnate, consummate
Found but in marble serenely quiescent
Wayward impetuously leapt into being
          With you and in you.

Rapturous, exquisite past all concealment
Love in a sigh breathed to perfect fruition
Seeing unclothed unashamed in the sunlight
          Glad adolescence.

Tremulous flesh in its riotous beauty
Flashing yet delicate past all expressing
The mirth of the world, and the joy of mere being;
                              Life at its zenith.

Eyes that fulfil all the yearnings of twilight
Mouth that steals open like dawn o'er the ocean
Figure more beautiful than (dared one imagine it)
                              God in his boyhood.

Now in thy nakedness, radiant, triumphant
Known by the salt waves in amorous transport
Kissed by the warm wind, caressed by the wavelets
                              Monarch of beauty.

Thus to have seen you is light for all ages
Just to have dreamed you were rapture for ever
But to have loved you is moment for lasting
                              For ever immortal.

Vibrant the future responds to your movement
Sinuous curves round all living to loving
Perfect contentment at last is accomplished
                              Full and sufficient.

Alan Stanley, 'The Dawn Nocturne (August Blue)', *Love Lyrics*, 1894

Silver mists on a silver sea,
And white clouds overhead
Sailing the grey sky speedily
To where the east turns red.
And one lone boat her sails has spread,
Sails of the whitest lawn,
That seems to listen for the tread
Of the tender feet of dawn.

The risen sun now makes the sky
An arching roof of gold,
Amber the clouds turn as they fly

Uncurling fold on fold;
The sun a goblet seems to hold
A draught of fervid wine,
And the young day no longer cold
Glows with a fire divine.

Stripped for the sea your tender form
Seems all ivory white,
Through which the blue veins wander warm
O'er throat and bosom slight,
And as you stand, so slim, upright
The glad waves grow and yearn
To clasp you circling in their might,
To kiss with lips that burn.

Flashing limbs in the waters blue
And gold curls floating free;
Say, does it thrill you through and through
With ardent love, the sea?
A very nymph you seem to be
As you glide and dive and swim,
While the mad waves clasp you fervently
Possessing every limb.

King of the Sea, triumphant boy,
Nature itself made thrall
To God's white work without alloy
On whom no stain doth fall.
Gaze on him, slender, fair, and tall,
And on the yearning sea
Who deigns to creep and cling, and crawl,
His worshipper to be.

John Gambril Nicholson, 'A Bather (for a painting by Edward Thomas)',[44] *Love in Earnest: Sonnets, Ballades, and Lyrics*, 1892

Clothed only in his wondrous loveliness
  He stands upon the margin of the stream –

The Summer's self were not a worthier theme
If language might but half his charms express: –
The sunlit land has donned its richest dress,
    And decked with gold the radiant meadows gleam;
    But he, whose garments hide his grace supreme,
Has cast them off beneath the sun's caress.

O Painter, who on Beauty's Self would seize,
    The Gods have left thee nothing to entreat,
    For surely thy contentment was complete
When, as a lily bends before the breeze,
This fair boy straightened both his naked knees
    And stooped to pluck the blossoms at his feet!

Frederick Rolfe, 'Ballade of Boys Bathing', *Art Review*, vol. 1:4, April 1890

(As dainty a sight as I wish to see.)
    Drifting along in a boat we were
On the coast of the land of the kilted knee,
    Under the sea-cliffs' shadow where
A flock of boys, slender and debonnaire,
    Laugh in a lovely disarray,
Fear they know not, nor ever a care
    The boys who bathe in St. Andrew's Bay.

Deep blue water as blue can be,
    Rocks rising high where the red clouds flare,
Boys of the colour of ivory,
    Breasting the wavelets, and diving there,
    White boys, ruddy, and tanned, and bare,
With lights and shadows of rose and grey,
And the sea like pearls in their shining hair,
    The boys who bathe in St. Andrew's Bay.

A summer night, and a sapphire sea,
    A setting sun, and a golden glare:
Hurled from the height where the wild rocks be,

Wondrous limbs in the luminous air,
Fresh as white flame, flushed and fair,
Little round arms in the salt sea spray,
And the sea seems alive with them everywhere,
    The boys who bathe in St. Andrew's Bay.

Envoy
Andrea! Set me out tinctures rare
    Give me a palette, and while I may
I'll fix upon canvas, if so I may dare,
    The boys who bathe in St. Andrew's Bay.

Charles Kains-Jackson, 'Sonnet on a Picture by Tuke',[45] *The Artist and Journal of Home Culture*, 1 May 1889

Within this little space of canvas shut
    Are summer sunshine, and the exuberant glee
    Of living light that laughs along the sea,
And freshness of kind winds; yet these are but
As the rich gem whereon the cameo's cut;
    The cameo's self, the boyish faces free
    From care, the beauty and the delicacy
Of young slim frames not yet to labour put.
The kisses that make red each honest face
    Are of the breeze and salt and tingling spray.
So, may these boys know never of a place
    Wherein, to desk or factory a prey,
That colour blanches slowly, nature's grace
    Made pale with life's incipient decay.

TOURISM

Two landscapes provide the scenes for opportunities for sensual or sexual contact between men in contemporary life: London, and the natural environment of labour and leisure. The middle-class white male tourist visits those places and spaces where he will find sexual partners, at home and abroad. It is possible to construct a map of homosexual London, marking the places where these men could meet one another, or purchase the sexual pleasures they sought, centred around W1, NW1 and WC1. In Albany Street there was both a barracks, a popular pick-up place, and next to the barracks a homosexual brothel. Boulton, Park and their associates spent a great deal of time in Brunswick Square and the Burlington Arcade. Close to Regent's Park, in Cleveland Street, there was an infamous male brothel, and a few hundred yards away, in Fitzroy Street, where, in addition to a homosexual 'introduction house', Taylor and Mason, amongst Wilde's fellow-accused, held drag parties at No. 46, while at No. 12 lived Simeon Solomon, painter and some-time paramour of Swinburne. Around the corner from Westminster Abbey, where William Banks MP was arrested for indecency behind 'a screen for urinating against the Abbey walls', is 13 Little College Street, then a homosexual brothel, where Alfred Taylor lived and Wilde visited.

As can be seen from a number of the legal cases in Chapter 2, loiterers in the street, especially in the evening, were taken to be debauchees in search of illicit pleasures, or were vulnerable to accusations of being up to no good. Urban space is regulated by strict rules of functionality and leisure, and, while certain trades were pursued in or through the streets, such spaces provided scope for encounters between members of different classes. John Gambril Nicholson's 'Your City Cousins' lists the plethora of types of working-class youth a man can meet in a day in London, and this catalogue serves to identify many of the stock characters of trial transcripts and newspaper reports: the groom, the telegraph boy, the clerk, the newspaper boy all occupy, with confidence and function, public spaces where they may be met and bargained with. The suspect nature of many of Wilde's friendships with men, in the eyes of the court and the media, is derived from anxieties about class, a breaking down of necessary boundaries. But the desirability of these young men is precisely dependent on them being inferior, different, other, since they are, as a result, sexier. Alphonse Conway, a newspaper seller on Worthing pier, and the recipient of the silver cigarette case, was 'a nice, pleasant creature', according to Wilde, and who could never look like an equal, no matter how he dressed. He called him Alphonse, but was never called Oscar in return. The class structure remains intact, whatever activities may have occurred. Such relationships between middle-class men and working-class men, and between white men and men of colour, share a set of assumptions about power and the innate sexual drive of the desired object.

Much of this tourist literature is distinguished by pronouncements or debates about the precise definition of the object of desire: he must be this old, with this kind of body, and this kind of attitude or experience. Symonds, in celebrating village lads or gondoliers, favours well-built, masculine youths, while Frederick Rolfe prefers something altogether younger and lither. In all cases, the boy or youth is objectified, dehumanized, particularly in texts where he becomes fruit or flower to be plucked. Class tourism and sexual colonialism part ways in their conceptualization of what makes these young men desirable. Where working-class youths derive their value from the authenticity of their work (seen from the eyes of middle-class men, usually of independent means), boys from Italy, India, North Africa, are sexy because they are languid, amoral and available.

One text in particular provides a vivid sketch of the terms and limits of this Orientalist fetish.[46] Kenneth Searight's manuscript entitled *Paidikion* is comprised of a large collection of stories and poems, and a catalogue of Searight's sexual encounters with boys in India and Naples between 1897 and 1917, numbering 129. Despite the advertised thirteen plates, only eight are actually present, spread throughout the manuscript. These are: a youth in a toga; nude youth outside cave; nude youth reclining on sofa; nude boy in armchair; nude boy and youth sitting on trapeze; nude boy standing; nude boy with waist-length hair lying on bed; nude boy leaning on stone urn in garden. The written contents of the manuscript are as follows:

1 'The Beloved Name' – 'boy' in twenty-four languages with space for thirteen other variants.
2 'Nox Amoris: a fragment' – a prose story of the first sexual experience of a young man with a soldier in the Horse Guards.
3 'Carmina Priapeia of Petronius Arbiter' – English translation.
4 'Amorous Education: a school story' – A schoolmaster teaches nine boys aged fourteen to seventeen in the arts of pederastic love.
5 'Two Pathan love songs to his boy'.
6 Measurements of the young male body.
7 'The Island: a Study in Solitude' – a shipwrecked man tries to force a seventeen-year-old youth to submit to sodomy and whips him until he yields. The youth escapes in the night and commits suicide. The man commits necrophilia and severs the boy's penis. 'And this one relic of the Island is with me now as I write.'
8 'Ten Little Bugger Boys' – a piece of doggerel fashioned after 'Ten little Indians'.

9   'Nel Bagno: a Neapolitan tale' – the hero visits a turkish bath in Naples and is seduced by a sixteen-year-old attendant. They engage in masturbation, fellatio, coprolagnia, urolagnia.

10 'Laddie: an Episode' – pederasty among tramps, inspired by an appendix to *Sexual Inversion*.

11 'Floreat Etona: or, where Waterloo was won' – erotic adventures of Eton schoolboys aged fourteen to sixteen.

12 'The Furnace: an autobiography in which is set forth the secret diversions of a paiderast' – a poem of 2,706 rhyming couplets. An extract is included below.

13 'Simla: the Tale of a Secret Society' – in which every possible sexual act between men and boys is performed.

14 'Kid: the strange story of a bugger-boy' – a thirteen-year-old homeless orphan is seduced by a man, taken to a brothel by a friend of the man and taught how to be a good prostitute.

15 'Paidology' – a list of sexual partners, detailing age, place, name, race and acts. At the bottom of each page the average age of the boys is calculated. The highest average is 15.8. The youngest boy is seven.

Such a record may be unique. It ceases with Searight's transfer to Afghanistan, which does not necessarily imply that the activities ceased. While the scale of the documentation is greater than any other writer on homosexual sexual experiences from the period, the objects, tone and framework of understanding are not markedly dissimilar (with the possible exception of 'The Island', which is entirely one of a kind, even when viewed in the context of the output of the Parisian pornographers), merely more obsessive and with less need for any degree of caution, given the privacy of the recording. But this text is an interesting object lesson in the difficulties of access to this material. The manuscript of *Paidikion* is in private hands, held seemingly anonymously, and only the briefest citations from it are available in print.[47] It would be interesting to know what happened to the final four little bugger boys, but only the handful of people who have seen the manuscript will ever know their fate.

Ten little Bugger Boys, drinking deep of wine
Got so tight at Fitz's Bar they counted only nine;
Nine little Bugger Boys, finding it was late
Left a lad in Leicester Square: and then there were eight.

Eight little Bugger Boys, dreaming still of heaven,
Met a lusty sodomite: and then there were seven.
Seven little Bugger Boys, in an awkward fix,
Saw a copper standing by; and then there were six.
Six little Bugger Boys – all now left alive –
Buggered one another til they reckoned only five!
Five little Bugger Boys, bottoms very sore,
Played at tossing Freddy off until there were four.

And if such a text as *Paidikion* was not only written, but survived, how much more material which documents the pleasures and trials of homosexuals and lesbians has yet to be discovered?

John Addington Symonds, 'Dearer to me', 1893[48]

Dearer to me is the lad village-born with sinewy members
Than the pale face of a fine town-bred effeminate youngling;
Dearer to me is a groom, a tamer of horses, a hunter,
Yea, or a sailor on board: but dear to me down to the heart's depth,
Dearest of all are the young, steel-thewed, magnificent soldiers –
Be it the massive form of a black-browed insolent guardsman,
Or a blue-eyed hussar with the down new-fledged on his firm lip –
Who with clanking spurs and martial tread when they meet me,
Know not how goodly they are, the sight of them how overwhelming.

John Gambril Nicholson, 'In Working Dress', *Love in Earnest: Sonnets, Ballades, and Lyrics*, 1892

'Twas on a hot midsummer day,
   When I had looked for you in vain
   In garden, stable, barn and lane,
I found you mowing in the hay.

I came upon you unaware.
  Suffused with sweat you swung the scythe;
  A stooping figure, strong and lithe,
With arms above the elbow bare.

In trousers of stiff corduroy,
  A cotton shirt, a leather belt,
  A drooping hat of dingy felt, –
I scarcely recognised my boy!

Behind you all unmarked I came,
  Watching how well your work you did;
  Your back was bent, your face was hid,
And dubiously I spoke your name.

You turned; and, hotter than before,
  With the broad hat your brow you fanned,
  And giving me a moist brown hand,
Glanced at the clumsy boots you wore.

For, as I gazed, you did not guess
  How fair you seemed in such disguise;
  Your deprecating down-cast eyes
Said, *Please excuse my working-dress!*

Not in your Sunday fineries,
  Nor clad in flannels for your play,
  But as you were that working-day
Of you my sweetest memory is!

John Gambril Nicholson, 'Your City Cousins', *Love in Earnest: Sonnets, Ballades, and Lyrics*, 1892

As I go down the street
A hundred boys a day I meet,
And gazing from my window high
I like to watch them passing by.

I like the boy that earns his bread;
The boy that holds my horse's head,

The boy that tidies up the bar,
The boy that hawks the *Globe* and *Star*.

Smart-looking lads are in my line;
The lad that gives my boots a shine,
The lad that works the lift below,
The lad that's lettered *G.P.O.*

I like the boy of business air
That guards the loaded van with care,
Or cycles through the city crowd,
Or adds the ledger up aloud.

I like the boy that's fond of play:
The office-boy cracks jokes all day,
The barber's 'prentice makes me laugh,
The bookstall-boy gives back my chaff.

When travelling home by tram or train
I meet a hundred boys again,
Behind them on the 'bus I ride
Or pace the platform by their side.

And though I never see you there
All boys your name and nature share,
And almost every day I make
Some new acquaintance for your sake.

Horatio Brown, 'Bored: at a London Music', *Drift*, 1900

Two rows of foolish faces blent
In two blurred lines; the compliment,
The formal smile, the cultural air,
The sense of falseness everywhere.
Her ladyship superbly dressed –
    I liked their footman, John, the best.

The tired musicians' ruffled mien,
Their whispered talk behind the screen,

The frigid plaudits, quite confined
By fear of being unrefined
His lordship's grave and courtly jest –
   I liked their footman, John, the best.

Remote I sat with shaded eyes,
Supreme attention in my guise,
And heard the whole laborious din,
Piano, 'cello, violin;
And so, perhaps, they hardly guessed
   I liked their footman, John, the best.

John Addington Symonds, 'Angelo Fusato', from *The Memoirs*, 1889[49]

While we were drinking our wine [Horatio] Brown pointed out to me two men in white gondolier uniform, with the enormously broad black hat which was then fashionable. They were servants of a General de Horsey; and one of them was strikingly handsome. The following description of him, written a few days after our first meeting, represents with fidelity the impression he made on my imagination.

> He was tall and sinewy, but very slender – for these Venetian gondoliers are rarely massive in their strength. Each part of the man is equally developed by the exercise of rowing; and their bodies are elastically supple, with free sway from the hips and a Mercurial poise upon the ankle. Angelo showed these qualities almost in exaggeration. Moreover, he was rarely in repose, but moved with a singular brusque grace. – Black broad-brimmed hat thrown back upon his matted *zazzera*[50] of dark hair. – Great fiery grey eyes, gazing intensely, with compulsive effluence of electricity – the wild grace of a Triton. – Short blond moustache, dazzling teeth; skin bronzed, but showing white and delicate through open front and sleeves of lilac shirt. – The dashing sparkle of this splendour, who looked to me as though the sea waves and the sun had made him in some hour of secret and unquiet rapture, was somewhat emphasized by a curious dint dividing his square chin – a cleft that harmonized with smile on lips and steady fire in eyes. – By the way, I do not know what effect it would have upon a reader to compare eyes to opals. Yet

Angelo's eyes, as I met them, had the flame and vitreous intensity of opals, as though the quintessential colour of Venetian waters were vitalized in them and fed from inner founts of passion. – This marvellous being had a rough hoarse voice which, to develop the simile of a sea-god, might have screamed in storm or whispered raucous messages from crests of tossing waves. He fixed and fascinated me.

Angelo Fusato at that date was hardly twenty-four years of age....This love at first sight for Angelo Fusato was an affair not merely of desire and instinct but also of imagination. He took hold of me by a hundred subtle threads of feeling, in which the powerful and radiant manhood of the splendid animal was intertwined with sentiment for Venice, a keen delight in the landscape of the lagoons, and something penetrative and pathetic in the man....Eight years have elapsed since that first meeting at the Lido. A steady friendship has grown up between two men brought by accident together under conditions so unpromising...the happy product of a fine and manly nature on his side and of fidelity and constant effort on my own....Well: I took him back to Casa Alberti; and what followed shall be told in the ensuing sonnet, which is strictly accurate – for it was written with the first impression of the meeting strong upon me.

I am not dreaming. He was surely here
    And sat beside me on this hard low bed;
    For we had wine before us, and I said –
    'Take gold: 'twill furnish forth some better cheer.'
He was all clothed in white; a gondolier;
    White trousers, white straw hat upon his head,
    A cream-white shirt loose-buttoned, a silk thread
    Slung with a charm about his throat so clear.
Yes, he was here. Our four hands, laughing, made
    Brief havoc of his belt, shirt, trousers, shoes:
    Till, mother-naked, white as lilies, laid
There on the counterpane, he bade me use
    Even as I willed his body. But Love forbade –
    Love cried, 'Less than Love's best thou shalt refuse!'

...I found him manly in the truest sense, with the manliness of a soldier and warm soft heart of an exceptionally kindly nature – proud and sensitive, wayward as a child, ungrudging in his service, willing and good-tempered,

334

though somewhat indolent at the same time and subject to explosions of passion. He is truthful and sincere, frank in telling me what he thinks wrong about my conduct, attentive to my wants, perfect in his manners and behaviour – due allowance made for his madcap temperament, hoarse voice and wild impulsive freedom.

I can now look back with satisfaction on this intimacy. Though it began in folly and crime, according to the constitution of society, it has benefited him and proved a source of comfort and instruction to myself. Had it not been for my abnormal desire, I could never have learned to know and appreciate a human being so far removed from me in position, education, national quality and physique. I long thought it hopeless to lift him into something like prosperity – really because it took both of us long to gain confidence in the stability of our respective intentions and to understand each other's character. At last, by constant regard on my side to his interests, by loyalty and growing affection on his side for me, the end has been attained.

John Addington Symonds, from 'In the Key of Blue', *In the Key of Blue and Other Prose Essays*, 1893

A symphony of blues and green,
Swart indigo and eau-marine.
Stripped to the waist two dyers kneel
On grey steps strewn with orange peel;
The glaucous water to the brink
Welters with clouds of purplish-pink:
The men wring cloth that drips and takes
Verditer hues of water-snakes,
While *pali* paled by sun and seas
Repeat the tint in verdigris.
Those brows, nude breasts, and arms of might,
The pride of youth and manhood white,
Now smirched with woad, proclaim the doom
Of labour and its life-long gloom.
Only the eyes emergent shine,
These black as coals, those opaline;
Lighten from storms of tangled hair,

Black curls and blond curls debonair,
Proving man's untamed spirit there.
A symphony of blues and red –
The broad lagoon, and overhead
Sunset, a sanguine banner, spread.
Fretty of azure and pure gules
Are sea, city, stagnant pools:
You, by my side, within the boat,
Imperially purple float,
Beneath a burning sail, straight on
Into the west's vermilion.
The triple azures melt and glow
Like flaunting iris-flowers arow;
One amethystine gem of three
Fused by the heaven's effulgency.
Now fails the splendour, day dies down
Beyond the hills by Padua's town;
And all along the eastern sky
Blue reassumes ascendency.
Lapped in those tints of fluor-spar,
You shine intense, an azure star,
With roses flushed that slowly fade
Against the vast aerial shade.
At Castelfranco, with a blouse
Venetian, blent of triple blues,
I walked all through the sleepy town,
Worshipped Madonna gazing down
From that high throne Giorgione painted
Above the knight and friar sainted,
Drank in the landscape golden-green,
The dim primeval pastoral-scene.
The blouse beside me thrilled no less
Than I to that mute loveliness;
Spoke little, turned aside, and dwelt
Perchance on what he dumbly felt.
There throbbed a man's heart neath the shirt,
The sash, the hose, a life alert,
Veiled by that dominating hurt.
Then swept a storm-cloud from the hills;

Eddying dust the city fills,
The thunder crashes, and the rain
Hisses on roof and flooded plain.
Ere midnight, when the moon sailed low,
Peering through veils of indigo,
We went abroad, and heard the wail
Of many a darkling nightingale,
Pouring as birds will only pour
Their souls forth when heaven's strife is o'er.
Those red walls, and the mighty towers,
Which lustrous ivy over-flowers,
Loomed through the murk divinely warm,
As palpitating after storm.
Hushed was the night for friendly talk;
Under the dark arcades we walk,
Pace the wet pavement, where light steals
And swoons amid the huge abeles:
Then seek our chamber. All the blues
Dissolve, the symphony of hues
Fades out of sight, and leaves at length
A flawless form of simple strength,
Sleep-seeking, breathing, ivory-white,
Upon the couch in candle-light.

Frederick Rolfe to C., 28 November 1909, from Venice

He found his patrons in this way. His first, the Count, had spoken to him on the Giardinetto where he was by chance lounging one morning, being out of work, and shirt being open as usual, because he was appassionated for the air, the Count had stroked his breast while saying that he was a fine boy. To whom he said that he was as God made him and preferred to be naked. Upon which the Count took him to the Osmarin for the day. Thereafter, he always went with his breast bare, even in Piazza, and soon Signiori walked after him, to whom he nodded in the first discreet corner and so he gained patrons. But, since the Club was moved to Padova, it was difficult for an honest lad – he is 16½ – to find a way of employing his nights. During the day he works as a stevedore along the Zattere or in the harbour of Marittima, earning 3.50 generally, of which he has to give 3 fr. to his father, also a stevedore and earning the same. His elder brother is doing military service. His cousin gondoles for a merchant, i.e. a grocer with whom he lives and sleeps. One younger brother of 12 earns 1.50 as a milk-boy. Beside these three there are a mother and grandmother, five sisters and three small brothers to be kept out of the joint earnings of 8 fr. a day. Naturally he wants to earn money for himself.

He assured me he knew incredible tricks for amusing his patrons. 'First, Sior, see my person', he said. And the vivacious creature did all which follows in about 30 seconds of time. Not more. I have said that we were sitting side by side of the little table [in the wineshop]. Moving, every inch of him, as swiftly and smoothly as cat, he stood up, casting a quick glance into the shop to make sure that no one noticed. Only the sleepy proprietor slept there. He rolled his coat into a pillow and put it on my end of the table, ripped open his trousers, stripped them down to his feet, and sat bare bottomed on the other end. He turned his shirt up right over his head, holding it in one hand, opened his arms wide and lay back along the little table with his shoulders on the pillow (so that his breast and belly and thighs formed one slightly slanting lane unbroken by the arch of the ribs, as is the case with flat distension) and his beautiful throat and his rosy laughing face strained backward while his widely open arms were an invitation. He was just one brilliant rosy series of muscles, smooth as satin, breasts and belly and groin and closely folded thighs with (in the midst of the black blossom of exuberant robustitude) a yard like a rose-tipped lance. And – the fragrance of his healthy youth and of the lily flower's dust was intoxicating. He crossed his ankles, ground his thighs together with a gently rippling motion, writhed his groin and hips once or twice and stiffened into the most inviting mass of fresh meat conceivable, laughing in my face as he made his offering of lively flesh. And the next instant he was up, his trousers buttoned, his shirt tucked in and his cloak folded around him. The litre of wine was gone. I called for another. 'Sior,' he said, 'half a litre this time, with permission.' So we made it half. Would I not like to take him to Padova from Saturday till Monday? Indeed I would. Nothing better. But because I see that you, my Amadeo, (i.e. Love God, quite a Puritan name) are a most discreet youth as well as a very capable one, I shall tell you my secret: for, in fact, you shall know that I am no longer a rich English but a poor, having been ruined by certain traitors and obliged to deny myself luxuries. To hear that gave him affliction and much dolour. But he wished to say that he was all and entirely at my disposal simply for affection; because, feeling sure that he had the ability to provide me with an infinity of diversions, each different and far more exciting than its predecessor, he asked me as a favour, as a very great favour, that I should afterwards recommend him to nobles who were my friends.

Theodore Wratislaw, 'To a Sicilian Boy', *Caprices*, 1893

Love, I adore the contours of thy shape,
Thine exquisite breasts and arms adorable;
The wonders of thine heavenly throat compel
Such fire of love as even my dreams escape:
I love thee as the sea-foam loves the cape,
Or as the shore the sea's enchanting spell:
In sweets the blossoms of thy mouth excel
The tenderest bloom of peach or purple grape.

I love thee, sweet! Kiss me, again, again!
Thy kisses soothe me, as tired earth the rain;
Between thine arms I find my only bliss;
Ah let me in thy bosom still enjoy
Oblivion of the past, divinest boy,
And the dull ennui of a woman's kiss!

Kenneth Searight, from 'The Furnace', *Paidikion: Volume 1: An Anthology or the Book of Hyakinthos and Narkissos with thirteen full page photographs from life*, manuscript written between 1897 and 1917

...I passed
From sensuous Bengal to fierce Peshawar
An Asiatic stronghold where each flower
Of boyhood planted in its restless soil

Is – *ipso facto* – ready to despoil
(Or to be despoiled by) someone else; the yarn
Indeed so has it that the young Pathan
Thinks it peculiar if he would pass
Him by without some reference to his arse.
Each boy of certain age will let on hire
His charms to indiscriminate desire,
To wholesome Buggery and perverse letches....
To get a boy was easier than to pick
The flowers by the wayside, for as quick
As one went out another one came in....
Scarce passed a night but I in rapturous joy
Indulged in mutual sodomy, the boy
Fierce-eyed, entrancing.

Aleister Crowley, 'Go into the highways and hedges and compel them *to come in*',[51] *White Stains*, 1898

Let my fond lips but drink thy golden wine,
My bright-eyed Arab, only let me eat
The rich brown globes of sacramental meat
Steaming and firm, hot from their home divine,
And let me linger with thy hands in mine,
And lick the sweat from dainty dirty feet
Fresh with the loose aroma of the street,
And then anon I'll glue my mouth to thine.
This is the height of joy, to lie and feel
Thy spiced spittle trickle down my throat;
This is more pleasant that at dawn to steal
Towards lawns and sunny brooklets, and to gloat
Over earth's peace, and hear in ether float
Songs of soft spirits into rapture peal.

Textual footnotes

1 The effeminate come, allured by the pleasure of being sodomised.
2 PE-DI-CA-RE – *pedicare*, meaning to sodomise.

NOTES

General introduction: strategies for liberation

1 A. E. Housman, *Last Poems*, XII, *c.* 1900.
2 See Chapter 2, 'The Wilde trials', for the speech by Wilde and the poem by Douglas from which the phrase comes.
3 Lord Rosebery, cited in Ronald Hyam, *Empire and Sexuality: The British Experience* (Manchester, 1990), p. 74.
4 Section 52; R v. Hare, 1934.
5 See Carpenter, *Homogenic Love, and its Place in a Free Society*, in Chapter 4.
6 John Lauristen and David Thorstad, *The Early Homosexual Rights Movement (1864–1935)* (New York, 1974), p. 47.
7 Havelock Ellis and John Addington Symonds, *Sexual Inversion*, volume I of *Studies in the Psychology of Sex* (London, 1897), p. 1.

1 The mute sin

1 *Peccatum Mutum (The Mute Sin, alias Sodomy), a Theological Treatise for the first time translated from the Latin of Rev. Father Sinistrari (xviith century)* (Paris, 1893).
2 Detachment of police officers working in a particular district.
3 Called or pressed into service.
4 Lit. little master.
5 Police officer of lowest rank.
6 Military drum-beater.
7 Maker of metal rims for wheels.
8 Boy kept for sexual purposes by man.
9 Priests.
10 Opening to a sewer in the street.
11 Of uncertain meaning.
12 Religious and social radicals opposed to infant baptism, the doctrine of transubstantiation and the right of the state to dictate religious beliefs and practices.
13 In 1857 William Dugdale was sentenced to twelve months in prison for selling obscene prints.
14 Eastern end of Regent Street, adjoining Piccadilly Circus.
15 Shop for making and selling mezzotints.
16 Offering for view or use the organ of excretion (not in OED).
17 Prostitutes.
18 Gatherings for drinking, smoking and singing.
19 Pimp for male prostitutes (not in OED).
20 Brothel (not in OED).
21 Opened a pawn shop (not in OED).
22 Brought to the ground, utterly failed.

23 Brothel.
24 Pretty (US).
25 A reference to a 'Hippodrome' theatre in Paris.
26 Perverse fools.
27 Patched together piece of nonsense.
28 Chanted.
29 Drinking dens.
30 Odd or drunken chap.
31 Equilaterally triangular boring tool.
32 Small, sharp-pointed tool for piercing holes.
33 Although now generally identified with Oscar Wilde, at the time of its first production, Bunthorne was generally believed to be a parody of Walter Pater, Oxford don and Renaissance scholar. Examples of his work are included in Chapter 4.
34 Queen Anne reigned 1702–14.
35 Empress of Napoleon, who held court at Navarre.
36 Homosexual.
37 Body-armour.
38 Georges Leopold Cuvier, eighteenth-century naturalist.
39 Embroidery in Berlin wool.
40 Boat-shaped feeding vessel for infants.
41 Edward Carpenter, *Towards Democracy*, published in four parts between 1891 and 1902, by T. Fisher Unwin.
42 Edward Carpenter, *Iolaus: Anthology of Friendship* (London, 1902).
43 Manchester Labour Society.
44 New Revised Standard Version of the Bible.
45 Sodom and Gomorrah.
46 A deliberate refusal to repent and accept salvation (Mark 3.29).
47 Carpenter did indeed eventually leave Sheffield, many years later, after the death of his long-term partner, George Merrill. He moved to a bungalow in Guildford, and died within a year.

2 Law

1 Re-enacted from the original statute passed under Henry VIII.
2 Error for Lollards. See Chapter 1, note 12.
3 Barrister of the Inner Temple.
4 He pierced his jugular vein with a small penknife, killing himself instantly.
5 Moody, vol. 1, Criminal Case 342.
6 Reekspear was executed, probably the last person in England or Wales to pay the death penalty for sodomy.
7 There follows a series of character witnesses, including servants, members of the nobility and clergymen.
8 Justice of the Peace, vol. 12, p. 761.
9 I have been unable to determine the fates of Gatehouse and Dowley.
10 Dennison, vol. 1, Case 364; *English Reports*, vol. 169, pp. 282–3.
11 I have been unable to determine the fate of Allen.
12 Cox's Criminal Law Cases, vol. 13.
13 I have been unable to determine the fate of Ransford.
14 In 1898 the law was amended to permit a condemned man to speak to the verdict.
15 Robert Sherard.

16 Sir Henry Irving.
17 Robert Louis Stevenson.
18 To my words they durst add nothing, and my speech dropped upon them (Douay-Rheims translation of the Vulgate Bible).
19 Douglas's house in Naples.
20 See H. Montgomery Hyde, *The Other Love* (London, 1970), pp. 146–52.
21 See Hyde, *The Other Love* for an account of this scandal involving a minor royal allegedly visiting a male brothel.

3 Science

1 Havelock Ellis, *A Note on the Bedborough Trial*, private publication, 1898.
2 Edward Stevenson. The book was privately published in Naples, in an edition of 125.
3 Nervous debility.
4 Edward Gibbon, *The Decline and Fall of the Roman Empire*, Chapter 20.
5 Gibbon, *Decline and Fall*, Chapter 40.
6 Anal intercourse.
7 Having phthisis, pulmonary consumption.
8 Having dropsy, a morbid condition.
9 J. L. Caspar and Carl Liman, *Handbuch der Gerichtlichen Medicin* (Berlin, 1889).
10 I have been unable to trace the reference.
11 A join like a seam between two organs or parts of the body.
12 I have been unable to trace the reference.
13 Statue of the Greek god of love, by Praxitiles, the greatest of the Athenian sculptors of the fourth century BC.
14 Almost certainly a reference to Symonds himself.
15 Extortion.
16 For want of something better.
17 I have been unable to trace the source of this quotation.
18 See Chapter 4, note 75.
19 I have been unable to trace the source of this quotation.
20 Hereditary taint.
21 *A Problem in Modern Ethics*.
22 Lapping the tongue on the other's genitals.
23 A female mind wrongly enclosed in a male body.
24 Jacques Joseph Magnan, author of *Leçons cliniques sur les maladies mentales* (Paris, 1890).
25 Marcel Gley, author of *Etudes de psychologie physiologique et pathologique* (Paris, 1903).
26 This has been identified as the biography of Roden Noel, whose poetry will be found elsewhere in this book. He is described in the preamble as 'a more genuine example of psychosexual hermaphroditism'.
27 The Bishop of Clogher, whose case appears in Chapter 2, was Roden Noel's uncle.
28 Pederasty, sodomy.
29 A medical word of unknown meaning.
30 Oral sex.
31 Between the thighs.
32 Wreck, derelict.
33 Match-making, pimping.

34 Intercourse between the thighs, anal intercourse, embracing without intercourse, mutual masturbation, oral masturbation.

35 'Eugenics and the mystical outlook', and the next extract, from 'Eugenics and spiritual parenthood', were both based on papers read to the Eugenics Education Society in 1911, and published in Mrs Havelock Ellis, *The New Horizon in Love and Life* (London, 1921).

---

4 Modes of defence

1 John Addington Symonds, *Studies of the Greek Poets*, 1893, p. 380.

2 Walter Pater, 'Wincklemann', *Studies in the History of the Renaissance*, 1873.

3 Pater, 'The Age of Athletic Prizemen', *Greek Studies: A Series of Essays*, 1895.

4 *The Memoirs of John Addington Symonds*, ed. Phyllis Grosskurth (London, 1984), p. 109.

5 Roden Noel in the introduction to his edition of *The Poems of Edmund Spenser*, 1887.

6 'A comparison of Elizabethan with Victorian poetry', *Essays Speculative and Suggestive*, 1893, pp. 391, 395.

7 Roden Noel, *The Plays of Thomas Otway*, pp. xlix, xxiii.

8 *The Memoirs of John Addington Symonds*, p. 63.

9 Carson's cross-examination of Wilde during the first trial, accusing the Marquis of Queensbury of libel.

10 *Blackwood's Edinburgh Magazine*, vol. cxlvi, no. 885, July 1889.

11 *Some Friends of Walt Whitman*, p.16.

12 Gosse to Whitman, 12 December 1873, cited in Horace Traubel, *With Walt Whitman in Camden (March 28–July 14, 1888)* (Carbondale, 1961), pp. 245–6.

13 Letter, November 1871, cited in Traubel, *With Walt Whitman*, p. 426.

14 Leander swam every night to visit his lover Hero, who guided him with a torch. One night the torch was extinguished, Leander drowned, and when the body washed ashore, Hero threw herself into the sea.

15 Two handsome young men and lovers who consented to be part of the human sacrifices performed by Epimenides. See Athenaeus, *Deipnosophistae* 13.602.

16 Phalaris, tyrant and torturer, roasted his victims inside a hollow brass bull, against whom his people rose and put him to death. See Juvenal, *Satires* 8.81, Pliny, *Natural History* 34.8.

17 Athenian general; see Livy 35.34.

18 Damon, a philosopher, was condemned to death by the tyrant Dionysius of Sicily, and obtained leave to return home to attend to his domestic affairs, undertaking to return to be executed at the appointed time. Pythias, his intimate friend, promised to undergo the punishment on Damon's behalf if he failed to return in time. Damon returned punctually, and Dionysius was so impressed by their fidelity to each other, he remitted the punishment, and begged them to let him share their friendship.

19 I Samuel 18.

20 During the Trojan war, Patroclus, friend and probable lover of Achilles, was killed by Hector, who was subsequently killed by Achilles in revenge. After Achilles' death, their ashes were mixed together. See Homer, *Iliad*, Plato, *Symposium* 180.

21 'In one of the pretty volumes of the *Bibliothèque Elzevirienne*...in one of these thirteenth century stories, *Li Amitiez de Ami et Amile*, that free play of human affection...makes itself felt in the incidents of a great friendship, a friendship pure and generous, pushed to a sort of passionate exaltation, and more than faithful unto death....The friendship of Amis and Amile is deepened by the romantic circumstance of an entire personal resemblance between the two heroes, through which they pass for

each other again and again, and thereby into many strange adventures' ('Two early French stories', *The Renaissance*, 1888).

22 *Richard Wagner's Prose Works*, trans. W. A. Ellis for the Wagner Society, London 1892.

23 Sodomy.

24 Things being changed that have to be changed, i.e. with necessary changes.

25 The period of Athenian cultural and commercial preeminence.

26 John Addington Symonds.

27 Baggage.

28 A beast with, variously, nine, fifty or a hundred heads, which, if one were severed, two would grow in its place, destroyed by Hercules as one of his labours.

29 'For you O democracy', *Calamus*.

30 Burton's complete translation of *The Thousand Nights and a Night* was published by the wholly spurious Kamashastra Society of Benares, which was in reality another imprint of Leonard Smithers' pornography publishing empire, and came out of Stoke Newington.

31 Accursed family of catamites, i.e. boys kept by men for sexual purposes.

32 Sir Charles Napier (1782–1853). In 1841 he was ordered to take control of Upper and Lower Sind, provinces of India, now part of Pakistan. In 1844 he began a campaign against the northern hill tribes. In 1847 he resigned from the government of Sind.

33 Moonshee, a native secretary or language teacher in India.

34 Brothels.

35 To agree with the buried person.

36 Ancient kingdom, now approximating to Iraq.

37 Babylon.

38 Those who attended the lectures of Plato at his school in the groves of Academus.

39 Muslim mystic and occult sects.

40 In Platonism, the name given to the creator of all things. In Gnosticism, a deity subordinate to the Supreme Being.

41 Causing cause.

42 The Persian nightingale, typically depicted, as in the poetry of Hafiz, as tragically in love with the rose.

43 Commonly called St Jerome, who travelled the world and wrote commentaries on the Gospels.

44 Plato, *Symposium* 179a.

45 The first three words of *Eclogue* 2: 'Corydon the shepherd was aflame for fair Alexis'.

46 'Nisus (famous for) the tender love of the boy (Euryalus)' (*Aeneid* 5.295). Book IX tells the story of the devoted friendship between Nisus and Euryalus.

47 Passive in sexual intercourse.

48 Active in sexual intercourse.

49 Lesbian.

50 Manly, butch.

51 Paolo Mantegazza, author of *Fisiologia dell' amore* (Milan, 1875).

52 One who submits to sexual intercourse, i.e. passive during sodomy.

53 In the rear.

54 Related to the surface of the body.

55 Hypersensitivity.

56 Lit. love in the rear, i.e. sodomy.

57 I have been unable to trace the source of the reference.

58 G. G. Adolph, *Dissertation inauguralis medica*, 1755: 'All habitual pederasts recognize one another quickly, often at a glance'.

59 Funnel-shaped.

60 Ambroise-Auguste Tardieu, *Etude medico* etc. (Paris, 1857).

61 Orpheus was torn to pieces by the Thracian women in a Bacchic orgy because he rejected them after his failed attempt to rescue Eurydice from Hades. Lyaeus turned the women into oak trees. The precise meaning of stigmata is not clear.

62 Ovid, *Metamorphoses* 10.79–80, 83–5. 'And Orpheus had shunned all love for women....He set the example for the Thracians by giving his love to young boys, and enjoying the springtime and first flower of their youth.'

63 'The colonists, when they came to Crete, adopted the constitution which they found already existing among the inhabitants' (Aristotle, *Politics* 2.10).

64 Herodotus asserts in the cited passage, 'This custom agrees with the rites known as Orphic and Bacchic (actually Egyptian and Pythagorean); for anyone initiated into these rites is similarly debarred from burial in a garment of wool.' The rites referred to are highly mysterious and sexual rituals indulged in by initiates of the cults of Orpheus and Bacchus, the details of which were not shared with non-members.

65 Canon George Rawlinson, author of *The Five Great Monarchies of the Ancient Eastern World*, 4 vols (1862–7).

66 *On the Malice of Herodotus*.

67 Lucian, *Affairs of the Heart* (now of doubtful authorship and published as the work of Pseudo-Lucian), chapter 54. 'Not even the affection of Achilles for Patroclus was limited to having him seated opposite....No, pleasure was the mediator even of *thei* friendship.'

68 Ephorus, an historian whose thirty books are lost, cited in Strabo, *Geography*.

69 'It is the Cretans we all hold to blame for making up the story of Ganymede.' Ganymede was a shepherd with whom Zeus fell in love, and who was carried off to Olympus by Zeus in the shape of an eagle to become the god's cup-bearer.

70 'We receive from the Cretans, because they were licentious in the love of boys, what was afterwards brought over to Sparta and the whole of Greece', Servius Maurus, *In Vergilii Aeneidos*, 10.325.

71 Inhabitants of Chalchis, the chief town of the island of Euboea.

72 Youth loved by Apollo and Zephyrus, the god of the west wind. Hyacinth returned Apollo's love, and Zephyrus destroyed him by blowing a quoit thrown by Apollo, so that it struck and killed the youth. Apollo transformed his blood into the flower that bears his name.

73 A beautiful young man with whom Heracles fell in love, and who accompanied him on the Argonauts' expedition to acquire the golden fleece. During a landing on the island of Mysia, Hylas drowned after being lured into the spring by nymphs. Heracles called in vain for Hylas, and, believing that the Mysians had kidnapped him, took hostages and ordered them to find Hylas. They continued to do this in an annual ceremony in which priests would call the name of Hylas three times.

74 Xenophon, *Constitution of the Lacedaemonians* 2.13: 'If someone, being an honest man, admired a boy's soul and tried to make of him an ideal friend to spend time with but without possessiveness, then he [Lycurgus] approved....But if it was obvious that it was the boy's beauty that was the real attraction, he banned the relationship as an abomination.'

75 Two citizens of Athens who conspired against the government of the city, headed by Hipparchus and Hippias, sons of Pisistratus (see p. 162 below).

76 Xenophon, *Symposium* 4.10. *Synop.* is an error for *Symp.*

77 I have been unable to trace the source of the quotation.

78 *Elegies*, Book II, no. 35.

79 Rival statesmen of Athens, the former banished for ten years by the latter.

80 Pseudo-Lucian, *Affairs of the Heart*, paragraphs 19–28.

81 'Did not rise unassailed' (a Latinized version of the original Greek of Pseudo-Lucian, *Affairs of the Heart* 54).

82 Juvenal, *Satires* 2.10: 'Have you the nerve to castigate vice, among our Socratic queens?'

83 A grove is so called because it excludes the light, i.e. a non-sequitor or absurd derivation.

84 'I leave them/To the nabob who spits his wine on the floor of Spartan marble:/Let him have the lot – the clack and whirr of the castanets' (Juvenal, *Satires* 11.171–3).

85 'Many youths and girls fell in love with him;/none of these youths and girls dared to touch him' (Ovid, *Metamorphoses* 3.339).

86 A Theban military leader, lover of Pelopidas, who defeated the Spartans in war, and who was killed fighting against them with the Eleans.

87 Battle fought between the confederate army of Thebans and Athenians, and the Macedonians, led by Philip the Second of Macedonia, where the former were defeated by an inferior force. Standard sources give a version in which Philip, after his victory, insulted the bodies of the dead and gloried in their fate. See Symonds, 'The Dantesque and Platonic ideals of love', p. 163 below.

88 Boys for hire.

89 Get away, lover, turn your back to me.

90 More debauchery among the men than among the women.

91 Doubtful chastity.

92 The Lex Scatinia de pudicitia enacted against those who kept catamites and those who prostituted themselves, for which the punishment was a fine.

93 The Lex Julia de adulterio et pudicitia punished the keeping of catamites and prostitution with death.

94 Pierre Bayle, *Dictionary*: 'That sort of Love was not then branded with infamy, as it is among Christians.'

95 Bald sodomite.

96 *Carmina* 57.

97 Suetonius, *Life of Caesar* 52.

98 Caesar conquered Gaul, Nicomedes conquered Caesar.

99 Whore of Bithynia.

100 Do you see how the sodomite ruled the world/circle [i.e. anus] with his finger?

101 Lit. little fish, i.e. boys.

102 Full-grown comrades.

103 An intertwined formation, usually applied to statues of wrestlers, but also applied in erotic contexts.

104 Seneca, *Natural Questions* 1.15.5, 'De ignibus (in aere existentibus)'.

105 Three in one bed, two endure sexual intercourse to the full.

106 The copulatory daisy-chain,
Five love-locked in links together.
(trans. Peter Whigham in *Epigrams
of Martial*, P. Sullivan and Peter
Whigham, London, 1987, p. 479)

107 *The Twelve Caesars* 1.2, 'De ordine imperatorum'; 2.5, 'Caligula Caesar'.

108 The catamites of [the emperors] Otho and Trajan.

109 Surname given to Emperor Marcus Aurelius Antonius because he had been a priest to that Phoenician deity. He was erratic and cruel, had four wives, professed himself a woman, made his horse a consul, chose a senate of women, and gave himself to one of his officers. He was beheaded at the age of eighteen in AD 222.

110 *Silura: The history of the oldest known rocks containing organic remains* (London, 1854).

111 A Gaul who attempted to plunder Apollo's temple at Delphi, who killed himself in a fit of intoxication induced by the enraged god.

112 'Tale of Kamar al-Zaman'.

113 'Tale of King Omar bin al-Nu'uman and his sons'.
114 'Abu Nowas with the three boys and the Caliph Harus Al-Rashid'.
115 'The man's dispute with the learned woman'.
116 Elucidation of obscenities.
117 A Spanish-language romance by Luis Hurtado (1587, pub. in three parts in English 1609–16).
118 Censor of morals.
119 To speak in Latin.
120 'Probably no European, even if he have lived half a century "in Orient lands", has ever gathered together such an appalling collection of degrading customs and statistics of vice as is contained in the notes to Captain Burton's translation of the "Arabian Nights". It is bad enough in the text of the tales to find that Captain Burton is not content with plainly calling a spade a spade, but will have it styled a dirty shovel; but in his notes he goes far beyond this, and the varied collection of abominations which he brings forward with such gusto is a disgrace and a shame to printed literature' (p. 183).
121 The well-being of the people is the highest law.
122 A courtesan of Corinth.
123 Wrestling-school.
124 J. Sylvester, trans. *Du Bartas, his divine weekes and workes* (London, 1641).
125 Henry Parry Liddon (1829–90), canon of St Paul's and a renowned preacher.
126 See note 123.
127 Handsome young man who despised love, and on whom rejected women took vengeance by calling on the goddess of retribution, Nemesis, who arranged for Narcissus to fall in love with his own reflection. He watched his reflection until he died.
128 Son of Hermes, messenger of the gods, and a nymph, loved by many gods, mortals and nymphs.
129 Greece.
130 See note 20.
131 See note 69.
132 Early Greek epic poems which together made up a history of the world from the earliest times. Very little is known of the authors or their works.
133 Athenian.
134 'When Achilles was lamenting the death of Patroclus, his unrestrained feelings made him burst out with the truth and say, "The converse of our thighs my tears do mourn/With duteous piety"', Pseudo-Lucian, *Affairs of the Heart* 54, probably from Aeschylus' *Myrmidons*.
135 *Deipnosophistae* 13.602.
136 One of the tribes of ancient Greece.
137 Theseus, son of Poseidon, and Pirithous, son of Zeus, were great friends who fought together against the Centaurs for Pirithous' nation, the Lapiths.
138 Orestes, exiled son of Agamemnon and Clytemnestra, was raised with Pylades, his cousin, who advised him in his vengeance against his mother for killing his father, and who fought and travelled alongside him all his life.
139 See note 18.
140 See note 15.
141 See note 75.
142 Aristotle, *Politics* 2.12.
143 See note 17.
144 See note 16.
145 See textual footnote 3.
146 Theban military leader who formed an inviolable friendship with Pelopidas.
147 See note 87.
148 Theban lyric poet.

149 Athenian tragic poet and playwright.
150 *Encomia*, Fragment 123, 'For Theoxenos of Tenedos'.
151 Pheidias, an Athenian sculptor, erected at Elis a 60 foot statue of Zeus in gold and ivory at the Temple of Zeus at Olympia, one of the seven wonders of the world. He is reputed to have carved 'Pantarkes is beautiful' on the statue's forefinger, an act that was considered blasphemous.
152 Maximus of Tyre, *Philosophical Orations* 21.
153 Plato, *Phaedrus* 246.
154 Plato, *The Republic* 4.438ff.
155 Plato, *The Republic* 7.514ff.
156 Plato, *Phaedrus* 249.
157 *Ibid.*
158 Plato, *Symposium* 202–3.
159 Maximus of Tyre, *Philosophical Orations* paragraph 5.
160 Pseudo-Lucian, *Affairs of the Heart*.
161 'A friendly chat', in which this confidence is given from one woman to another: 'He brought two of them with him – at first glance my eyes started out of my head; I may tell you – we are alone – they were firmer than the real article, and not only that, but as soft as sleep, and the straps more like wool than leather; a kinder craftsman to a woman you could not possibly find.'
162 Cicero's second *Philippic* represents Mark Antony as a conniving, sexually perverted murderer and thief.
163 *The Memoirs of John Addington Symonds: The Secret Homosexual Life of a Leading Nineteenth-Century Man of Letters*, ed. Phyllis Grosskurth (Chicago, 1984).
164 See note 73.
165 Aromatic sedge plant.
166 A gentle breeze.
167 See note 69.
168 Without a roof.
169 A stylized representation of the acanthus leaf, used in decoration of columns.
170 Pin for fastening Greek tunic.
171 See note 127.
172 Mountain nymphs.
173 *Sir Edmund Gosse: The Augustan Books of Modern Poetry* (London, n.d.).
174 A town in Sicily, now Castro Janni, near a plain from which Proserpina was abducted by Pluto.
175 Also called Ceres, goddess of corn and mother of Proserpina who was taken to Hades by Pluto. Demeter gained Zeus's agreement to have her daughter returned, provided she had not eaten anything while in Hades. Because Proserpina had eaten six pomegranate seeds, she was only permitted to return to the world for six months of each year. This myth explains the origin of the seasons, since Ceres goes into mourning for six months of every year.
176 Dionysus, attended by his female devotees the Meanads, Pan and all the satyrs, all armed with cymbals, thyrsi (spears tipped with an ornament like a pine cone) made an expedition to the East, drawn in a chariot by a lion and a tiger, and conquered all the land he passed through without bloodshed, teaching the people how to make wine and honey.
177 Ancient Greek hero and warrior.
178 Wild thyme.
179 A Christian iconographic representation of eloquence.
180 Capital city of the island of Lesbos.
181 One of the rivers of Hades, the waters of which induced forgetfulness of all things on earth.

182 Certain actors from Britain.

183 'Passionate Chimera, crowning effort of art and pleasure, charming monster, how I love you with your manifold beauty.' I have been unable to trace the source of this quotation, if, indeed, it is one.

184 The title of an essay by A. C. Swinburne, in *Studies in Prose and Poetry*, in which he gives mitigated praise to Whitman's poetry, and observes that 'the present writer at any rate most decidedly never intended to convey by a tribute of sympathy or admiration which may have earned for him the wholly unmerited honour of an imaginary enlistment in the noble army of Whitmaniacs'.

185 Dear man, honoured master, I cannot do it!

186 Between this entry and the next Johnston paid a visit to Whitman in Camden.

187 Punctuation as in the original.

188 Davos Platz, Switzerland.

189 I have been unable to trace this case. 'Labouchere's Clause' is a reference to the amendment to the 1885 Criminal Law Amendment Act proposed by Henry Labouchere MP, which made the penalty for sodomy life imprisonment, and that for gross indecency up to two years with hard labour. See the introduction to chapter 2 above.

190 The Society for the Study of Sex Psychology, to which this essay was delivered in lecture form.

---

5 Love

1 The two works which are most influential in developing this view of pre-twentieth-century relationships between women are Elizabeth Mavor, *The Ladies of Llangollen: A Study in Romantic Friendship* (Harmondsworth, 1973) and Lillian Faderman, *Surpassing the Love of Men: Romantic Friendship and Love between Women from the Renaissance to the Present* (London, 1985).

2 *Edward Cracroft Lefroy: His Life and Poems*, from Appendix, 'Thirty sonnets not included in the 1885 volume'.

3 Paint a picture of.

4 Because I have loved much.

5 This poem is regarded as an answer to Edward Cracroft Lefroy's 'A palaestral study' (see p. 160 above).

6 In the published version of this poem, in *New and Old* (1880), lines 8–10 read: 'Or if the spark of heaven-born fire that lights/Love in both breasts from boyhood, thus have wrought/Our spirits to communion.'

7 Three, four or seven nymphs, daughters of Hesperus, who guarded, with the aid of a dragon, the garden on the Isle of the Blessed, in which grew golden apples.

8 Fungi.

9 Silver-girded.

10 Margin.

11 A youth with the divine beauty of Phoebus Apollo.

12 Black volcanic glass.

13 Precious stone spotted or streaked with red.

14 Sacramental oil mixed with balm.

15 A fabulous tree from Java, so deadly it would poison every animal and plant within fifteen miles of it.

16 Nevertheless.

17 The names here are those given to different classes of angels.

18 Corpse.

19 This poem, translating as 'Theme and variation', originally appeared in the privately printed *Pamphlet I*. In John Addington Symonds, *Many Moods* (1878), the same title appears, but there the poem consists of Symonds's 'Variazioni' as 'Tema', with six different variations on that theme.

20 Benson here describes the beginning of the relationship between Minnie Benson, wife of the then Archbishop of Canterbury, and Lucy Tait, her constant companion, who lived in the family home from six years before Minnie Benson's husband's death, and who is described by her son as 'the friend of her heart'.

21 Thomas James Wise and John Alexander Symington, *The Brontes*, vol. 1 (Oxford, 1932), pp. 153–4.

22 Michael Field, 'Works and days' (1888).

23 The earliest pseudonym adopted by Katherine Bradley.

24 Ellipsis as text.

25 Both this and the next poem were eventually published in *The Wattlefold: Unpublished Poems by Michael Field* (1930).

26 From *An Anthology of 'Nineties' Verse*, ed. A. J. A. Symons (1928).

27 Quoted in Samuel Edwards, *George Sand: A Biography of the First Modern, Liberated Woman* (New York, 1972).

28 In this extract from his biography, Ellis writes as both participant in and scientific observer of his wife's relationships with other women.

29 Havelock Ellis, 'Whitman', *The New Spirit* (1890): 'Defective scientific perception is perhaps as responsible as any failure of moral insight for the vigorous manner in which an element of "manly love" flourishes, in "Calamus" and elsewhere. Whitman is hardy to enough to assert that he expects it will to a large extent take the place of love between the sexes. "Manly love", even in its extreme form, is certainly Greek, as is the degradation of women with which it is always correlated.'

30 Shakespeare, *Romeo and Juliet*, Act III scene i.

31 James Hinton, a doctor and scientist (1822–75), who developed theories of the relationship between science and religion, and who taught that real freedom comes from the uniting of service and pleasure. His life and work are described at length in Mrs Havelock Ellis, *Three Modern Seers* (1910).

32 The Ellis house in Cornwall was in Carbis Bay.

33 Ellipsis as original text.

6 Sex

1 Silvio Venturi, *Le degenerazioni psico-sessuali nella vita degli individui e nella storia delle societa* (1892).

2 John Addington Symonds to Edward Carpenter, 29 Dec. 1892 and 29 Jan. 1893, cited in Wayne Koestenbaum, *Double Talk: The Erotics of Male Literary Collaboration* (London, 1989), p. 47.

3 Humorous compositions.

4 Wits.

5 A composition made by joining scraps of writing by various authors.

6 A very large penis.

7 Wine of wit.

8 Writings.

9 Detailed discussion, appendix.

10 Fellatio.

11 Lit. clasp or buckle.

12 Lit. chattering belly.
13 For a full discussion of the genesis of this text, see the introduction and appendices to John McRae's edition of *Teleny*, described as being by 'Oscar Wilde and Others' (London, 1986).
14 Cavalryman in the Turkish army.
15 Sodom and Gomorrah.
16 Master of languages/of tongues.
17 Stampede, headlong flight.
18 This poem appears in the first version of the book only, which was suppressed within days of its appearance. The replacement volume is identical, except that in the place of this poem and 'To a Sicilian boy' (see p. 339 below), two different poems are inserted into the binding, printed on different paper.
19 Song of Solomon, 5.2.
20 Song of Solomon, 8.7.
21 Song of Solomon, 2.17 etc.
22 Swinburne's Letters, vol. ii, p. 76. His cousin was Thomas Ashburnham.
23 'Pelleas and Ettare', from Tennyson's 'Idylls of the King', the story of a youth seeking to become a knight who falls in love with a heartless and faithless woman.
24 *Henry IV Part 2*, III, i, 29.
25 My old friend, i.e. Richard Monckton Milnes, Lord Houghton.
26 *King Lear*, III, iii, 53.
27 A.C. Swinburne, 'Anactoria', *Poems and Ballads: First Series* (1865).
32 A.C. Swinburne, 'Sapphics', *Poems and Ballads: First Series*.
33 A.C. Swinburne, 'Ad Catullum', *Poems and Ballads: Second Series* (1878).
30 Tertullian, *Apologeticus*, chapter 50: 'The blood of the martyr is the source of the church.'
31 Marquis de Sade, *Justine, or Good Conduct Well Chastised* (1791): 'O sir, is it possible to take pleasure in the sight of suffering, in seeing the story of the blood? You see it, little sodomite, replies this immoral man: yes, whore, you see it!'
32 Receive, Supreme Being, the sad offering of my sufferings.
33 *The Whippingham Papers; A Collection of Contributions in Prose and Verse, chiefly by the author of the 'Romance of Chastisement'* (London, 1888), an anthology attributed in whole or in part to Swinburne. Included here are stanzas 26–30 and stanza 50 to the end of the poem.
34 Person afflicted by nervous disease.
35 Two nations who will wage war with Satan against the people of God, and who signify the imminence of the Apocalypse. See Revelation 20.8; Ezekiel 38, 39.
36 Sodomy.
37 Dedication.
38 *The Confessions of Aleister Crowley: An Autohagiography*. The first two volumes were published in 1929. The full six-volume edition appeared for the first time in 1969, edited by John Symonds.
39 Letter quoted in K.-H. Ulrichs, *'Memnon': Die Geschlechtsnatur des mannliebenden Urnings*; see Hubert Kennedy, *Ulrichs: The Life and Works of Karl Heinrich Ulrichs, Pioneer of the Modern Gay Movement* (Boston, 1988).
40 See, for example, the highly sentimental story 'Narcissus' by Count Eric Stenbock, from *Studies of Death: Romantic Tales* (1894), in which a disfigured recluse takes a blind boy to live with him.
41 Author, whose real name was John Francis Bloxham, of 'The Priest and the Acolyte', the story of a love-affair between a priest and an altar-boy, which was printed, under the name of 'X', in *The Chameleon*, and which Wilde, during Queensbury's libel trial, described as 'disgusting, perfect twaddle'.
42 Howard Overing Sturgis, *Tim* (1891).

43 E. F. Benson wrote a large number of novels which may be successors to *Tim*, called *Alan, Colin, Mike, Peter* etc.

44 I have been unable to trace this painter.

45 H. S. Tuke, Royal Academician, and painter of many 'bathing-boy' pictures.

46 See Edward Said's *Orientalism* (London, 1978) for an excellent discussion of how the 'exotic' becomes the 'erotic'.

47 My knowledge of this text comes entirely from two published sources: Ronald Hyam, *Empire and Sexuality: The British Experience* (Manchester, 1990) and Toby Hammond, '*Paidikion*: a paiderastic manuscript', *International Journal of Greek Love* (New York), vol. 1, no. 2, 1966.

48 Translated from a fragment from the works of Ulrichs, in *Walt Whitman: A Study* (1893), pp. 50–1 in reference to Whitman's lines, 'The boy I love, the same becomes a man.'

49 First published as *The Memoirs of John Addington Symonds: The Secret Homosexual Life of a Leading Nineteenth-Century Man of Letters*, ed. Phyllis Grosskurth (Chicago, 1984).

50 Long hair worn by men.

51 Luke 14.23.

SELECT BIBLIOGRAPHY

Place of publication is London unless otherwise indicated.

Aldrich, Robert, *The Seduction of the Mediterranean: Writing, Art and Homosexual Fantasy*, Routledge, 1993.

Altmann, Dennis *et al.*, *Which Homosexuality: Essays from the International Conference on Lesbian Studies*, Gay Men's Press, 1989.

Bartlett, Neil, *Who was that Man? A Present for Mr Oscar Wilde*, Serpent's Tail, 1988.

Bleys, Rudi C., *The Geography of Perversion: Male-to-Male Sexual Behaviour outside the West and the Ethnographic Imagination 1750–1918*, Cassell, 1996.

Borland, Maureen, *Wilde's Devoted Friend: A Life of Robert Ross 1869–1918*, Oxford, Lennard, 1990.

Bristow, Joseph (ed.), *Sexual Sameness: Textual Differences in Lesbian and Gay Writing*, Routledge, 1992.

Brome, Vincent, *Havelock Ellis, Philosopher of Sex: A Biography*, Routledge and Kegan Paul, 1979.

Carpenter, Edward, *Towards Democracy*, Gay Men's Press, 1985.

Cooper, Emmanuel, *The Sexual Perspective: Homosexuality and Art in the Last 100 Years in the West*, Routledge and Kegan Paul, 1986.

Coote, Stephen, *The Penguin Book of Homosexual Verse*, Penguin, 1986.

Craig, Alec, *The Banned Books of England and Other Countries: A Study in the Conception of Literary Obscenity*, George Allen and Unwin, 1962.

Dollimore, Jonathan, *Sexual Dissidence: Augustine to Wilde, Freud to Foucault*, Oxford, Clarendon Press, 1991.

Duberman, Martin Bauml, Martha Vicinus and George Chauncey Jr (eds), *Hidden from History: Reclaiming the Gay and Lesbian Past*, Penguin, 1991.

Ellmann, Richard, *Oscar Wilde*, Penguin, 1988.

Faderman, Lillian, *Surpassing the Love of Men: Romantic Friendship and Love between Women from the Renaissance to the Present*, The Women's Press, 1985.

Fletcher, Ian (ed.), *British Poetry and Prose 1870–1905*, Oxford, Oxford University Press, 1987.

Grosskurth, Phyllis (ed.), *The Memoirs of John Addington Symonds: The Secret Homosexual Life of a Leading Nineteenth-Century Man of Letters*, Chicago, University of Chicago Press, 1984.

Hammond, Toby, '*Paidikion*, a paiderastic manuscript', *The International Journal of Greek Love*, New York, vol. 1, no. 2, 1966.

Harrison, Fraser, *The Dark Angel: Aspects of Victorian Sexuality*, Fontana, 1979.

Hobby, Elaine and Chris White (eds), *What Lesbians Do in Books*, The Women's Press, 1991.

Hyam, Ronald , *Empire and Sexuality: The British Experience*, Manchester, Manchester University Press, 1990.

Hyde, H. Montgomery, *The Other Love*, Heinemann, 1970.

Irwin, Robert, *The Arabian Nights: A Companion*, Allen Lane, 1994.

Kellogg, S. (ed.), *Essays on Gay Liberation*, New York, Harrington Park Press, 1989.

Kennedy, Hubert, *Ulrichs: The Life and Works of Karl Heinrich Ulrichs, Pioneer of the Modern Gay Movement*, Boston, Alyson Publications, 1988.

Koestenbaum, Wayne, *Double Talk: The Erotics of Male Literary Collaboration*, Routledge, 1989.

Lambert, J. W. and Michael Ratcliffe, *The Bodley Head 1887–1987*, The Bodley Head, 1987.

Levey, Michael, *The Case of Walter Pater*, Thames and Hudson, 1978.

Licata, Salvatore and Robert Petersen (eds), *The Gay Past: A Collection of Historical Essays*, New York, Harrington Park Press, 1981.

Maas, Henry, J. L. Duncan and W. G. Good, *The Letters of Aubrey Beardsley*, Oxford, Plantin, 1990.

McRae, John (ed.), 'Oscar Wilde and others', *Teleny*, Gay Men's Press, 1986.

Marcus, Steven, *The Other Victorians: A Study of Sexuality and Pornography in Mid-Nineteenth Century England*, Corgi, 1966.

Mavor, Elizabeth, *The Ladies of Llangollen: A Study in Romantic Friendship*, Penguin, 1973.

Mort, Frank, *Dangerous Sexualities: Medico-Moral Politics in England Since 1830*, Routledge and Kegan Paul, 1987.

Pearsall, Ronald, *The Worm in the Bud: The World of Victorian Sexuality*, Penguin, 1983.

Perrin, Noel, *Dr Bowdler's Legacy: A History of Expurgated Books in England and America*, Boston, Nonpareil, 1992.

Porter, Roy and Lesley Hall, *The Facts of Life: The Creation of Sexual Knowledge in Britain 1650–1950*, Yale University Press, 1995.

Raitt, Suzanne (ed.), *Volcanoes and Pearl Divers: Essays in Lesbian Feminist Studies*, Onlywomen Press, 1995.

Reade, Brian, *Sexual Heretics: Male Homosexuality in English Literature from 1850 to 1900*, Routledge and Kegan Paul, 1970.

Said, Edward, *Orientalism*, Penguin, 1978.

Shires, Linda (ed.), *Rewriting the Victorians: Theory, History and the Politics of Gender*, Routledge, 1992.

Silverstolpe, Frederic, 'Benkert was not a doctor: on the non-medical origins of the homosexual category in the nineteenth century', *Homosexuality, Which Homosexuality? International Scientific Conference on Gay and Lesbian Studies*, Amsterdam, Free University/Schorer Foundation, 1987.

Sinfield, Alan, *The Wilde Century: Effeminacy, Oscar Wilde and the Queer Moment*, Cassell, 1994.

Small, Ian (ed.), *The Aesthetes: A Sourcebook*, Routledge and Kegan Paul, 1979.

Weeks, Jeffrey, *Coming Out: Homosexual Politics in Britain from the Nineteenth Century to the Present*, Quartet, 1977.

Weeks, Jeffrey and Sheila Rowbotham, *Socialism and the New Life: The Personal and Sexual Politics of Edward Carpenter and Havelock Ellis*, Pluto, 1977.

Wurgaft, Lewis D., *The Imperial Imagination: Magic and Myth in Kipling's India*, Middletown, Connecticut, Wesleyan University Press, 1983.

INDEX

abnormal(s) 4, 63, 64, 69, 73, 74, 75, 76, 77, 83, 85, 86, 88, 91, 94, 95, 96, 104, 113, 114, 115, 147, 152, 163, 217, 226, 319, 335
abnormality 5, 94, 96, 97, 100, 114, 115
absinthe 312
Abu Nowas 152, 233, 349
abuse 29, 61, 62, 147, 148, 149, 267, 316
Achilles 120, 126, 139, 148, 161, 163, 167, 208, 215, 345, 347, 349
Actaeon 234
actor 15, 72, 192, 197, 198, 199, 201, 205, 207
Adam 231, 232
adhesiveness 214, 217; *see also* amativeness; Whitman, Walt
Admetus 173–4
adolescence 75, 317, 319, 322
Adolph, Dr G. G. 147, 346
Adonis 121, 122
Adult League 66
adultery 29, 71, 153, 312
Æolia 171
Æschines 72, 150, 161, 163, 167, 168, 233
Aeschylus 126, 149, 349
affection(s) 57, 80–1, 83, 88, 93–4, 96, 102, 119, 125, 131, 134, 137, 139, 146, 154, 161–4, 208, 210, 212, 235, 277, 319–20, 335, 338, 345, 347
Afghanistan 145, 329
Africa 145, 228, 328
African tribes 126
Agamemnon 349
Agathocles 169
Agathon 149
Agnon the Academic 149
agony 292, 301, 311, 314
Alcaeus 149
Alcibiades 149, 172, 230, 232, 233
alcoholism 69
Aleutridae 232
Alexander 126, 163, 208, 352
Alhambra 45
alien 115, 199, 302
allegorical 236, 282

allegory 196, 234, 251
Allen, Henry 43, 44
amativeness 214, 217; *see also* adhesiveness; Whitman, Walt
Amazons 18
America(n) 23, 67, 94, 101, 110, 118, 122, 127, 142, 212, 222, 226; *see also* U.S.A.
Amis and Amile 127, 345
Anacreon 126, 149, 150
Anactoria 310, 353
anal 344; *see also* anum; anus
anatomical 78, 98, 147
ancestry 82, 102, 111
androgynes 231
androgynous 171, 232
androgyny 68
angel(s) 159, 256–8, 273, 352
Annandale Observer 220
anonymous 7, 168, 281, 285
Anthology of 'Nineties' Verse, An 271
Antichrist 312
Antinoüs 151, 206
anum, per 65
anus 286, 288, 348
aphrodisiacs 284
Aphrodite 120, 165, 178, 181, 182, 230, 266
Apollo 50, 132, 148, 173, 174, 181, 270, 347, 349, 351
appetite(s) 20, 23, 63, 72, 75, 77–82, 85, 89, 110, 137, 164, 217, 251
Arab(s) 153, 285, 340
Arabian Nights 116, 233, 349; *see also* The Book of the Thousand Nights and a Night
Archangel Gabriel 62
Archias the Bacchiad 170
Argonauts 347
Aristides 149
Aristog(e)iton 87, 148, 162, 171
Aristophanes 153, 168, 169, 170, 233
Aristotle 75, 134, 148, 149, 347, 349
Aristrippus 149
arm(s) 42, 71, 90, 97, 125, 132, 142, 162, 163, 174, 176, 177, 178, 210, 242, 261,

The Intersexes 68, 104
'The New Chivalry' 117, 154
The New Minnesinger and Other Poems 266
The New Spirit 274, 352
'The Picture of Dorian Gray', 51
The Pixy 277
The Star 60
Theban(s) 72, 87, 163, 216, 348, 350
Themistocles 149
Theocritus 126, 160, 175, 242
Theodectes 149
Theodosius 71
Theodotus 169
Theognis 126, 149
Theseus 148, 162, 199, 349
Theseus and Pirithous 148
Thessalians 125
thighs 311, 338, 349
third sex 319
throat 245, 255, 258, 278, 324, 334, 338, 339, 340
Tiberius 150
Timaeus 148
Timarchus 150, 168, 233
Times 2, 9, 10, 11, 32, 35, 36, 40, 129, 342
tombstone 61
tongue(s) 204, 228, 253, 259, 283, 286, 304–5, 315, 344, 353
Towards Democracy 20, 236, 247, 343; *see also* Carpenter, Edward
Transmutation 137, 138
Traubel, Horace 345
treason 26
trials 26, 50, 59, 163, 192, 330
tribad(e)(s) 146, 149, 171, 172, 259
tribadism 283
tribassare 231
Trinity 264
trousers 312, 331, 334, 338
Tuke, Samuel 326, 354
Turkey 63
Turkish 353
Turkistan 145
Turks 81, 87
tyrant(s) 125, 138, 141, 162, 169, 345

Ulrichs, K.-H. 3, 4, 5, 66, 68, 73, 74, 75, 76, 77, 78, 80, 81, 82, 83, 84, 85, 86, 87, 88, 89, 100, 129, 352, 354

unclothed 290, 322; *see also* bare; naked(ness); stripped
Underneath the Bough: A Book of Verses 269; *see also* Michael Field
unisexuality 69
unnatural 2, 21, 22, 25, 27, 28, 32, 39, 40, 42, 43, 46, 49, 51, 57, 62, 63, 64, 71, 72, 82, 85, 107, 122, 133, 137, 148, 238
unnatural offences 3, 25, 62
Uraniad(s) 69, 107–10, 112
Uranian(s) 4–5, 68, 105, 106–10
Uraniaster(s) 76, 84, 86
Uranisme et unisexualité 259; *see also* Raffalovich, M.A.
Uranos 229
Urning(s) 4, 74, 76–8, 80–9, 105, 130–1, 136, 229, 352
urolagnia 66, 329; *see also* coprolagnia
U.S.A. 101, 227, 143, 144, 163, 227; *see also* America

valet(s) 32, 53, 230
Vatican 80
venereal 44, 72, 103, 146
Venetian 232, 333, 336
Venice 25, 90, 121, 122, 334, 337
Venturi, Silvio 282, 352
Venus 72, 121, 128, 180, 189, 231, 245, 313
Venus and Adonis 121, 189
Vere Street 2, 10–13
vice(s) 2, 13, 21, 23, 33, 39, 60, 63, 64, 71, 72, 85–8, 90, 99, 103, 118, 122, 145, 151, 153, 155, 163, 167, 171–3, 190, 216, 251, 260, 281, 289, 312, 313, 316, 348, 349
victim(s) 21, 26, 32, 50, 82, 104, 110, 116, 237, 317, 345
violation 28, 33, 47
Virey 147
Virgil 126, 146, 153, 172
Virgin Mary 173, 243, 266
virgin(ity) 189–90, 245, 319
Vision of Love Revealed in Sleep, A 282, 289
Vishnu 232
Voltaire 185
vulva 78; *see also* cunt

Wagner, Richard 128, 138, 229, 346